THE

CHARTER

AND

ORDINANCES

OF THE

CITY OF BOSTON,

TOGETHER WITH THE

ACTS OF THE LEGISLATURE

RELATING TO THE CITY:

COLLATED AND REVISED

PURSUANT TO AN ORDER OF THE CITY COUNCIL,

BY

PELEG W. CHANDLER.

BOSTON:
JOHN H. EASTBURN, CITY PRINTER.
1850.

CITY OF BOSTON.

In Common Council, Feb. 14, 1850.

Ordered, That Messrs. Brooks, Minot, and Haskell, with such as the board of mayor and aldermen may join, be a committee to cause the revision and printing of all the city ordinances, with such other matters as they may deem expedient—and that said committee be authorized to employ such assistance as may be necessary, and that the expense thereof be charged to the appropriation for incidental expenses and miscellaneous claims.

Sent up for concurrence.

FRANCIS BRINLEY, *President.*

In the Board of Mayor and Aldermen, Feb. 18, 1850.

Read and concurred, and Aldermen Rogers and Grant were joined.

JOHN P. BIGELOW, *Mayor.*

At a meeting of the committee on the revision of the city ordinances, held March, 15, 1850, it was

Voted, That Peleg W. Chandler, Esq., be employed to re-arrange, revise and prepare for publication, the city ordinances, in such manner as he may deem the interest of the city to require, with power to engage such assistance as he may need during the progress of the work.

Voted, That Messrs. Rogers and Minot be a committee to carry the above vote into effect.

Attest, WM. G. BROOKS, *Secretary.*

PREFACE.

The necessity of revising and printing the city ordinances has long been felt by the city council; and commissioners, appointed in previous years for this purpose, have devoted more or less time to the subject. For reasons, however, which it is not necessary to state here, but little progress seems to have been made, up to the present year. Meanwhile, the old collection of ordinances being out of print, and great inconvenience being occasioned by that fact, the city council, in February last, appointed a committee, with instructions to cause the revision and printing of all the city ordinances, with such other matter as they might deem expedient, and they were authorized to employ such assistance as might be necessary. The committee subsequently employed the city solicitor to re-arrange, revise and prepare for publication, the city ordinances, in such manner as he might deem for the interest of the city, with power to engage such assistance as he might need during the progress of the work.

In accordance with these votes the present volume has been prepared. It contains (1) a summary or digest of all the acts of the legislature relating to the city of Boston, and of such general laws as it seemed to be desirable to insert; (2) the ordinances of the city; and (3) such notes, references to judicial decisions, and such historical statements, as were deemed necessary and proper.

In regard to the legislative provisions, it has often been a difficult question to determine what acts of the legislature should be incorporated in the present volume. Of course, all the special laws now in force relating to the city should be inserted. As to the general laws, it was thought that no fixed rule could safely be adopted, but that each case should depend on a careful judgment, based upon all the facts and considerations affecting the case. Some statutes, although general in their form, are more particularly applicable to Boston than to any other part of the commonwealth. In others, there are specific duties to be performed in this city in a different manner from what they are required to be performed in other places; while there are other statutes so general and universal in their application, that it was thought best to insert them for that reason.

In this department of the work there has been much difficulty and embarrassment from the fact, that when the general laws of the commonwealth were revised in 1835, there were a large number of special acts relating to the city of Boston, growing out of its peculiar wants, condition and circumstances, which were not expressly revised or repealed, and the Revised Statutes provided that this city should continue to have and exercise all the powers and privileges, and be subject to all the duties and liabilities, mentioned in the act establishing the city of Boston, and in the several acts specially relating to said city. At the same time, the Revised Statutes contain many general provisions upon the same subjects that are included in the special laws relating to the city of Boston, which obviously supersede and were intended to supersede the special provisions. The same fact is more obvious in many subsequent statutes, where the legislature have made general provisions, in effect extending special acts to all the towns in the commonwealth. Whether a general act is to be deemed an implied repeal of a special prior act, is of course a question depending upon a careful comparison of the two acts. In the present volume, the principles laid down in the case of *Brown v. City of Lowell*, (8 Metcalf's Rep. 172,) have been adopted as the rule of action. No special act has been regarded as repealed by implication by a general act, unless the latter contained strong terms upon which to found such a conclusion, and even then, such notes and references have been made as will enable the reader easily to examine the point for himself.

It will be noticed that the statutes have not been inserted at length, but are presented rather in the form of a digested summary, although the language of the acts has been generally used. It would have been much less laborious to insert the various statutes in chronological order, without undertaking to state precisely what the law now is, but it is obvious that this would have left a labor, always embarrassing and sometimes very difficult, to be performed by every person who should consult the work, in order to ascertain the *present state of the law* on a given subject. The City Charter, for instance, has been amended so often and in so many different parts, that it is necessary to consult several different acts of the legislature to find out what the present chartered rights and duties of the city are. Much trouble is saved by presenting a digested summary of the law as it now stands, the various amendments being all incorporated, and the original altered so as to correspond with the subsequent statutes. This course has been attended with considerable labor and constant liability to error; but all the statutes are so constantly referred to in the margin, and the notes are so frequent, that the means of correcting any error are always near at hand.

It is hardly necessary to state in this connection, that this work is intended for *popular* rather than *professional* use; and members of the legal profession will not, of course, be content with any digest of the statutes, but will go to the originals, an examination of which this work is not intended to supersede, although it is hoped that it may be of some use to them *in pointing the way.*

The ordinances contained in this volume have in general been recently revised and passed by the city council. When the committee was appointed, it was their understanding, and they had reason to know that it was the understanding of the city council, that the volume should be printed during the present year. It was not supposed that there would be time for any thing like a general revision of the ordinances, which would necessarily require much labor, from the fact that there had been no general revision since 1833. But upon examination it was found that there were so many ordinances upon the same subjects; there had been so many alterations and amendments, repeals and partial repeals, that it was impossible to make any useful collection without revising and submitting many of the ordinances to the city council for its approval. This has been done with most of them, and in some instances important alterations have been made. In those instances where no alterations seemed necessary, the ordinances have been printed from the original records, with this difference, that where there are several on one subject, they are placed together and the sections numbered continuously as one ordinance; but in all cases the dates of the ordinances are given in the margin.

When it is considered that the plan of this revision was not matured and the work itself was not actually commenced until the latter part of March last; that all the general and special laws relating to the city have been collated and digested, with notes and references to the leading decisions; that nearly all the old ordinances of the city have been revised; and that several new and important ordinances have been made, it will not be denied, probably, that the work has been printed as soon as could reasonably be expected.

Boston, *November*, 1850.

CONTENTS.

LIST OF ORDINANCES,

CONTAINED IN THIS VOLUME.

LIST OF STATUTES,

CITED IN THIS VOLUME.

Revised Statutes.

TABLE OF CASES,

CITED IN THIS VOLUME.

CITY CHARTER AND ORDINANCES,

AND

STATUTES RELATING TO THE CITY OF BOSTON.

ERRATA.

On page 22, in the margin, for "R. S. 16," read "R. S. 15."
On page 75, in the 22d line, strike out the second "not."
On page 93, in the note, add a reference to Rev. Stat. c. 141, §§ 6, 7, 8.
On page 172, in the 3d, 14th, and 20th lines of the margin, for "Ibid," in each case, read "1847, 234."
On page 276, in the 3d line of the note, for "*Dorr*," read "*Dow*."
On page 301, in the 2d line of the note, for 1835, read 1838.
On page 341, in the 21st line of the margin, for "R. S. § 20," read "R. S. 23, § 20"; and, in the 27th line of the margin, for "§ 20," read "§ 21."
On page 366, second column, 2d line, for "assistants," read "an assistant."
On page 568, in the 39th line, for "only," read "evenly."

CITY OF BOSTON.

CITY CHARTER AND AMENDMENTS.

1. Corporate name and general powers. Power to amend the charter. To be adopted by the citizens.
2. City council and other city officers.
3. Division into twelve wards. Each ward to include an equal number of voters.
4. Annual municipal election. Warden and clerk. Absence of warden or other officers. Inspectors. Warden, clerk, and inspectors to be under oath.
5. Power of warden to preserve order. Provisos.
6. Election of mayor. No choice. Decease, inability, or absence of mayor.
7. Proceedings in case of no choice of mayor before the commencement of the municipal year.
8. Refusal of mayor elect to accept. Absence of mayor elect.
9. Proceedings in case no mayor is chosen, or a full board of aldermen is not elected. In case neither a mayor nor any alderman is elected.
10. Who is to discharge the duties when no mayor is elected.
11. Election of aldermen.
12. Death or resignation of aldermen.
13. Vacancy in board of aldermen, common council, or other offices.
14. Election of common council. No choice. Adjournment. Certificate of election. Council shall decide questions of elections, &c.
15. Qualifications of voters at municipal elections.
16. Commencement of municipal year. Oath of office.
17. Mayor and aldermen to compose one board. City clerk. His powers and duties.
18. Common council a separate body. President. Clerk. Sittings to be public. Quorum.
19. Compensation of the mayor. His powers and duties.
20. Powers and duties of mayor and aldermen.
21. May license theatrical exhibitions, &c.
22. May be chosen surveyors of highways.
23. May have the powers of county commissioners, except, &c.
24. Powers of city council. By-laws. Provisos. Assessment of

Corporate name and general powers. 1821, 110, § 1.

I. By an act of the legislature of Massachusetts, passed on the twenty-third day of February, eighteen hundred and twenty-two,[1] it was provided that the inhabitants of the town of Boston for all purposes, for which towns were by law incorporated in this commonwealth, should continue to be one body politic, in fact and in name, under the style and denomination of the City of Boston, and as such should have, exercise and enjoy, all the rights, immunities, powers and privileges, and should be subject to all the duties and obligations, then incumbent upon and appertaining to said town, as a municipal corporation. The legislature reserved the right to amend or alter this act whenever they might deem it expedient; and it was to be void unless the inhabitants of the town at a legal meeting should determine to adopt the same within twelve days. It was adopted on the fourth day of March in the same year, and the town immediately became a city.

Power to amend the charter. Ibid, § 30.

To be adopted by the citizens. Ibid, § 31. Boston Records, vol. 10, p. 457. 1 Pick. Rep., 375.

---

1 The act establishing the city of Boston was passed February 23, 1822, but is to be found and is properly cited as the stat. of 1821, ch. 110. For the act as originally adopted, and some of the principal acts of amendment, see the appendix to this volume.

II. The administration of all the fiscal, prudential, and municipal concerns of the city, with the conduct and government thereof, is vested in one principal officer, to be styled the mayor, one select council, consisting of eight persons, to be denominated the board of aldermen, and one more numerous council to consist of forty-eight persons, to be denominated the common council; which boards in their joint capacity are denominated the city council—together with such other board of officers as are hereinafter specified.

City council and other city officers.
1821, 110, § 1.

III. By the second section of the city charter it was made the duty of the selectmen of Boston, as soon as might be after the passing of the act, to cause a new division of the town to be made into twelve wards, in such manner as to include an equal number of inhabitants in each ward, as nearly as conveniently might be, consistently with well defined limits; including, in such computation of numbers of inhabitants, persons of all descriptions, and taking the last census, made under the authority of the United States, as a basis for such computation. Power was given to the city council, from time to time, not oftener than once in ten years, to alter such divisions of wards, in such manner as to preserve, as nearly as might be, an equal number of inhabitants in each ward. This last provision has recently been amended, to the effect, that the division of the city into wards is to be so made as to include an equal number of *legal voters* in each ward.

Division into twelve wards.
1821, 110, § 2.

Each ward to include an equal number of voters.
1850, 167, § 1.
(Adopted by city council, April 29, 1850. City Records, vol. 28, p. 160.)

IV. On the second Monday of December annually, the citizens qualified to vote in city affairs are required to meet within their respective wards, at such time and place as the mayor and aldermen may by their warrant direct and appoint; and the said citizens shall then choose by ballot one warden and one clerk, who shall be resident in said ward, who shall hold their offices for one year, and until others are appointed in their stead. It shall be the duty of the warden to preside at all meetings of the citizens of the ward and to preserve order therein. It shall be the duty of the clerk to make a fair and true record, and keep

Annual Municipal election.
1821, 110, § 3.
1824, 49, § 1.
(Adopted by the inhabitants, Feb. 25, 1825. Boston Records, vol. 10, p. 505.)

Warden and clerk.

an exact journal of all the acts and votes of the citizens, at the ward meetings; to deliver over such records and journals, together with all other documents and papers held by him, in his said capacity, to his successor in office. In case of the absence of the warden at the opening of any annual meeting it shall be the duty of the clerk to call the citizens to order and preside until a warden is chosen by ballot.[1] If at any other meeting the warden be absent, the clerk is to preside until a moderator or warden *pro tempore* shall be chosen, which may be done by nomination and hand vote if the clerk so direct. The act of 1845, ch. 217, § 3, provides, however, that in case of the absence of any or either of the ward officers, at any meeting for elections, or other purposes, such office may be filled, *pro tempore*, by the legal voters present, which may be done by nomination and hand votes, if the voters present so determine. At the same meeting five inspectors of elections are to be chosen for the ward, being residents therein, by ballot, to hold their offices for one year. It shall be the duty of the warden and inspectors in each ward, to receive, sort, count and declare all votes, at all elections within such ward. And the warden, clerk, and inspectors, so chosen, shall respectively be under oath, faithfully and impartially to discharge their several duties, relative to all elections; which oath may be administered, by the clerk of such ward, to the warden, and by the latter to the clerk and inspectors, or by any justice of the peace of the county of Suffolk; and a certificate of such oath's having been administered shall be entered in the record or journal, to be kept by the clerk of such ward.

Absence of warden or other officers.

1845, 217, § 3. (Adopted by city council, Oct. 6, 1845. City Records, vol. 23, p. 406.)

Inspectors.

Warden, clerk and inspectors to be under oath.

Power of warden to preserve order. 1821, 110, § 4.

V. The warden, or other presiding officer of a ward meeting, shall have full power and authority to preserve order and decorum therein, and to repress all riotous, tumultuous, and disorderly conduct therein, and for that purpose to call

[1] This was the original provision in the charter, but the fair inference from the act of 1845, ch. 217, § 3, which is incorporated in the text, is, that any ward office in case of absence may be filled *pro tempore*, by nomination and hand vote, if the voters present so determine.

to his aid, any constable, or other peace officer, and also to command the aid and assistance of any citizen or citizens, who may be present; and any peace officer, or other citizen, neglecting or refusing to afford such aid, shall be taken and deemed to be guilty of a misdemeanor. The warden shall also have power and authority, by warrant, under his hand, to cause any person or persons who shall be guilty of any riotous, tumultuous, or disorderly conduct at such meeting, to be taken into custody, and restrained: *Provided, however*, that such restraint shall not continue after the adjournment or dissolution of such meeting: *And Provided, further*, that the person, so guilty of such disorderly conduct, shall be liable, notwithstanding such restraint, to be prosecuted and punished, in the same manner, as if such arrest had not been made.

Provisos.

VI. The citizens qualified to vote in city affairs, at their respective ward meetings, to be held on the second Monday in December annually, shall be called upon to give in their votes for one able and discreet person, being an inhabitant of the city, to be mayor of said city, for the term of one year. And all the votes so given in, in each ward, being sorted, counted, and declared by the warden and inspectors of elections, shall be recorded at large, by the clerk, in open ward meeting: and in making such declaration and record, the whole number of votes or ballots, given in, shall be distinctly stated, together with the name of every person voted for, and the number of votes given for each person respectively; such numbers to be expressed in words at length; and a transcript of such record, certified and authenticated by the warden, clerk, and a majority of the inspectors of elections for each ward, shall forthwith be transmitted or delivered by such ward clerk, to the clerk of the city. And it shall be the duty of the city clerk, forthwith to enter such returns, or a plain and intelligible abstract of them, as they are successively received, upon the journal of the proceedings of the mayor and aldermen, or some other book to be kept for that purpose. And it shall be the duty of the mayor and aldermen to meet to-

Election of mayor. Ibid, § 5. 1824, 49, § 1. (Adopted by inhabitants, Feb. 25, 1825. Boston Records, vol. 10, p. 505.) R. S. 4, § 12.

gether, within two days after such election, and to examine and compare all the said returns, and to ascertain whether any person has a majority of all the votes given for mayor; and in case a majority is so given, it shall be their duty to give notice thereof, in writing, to the person thus elected, and also to make the same known to the inhabitants of said city. But if, on such an examination no person appears to have a majority of all the votes given for mayor, the mayor and aldermen for the time being, shall issue their warrants for meetings of the respective wards, for the choice of a mayor, at such time and place, as they shall judge most convenient; and the same proceedings shall be had in all respects, as are herein before directed, until a mayor shall be chosen by a majority of all the voters, voting at such elections. And in case of the decease, inability, or absence of the mayor, and the same being declared and a vote passed by the aldermen and common council, respectively, declaring such cause, and the expediency of electing a mayor, for the time being, to supply the vacancy thus occasioned, it shall be lawful for the aldermen and common council to meet in convention, and elect a mayor to hold the said office until such occasion shall be removed, or until a new election.

No choice.

Decease, inability or absence of mayor.

Proceedings in case of no choice of mayor before the commencement of the municipal year. 1830, 7, § 1. (Adopted by citizens, June 16, 1830. Boston Records, vol. 10, p. 516.)

VII. Whenever, on examination by the mayor and aldermen of the returns of votes given for mayor at the meetings of the wards holden for the purpose of electing that officer, last preceding the first Monday of January, in each year, no person shall appear to have a majority of all the votes given for mayor, the mayor and aldermen, by whom such examination is made, shall make a record of that fact, an attested copy of which it shall be the duty of the city clerk to produce and read, on the first Monday of January, in the presence of the members returned to serve as aldermen and common councilmen; and thereupon the oaths prescribed by law may be administered to the members elect, by any one of the justices of the supreme judicial court, or any judge of any court of record holden in said city, or by any justice of the peace for the county of Suffolk; and thereupon the members of the board of aldermen shall proceed to elect a chairman, and the common council a president, in their respective chambers, and being respectively organized, shall proceed to business in the same manner as is provided in the seventeenth section below, in case of the absence of the mayor:—and the board of aldermen shall forthwith issue their warrants for meetings of the citizens of the respective wards, for the choice of a mayor, at such time and place as they shall judge most convenient; and the same proceedings shall be had, in all respects, as are directed in and by the provisions of the preceding section and repeated from time to time, until a mayor shall be chosen, by a majority of all the voters voting at such elections.

Refusal of mayor elect to accept. 1830, 7, § 2. Ibid.

VIII. In case any person elected mayor of the city shall refuse to accept the office, the same proceedings shall be had in all respects, as are herein before directed in cases wherein there has been no choice of mayor, until a mayor be chosen by a majority of votes. And in case of the unavoidable absence by sickness or otherwise, of the mayor elect, on the first Monday in January, the city government shall organize itself in the mode herein before provided, and may proceed to business in the same manner as if the mayor were present.

Absence of mayor elect.

Proceedings in case no mayor is chosen, or a full board of aldermen is not elected. 1845, 217, § 1. (Adopted by city council, Oct. 6, 1845. City Records, vol. 23, p. 406.)

IX. Whenever it shall appear, by the regular returns of the elections of the city officers, that a mayor has not been chosen, or that a full board of aldermen has not been elected, such of the board of aldermen, whether they constitute a quorum or not, as may have been chosen, shall issue their warrant, in usual form, for the election of a mayor, or such members of the board of aldermen as may be necessary, and the same proceedings shall be had and repeated, until the election of a mayor and aldermen shall be completed, and all vacancies be filled in the said board; and in case neither a mayor nor any aldermen shall be elected at the usual time for electing the same, and after the powers of the former mayor, and mayor and aldermen,

In case neither a mayor nor any alderman is elected.

shall have ceased, it shall be the duty of the president of the common council, to issue his warrant, in the same manner as the board of aldermen would have done, if elected, and the same proceedings shall be had and repeated, until a mayor, or one or more aldermen, shall be elected.

Who is to discharge the duties when no mayor is elected. 1845, 217. § 4. Ibid.

X. In case of the non-election of a mayor, the chairman of the board of aldermen shall discharge all the duties incumbent on the mayor of the city, prescribed by the city charter, or any other law, or any ordinance of the city, which now or hereafter may be required of him, until a mayor shall be chosen and duly sworn to the discharge of his duties; and such chairman, with the board of aldermen, shall discharge all the duties incumbent on the mayor and aldermen.

Election of aldermen. 1821, 110, § 6. 1824, 49, § 1. (Adopted by citizens, Feb. 25. 1825. Boston Records, vol. 10, p. 505.)

XI. The citizens in their respective ward meetings, to be held on the second Monday of December, annually, shall be called upon to give in their votes for eight persons, being inhabitants of said city, to constitute the board of aldermen, for the ensuing year; and all the votes so given, being sorted, counted, and declared by the warden and inspectors shall be recorded at large, by the clerk, in open ward meeting; and in making such declaration and record, the whole number of votes or ballots given in shall be particularly stated, together with the name of every person voted for, and the number of votes given for each person; and a transcript of such record, certified by the warden and clerk, and a majority of the inspectors of each ward, shall, by the said clerk, within two days, be transmitted to the city clerk; whereupon the same proceedings shall be had, to ascertain and determine the persons chosen as aldermen, as are herein before directed in regard to the choice of mayor, and for a new election, in case of the whole number required not being chosen at the first election. And each alderman, so chosen, shall be duly notified in writing of his election by the mayor and aldermen for the time being.

XII. In case of the death or resignation of any member of the board of aldermen, the citizens of Boston shall have power to fill such vacancy, at any regular meeting that may thereafter be convened for that purpose.

Death or resignation of aldermen.
1824, 28, § 6.

XIII. Whenever it shall appear to the mayor and aldermen, that there is a vacancy in either the board of aldermen, or in the common council, or in any of the city or ward offices, it shall be the duty of the mayor and aldermen to issue their warrant for elections, in due form, to fill all such vacancies in each and all of the said boards and offices, at such time and place as in their judgment may be deemed advisable.

Vacancy in board of aldermen, common council, or other offices.
1845, 217, § 2. (Accepted by city council, Oct. 6, 1845. City Records, vol. 23, p. 406.)

XIV. The citizens of each ward, qualified to vote as aforesaid, at their respective ward meetings, to be held on the second Monday of December, annually, shall be called upon to give in their votes for four able and discreet men, being inhabitants of said ward, to be members of the common council; and all the votes given in as aforesaid, in each ward, being sorted, counted, and declared by the warden and inspectors, if it appear that four persons have a majority of all the votes given at such election, a public declaration thereof, with the names of the persons so chosen, shall be made in open ward meeting, and the same shall be entered at large, by the clerk of such ward, in his journal, stating particularly the whole number of votes given in, the number necessary to make a choice, and the number actually given for each of the persons, so declared to be chosen. But, in case four persons are not chosen at the first ballot, a new ballot shall be opened for a number of common councilmen, sufficient to complete the number of four; and the same proceedings shall be had, as before directed, until the number of four shall be duly chosen; *Provided, however*, that if the said elections cannot conveniently be completed on such day, the same may be adjourned to another day, for that purpose, not longer distant than three days. And each of the persons so chosen as a member of the common council, in each ward, shall, within

Election of common council.
1821, 110, § 7, 1824, 49, § 1. (Adopted by citizens, Feb. 25, 1825. Boston Records, vol. 10, p. 505.)

No choice.

Adjournmen

Certificate of elections.

two days of his election, be furnished with a certificate thereof, signed by the warden, clerk, and a majority of the inspectors of such ward; which certificate shall be presumptive evidence of the title of such person to a seat in the common council; but such council, however, shall have authority to decide ultimately upon all questions relative to the qualifications, elections, and returns of its members.

Council shall decide questions of elections, &c.

Qualifications of voters at municipal elections, &c. 1821, 110, § 8.

XV. Every male citizen of twenty-one years of age and upwards, excepting paupers, and persons under guardianship, who shall have resided within the commonwealth one year, and within the city six months next preceding any meeting of citizens, either in wards, or in general meeting, for municipal purposes, and who shall have paid by himself or his parent, master, or guardian, any state or county tax, which, within two years next preceding such meeting, shall have been assessed upon him, in any town or district in this commonwealth, and also every citizen who shall be, by law, exempted from taxation, and who shall be in all other respects qualified as above mentioned, shall have a right to vote at such meeting, and no other person shall be entitled to vote at such meeting.

Commencement of municipal year. 1821, 110, § 9. 1824, 49, § 2. (Adopted by citizens, Feb. 25, 1825. Boston Records, vol. 10, p. 505.)

Oath of office.

XVI. The mayor, aldermen, and common councilmen, chosen as aforesaid, shall enter on the duties of their respective offices on the first Monday of January, and before entering on the duties of their offices, shall respectively be sworn, by taking the oath of allegiance and oath of office, prescribed in the constitution of this commonwealth, and an oath to support the constitution of the the United States. And such oaths may be administered to the mayor elect, by any one of the justices of the supreme judicial court, or any judge of any court of record, commissioned to hold any such court, within the said city, or by any justice of the peace for the county of Suffolk. And such oaths shall and may be administered to the aldermen and members of the common council, by the mayor, being himself first sworn as aforesaid; and a certificate of such oaths having been taken, shall be entered in the journal of the mayor and aldermen, and of the common council, respectively by their respective clerks.[1]

Mayor and aldermen to compose one board. 1821, 110, § 10. See also 1845, 217, § 4, and 1846, 50.

XVII. The mayor and aldermen, thus chosen and qualified, shall compose one board, and shall sit and act together as one body, at all meetings, of which the mayor, if present, shall preside; but in his absence, the board may elect a chairman, for the time being. The said board, together with the common council, in convention, shall have power to choose a clerk, who shall be sworn to the faithful discharge of the duties of his office, who shall be chosen for the term of one year, and until another person is duly chosen to succeed him; removable, however, at the pleasure of the mayor and aldermen; who shall be denominated the clerk of the city, and whose duty it shall be to keep a journal of the acts and proceedings of the said board, composed of the mayor and aldermen; to sign all warrants issued by them, and to do such other acts in his said capacity, as may, lawfully and reasonably, be required of him; and to deliver over all journals, books, papers, and documents, entrusted to him as such clerk, to his successor in office, immediately upon such successor being chosen and qualified as aforesaid, or whenever he may be thereto required by the said mayor and aldermen. And the city clerk thus chosen and qualified, shall have all the powers, and perform all the duties belonging, at the time of the act of incorporation, to the town clerk of the town of Boston, as if the same were particularly and fully enumerated, except in cases where it is otherwise expressly provided.

City clerk.

His powers and duties.

---

[1] The statute of 1824, c. 49, § 2, cited in the margin of § XVI in the text, provides that all the officers chosen on the second Monday of December by virtue of said act, shall enter on the duties of their respective offices on the first Monday of January in each year. This provision includes not only the mayor, aldermen and common councilmen, but also the wardens, clerks of the wards, inspectors of elections, overseers of the poor and school committee. See the act, as printed at large in the Appendix, p. 471, *post*.

Common council a separate body. 1821, 110, § 11.

XVIII. The persons so chosen and qualified, as members of the common council of the said city, shall sit and act together as a separate body, distinct from that of the mayor and aldermen, except in those cases in which the two bodies are to meet in convention; and the said council shall have power, from time to time, to choose one of their own members to preside over their deliberations, and to preserve order therein, and also to choose a clerk, who shall be under oath faithfully to discharge the duties of his office, who shall hold such office, during the pleasure of said council, and whose duty it shall be to attend said council, when the same is in session, to keep a journal of its acts, votes, and proceedings, and to perform such other services, in said capacity, as said council may require. All sittings of the common council shall be public; also all sittings of the mayor and aldermen, when they are not engaged in executive business. Twenty-five members of the common council shall constitute a quorum for the transaction of business.

President. Clerk. Sittings to be public. Quorum.

XIX. The mayor of the said city, thus chosen and qualified, shall be taken and deemed to be the chief executive officer of said corporation; and he shall be compensated for his services by a salary, to be fixed by the board of aldermen and common council, in city council convened, payable at stated periods; which salary shall not exceed the sum of five thousand dollars annually, and he shall receive no other compensation or emoluments whatever; and no regulations enlarging or diminishing such compensation shall be made, to take effect until the expiration of the year, for which the mayor then in office shall have been elected. And it shall be the duty of the mayor to be vigilant and active at all times, in causing the laws for the government of said city to be duly executed and put in force; to inspect the conduct of all subordinate officers in the government thereof, and as far as in his power, to cause all negligence, carelessness, and positive violation of duty to be duly prosecuted and punished. He shall have power,

Compensation of the mayor. 1821, 110, § 12. His powers and duties.

whenever in his judgment, the good of said city may require it, to summon meetings of the board of aldermen and common council, or either of them, although the meeting of said boards, or either of them may stand adjourned to a more distant day. And it shall be the duty of the mayor, from time to time, to communicate to both branches of the city council all such information, and recommend all such measures as may tend to the improvement of the finances, the police, health, security, cleanliness, comfort, and ornament of the said city.

XX. The administration of police, together with the executive powers of the said corporation generally, together also with all the powers heretofore vested in the selectmen of the town of Boston, either by the general laws of this commonwealth, by particular laws relative to the powers and duties of said selectmen, or by the usages, votes or by-laws of said town, are vested in the mayor and aldermen, as hereby constituted, as fully and amply as if the same were herein specially enumerated.

Powers and duties of mayor and aldermen. 1821, 110, § 13. 1832, 166, repealed by Rev. Stat. 2 Metc. 220. 15 Pick. 243.

XXI. The mayor and aldermen shall have power to license all theatrical exhibitions, and all public shows, and all exhibitions, of whatever name or nature, to which admission is obtained on payment of money, on such terms and conditions as to them may seem just and reasonable; and to regulate the same, from time to time, in such manner as to them may appear necessary to preserve order and decorum, and to prevent interruption of peace and quiet. And any person or persons who shall set forth, establish, or promote any such exhibition or show, or publish, or advertise the same, or otherwise aid or assist therein, without a license so obtained as aforesaid, or contrary to the terms or conditions of such license, or whilst the same is suspended, or after the same is revoked by said mayor and aldermen, shall be liable to such forfeiture, as the city council may, by any by-law made for that purpose prescribe.[1]

May license theatrical exhibitions, &c. 1821, 110, § 14. But see 1849, 231, § 1, 2. 9 Pick. 415.

[1] This section appears to be superseded by stat. 1849, c. 231. See Amusements.

May be chosen surveyors of highways. 1823, 2.

XXII. The city council have the power and authority of electing, if they see fit, the mayor and aldermen, surveyors of highways for the city.

May have the powers of county commissioners, except, &c. R. S. 24, § 54.

XXIII. In the county of Suffolk, the mayor and aldermen of the city of Boston shall, within the said city, have the like powers and perform the like duties, as are exercised and performed by the commissioners of other counties, saving to any party aggrieved the right of trial by jury in the court of common pleas, in cases of the laying out, altering and discontinuing of ways, and assessing damages therefor.

Ibid, § 55. Ibid, 14, § 29.

Powers of city council. 1821, 110, § 15.

XXIV. All other powers by law vested, at the time of the act of incorporation, in the town of Boston, or in the inhabitants thereof, as a municipal corporation, are vested in the mayor and aldermen, and common council of the said city, to be exercised by concurrent vote, each board, as hereby constituted, having a negative upon the other. More especially they shall have power to make all such needful and salutary by-laws, as towns by the laws of this commonwealth have power to make and establish, and to annex penalties, not exceeding twenty dollars, for the breach thereof, which by-laws shall take effect and be in force from and after the times therein respectively limited, without the sanction or confirmation of any court, or other authority whatsoever; *Provided*, that such by-laws shall not be repugnant to the constitution and laws of this commonwealth:[1] *And provided also*, that the same shall be liable to be annulled by the legislature thereof. The said city council shall also have power, from time to time, to lay and assess taxes for all purposes, for which towns are by law required or authorized to assess and grant money,[2] and also for all purposes, for which

By-laws.

Provisoes.

Assessment of taxes.

---

[1] For general powers of city councils to make by-laws, see Ordinances and By-laws. See also stat. 1847, c. 262.

[2] The city council are the agents and trustees of the inhabitants of Boston, with a limited authority; they can perform no act in the execution of their trust, unless warranted by some general or special law of the

county taxes may be levied and assessed, so long as the town of Chelsea shall not be liable to taxation therefor; *Provided, however*, that in the assessment and apportionment of all such taxes upon the polls and estates of all persons liable to contribute thereto, the same rules and regulations shall be observed as are now established by the laws of this commonwealth, or may be hereafter enacted, relative to the assessment and apportionment of town taxes. The said city council shall also have power to provide for the assessment and collection of such taxes, and to make appropriations of all public moneys, and provide for the disbursement thereof, and take suitable measures to ensure a just and prompt ac-

1822, 85.

Proviso.

Collection of taxes.

---

commonwealth, either in express terms or by reasonable inference. The general authority of towns to raise money by the assessment of taxes on the inhabitants, was given by the statute of 1785, ch. 75, § 7, "for the settlement, maintenance and support of the ministry, schools, the poor, and other necessary charges arising within the same town," the most of which provision is re-enacted in the Revised Statutes, ch. 15, § 12. The only difficulty in the construction of this provision has been as to what are "other necessary charges," for which towns are authorized to raise money. Upon this point there have been several decisions. In the case of *Stetson v. Kempton*, (13 Massachusetts Reports 272,) it was held, that towns have no authority in time of war and hostile invasion, to raise money to give additional wages to the militia and for other purposes of defence. The court say, that the erection of public buildings for the accommodation of the inhabitants, such as town houses to assemble in, and market houses for the sale of provisions, may also be a proper town charge, and may come within the fair meaning of the term *necessary*, for these may be essential to the comfort and convenience of the citizens. But it cannot be supposed that the building of a theatre, a circus, or any other place of mere amusement, at the expense of the town, could be justified under the term *necessary town charges*. Nor could the inhabitants be lawfully taxed for the purpose of raising a statue or a monument, these being matters of taste, and not of necessity; unless in populous and wealthy towns, they should be thought suitable ornaments to buildings or squares, the raising and maintenance of which are within the duty and care of the governors or officers of such towns. In *Allen v. Inhabitants of Taunton*, (19 Pick. Rep. 485,) it was held, that a town is authorized to appropriate money for the repair of fire engines, used for the purpose of extinguishing fires therein, whether they belong to the town or were purchased by private subscription; and in the case of *Hardy v. Inhabitants of Waltham*, (3 Metcalf's Rep. 163,) it was held, that a town has authority to appropriate money for the construction of reservoirs for water to supply fire engines. In the case of *Spaulding v. City of Lowell*, (23 Pick. Rep. 71,) it was held, that cities and towns in this commonwealth, by virtue of their general powers,

Assessors to be chosen.

count thereof; and for these purposes, may either elect such assessors, and assistant assessors, as may be needful, or provide for the appointment or election of the same, or any of them, by the mayor and aldermen, or by the citizens, as in their judgment may be most conducive to the public good, and may also require of all persons entrusted with the collection, custody, or disbursement of public moneys, such bonds with such conditions and such sureties, as the case may in their judgments require.

Bonds, &c., may be required.

City council may provide for the appointment of city officers. 1821, 110, § 16.

XXV. The said city council shall have power, and they are authorized to provide for the appointment or election of all necessary officers, for the good government of said city, not otherwise provided for; to prescribe their duties, and fix their compensation, and to choose a register of deeds, whenever the city shall compose one county. The city council also shall have the care and superintendence of

Register of deeds.

---

have authority in their corporate capacity, to build a market house, to appropriate money therefor, and to assess the same upon the inhabitants. "To bring any particular subject," the court remark, "within this description of necessary town charges, it must appear to be money necessary to the execution of some corporate power, the enjoyment of some corporate right, or the performance of some corporate duty, as established by law, or *long usage*." A town has no authority to raise money to aid in the construction of a road which by law is to be made at the expense of the county, and consequently a tax laid by the town for the purpose of collecting the money is illegal and void. A vote by a town appointing a committee to appropriate money for constructing such road, is an illegal and void act; and a contract for constructing it entered into by the committee in behalf of the town, will not be binding upon the town. *Parsons v. Inhabitants of Goshen*, (11 Pick. Rep. 396.) A town has authority to provide for the support of a public clock, and to assess the expense thereof upon the inhabitants of the town. *Willard v. Inhabitants of Newburyport*, (12 Pick. Rep. 227.) A town is authorized to indemnify its officers, against any liability which they may incur in the bona fide discharge of their duties, although it turn out that they have exceeded their legal rights and authority. *Nelson v. Milford*, (7 Pick. Rep. 18); *Bancroft v. Lynnfield*, (18 ibid, 566.) By the act of 1847, ch. 37, whenever any city or town shall have voted to raise by taxation, or by pledge of its credit, or to pay over, from moneys in its treasury, any sum or sums of money, for any other purpose or purposes, than those for which it may have the legal right and power so to do, the supreme judicial court is authorized to interfere and prevent the same, upon the suit or petition of any ten inhabitants of such city or town who are liable to be taxed therein.

the public buildings, and the care, custody, and management of all the property of the city, with power to lease or sell the same, except the common and Faneuil Hall, with power also to purchase property, real or personal, in the name, and for the use of the city, whenever its interest or convenience may in their judgment, require it.[1]

Care and custody of city property.

Power to purchase property.

XXVI. All the power and authority by law vested, at the time of the act of incorporation, in the board of health for the town of Boston, relative to the quarantine of vessels, and relative to every other subject whatsoever, shall be and the same is hereby transferred to, and vested in the said city council, to be carried into execution by the appointment of health commissioners, or in such other manner as the health, cleanliness, comfort, and order of the city may, in their judgment, require, subject to such alterations as the legislature may from time to time adopt.[2] The mayor and aldermen of said city, and the said common council shall as soon as conveniently may be, after their annual organization, meet together in convention, and elect some suitable and trustworthy person to be the treasurer of said city, who shall also be county treasurer.

Board of health. 1821, 110, § 17. 12 Pick. 184.

City treasurer. 1821, 110, § 18.

County treasurer. R. S. 14, § 47.

XXVII. The citizens at their respective ward meetings, to be held on the second Monday of December annually, shall elect by ballot one person in each ward, to be an overseer of the poor; and the persons thus chosen shall together constitute the board of overseers for said city, and shall have all the powers and be subject to all the duties, by law appertaining, at the time of the act of incorporation, to the overseers of the poor for the town of Boston, until the same shall be altered or qualified by the legislature.[3]

Overseers of the poor. 1821, 110, § 19. 1824, 49, § 1. (Adopted by citizens, Feb. 25, 1825. Boston Records, vol. 10, p. 505.)

---

[1] For other powers of the mayor and aldermen, and of the city council, on various subjects, see the several titles, *post*.

[2] See Revised Statutes, c. 21, § 2, repealed by stat. 1847. c. 229. See also stat. 1849, c. 211.

[3] As to the corporate power of the overseers of the poor of Boston, see *Overseers of the Poor of Boston v. Sears*. (22 Pick. Rep. 122.)

School committee. 1835, 128, § 1. (Adopted by citizens in ward meetings, April 29, 1835. Records of returns of votes from the wards, April 29, 1835.) 1821, 110, § 19.

XXVIII. The school committee of the city of Boston shall consist of the mayor, of the president of the common council, and of twenty-four other persons, two of whom shall be chosen in each ward, and who shall be inhabitants of the wards in which they are chosen; said twenty-four members to be chosen by the inhabitants at their annual election of municipal officers; and said school committee shall have the care and superintendence of the public schools.

Accountability of all boards and officers for public money. 1821, 110, § 20. Annual financial statement.

XXIX. All boards, and officers, acting under the authority of the said corporation, and entrusted with the expenditure of public money, shall be accountable therefor to the city council in such manner as they may direct. And it shall be the duty of the city council to publish and distribute, annually, for the information of the citizens, a particular statement of the receipts and expenditures of all public moneys, and a particular statement of all city property.

Mayor may nominate certain officers. 1821, 110, § 21. Members of city council not eligible to salaried office.

XXX. In all cases in which appointments to office are directed to be made by the mayor and aldermen, the mayor shall have the exclusive power of nomination; such nomination, however, being subject to be confirmed or rejected by the board of aldermen: *Provided, however*, that no person shall be eligible to any office, the salary of which is payable out of the city treasury, who at the time of his appointment, shall be a member either of the board of aldermen or common council.

Number of representatives to general court. 1821, 110, § 22. 1831, 38.

XXXI. It shall be the duty of the two branches of the city council, in the month of October, in each year, after their annual organization, to meet in convention, and determine the number of representatives, which it may be expedient for the corporation to send to the general court in such year, within its constitutional limits, and to publish such determination, which shall be conclusive; and the number thus determined shall be specified in the warrant calling a meeting for the election of representatives; and neither the mayor, nor any aldermen, or members of the common council, shall, at the same time, hold any other office under the city government.

Members of city council to hold no other office, &c.

XXXII. All city officers, after their election, shall be held to discharge the duties to which they have been elected, being residents of the ward at the time of their election, notwithstanding their removal afterwards out of their ward into any other ward of the city.

Officers to discharge their duties notwithstanding removal into other wards. 1845, 217, § 5. (Adopted by city council. City Records, vol. 23, p. 406.)

XXXIII. All elections for governor, lieutenant governor, senators, representatives, representatives to congress, and all other officers, who are to be chosen and voted for by the people, shall be held at meetings of the citizens qualified to vote in such elections, in their respective wards, at the time fixed by law for those elections respectively. And at such meetings, all the votes given in, being collected, sorted, counted, and declared by the inspectors of elections, in each ward, it shall be the duty of the clerk of such ward to make a true record of the same, specifying therein the whole number of ballots given in, the name of each person voted for, and the number of votes for each, expressed in words at length. And a transcript of such record, certified by the warden, clerk, and a majority of the inspectors of elections in such ward, shall forthwith be transmitted or delivered by each ward clerk to the clerk of the city. And it shall be the duty of the city clerk forthwith to enter such returns, or a plain and intelligible abstract of them, as they are successively received, in the journals of the proceedings of the mayor and aldermen, or in some other book kept for that purpose. And it shall be the duty of the mayor and aldermen to meet together within two days after every such election, and examine and compare all the said returns, and thereupon to make out a certificate of the result of such election, to be signed by the mayor and a majority of the aldermen, and also by the city clerk, which shall be transmitted, delivered, or returned, in the same manner as similar returns are by law directed to be made by the selectmen of towns; and such

Elections of national and state officers. 1821, 110, § 23. R. S. 5, § 11; 6, § 9, 18.

Examination and return of votes.

Certificate.

certificates and returns shall have the same force and effect in all respects, as like returns of similar elections made by the selectmen of towns. At the election of governor, lieutenant governor, and senators, it shall be the duty of the mayor and aldermen to make and seal up separate lists of persons voted for as governor, lieutenant governor, and senators of the commonwealth, with the number of votes for each person, written in words at length against his name, and to transmit said lists to the secretary of the commonwealth or to the sheriffs of their respective counties. The mayor and aldermen shall, within three days next after the day of any election of electors of president and vice president of the United States, held by virtue of the laws of this commonwealth, or of the United States, deliver, or cause to be delivered the lists of votes therefor, sealed up, to the sheriff of the county, and the said sheriff shall within four days after receiving said lists, transmit the same to the office of the secretary of the commonwealth, or the said mayor and aldermen may, and when the office of sheriff is vacant, he or they shall themselves transmit the said lists to the said office within seven days after the election, and all votes not so transmitted shall be rejected. In all elections for representatives to the general court, in case the whole number proposed to be elected shall not be chosen by a majority of the votes legally returned, the mayor and aldermen shall forthwith issue their warrant for a new election, and the same proceedings shall be had in all respects as are herein before directed, until the whole number shall be elected.[1]

Separate lists of votes for governor, &c. to be transmitted to the secretary or to sheriffs. R. S. 5, § 1.

Votes for electors of president, &c., how and when to be transmitted to the secretary. 1844, 167, § 1.

Proceedings in case representatives are not chosen.

XXXIV. Prior to every election of city officers, or of any officer or officers under the government of the United States or of this commonwealth, it shall be the duty of said mayor and aldermen to make out lists of all the citizens of

Mayor and aldermen to make lists of voters prior to every election. 1821, 110, § 24. R. S. 3.

[1] This section of the city charter contains also a provision for taking the sense of the town upon the question, whether the election for State and United States officers should be holden in general meeting; which question was decided by the inhabitants in the negative, at a meeting held Monday, March 4, 1822. See Boston Records, vol. 10, p. 457.

each ward, qualified to vote in such election, in the manner in which selectmen and assessors of towns are required to make out similar lists of voters, and for that purpose they shall have free access to the assessors' books and lists, and be entitled to the aid and assistance of all assessors, assistant assessors, and other officers of said city. And it shall be the duty of said mayor and aldermen to deliver such list of the voters in each ward, so prepared and corrected, to the clerk of said ward, to be used by the warden and inspectors thereof at such election; and no person shall be entitled to vote at such election, whose name is not borne on such list. And to prevent all frauds and mistakes in such elections, it shall be the duty of the inspectors, in each ward, to take care that no person shall vote at such election, whose name is not so borne on the list of voters, and to cause a mark to be placed against the name of each voter on such list, at the time of giving in his vote.

Inspectors to allow no one to vote whose name is not on the list.

XXXV. It shall be the duty of all ward officers authorized to preside and act at elections of city officers to attend and perform their respective duties, at the times and places appointed for elections of any officers, whether of the United States, state, city, or wards, and to make and sign the regular returns of the same.

Duties of ward officers at all elections. 1845, 217, § 3. (Adopted by city council. City Records, vol. 23, p. 406.)

XXXVI. General meetings of the citizens, qualified to vote in city affairs, may from time to time be held to consult upon the common good, to give instructions to their representatives, and to take all lawful measures to obtain a redress of any grievances, according to the right secured to the people by the constitution of this commonwealth. And such meetings shall and may be duly warned by the mayor and aldermen, upon the requisition of fifty qualified voters of said city.

General meetings of the citizens. 1821, 110, § 25.

XXXVII. All warrants for the meetings of the citizens, for municipal purposes to be had either in general meetings or in wards, shall be issued by the mayor and aldermen, and shall be in such form, and shall be served,

Warrants for meetings to be issued by mayor and aldermen. 1821, 110, § 26.

executed, and returned at such time, and in such manner, as the city council may, by any by-law, direct and appoint.

City of Boston to have all the powers, &c. conferred by charter, &c. R. S. 16, § 86.

XXXVIII. The city of Boston shall continue to have and exercise all the powers and privileges, and be subject to all the duties and liabilities, mentioned in the act establishing said city of Boston, and in the several acts specially relating to said city.

SEAL OF THE CITY.

An Ordinance to establish the City Seal.

Ordinance to establish the city seal. Passed Jan. 2, 1823.

Be it ordained by the Mayor, Aldermen and Common Council of the City of Boston, in City Council assembled, That the design hereto annexed, as sketched by John R. Penniman, giving a view of the city, be the device of the city seal; that the motto be as follows, to wit: "Sicut patribus, sit Deus nobis;" and that the inscription be as follows, to wit: "Bostonia condita, A. D. 1630. Civitatis regimine donata, A. D. 1822."

ACTIONS.

1. All actions, suits and prosecutions against the city of Boston, may be brought in the county where the plaintiff lives, or in either of the counties of Suffolk, Essex, Middlesex or Norfolk.

Actions, &c., against the city of Boston where they may be brought. R. S. Act of amendment, § 13.

2. All actions, suits and prosecutions by the city of Boston, or by any officer for the use of the said city, may be brought in either of the four counties mentioned in the preceding section; but any such action, suit or prosecution, if brought in the county of Suffolk, may be removed to one of the said other counties, in the manner provided in the following section.

Actions, &c., by the city of Boston, where they may be brought, and when and to what counties they may be removed. Ibid.

3. The defendant or tenant, at the term at which his appearance is entered, may file a motion in writing for the removal of the suit to some other county, and the court shall thereupon order it to be removed to such one of the said other three counties as the attorney of the city of Boston shall elect, to be there heard and determined in any court proper to try the same; and the attorney of the said city shall enter the same accordingly, in the court so designated, at the next term thereof, and shall file therein certified copies of the writ or other process, and of the order of removal.

Such suits, how removed, entered, &c. Ibid.

4. The court to which the suit is so removed shall have jurisdiction thereof, and all the proceedings therein shall be conducted in like manner as if the suit had been originally commenced in that county.

How conducted. Ibid.

Inhabitants of Boston not disqualified by interest from acting as jurors, &c. Ibid.

5. No person shall be disqualified from acting as a magistrate, juror, appraiser, or officer of any kind, in any suit or process in which the city of Boston is interested, by reason of any interest that he may have as an inhabitant of the said city.

Mayor and aldermen may authorise any person to enter into recognizance. Ibid, § 4.

6. When any city shall be required to enter into a recognizance, the mayor and aldermen may, by an order or vote authorise any person to enter into the recognizance in the name and behalf of the city, and such recognizance shall be binding on the city, and on the inhabitants thereof, like any other contract lawfully made by such city.

In prosecutions, it shall be sufficient to set forth the offence, without setting forth the special act, by-law, ordinance, or any part thereof. 1824, 28, § 5.

7. In all prosecutions by complaint before the police court for the city of Boston, founded on the special acts of the legislature, the by-laws of the town of Boston, or the ordinances or the by-laws of the city of Boston, it shall be sufficient to set forth, in such complaint, the offence fully and plainly, substantially and formally; and in such complaint it shall not be necessary to set forth such special act, by-law, ordinance or any part thereof.

ALIEN PASSENGERS.

STATUTES.

1. Governor and council to appoint superintendent of alien passengers. Oaths. Bonds. Superintendent to give notice to pilots of the place of examination.
2. Salary. Proviso.
3. Duties. Prosecutions.
4. To examine into condition of passengers arriving, &c. Master of vessel to make report under oath.
5. Lunatics, idiots, &c., not permitted to land till bond given by master, &c. Proviso. Proviso as to such as are sick or destitute, when the master refuses to support them.
6. Superintendent to render accounts. Balance to be paid into the state treasury.
7. Abstract of reports and bonds to be published. Copy of abstract to be sent to each city and town.

1. The governor, with the advice and consent of the council, shall appoint and commission some suitable person to be superintendent of alien passengers in each city and town of the commonwealth, when it may be necessary for the execution of the provisions herein contained, who, before entering upon the duties of his office, shall be duly sworn, and shall give bonds to the state treasurer, with sufficient sureties for the performance thereof, in such sum as shall be specified by the governor in his commission, and who shall hold said office until another shall be appointed, commissioned, and qualified in his stead. And the superintendent shall, from time to time, notify the pilots of the port of the said city, or town, of the place or places where the said examination is to be made; and the said pilots shall be required to anchor all such vessels at the place so appointed, and shall require said vessels there to remain until such examination shall be had; and any pilot who shall refuse or neglect to perform the duty imposed upon him by this section, or who shall, through negligence or design, permit any alien passenger to land, before such examination shall be had, shall forfeit to the city or town a sum not less that fifty, nor more than two thousand dollars.

Governor and council to appoint superintendents of alien passengers. 1848, 313, § 1.

Oath. Bonds.

Superintendent to give notice to pilots of the place of examination.

Penalty.

2. The governor, with the advice and consent of the council, shall determine the salary of each superintendent of alien passengers, by him appointed, and shall specify the same in his commission; *provided, however*, that such salary shall never exceed the net amount of alien-passenger money received by such superintendent, according to the provisions of this act.

Salary. Ibid, § 2.

Proviso.

Duties. Ibid, § 3.

3. The superintendents of alien passengers shall have a care and oversight of all causes and matters arising under this act, in the city or town for which they are appointed; and whenever a breach of any of its provisions shall come to their knowledge, they shall, with the advice of the district attorney for their district, institute prosecutions, by indictment or otherwise, for the forfeitures incurred.

Prosecutions.

To examine into condition of passengers arriving, &c. Ibid, § 4.

4. When any vessel shall arrive at any port or harbor within this state, with alien passengers on board, who have never before been within the state, the superintendent of the city or town where it is intended to land such passengers, shall go on board such vessels, and shall examine into the condition of said passengers; and the master or commanding officer of such vessel shall, within twenty-four hours after such arrival, make a report in writing, under oath, to said superintendent, of the name, age, sex, occupation, place of birth, last place of residence, and condition, of every such passenger; and none of them shall be landed, or be permitted to land, until such report shall be made, except as is hereinafter provided.

Master of vessel to make report under oath.

No alien passenger permitted to land till report made.

Lunatics, idiots, &c., not permitted to land till bond given by master, &c. Ibid, § 5.

5. [If, on examination, there shall be found, among said passengers, any lunatic, idiot, maimed, aged, or infirm person, incompetent, in the opinion of the superintendent so examining, to maintain themselves, or who have been paupers in any other country, no such alien passengers shall be permitted to land until the master, owner, consignee, or agent of such vessel, shall make and deliver, to said superintendent, a bond to the commonwealth, with such sureties as are undoubted and satisfactory, in the sum of one thousand dollars, that no such lunatic or indigent passenger shall ever become a city, town, or state charge, from the date of said bond; *provided, however*, that if it shall be made to appear to said superintendent, by undoubted evidence, that any passengers on board such vessel are in such condition, as to health, property, capacity and character, that they are not likely to become chargeable to any city or town, he may permit them to be landed, on payment to him, by said master, consignee, or agent, of the sum of two dollars for each passenger so landed; and the names of all such

Proviso.

passengers shall be certified by said superintendent on the back of the report; *and provided, further*, that if any such passengers are so sick or destitute as to require relief, and if said master shall refuse to report them, or if said master, owner, consignee, or agent, shall refuse to give such bond as is herein required, the said superintendent may permit them to be landed; and in such cases, any city or town, that shall be put to any expenses for the support, sickness, or burial, of any such passenger, within ten years of the time he was so landed, may maintain an action of debt against said master, owner, consignee, or agent, and recover all expense incurred as aforesaid; and said commanding officer, owner, consignee, or agent, shall be liable to the penalties provided in the tenth section of this act.[1]]

Proviso as to such as are sick or destitute, when the master refuses to support them.

6. Every superintendent of alien passengers shall, on the third Wednesday of January, April, July, and October of each year, render an account, to the treasurer of the commonwealth, of all the money received by him and his assistants, under the provisions of this act, up to the first days of said months of January, April, July, and October; and, after deducting therefrom the amount of salary due to him up to which said quarterly accounts shall severally extend, shall pay the balance into the state treasury; and the treasurer shall, as soon as may be after the third Wednesday of January of each year, lay said accounts before the legislature.

Superintendents to render accounts. Ibid, § 6. But see *post*, p. 30.

Balance to be paid into state treasury.

7. The treasurer of the commonwealth shall cause to be published, monthly, in some convenient form for reference, an abstract of the reports and bonds deposited with him by superintendents, as provided in the seventh section,[2]

Abstract of reports and bonds to be published. Ibid, § 7. 1850, 105, § 3.

---

[1] This section is mainly if not entirely superseded by the first section of the act of 1850, c. 105. See p. 29, *post*. See also, *Norris v. City of Boston*, (4 Metcalf's Rep. 282.) *Smith v. Turner*, (7 Howard's U. S. Rep. 283.) *Norris v. City of Boston*, (ibid.)

[2] The intention here was, probably, to refer to the "seventh section" of the act as *originally reported*. In the act as it *finally passed*, that section was struck out. See Senate Documents, 1848, No.'s 46, 116, 122.

which abstract shall contain an alphabetical list of all the names of alien passengers that shall have been reported up to the time of publishing said abstract, and not previously published, with the reported age, sex, occupation, place of birth, and last place of residence, of each of said aliens; also the time and place of their landing, the name of the vessel from which they were landed, and, if bonds of indemnity shall have been given as is provided in the fifth section, the names of the obligors in said bonds, and their residences, and also the names of such alien passengers as shall have been permitted to land by any superintendent, under the second proviso contained in said fifth section; together with the name of the vessel from which they were landed, the time when landed, with the names respectively of the master, commanding officer, owner, consignee, or agent, of such vessel; and the treasurer shall forward a copy of said abstract, when so published, monthly, to the clerks of the several towns and cities in the commonwealth.[1]

Copy of abstract to be sent to each city and town. 1848, 313, § 7. 1850, 105, § 3.

Overseers of the poor to perform duties of superintendents in certain cases. 1848, 313, § 8.

8. The overseers of the poor, in any town where there may be no superintendent of alien passengers, or where such superintendent shall be unable to perform his duties by reason of absence or ill health, shall perform the duties and exercise the authority herein conferred on such superintendents, and shall in like manner render their accounts to the state treasurer, and pay over the money so received, deducting therefrom a reasonable compensation for their services.

Penalty for landing passengers with intent to avoid, &c. Ibid, § 9.

9. If any master, or commanding officer of any vessel, shall land any such alien passengers at any place within this state other than those to which said vessel is destined, with intent to avoid the requirements of this act, such master or commanding officer shall forfeit the sum of one hundred dollars for every such passenger so landed.

Penalty for landing passengers without complying with law. Ibid, § 10.

10. If any master or commanding officer of any vessel shall land, or permit to be landed, in this state, any alien passengers as aforesaid, without complying with the fore-

[1] So much of this section as relates to alien passengers not bonded, was repealed by stat. 1849, c. 34.

going provisions, said master or commanding officer, and the owner or consignee thereof, shall severally forfeit the sum of five hundred dollars for every such alien passenger so landed; *provided*, always, that the provisions in this act shall not extend to seamen sent from foreign places by consuls or vice-consuls of the United States, nor to vessels coming on shore in distress, or to any alien passenger taken from any wreck, where life is in danger.[1] **Proviso.**

11. Any master, owner, consignee, or agent of any vessel, or any passenger-carrier by water, who shall bring or aid in bringing into this commonwealth, any alien never before within the state, shall, for each and every such alien, give a bond to the commonwealth with good and sufficient sureties, to be approved by the superintendent of alien passengers, in the penalty of one thousand dollars, with a condition that no such alien shall ever become a city, town or state charge as a pauper, and in default of giving such bond, shall forfeit and pay to the use of the commonwealth, the sum of one thousand dollars for every such alien so brought into the state, to be recovered by action of debt, in any court competent to try the same; *provided*, that it shall be at the option of every such master, owner, consignee, or agent of any vessel, or passenger-carrier by water, to pay to the superintendent of alien passengers, for the use of the commonwealth, in place of such bond, the sum of two dollars for every such alien, who is not, in the opinion of the superintendent, a pauper, lunatic, or idiot, or maimed, aged, infirm or destitute, or incompetent to take care of himself or herself, without becoming a public charge as a pauper; *and provided, also*, that this act shall not extend to seamen sent from foreign ports by consuls or vice-consuls of the United States, nor to ambassadors, consuls, or public ministers, or other persons representing foreign states, nor to persons coming on shore from vessels in distress, nor to any alien passenger taken from any wreck where life is in danger.

Master, owner, &c., of vessel, to give bond for every alien passenger.
1850, 105, § 1.
Penalty.
May pay $2 instead.
Proviso.

---

[1] The stat. of 1848, c. 313, § 11, repealed stat. 1837, c. 238; 1840, c. 96; and 1845, c. 76.

Superintendent may make demand for bonds and examinations. Ibid, § 2.

12. The superintendent of alien passengers in any city or town of this commonwealth, may make all demands for bonds under the preceding section, and all examinations of alien passengers, brought or coming into this state by water, necessary to enforce the provisions of all acts in relation to alien passengers.

Paupers may be sent home. R. S., 46, § 17. 1850, 105, § 4.

13. Upon the complaint of superintendents of alien passengers, justices of the peace may, by warrant directed to, and to be executed by any constable, or any other person therein designated, cause any pauper, residing or found in their towns, having no lawful settlement, within this state, to be sent and conveyed, at the expense of the state by land or water, to any other state, or to any place beyond sea, where he belongs, if the justice thinks proper, and if he may conveniently be removed; but if he cannot be so removed, he may be sent to and relieved, and employed in the house of correction or work-house at the public expense.[1]

Expenses for support of bonded alien to be paid by commonwealth. Ibid, § 6.

14. Whenever any city or town shall have incurred any expense or charge for the support of any alien for whom a bond has been given, under the foregoing provisions, the claims of such city or town therefor, upon being approved by the auditor, may be paid by the treasurer of the commonwealth, whose duty it shall be to cause the same to be forthwith collected of the obligors in such bond, and paid into the treasury of the commonwealth.

Superintendents to make annual returns of receipts and expenditures. 1850, 292, § 1. See *ante*, p. 27.

15. The superintendents of alien passengers shall, on or before the fifteenth day of December of each year, make returns of all moneys by them received and expended, to the treasurer of the commonwealth, and said returns shall show the details of every account for which said moneys have been received and expended.

---

[1] The act of 1850, c. 105, § 5, repealed all acts and parts of acts, inconsistent with that act.

AMUSEMENTS.

1. The mayor and aldermen of any city, or the selectmen of any town, may license all theatrical exhibitions, public shows, public amusements, and exhibitions of every description, to which admission is obtained upon payment of money, or the delivery of any valuable thing, or by any ticket, or voucher, obtained for money, or any valuable thing, upon such terms and conditions as they shall think reasonable; and they may revoke or suspend the same whenever there shall appear to them to be sufficient cause for such revocation or suspension.

Mayor and aldermen may license theatrical and other exhibitions, &c.
9 Pick. 415.
See *ante*, p. 13.
1849, 231, § 1.

2. Any person who shall offer to view, or shall set up, set on foot, maintain, or carry on, or shall publish, or otherwise assist in, or promote any such exhibition, show, or amusement, as mentioned in the preceding section, without a license as therein specified, shall be punished by a fine not exceeding five hundred dollars for each offence.

Penalty for exhibition without a license.
Ibid, § 2.

3. Any person who shall get up and set on foot, or cause to be published, or otherwise aid in getting up and promoting any masked ball, or other public assembly, at which the company wear masks, or other disguises, and to which admission is obtained upon payment of money, or the delivery of any valuable thing, or by any ticket or voucher obtained for money, or any valuable thing, shall be punished by a fine not exceeding five hundred dollars; and for a repetition of the offence, by imprisonment in the common jail or house of correction, not exceeding one year.

Masked balls forbidden, under penalty.
Ibid, § 3.

AUCTIONEERS.

STATUTES.

1. Mayor and aldermen may license auctioneers.
2. Conditions to be inserted in the license.
3. Penalty for selling in Boston, contrary to license.
4. Tenants, &c. answerable, if they permit unlicensed sales in their premises.

Mayor and aldermen may license auctioneers. 1821, 110, § 13. 1795, 8, § 1.

1. By the operation of the city charter, transferring all the powers of the selectmen of Boston to the mayor and aldermen, and of the statute of 1795, c. 8, § 1, in force when the city charter was adopted, the power of licensing auctioneers in Boston, is in the mayor and aldermen.

Conditions to be inserted in the license. R. S. 29, § 13.

2. In all licenses granted to auctioneers in the city of Boston, the mayor and aldermen may make such conditions, respecting the places of selling goods and chattels by auction, within said city, as they shall think expedient.

Penalty for selling in Boston, contrary to license. Ibid, § 14.

3. If any person shall make any sale by auction in the city of Boston, at any place not authorized by his license, he shall be subject to the like penalties as for selling by auction without license; and the same shall be recovered, by action of debt, or by indictment, to the use of the city of Boston.

Tenants, &c., answerable, if they permit unlicensed sales in their premises. 1819, 132, § 2.

4. The owner, tenant or occupant of any house or store, having the actual possession and control of the same, who shall allow or permit any person, licensed as aforesaid, to sell any goods or chattels by public auction or out cry, in his said house or store, or in any apartment or yard appurtenant to the same, contrary to the conditions, limitations or restrictions, annexed to the license of such person, shall be liable and subject to the same penalties and forfeitures, to be prosecuted for and recovered in the same manner, as if such owner, occupant or tenant, had knowingly allowed or permitted any unlicensed person, to sell any goods or chattels, by public auction, or out cry, in his said house and store, or in any apartment or yard appurtenant thereunto.[1]

[1] For general laws respecting sales by auctioneers, see Rev. Stat. c. 29; also stat. 1837, c. 233; 1839, c. 111; 1843, c. 21; 1844, c. 36, 90; 1847, c. 264; 1849, c. 138; 1850, c. 42.

BOATS AND LIGHTERS.

STATUTES.

1. Weighers of Lighters, &c., to be appointed by the mayor and aldermen.
2. Lighters, &c., to be marked.
3. Duty of weighers.
4. Deduction may be made of one ton for every inch, &c.
5. Persons on board, to keep between bulk head and fore chains, under penalty.
6. Marks to be examined every year.
7. Fees.
8. Penalty for neglecting to have lighters weighed.
9. Penalty for falsely placing marks, &c.
10. City council authorized to make ordinances, &c., weighing and marking vessels.

1. By the Revised Statutes, the mayor and aldermen of the city of Boston are required to appoint, in the months of March or April, annually, one or more weighers of vessels, who shall be sworn to the faithful discharge of the duties of that office.

Weighers of lighters, &c., to be appointed by the mayor and aldermen. R. S. 31, § 1.

2. Every lighter or other vessel employed in transporting any stone sold by weight, or any gravel or sand, is required to be marked on the stem and stern post, nearly level with the bend of such vessel, with stationary marks of bar iron, not less than six inches in length, and two and a half inches in breadth, fastened with two good and sufficient iron bolts, driven through said stem and stern post, and riveted into the said bar iron, from which all other marks shall take their distance, in feet, inches, and parts of inches, as the distance may require, from the lower edge of the said stationary marks to the lower edge of the other marks; which marks shall be as follows, namely; light water marks, not less than four inches in length and one inch and a half in breadth; and every four tons above said light water marks, legibly cut, or cast, in figures, of 4, 8, 12, 16, 20, and so forth, up to the full capacity of the vessel; and said figures shall express the weight, which such vessel is capable of carrying, when the lower part of the respective numbers aforesaid shall touch the water; and all the said marks shall be of good and sufficient lead or

Lighters, &c. to be marked. Ibid, § 2.

copper, fastened on the stem and stern post of each vessel with sufficient nails not less than one inch in length.

Duty of weighers.
Ibid, § 3.

3. Every such weigher shall furnish all the requisite marks and nails, when thereto requested, and shall cause all such lighters and other vessels to be weighed and marked in conformity with the provisions of the preceding section, and during the time of so weighing and marking them, all the persons, employed on board of said vessels, shall be stationed between the bulk head and the fore chains thereof; he shall also keep a correct account of the distance of each mark, below the stationary marks, in feet, inches and parts of inches, in a book to be kept for that purpose, and give a certificate thereof, expressing the distance as aforesaid, to the master of every such vessel.

Deduction may be made of one ton for every inch, &c.
Ibid, § 4.

4. In taking the tonnage of every such vessel, a deduction may be made of one ton, for every inch that the light water marks may be under water, after such vessel shall have discharged their loading.

Persons on board, to keep between bulk head and fore chains, under penalty.
Ibid, § 5.

5. Every person, on board of any such vessel, who shall not keep within the bounds of the bulk head and fore chains, during the time of taking her marks, or while any weigher shall be employed in weighing or marking as aforesaid, unless in case of absolute necessity, shall forfeit a sum not exceeding twenty dollars for every offence.

Marks to be examined every year.
Ibid, § 6.

6. All such vessels shall have their marks examined in the month of June in each year, by a sworn weigher, who shall ascertain if their marks agree with their former certificates, and, if so, shall certify the same accordingly; and in case such marks should not agree with the former certificates, the said weigher shall keep such certificates in his possession, to be used as evidence against the master or owner of said vessel, in any prosecution under the provisions of this chapter; and such vessel shall, moreover, in such case, be weighed again.

Fees.
Ibid, § 7.

7. Every weigher of vessels shall be entitled to receive, from the owner or master of each vessel, weighed and marked according to the provisions of this chapter, the following fees, to wit; twenty cents for every ton of such vessel, and four dollars for furnishing marks, nails, and

other necessary articles, and fastening the same, and giving the certificate, as before provided; and for the services required of him by the preceding section, he shall receive one dollar and fifty cents.

8. Every owner or master of any such vessel, who shall neglect to have the same weighed, marked and examined, according to the provisions of this chapter, or who shall remove any marks, or alter his certificate, shall forfeit a sum not exceeding three hundred dollars for every offence.

Penalty for neglecting to have lighters weighed. Ibid, § 8.

9. Every such weigher, who shall be guilty of placing any such mark, contrary to the provisions of this chapter, or who shall give a false certificate, shall forfeit a sum not exceeding three hundred dollars for every offence.

Penalty for falsely placing marks, &c. Ibid, § 9.

10. A statute was passed in 1848, authorizing the city council of the city of Boston to establish any ordinances and regulations respecting the weighing and marking of lighters, and other vessels employed in the transportation of stones, gravel, sand, or other ballast, and for the inspection and weighing such ballast within the city of Boston, including the appointment and compensation of weighers, markers, inspectors, or other officers necessary to carry such ordinances and regulations into effect, as they may deem expedient, and to affix penalties for the breach thereof, not exceeding those provided above; and providing that the adoption of any such ordinance or regulation shall supersede the foregoing provisions, within said city, so far as the same shall be inconsistent with, or repugnant to said provisions.

City council authorized to make ordinances, &c. respecting weighing and marking of vessels. 1848, 308.

BOUNDARY LINES.

STATUTES, &c.

1. Line between Boston and Roxbury.
2. Ratification of the line agreed upon between Boston and Roxbury.
3. Line between Boston and Roxbury declared.
4. Line between Boston and Roxbury modified.

5. Line between Boston and Roxbury altered.
6. Further altered.
7. Further altered. Proviso as to election of senators.
8. Mayor and aldermen of Boston shall cause monuments to be erected, &c.
9. Mayor and aldermen of Boston to furnish lists of voters to Roxbury. Penalty.
10. Annexation of part of Dorchester to Boston, (S. Boston.)
11. Lots of land to be set apart for public use, in South Boston.
12. Selectmen authorized to lay out streets in South Boston. Provisoes.
13. Thompson's Island annexed to Boston.
14. Line between Boston and Brookline. Suffolk and Norfolk counties. Proviso as to wooden buildings.
15. Land annexed to ward No. 6.

PERAMBULATIONS.

16. Boston and Roxbury.
17. Boston and Dorchester.
18. Boston and Brookline.

Line between Boston and Roxbury.

(Selectmen's minutes, from 1786 to 1792, p. 119.)

1. It appears, from the records of the selectmen of the town of Boston, May 20, 1788, that the following boundary line between Boston and Roxbury was agreed upon by the selectmen of both towns, and the agreement was accepted by the selectmen of Boston, to wit;—Beginning at the mouth of the creek which opens into the bay leading to Cambridge, and as the creek runs until it comes in a range with the fence and trees between the land now occupied by the widow Susannah Davis, formerly John Richardson, Esquire's, and the land now belonging to the heirs of Samuel Wells, Esq., deceased, formerly Mr. Minot's, then across the street or highway, until it comes to a large stone standing endwise in the fence on the easterly side of said street or highway, and from thence south forty-three degrees east to a large stone standing endwise in the ground about eighty feet from the said street or highway, marked B. on the easterly side, and R. on the westerly side, and from thence the same course to a large stone standing in the meadow, marked B. on the northwesterly side, and R. on the southeasterly side; from thence turning and running north fifty-eight degrees, east by a straight line until it comes to a stone affixed in Lamb's Dam, (so called) and from thence to the creek, and as said creek runs into the bay between the towns of Boston and Dorchester.

Ratification of the line agreed upon between

2. An act was passed, April 30, 1787, for altering part of the boundary line between the towns of Boston and

Roxbury, and for ratifying an agreement made between the said towns for that purpose, reciting, that that part of the boundary line between the towns of Boston and Roxbury, which crossed *Lamb's Meadow*, so called, was nearly obliterated, and that the selectmen of said towns had petitioned the general court, that a new direct line might be established in lieu thereof, agreeably to a plan mutually agreed on by the said towns; and that it appeared reasonable that said agreement should be ratified and confirmed: and declaring that the agreement entered into between the towns of Boston and Roxbury, for altering that part of the boundary line between the said towns, which crossed *Lamb's Meadow*, so called, be ratified and confirmed. **Boston and Roxbury.** 1786, 87, § 1.

3. It was also provided, that a line in lieu of the aforesaid obliterated boundary line, should in all future perambulations thereof, be run in the following manner, that is to say, by a straight line in the same direction with the then existing line from the road leading from Boston to Roxbury, from the most easterly boundary-marked stone in the said *Lamb's Meadow*, one chain and forty-one links; thence turning and running north fifty-eight degrees east, by a straight line across the said meadow, until it strikes the ancient boundary mark in *Lamb's Dam*, so called. **Line between Boston and Roxbury declared.** Ibid, § 2.

4. By an act passed in 1836, it was provided, that the following lines, which have been mutually agreed upon between the city of Boston and the town of Roxbury, shall thereafter constitute and be considered the boundary lines in the section to which they refer, between said city and said town, to wit; beginning at a stone monument on the southwesterly side of the dyke that forms the southwesterly boundary of the Empty Basin, so called, from which point the centre of the steeple of Park Street meeting-house, in said city, bears north, fifty-three degrees east, this line to run in this direction from the point above mentioned, about two hundred and ninety rods, until it strikes the centre of the main channel westerly of the rope-walk lands, in said city; thence turning and running northerly in the centre of said channel, about one hundred and twenty-five rods, to a point two hundred feet distant, southerly, from the main **Line between Boston and Roxbury, modified.** 1836, 37.

branch of the Mill Dam, or Western Avenue; thence turning nearly at right angles, and running westerly nearly on a parallel line with said Mill Dam, until it strikes the branch thereof leading to Roxbury, at which point a stone monument has been erected. And the territory and jurisdiction on either side of the said lines as thereby established, were accordingly confirmed to said city and town respectively.

Line between Boston and Roxbury altered. 1837, 202, § 1.

5. By an act passed in 1837, the boundary line between the city of Boston and the town of Roxbury, which then ran on the easterly side of Plymouth Street, was altered, so that the same was thereafter established as follows, to wit; beginning at a stone monument, which then marked the south corner bound of said city, being one hundred and forty-one feet easterly of said Plymouth Street, and from the said monument running on a straight line in a northeasterly direction to the Centre Point, (so called,) where the Roxbury old and new channels form a junction, being about four thousand five hundred feet from the said monument.

Further altered. Ibid, § 2.

6. The boundary line between the said city and town which then passed over a part of Tremont Street, in said city, was also altered, so that the same was thereafter established as follows, to wit; beginning on the southeasterly side of said Tremont Street, at the centre of a bridge then erected across the creek which divides the said city from said town, and thence running northwesterly at right angles with said Tremont Street, about two hundred and fifty feet, until it intersects the then boundary line between said city and town, in the middle of said creek.

Further altered. 1850, 281, § 1.

7. The boundary line between the city of Boston and the city of Roxbury, southeasterly of Harrison Avenue, was altered and established, by an act passed in 1850, as follows, to wit; beginning at a point in the present boundary line at the centre of the Roxbury Canal, (so called,) thence running in the centre of said canal to a point in the same, situate one thousand and seven feet from the southeasterly side of Harrison Avenue, measuring southeasterly and in the range of the westerly side of Worcester Street

in said Boston, thence running in a straight line northeasterly about twenty-six hundred and twenty-two feet to a pile monument in the Roxbury Channel in the present line; and all that portion of land or flats northwest of the line thereby established, was thereby annexed to and made part of the said city of Boston, in the county of Suffolk: *Provided*, however, that the territory so transferred, shall, for the purpose of electing senators, continue to be and remain, a part of the city of Roxbury; and that all the inhabitants residing upon it shall, until otherwise constitutionally provided, always enjoy, in relation to the election of senators, all the rights and privileges of, and in relation to, voting in the said city of Roxbury, which they would have possessed if this act had not passed, such voting to be in the ward, whereof the place of voting shall be for the time being, nearest the westerly corner of the said territory.

Proviso as to election of senators.

8. The mayor and aldermen of the city of Boston shall cause suitable monuments to be erected and continued, showing the line between the said city of Boston, as it has existed by said territory hitherto, and shall cause the same to be perambulated in like manner and with the like penalties for neglect, as now by law is or are provided in respect to other boundary lines of cities and towns, such penalties to be recovered against the said city of Boston.

Mayor and aldermen of Boston shall cause monuments to be erected. Ibid, § 2.

9. The mayor and aldermen of the city of Boston shall annually furnish to the city authorities of Roxbury, forty-eight hours at least before any senatorial election, correct lists, so far as may be ascertainable from the records and doings of the said city of Boston or any of its officers, of all persons resident in the territory hereby set off, who shall be entitled to vote for senators as aforesaid, in the said city of Roxbury: and the said city of Boston, for every neglect of its said mayor and aldermen so to furnish such list, shall forfeit the sum of one hundred dollars; and for the making of a false return in respect to any part of such list, shall forfeit the sum of twenty dollars for every name in respect to which a false return shall have been made; to be recovered in the same manner as is provided

Mayor and aldermen of Boston to furnish lists of voters to Roxbury. Ibid, § 3.

Penalty.

by the fourth section of the third chapter of the Revised Statutes, in respect to penalties for neglect or false returns by collectors of towns.

Annexation of part of Dorchester to Boston, (South Boston.) 1803, 111, § 1.

10. By the act of annexation of South Boston, passed March 6, 1804, it was provided that all that part of Dorchester, lying northeast of the following line, viz: Beginning at a stake and stones at Old Harbor, so called, at the southwest corner of land formerly belonging to John Champney, running north thirty-seven and one half degrees west, to a large elm tree, marked D. on the southwest side, and B. on the northeast side, standing on land belonging to the heirs of Thomas Bird, deceased; then running the same course to a heap of stones on the southeast side of the road; thence across the road, the same course, to a heap of stones on the northwest side; thence on the same course to a black oak tree, standing on a small hummock, marked D. on one side, and B. on the other side, upon land of Ebenezer Clap, jr.; thence the same course till it comes to Boston Harbor, with the inhabitants thereon, be annexed to the town of Boston, in the county of Suffolk, and be considered and deemed to be a part of the town of Boston.

Lots of land to be set apart for public use in South Boston. Ibid, § 2.

11. It was further provided by the same act, that the proprietors of the said tract, should assign and set apart three lots of land on the same, for public use, viz: one lot for the purpose of a public market place, one lot for a school house, and one lot for a burial ground, to the satisfaction and acceptance of the selectmen of the town of Boston; or in case the said selectmen and proprietors should not agree upon the said lots, it should be lawful for the supreme judicial court, at any session thereof in the said county of Suffolk, upon application of the said selectmen, to nominate and appoint three disinterested freeholders within the commonwealth, and not inhabitants of said town of Boston, to assign and set off the three lots aforesaid, by metes and bounds; and the report of the said freeholders, or any two of them, being made and returned to, and accepted by the said court, at any session thereof in said county, should be final and binding upon all parties; and the lots of land by them assigned and set off as afore-

said, should thenceforth vest in the said town of Boston forever, without any compensation to be made therefor by the town; but if the person or persons whose land should be assigned and set apart as aforesaid, should demand compensation therefor, the same should be appraised by three freeholders to be appointed as aforesaid, who should also assess upon the other proprietors, the sum or sums which each should be holden to pay to the person whose lands might be thus assigned for public use; and the report of said freeholders or any two of them, being made and returned to, and accepted by said court, judgment thereon should be final, and execution awarded as in cases of reports by referees, under a rule of court.

12. The selectmen of Boston were authorized to lay out such streets and lanes through the said tract, as in their judgment might be for the common benefit of the said proprietors and of said town of Boston; a reasonable attention being paid to the wishes of the proprietors; and in case of disagreement between the selectmen and proprietors, or either of them, the same proceedings were to be had as were provided by law in other cases for laying out town ways: *provided, only*, that no damages or compensation should be allowed to any proprietor for such streets and lanes as might be laid out within twelve months from the passing of this act: *and provided, also*, that the town of Boston should not be obliged to complete the streets laid out by their selectmen pursuant to this act, sooner than they might deem it expedient so to do.[1]

Selectmen authorized to lay out streets in South Boston. Ibid, § 3.

Provisoes.

13. By a statute passed March 25, 1834, it was enacted, that Thompson's Island, lying in the harbor of Boston, and previously a part of the town of Dorchester, with the inhabitants thereon, should be annexed to the city of Boston, in the county of Suffolk; and should be considered and deemed to be a part of the city of Boston; *provided*, that said island should revert to the town of

Thompson's Island annexed to Boston. 1834, 102.

Provisoes.

[1] As to the streets in South Boston, see *Commonwealth v. City of Boston*, (16 Pick. Rep. 442;) *Wright v. Tukey*, and *Bowman v. City of Boston*, decided in the supreme judicial court, March term, 1849.

Dorchester, in one year after it should cease, by the voluntary act of the proprietors, to be used for the purposes of a farm school, or other charitable public purposes, and should be appropriated to any other use; *and provided, also*, that nothing in the act contained should destroy or affect any lawful right that the inhabitants of the said town of Dorchester then had, to dig and take clams on the banks of said island. The island is exempted from taxation, so long as it shall continue to be appropriated to the use of the Boston Farm School, or to any similar public charity.[1]

Line between Boston and Brookline. 1824, 90, § 1.

14. By an act passed February 22, 1825, it was provided, that the agreement made by and between the mayor and aldermen of the city of Boston, for and in behalf of said city, and the selectmen of the town of Brookline, in behalf of said town, relative to the boundary lines between the said city and town, be ratified and confirmed, and that henceforth the boundary lines between the said city and town, should be as follows, viz. beginning at a point marked (*a*) on a plan drawn by S. P. Fuller, 1123 feet distant westerly from the westerly side of the filling sluices of the Boston and Roxbury mill dam; thence running northwesterly from the said point (*a*) at an angle of 115 degrees from the mill dam, until it strikes the centre of the channel of Charles River, and also running from the said point (*a*) southerly, at an angle of 103 degrees forty minutes, until it strikes the centre of the channel of Muddy River, at a point where the respective boundaries of Boston, Brookline, and Roxbury meet each other. It was further enacted, that the boundary lines between the counties respectively of Suffolk and Norfolk, so far as they were affected by the act, should thereafter conform to the said boundary lines between the said city and town, and the same were declared and established to be the boundary lines between the said counties respectively, any thing in any former act to the contrary notwithstanding: *provided, however*, that the several laws regulating the erection of buildings within

Suffolk and Norfolk counties. Ibid, § 2.

Proviso as to wooden buildings.

[1] For enactments respecting the Boston Asylum and Farm School, see 1813, c. 153; 1823, c. 53; 1833, c. 135; 1835, c. 28; and 1838, c. 16.

the city of Boston, should not extend to the land thereby transferred from the said town of Brookline, to the said city.

15. By an act passed March 3, 1826, the tract of land annexed to the city of Boston by the preceding act, was made a part of ward numbered six, in said city.

Land annexed to ward 6. 1825, 128.

PERAMBULATIONS.[1]

16. The mayor and aldermen of Boston and Roxbury, on the 25th of November, 1846, made a perambulation of the line between Boston and Roxbury, pursuant to the Revised Statutes, and run the line and renewed the bound marks between the city of Boston and the city of Roxbury, as follows, to wit: Beginning in the centre of the channel dividing the city of Roxbury and the town of Dorchester, at the point where the line dividing the city of Boston from the town of Dorchester intersects the centre of said channel; from thence running northerly by the centre of said channel until it meets the centre of another channel; then running westerly through the centre of the last mentioned channel to a monument placed therein; then running in a southwesterly direction about 4500 feet to a stone monument standing in a meadow which marks the south bounds of the city of Boston, which monument is marked B. on the northeasterly side and R. on the southwesterly side; from thence running northwesterly five hundred and forty-two feet and one half foot, to a stone post two hundred and fifteen feet from the former line of Washington Street; thence continuing the same course two hundred and fifteen feet to a stone post standing in Washington Street, marked B. on the northeasterly side, and R. on the southwesterly side; from thence across said street to the fence dividing the land now or formerly belonging to Isaac Scott and others, (formerly also of Minot,) from land now or formerly belonging to Susannah and Sarah Davis, (formerly also of John Richardson, Esq.;) thence by said fence and the line

Perambulation of line between Boston and Roxbury, Nov. 25, 1846. City Records, vol. 24, p. 601.

[1] For general provisions respecting the boundaries of towns, and the perambulation of the same, see Rev. Stat., c. 15, § 1–7.

thereof continued to the creek, formerly opening into the bay leading to Cambridge, but now into the full basin of the Boston and Roxbury Mill Corporation; thence through the centre of said creek to the centre of the bridge across Tremont Street; thence by a line running northwesterly at right angles with said Tremont Street, about two hundred and fifty feet, to the middle of said creek; thence by the centre of said creek to a stone post standing on the dyke of said corporation, dividing said full basin from the receiving basin of said corporation, marked B. on the southeasterly side, and R. on the northwesterly side; from thence running north fifty-three degrees east, in a direction to the steeple of Park Street meeting-house in Boston, about two hundred and ninety rods to the centre of the main channel westerly of Charles and Pleasant Streets in Boston; from thence northerly through the centre of said channel to a point two hundred feet distant southerly from the mill dam, or Western Avenue, running westerly by a straight line to a stone post, standing on the easterly side of the branch of the said mill dam leading to Roxbury, marked B. on the northerly side, and R. on the southerly side; thence across said branch dam to another stone post standing on the westerly side thereof, and marked B. on the northerly side, and R. on the southerly side; thence by the centre of the channel, in said full basin, to the line dividing Boston and Roxbury from Brookline.[1]

Between Boston and Dorchester. Ibid, p. 599.

17. The line between Boston and Dorchester was perambulated on the same day, by the mayor and aldermen of Boston and the selectmen of Dorchester, as follows: Beginning at Old Harbor, so called, at the southwest corner of land formerly belonging to John Champney, running north, thirty-seven and one half degrees west, to a stone post marked B. on the northeast side, and D. on the southwest side; then running the same courses to another stone post, standing near Dorchester Street, marked B. on the northeast side, and D. on the southwest side; then across

---

[1] The line thus perambulated was altered by the statute of 1850, c. 281. See *ante*, pp. 38, 39

said Dorchester Street, and continuing the same course, to a stone post standing on the Dorchester Turnpike, marked B. on the northeast side, and D. on the southwest side; then continuing the same course until it comes to Boston Harbor, being the same line described in the act entitled, "An act to set off the northeast part of the town of Dorchester, and to annex the same to the town of Boston."

18. The line between Boston and Brookline was also perambulated as follows: Beginning at a stone post marked *Bo.* on the easterly side, and *Br.* on the westerly side, standing on the Boston and Roxbury Mill Dam, westerly from the new filling sluices erected in said dam, (the old sluices referred to in the act of February 22d, 1825, entitled "an act relative to the boundary lines of the city of Boston and to the town of Brookline" having been removed;) thence running northwesterly from said post, at an angle of one hundred and fifteen degrees from the mill dam, until it strikes the centre of the channel of Charles River, and also running from the said post, southerly, at an angle of one hundred and three degrees forty minutes, until it strikes the centre of the channel of Muddy River, at a point where the respective boundaries of Boston, Brookline, and Roxbury meet each other, being the same lines mentioned and described in the above recited act.

Between Boston and Brookline. Ibid, p. 600.

BRIDGES.

STATUTES.

1. Incorporation of Boston South Bridge.
2. Width, and manner of building and maintaining said bridge.
3. Proprietors authorized to transfer the franchise and materials to the city of Boston; to be toll free. Provision for surrender to the commonwealth, in case, &c.
4. Provision for discontinuance of the bridge, in case, &c.
5. Transfer of Boston South Bridge to the city.
6. Boston Free Bridge Corporation. Authority to build a bridge.

BOSTON SOUTH BRIDGE.

Incorporation of Boston South Bridge. 1803, 113, §§ 1, 2, 3, 5, 6, 8.

1. By an act passed March 6, 1804, William Tudor, Gardiner Greene, Jonathan Mason and Harrison Gray Otis, and those who should become their associates, were made a corporation, under the name of "The Proprietors of the Boston South Bridge." Provisions were made for organization, the rates of toll, the amount to be paid to vessels passing the draw, and the indemnity to be paid to persons whose land should be taken; and a penalty of not more than fifty nor less than twenty dollars was imposed upon the corporation, for every neglect or refusal to open the draw, or unnecessary detention of any vessel about to pass. It was also provided that the act should be void, if the corporation should refuse or neglect to build and complete the bridge for the space of three years. The provision for the payment to vessels passing the draw was repealed by an act passed March 12, 1830.

Ibid, § 7.

1829, 119.

Width and manner of building and maintaining said bridge. 1803, 113, § 4.

2. The fourth section of the same act provided, that the bridge should be built of good and sufficient materials, not less than forty feet wide, and well covered with plank or timber, suitable for such a bridge, with sufficient rails on each side for the safety of travellers and protection of foot passengers; that it should be kept accommodated with not less than twenty lamps, which should be well supplied with oil, and lighted in due season, and kept burning until

midnight; that there should be made a good and sufficient draw or passage way, at least thirty feet wide, in the channel over which said bridge should be built, proper for the passing and repassing of vessels, through which vessels might pass free of toll; that there should be erected at said draw and maintained in good repair, a well constructed and substantial pier or wharf on each side of the bridge, and adjoining to the draw, every way sufficient for vessels to lie at securely; that the draw should be lifted for all vessels without delay and without toll, except for boats passing for pleasure; that the proprietors might make the leaves of the draw twenty feet long, instead of the width of the bridge; and that the bridge should be kept in good, safe and passable repair for the term of seventy years from the day of the first opening of the bridge for passengers, and at the expiration of said term should be surrendered to the commonwealth, who should be deemed the successor of the corporation.

3. On the 23d of June, 1831, after the Boston Free Bridge had been built, and the Boston South Bridge was greatly diminished in value, in consequence thereof, an act was passed, authorizing and empowering the proprietors of the Boston South Bridge to sell, assign, and transfer to the city of Boston, the franchise and materials of said Boston South Bridge, to have and to hold the same to the said city and its successors forever; *provided*, that no toll or duty should ever be exacted or paid for any travel over said bridge, or passing the draw of the same, and the said city should always be held liable to keep said bridge and draw in good repair, and to raise the draw of said bridge, and afford all necessary and proper accommodation to vessels that have occasion to pass the same by night or by day, and should keep said bridge sufficiently lighted. This act also authorized the proprietors to surrender the franchise to the commonwealth, in case the city of Boston should not, before the 15th of September in the same year, pay them such sum as should be agreed upon, and receive a transfer.

Proprietors authorized to transfer the franchise and materials to the city of Boston. 1831, 71, § 1.

To be toll free.

Provision for surrender to commonwealth, in case, &c. Ibid, § 2.

4. By an additional act, passed March 16, 1832, the proprietors of the Boston South Bridge were authorized to

Provision for discontinuance of the bridge, in case, &c.

1832, 136, § 1. discontinue said bridge, as a pass way, and at any time between the passing of this act, and the first day of August then next, if the city of Boston, before the first day of May then next, should not pay to said proprietors such sum of money as might be agreed upon by them and the said city, for a transfer and assignment of the franchise and materials of said bridge, as above provided, and to take up and remove the materials.

Transfer of Boston South Bridge to the city. City Records, vol. 10. pp. 78, 97.

5. On the 12th of March, 1832, the joint committee of the city council upon the subject was authorized to agree with the proprietors of the Boston South Bridge for the purchase of their franchise. On the 2d of April they made their report, that the proprietors offered to sell, for a sum not less than thirty-five hundred dollars; and recommended that the offer be accepted. This report was accepted by the city council. A vote was passed by the corporation, April 19, 1832, authorizing the president and clerk to execute a deed to the city; and a deed was executed accordingly, dated April 19, in consideration of $3500, conveying to the city of Boston and its successors "all that the franchise and also all the materials of the Boston South Bridge, together with the buildings, rights, wharves and real estate of the said corporation, and every part and parcel thereof, whatsoever the same may be, and wheresoever situate, with all the privileges, appurtenances and immunities of every description to the granted premises and any part thereof in any wise appertaining,"—"subject nevertheless always to all the provisoes, terms, duties, conditions and tenure in the aforesaid acts of the said commonwealth set forth and expressed."

Records of Suffolk deeds. Lib. 360, fol. 50.

BOSTON FREE BRIDGE.

Boston Free Bridge Corporation. Authority to build a bridge. 1825, 147, § 1, 2.

6. The Boston Free Bridge Corporation was incorporated March 4, 1826. The corporation was authorized and empowered to build and construct, or cause to be built and constructed, a free bridge, with one or more suitable and sufficient draws, across the water and over the channel, in or near a direction in a straight line from or near Sea street, in Boston, to the newly made land at South Boston,

and nearly in the direction of the Dorchester turnpike, and to erect a wharf or pier on each side of said bridge, near said draws, for the accommodation of vessels passing through said bridge; such bridge and wharves to be built in such manner as the city government of Boston should approve: *Provided, however*, that said corporation should be holden to make compensation to any person, or corporation, whose land should be appropriated to the use of said bridge.

7. It was further enacted that no toll or duty should ever be exacted or paid, for any travel over said bridge, or passing the draws of the same; and that said corporation should always be held liable to keep said bridge and draws in good repair, and to raise the draw of said bridge, and afford all necessary and proper accommodation to vessels, that should have occasion to pass the same by night or by day, and should keep said bridge sufficiently lighted; and if any vessel should be unreasonably delayed or hindered in passing said draw, by the negligence of said corporation or their agents, in discharging the duties enjoined on them by this act, the owners or commanders of such vessels should recover reasonable damage therefor, of said corporation, in an action on the case, before any court proper to try the same; and if the said corporation should not, within three years from the passing of this act, locate, construct, build, and complete said bridge, agreeably to the provisions of this act, then the act should be null and void: *Provided*, that whenever the city government of Boston should assume the care and obligations of keeping said bridge in repair, lighting the same, and providing facilities for raising said draw or draws, as aforesaid, then the obligations imposed on said corporation to that effect, should be annulled, and the same should devolve on the said city government; in which case the damages mentioned in this section should be sued for, before any court proper to try the same, in either of the counties of Middlesex or Essex. But unless the city government should assume the care and obligations aforesaid, the said corporation, before commencing the building of said bridge, should furnish ade-

Obligations imposed upon the corporation. Ibid, § 3.

Obligations to devolve on city government, when they shall assume the care of bridge.

7

quate security, to the satisfaction of the said city government, for the due performance of the obligations and duties imposed on said corporation by the provisions of this act.

Compensation for land taken. Ibid, § 4.

8. The fourth section provided for the mode of recovery of compensation for land taken.

City of Boston at liberty to erect said bridge. Ibid, § 5.

9. It was further enacted, that if the city government of Boston should, within three months from the passing of this act, determine, by a concurrent vote of both branches of the said city government, to erect said bridge, they should be at liberty so to do, on the same terms and conditions as said Boston Free Bridge Corporation were otherwise, by the provisions of this act, authorized to erect the same.[1]

Surrender of the Free Bridge, &c. to the city of Boston. City Records, vol. 5, p. 44.

10. On the 5th of February, 1827, the city council passed a resolve, that, in case the Boston Free Bridge Corporation should build a bridge, such as the city council should direct and approve, and should locate it to the satisfaction of said council, it would be expedient for the city to accept the same; and to assume the care and obligation of keeping said bridge in repair, and to provide for lighting the same, and for raising the draw or draws thereof as long as South Boston should remain a part of the city of Boston, upon such terms and conditions as should be required by the city council. On the 11th of August, 1828, a committee was appointed by the city council, with full power to accept from the Boston Free Bridge Corporation the surrender of the free bridge, with its abutments, on the compliance by the corporation with the terms and conditions prescribed, and to submit all matters in dispute to arbitration. The committee reported, October 7, 1828, that they had submitted the same to the arbitration of Loammi Baldwin, Samuel Hubbard and Willard Phillips, Esquires, who had made an award; and that the requisite deeds had been delivered, on the second of October, and the sum of sixteen hundred and seven dollars, paid to the city by the corporation, upon which delivery and payment, the obliga-

City Records, vol. 6, p. 262.

Ibid, p. 306.

---

[1] This act repealed a previous act, passed Feb. 25, 1825, (1824, c. 115,) establishing a free bridge.

tion of the care and superintendence of the bridge and streets devolved upon the city, by force of said award. The corporation also gave notice of their election to complete the northerly abutment, and claimed the return of four hundred and seventy-four dollars, according to the award, which was returned accordingly. By the deed of the corporation, which was executed by Francis J. Oliver, the president, on September 26, 1828, pursuant to a vote of the corporation, passed September 24, the Boston Free Bridge Corporation surrendered and conveyed the said bridge and abutments, wharves, &c. to the city of Boston, upon the terms and conditions on which the said city agreed to accept the same, by the resolve of February 5, 1827; and also assigned to the city a deed from Gardner Greene, dated August 21, 1828, and a deed from John T. Apthorp and others, dated August 1, 1828, and conveyed to the city all the lands and flats and rights and privileges acquired thereunder.

Records of Suffolk deeds. Lib. 331, fol. 13.

11. By a subsequent act, the city of Boston is authorized to construct and maintain such wharves or piers, on either or both sides of the Free Bridge mentioned in the act of 1825, c. 147, (§§ 6, 7, above) as shall be necessary for the preservation and safety of said bridge, *provided, however*, that the said wharves or piers shall not extend in width from the sides of said bridge more than twenty-five feet.

City of Boston authorized to maintain wharves or piers, on both sides of the Free Bridge. 1830, 121, § 1.

12. If any person shall wilfully do any injury or damage to said bridge, said wharves or piers, or shall disturb or hinder the said city in the occupation of said wharves or piers, for the purpose aforesaid, the person so offending shall forfeit and pay, for each offence, a penalty not less than fifty dollars, nor more than one hundred dollars, to the use of the commonwealth, to be recovered by indictment, or information in any court of competent jurisdiction, and such person so offending shall be further liable to answer in damages to the city of Boston, *provided*, that nothing in this act shall be construed as intending to impair or affect the lawful rights of any person whatsoever.

Penalty for injury to bridge, &c. Ibid, § 2.

Right to use wharves, &c. shall cease, in case, &c. Ibid, § 3.

13. Whenever the wharves or piers erected, or which shall be erected by the authority of the said act, shall be used or improved for any purpose or purposes than those therein specified, all right and authority to maintain them shall cease, and be void.

Wharves, &c. not to be within forty feet of other wharves, &c. 1831, 46.

14. No part of the wharves or piers, which the city of Boston is authorized to construct by virtue of the act last cited, shall be maintained within the distance of forty feet of any wharf or pier which shall have been or may hereafter be lawfully constructed by any individual or individuals.

CHELSEA POINT BRIDGE.

City of Boston authorized to purchase Chelsea Point Bridge. 1849, 106, § 1.

15. By an act passed April 17, 1849, the city of Boston was authorized and empowered to purchase the franchise of Chelsea Point Bridge, with all the rights and property incident thereto.

A highway authorized to be laid out over said bridge. Ibid, § 2.

16. The mayor and aldermen of the city of Boston, as county commissioners therein, were authorized and empowered to lay out a highway over so much of Chelsea Point Bridge, and the tide waters thereat, as is within the city of Boston; and the commissioners appointed by the court of common pleas holden at Boston, by the order of said court, dated March 15, 1848, to perform the duties of county commissioners, as in said order specified, or those at any time thereafter holding the like authority, were authorized and empowered to lay out a highway over so much of said Chelsea Point Bridge, and the tide waters thereat, as is within the town of North Chelsea: *provided*, the assent of the proprietors of Chelsea Point Bridge shall be first obtained.

Proviso.

Highway authorized over certain tide waters. Ibid, § 3.

17. The commissioners appointed by the court of common pleas, as aforesaid, or those who might thereafter be appointed to the like authority, were authorized and empowered to lay out and construct a highway over the tide waters between the easterly shore of Pulling Point, and the neck of land leading to Point Shirley, in North Chelsea, so as to form a continuous highway from East Boston to Point Shirley.

CHELSEA FREE BRIDGE.

18. By another act, passed April 17, 1849, the mayor and aldermen of the city of Boston as county commissioners therein, were authorized and empowered to lay out and construct a highway over so much of Chelsea Free Bridge, and the tide waters thereat, as are within the city of Boston; and the county commissioners appointed by the court of common pleas of the commonwealth of Massachusetts, holden at Boston in and for the county of Suffolk, by the order of said court, dated October 16, 1848, to perform the duties of county commissioners, as in said order specified, or those at any time thereafter holding the like or similar authority, were authorized and empowered to lay out and construct a highway, over so much of Chelsea Free Bridge, and the tide waters thereat, as are within the town of Chelsea. The said bridge to be maintained with good and sufficient materials, and not less than twenty-five feet wide, with sufficient railings for the protection of passengers, and a good and sufficient draw, not less than twenty feet wide, with proper piers above and below said draw, for the accommodation of vessels passing through the same.[1]

Highway to be laid out over Chelsea Free Bridge and the tide waters thereat. 1849, 109, § 1.

Bridge, how to be maintained.

Draw.

---

[1] By a resolve of the mayor and aldermen, passed May 6, 1850, so much of the Chelsea Free Bridge as is within the city of Boston, was taken and laid out as a public highway, in the way and manner that the same was then made.

For acts in relation to Charles River and Warren Bridges, see 1784, c. 53; 1791, c. 62; 1792, c. 21, 87; 1795, c. 76; 1799, c. 41; 1827, c. 127; 1832, c. 170; 1833, c. 219; 1834, c. 131; 1835, c. 155; a resolve, passed April 16, 1836; 1841, c. 88; 1842, c. 48; and 1850, c. 40.

For West Boston, Canal and Hancock Free Bridges, see 1791, c. 62; 1792, c. 21, 87; 1795, c. 76; 1799, c. 41; 1803, c. 100; 1806, c. 88; 1807, c. 61; 1809, c. 112; 1819, c. 75; 1822, c. 19; 1846, c. 146; 1848, c. 120; and 1850, c. 257.

For Boston and Roxbury Mill Corporation, (Mill Dam,) see Stat. 1814, c. 39; 1816, c. 40; 1819, c. 65; 1822, c. 34; 1824, c. 26; 1833, c. 120.

ORDINANCE OF THE CITY.

Superintendents of Boston South Bridge and Boston Free Bridge to be chosen. May 6, 1850.

SECT. 1. In the month of January or February, annually, there shall be chosen, by concurrent vote of the city council, to be first voted upon by the mayor and aldermen, a superintendent of the Boston South Bridge, and also a superintendent of the Boston Free Bridge, who shall each hold his office until removed or a successor be appointed, and shall receive such compensation for his services as the city council shall authorize and establish; and shall be removable at the pleasure of the city council. And in case either of said offices shall become vacant by death, resignation or otherwise, a successor shall be forthwith chosen in the manner above described.

Their duties.

SECT. 2. It shall be the duty of the superintendent of the Boston Free Bridge to take charge of the said Free Bridge, and it shall be the duty of the superintendent of the Boston South Bridge to take charge of the said South Bridge. And each superintendent shall take charge of the bridge of which he is superintendent, by night and by day, and cause the draw thereof to be opened at all times, when required for the free passage of vessels, and to cause the same to be closed, forthwith, and with all possible expedition, not permitting more than one vessel to pass at any one opening of the draw, unless the bridge shall be free of passengers while the draw is up, in which case, he shall use his discretion as to the number of vessels to be permitted to pass, prior to the closing of the said draw. And each superintendent shall take care of the bridge of which he is superintendent, and of the abutments and wharves, connected therewith, and shall see that at all times they are in a safe and satisfactory condition, and free of all incumbrances; that the lamps thereon are well lighted, that the railing and planks are in good order, and the snow and ice removed from the sidewalks in winter; subject at all times to the authority, control and direction of the mayor and aldermen for the time being, relative to the duties hereinbefore expressed, and also relative to any other duties respecting said bridges and wharves, and the abutments connected therewith, which the said mayor and aldermen may from time to time order and prescribe.

SECT. 3. Any person or persons who shall deface, break or injure either of said bridges or wharves, or shall unnecessarily open or obstruct the passage of either of said draws, without the consent of the superintendent of such bridge, or shall, without such consent, make fast to such bridge any scow or other vessel, shall, upon conviction thereof, pay a fine not less than three dollars, and not exceeding twenty dollars. Penalty for injuring bridges, &c.

BUILDINGS.

STATUTES.

1. No building shall be erected within the city of Boston, and used and improved as a stable for the taking in and keeping horses or chaises or other carriages, upon hire or to let, commonly called livery stables, within one hun- Livery stables not to be erected within 170 feet of any church. 1810, 124, § 1. See also R. S. 58, § 4.

dred and seventy feet of any church or meeting-house erected for the public worship of God.[1]

Penalty. Ibid, § 2.

2. For any offence against the preceding provision, the owner or owners, keeper or keepers of such building, shall forfeit and pay the sum of one hundred dollars for every calendar month during which the same shall be so used and improved, to be recovered by action of debt, one half thereof to enure for the use of the poor of the city of Boston, the other half thereof to him or them who shall sue for the same.

Wooden buildings in Boston, more than sixteen feet high, forbidden, except under certain restrictions. 1835, 139, § 1. (Accepted by citizens, May 13, 1835. Boston Records of general meetings after 1830, p. 6.)

3. No wooden building of more than sixteen feet in height, from the ground or foundation thereof, shall be erected in the city of Boston, except under the following limitations and restrictions, namely; the dimensions of such building on the ground not to exceed twenty-five feet by fifty feet; or, being in any other proportion, not to cover more than twelve hundred and fifty superficial feet of land; the walls not to exceed twenty feet in height from the under side of the sills, which sills may be three feet six inches above the level of the street, to the eaves of the roof; the roof, in the highest point thereof, not to rise more than thirty-two feet from the under side of the sills aforesaid, and there shall be at least one scuttle at or near the highest point of said roof.

Two or more such buildings in connexion, or within three feet, shall have brick or stone wall between them. Ibid, § 2.

4. When two or more such two story buildings as are provided for in the preceding section shall be erected in connexion, or within three feet of each other, or within three feet of any other wooden building, more than sixteen feet in height, there shall be an entire brick or stone wall between them, commencing from the foundation of said wall, and carried to the height of twelve feet above the level of the street, at least twelve inches in thickness, and the residue of said wall shall be at least eight inches in thickness; and in case any openings are made through said walls, the same shall be secured against fire by iron doors applied to such openings; *provided*, that such brick or

Proviso as to neck lands.

---

[1] There was a proviso in this act, respecting stables then in part erected, which proviso has ceased to be material.

stone walls may be dispensed with by consent, in writing, of the mayor and aldermen of the city of Boston, on what are commonly called the neck lands, in said city.[1]

5. If any person or persons shall violate the provisions of the two preceding sections, such person or persons, on conviction thereof, in any court competent to try the same, shall forfeit and pay for every such offence, a sum not less than fifty nor more than five hundred dollars, and shall be liable to a like prosecution and penalty for each and every year after such conviction, until said building or buildings, erected contrary to the provisions aforesaid, shall be removed or made to conform thereto; and the said penalties and forfeitures incurred by virtue of this act may be recovered by indictment, to the use of the city of Boston, or by an action of debt in any court competent to try the same, one half to the use of the person or persons who shall sue therefor, and the residue to the use of the said city.

Penalty. Ibid, § 3.

How recovered.

6. It shall be the duty of the board of engineers of the said city, to cause suits to be commenced without delay against each and all who shall violate the provisions of the three preceding sections, and to prosecute the same to final judgment.

Duty of board of engineers to prosecute. Ibid, § 4.

7. An act passed March 27, 1847, provided, that any building thereafter erected in the city of Boston, contrary to the provisions of the four preceding sections, shall be deemed and taken to be a common nuisance; and the mayor and aldermen of the said city shall have the same power and authority to abate and remove any such building as are given to the board of health, in the tenth and eleventh sections of the twenty-first chapter of the Revised Statutes; *provided, however*, that nothing in this section shall be construed as affecting any remedies already given, in the four preceding sections.

Further remedy. 1847, 132.

8. The city council of the city of Boston may authorize the erection of wooden buildings in those parts of said city called South Boston and East Boston, upon such terms and

City council may authorize and regulate wooden buildings in South and East Boston. 1850, 280, § 1.

---

[1] The remainder of this section, as it stood in the original act, and the 5th section of the same act, were repealed by stat. 1850, c. 280, § 2.

(Accepted by city council, May 16, 1850.) conditions, and subject to such limitations and restrictions, as they may deem expedient.[1]

City council may make rules respecting balustrades. 1848, 278.

9. The city council of any city, in this commonwealth, shall have power, from time to time, to make and adopt such rules and regulations, for the erection and maintenance of balustrades, or other projections, upon the roofs or sides of buildings in such city, as, in their judgment, the safety of the citizens may require. And the city council of any city may annex penalties, for the violation of any such rules and orders, not exceeding twenty dollars in any one instance; which penalties may be recovered, for the use of the city, by complaint before the police court of such city, or any justice of the peace in a city where no police court is established:

Proviso.

provided, that no such rule or order shall take effect, or go into operation, until the same shall have been published at least sixty days in some newspaper printed in such city, or the county within which such city is included.

ORDINANCE OF THE CITY.

Notice shall be given of intention to build, &c. Nov. 14, 1833.

SECT. 1. All persons, intending to erect, or to make any alterations in the external walls of any building or buildings of any description, any part of which is to be placed upon or within ten feet of any of the public streets, squares, alleys or lanes of the city, shall, before he or they proceed to build or erect the same, or to lay the foundation thereof, or to make the said alterations, give notice in writing of such their intention to the mayor and aldermen, fifteen days at least before doing any act for carrying such their intention into execution, in order that any encroachment or any other injury or inconvenience to the said public streets, squares,

---

[1] The stat. of 1850, c. 280, § 2, repealed stat. 1817, c. 171, §§ 1, 2, 3, 4, 5, 7, 8, 15; 1821, c. 26, 31; 1822, c. 16; 1829, c. 34; so much of stat. 1835, c. 139, § 2, as relates to South Boston and East Boston, together with § 5, of the same act.

lanes, or alleys, which might otherwise happen, may be thereby prevented, and in default thereof, that the city be considered as discharged from all damages, of any nature whatsoever, resulting from the failure to give notice as above provided, particularly from all such damages or expenses as have been enhanced or occasioned by reason of any thing done previously to, or without such notice.

Numbers of buildings. Nov. 14, 1833. May 16, 1850.

SECT. 2. The mayor and aldermen shall have power to cause numbers of regular series, to be affixed to, or inscribed on, all dwelling houses and other buildings erected or fronting on any street, lane, alley, or public court within the city of Boston, at their discretion; and shall also have power to determine the form, size, and material of such numbers, and the mode, place, succession and order, of inscribing or affixing them on their respective houses or other buildings.

Penalty for numbering contrary to directions. May 16, 1850.

And any owner or occupant of any building or part of a building, who shall neglect or refuse to affix to the same the number designated by the mayor and aldermen, or by some person by them duly authorized, or who shall affix to the same, or retain thereon more than one day, any number contrary to the direction of the mayor and aldermen, or person so authorized, shall forfeit and pay a sum not less than one dollar, nor more than twenty dollars, and a like sum for every subsequent offence.

Cellar doors and platforms, to be kept in good repair. Nov. 14, 1833.

SECT. 3. Whenever any cellar door or the platform thereof shall project into any of the streets, lanes, alleys, public squares or places within the city, it shall be the duty of the owners and occupants of the buildings or estate to which the same belong to keep the same in good repair. And if at any time the said cellar doors or platforms are out of repair, so that in the opinion of the mayor and aldermen the safety of the inhabitants is thereby endangered, the mayor and aldermen are hereby authorized to notify the said owners and occupants of the fact; and if said owners or occupants neglect or refuse for the space of twenty-four hours to repair the same, the said mayor and aldermen shall forthwith cause the same to be repaired at the expense of said owners or occupants, and said owners and occupants shall in case of such neglect or refusal as aforesaid, be further liable to a penalty of not less than one nor more than twenty dollars, for each and every day that said cellar door or the platform thereof shall continue to be out of repair.

Cellar doors to be lighted when open at night.

SECT. 4. Whenever any of the cellar doors before mentioned are open or the platforms thereof removed at any time during the night, it shall be the duty of the occupant of the cellar to which the same belongs, to cause a sufficient light to be so placed that the opening of said door or removal of said platform shall at all times during the night, be distinctly visible. And any person offending against the provisions of this section shall forfeit and pay a sum not less than one nor more than twenty dollars.

Defacing buildings, &c. (See R. S. 126, § 42.)

SECT. 5. Any person or persons, who shall be guilty of defacing any building or buildings, fence, sign, or other property, in the city, by cutting, breaking, daubing with paint, or in any other way defacing or injuring the same, shall upon conviction thereof, pay a fine not exceeding twenty dollars.

Wooden buildings permitted in South and East Boston, under certain limitations. May 16, 1850.

Brick partition walls to be put up in certain cases.

SECT. 6. It shall be lawful to erect wooden buildings in those parts of the city called South Boston and East Boston, which shall not be more than thirty-two feet high from the ground to the highest part thereof; *provided*, however, that no wooden building except for mechanical purposes shall be erected in a range of more than fifty feet in extent, without the intervention of a brick partition wall, of at least eight inches in thickness, such wall to extend six inches at least above the surface of the roof; and no wooden building shall be altered for a dwelling house contrary to this provision.[1]

---

[1] For buildings belonging to the city, see Public Buildings. For certain provisions respecting bow windows, cellar doors, steps, &c., see Streets.

CARRIAGES.

STATUTES.

Travellers, to take the right hand side of roads, &c. R. S. 51, § 1. 1 Pick. 345. 4 Pick. 125. 23 Pick. 201. 8 Metc. 213. 11 Metc. 403.

1. Whenever any persons shall meet each other on any bridge or road, travelling with carriages, wagons, carts, sleds, sleighs or other vehicles, each person shall seasonably drive his carriage or other vehicle to the right of the middle of the travelled part of such bridge or road, so that the respective carriages or other vehicles aforesaid may pass each other without interference.

Bells to be used with sleighs. R. S. 51, § 2.

2. No person shall travel on any bridge or road, with any sleigh or sled drawn by one or more horses, unless there shall be at least three bells attached to some part of the harness thereof.

Penalties, and how to be recovered. Ibid, § 3.

3. Every person, offending against the provisions of the two preceding sections, shall for each offence forfeit a sum not exceeding twenty dollars, to be recovered on complaint before any justice of the peace, in the county where the offence shall have been committed; and he shall further be liable to any party for all damages sustained by reason of such offence; provided, that every such complaint shall be made within three months after the offence shall have been committed, and that every such action for damages shall be commenced within twelve months, after the cause of action shall have accrued.

Drivers of stage coaches, &c. not to leave their horses, without, &c. Ibid, § 4.

4. If any driver of a stage coach, or other vehicle, for the conveyance of passengers for hire, shall, when any passenger is within or upon such coach or vehicle, leave the

horses thereof without some suitable person to take the charge and guidance of them, or without fastening them in a safe and prudent manner, he may be punished by imprisonment not exceeding two months or by fine not exceeding fifty dollars.

5. The mayor and aldermen of any city in this commonwealth shall have power, from time to time, to make and adopt such rules and orders, as to them shall appear necessary and expedient, for the due regulation, in such city, of omnibuses, stages, hackney coaches, wagons, carts, drays, and all other carriages and vehicles whatsoever, used or employed, wholly or in part, in such city, whether by prescribing their routes and places of standing, or in any other manner whatsoever; and whether such carriages and other vehicles as aforesaid are used for burden or pleasure, or for the conveyance of passengers or freight, or otherwise, and whether with or without horse or other animal power; *provided*, that nothing contained in this act shall be construed to abridge or impair the rights of cities to make such by-laws and regulations, touching the subjects above provided for, as they now possess, by virtue of their charters, or the amendments thereof.

Mayor and aldermen may adopt rules and orders for the regulation of carriages. 1847, 224, § 1.

Com. v. Stodder, S. J. C., March T. 1849. 11 Law Rep. 547.

Proviso.

6. The mayor and aldermen of any city may annex penalties for the violation of any such rules and orders as are authorized in the preceding section, not exceeding twenty dollars in any one instance; which penalties may be recovered for the use of the city, by complaint before the police court of such city, or any justice of the peace in a city where no police court is established: *provided*, that no such rule or order shall take effect, or go into operation, until the same shall have been published at least one week in some newspaper printed in such city or the county within which such city is included.[1]

Penalties. 1847, 224, § 2.

Rules, &c., to be published.

7. The mayor and aldermen are authorized to demand and receive the sum of one dollar, and no more, for a

Fee for license. 1850, 275.

[1] The third section of this act repeals stat. 1796, c. 32; the 7th section and part of the 5th section of stat. 1799, c. 31; and the 2d and 3d sections of stat. 1809, c. 28.

license to any person to set up and use within the city, any carriage or vehicle mentioned in the two preceding sections.

RULES AND ORDERS OF THE MAYOR AND ALDERMEN.[1]

HACKNEY CARRIAGES.

Hackney carriage defined. May 13, 1850.

SECT. 1. Every hack, stage coach, omnibus, cab, chariot, coachee, barouche, landau, or other vehicle, whether on wheels or runners, drawn by one or more horses, or other animal power, which shall be used in the city of Boston for the conveyance of persons for hire, from place to place within said city, shall be deemed a hackney carriage within the meaning of these regulations.

License required.

SECT. 2. No person shall set up, use or drive, in the city of Boston, any hackney carriage for the conveyance of persons for hire from place to place within said city, without a license for such carriage from the mayor and aldermen, under a penalty of not less than five nor more than twenty dollars, every time such carriage is used.

Mayor and aldermen may license and revoke.

SECT. 3. The mayor and aldermen will, from time to time, grant licenses to such persons, and upon such terms, as they may deem expedient, to set up, use or drive hackney carriages for the conveyance of persons for hire, from place to place within the city, and they may revoke such licenses at their discretion; and a record of all licenses so granted shall be kept by the city marshal.

Fee for license. City marshal to make quarterly report.

SECT. 4. For every license so granted there shall be paid to the city marshal the sum of one dollar for the use of the city; and the city marshal shall make a quarterly report to the mayor and aldermen of all sums so received, and shall pay over the same to the city treasurer.

---

[1] These rules and orders were published in the Boston Daily Advertiser one week, commencing May 15, 1850, and ending May 22, 1850.

SECT. 5. All licenses granted as aforesaid, shall expire on the first day of July next after the date thereof, and no license shall be sold, assigned or transferred, without the consent of the mayor and aldermen, endorsed thereon by the city marshal. When license shall expire. Shall not be transferred without, &c.

SECT. 6. The person in whose name a license is taken out for a hackney carriage, shall, for all the purposes of these rules and orders, be considered as the owner of the same, and liable to all forfeitures and penalties herein contained; unless upon the sale of the said carriage, notice be given to the city marshal, and the license delivered to him. Who shall be liable.

SECT. 7. Any person who may be licensed as aforesaid, either as owner or driver of any hackney carriage, who shall continue to use any such carriage, and shall neglect or refuse to take out and pay for his license within thirty days after notice that the same has been granted, shall be liable to a fine of not less than one dollar, and not more than twenty dollars, for each and every day thereafter, that he or they shall so refuse or neglect to take out said license. Neglect to take out license after it is granted.

SECT. 8. Hackney carriages shall be marked and numbered in the manner following, viz:—Every hack or landau which stands on the owner's premises, shall be marked on the outside, and upon each side, on the sill or rocker, immediately below the doors, with the number of the license, with white, gilded or plated figures, in the Arabic character, of not less than one and a half inches in size, on a dark ground, or with a dark figure of the same kind and size upon a light ground, and no other figure or device within four inches of the same. Stage coaches shall be numbered in like manner on the top rail of the doors. Omnibuses shall be numbered in like manner on the lower panel of the door. Cabs shall be numbered in like manner on the centre of the top panel of the door, immediately below the glass. Every hackney carriage, when driven or used in the night time, shall have fixed upon some conspicuous part of the outside thereof, two lighted lamps, with plain glass fronts and sides, and having the number of the license of such hackney carriage in figures Manner of marking and numbering.

of at least one and a half inches in size, of the like character, painted with black paint upon the sides and front of each of said lamps, in such a manner that the same may be distinctly seen and known, when the same may be standing or driving. The name of the owner and driver, and the number of the license, together with the rates of fare, shall be printed on a card and placed in all hackney carriages in the most conspicuous place for the information of passengers. And if any owner or driver of any hackney carriage shall use or drive any such carriage, or permit the same to be used and driven, without complying with the foregoing requisitions, or use, or drive, or permit to be used or driven, any such carriage in the night time, without its lamps being lighted and numbered as aforesaid; said owner and driver shall be liable to a fine of not less than two nor more than twenty dollars for each offence.

No other number shall be used.

SECT. 9. No owner or driver of any hackney carriage shall use or suffer such carriage to be used with any other number upon the same than that assigned by the mayor and aldermen; nor with such number placed on any other part of such carriage than that designated in the preceding section, under a penalty of not less than five, nor more than twenty dollars, every time such carriage is used.

Carriage and horses shall not be left, unless in care of suitable person.

SECT. 10. No owner, driver, or other person having charge of any licensed hackney carriage, shall leave such carriage and horses when harnessed, unless in the care of some suitable person, under a penalty of not less than five nor more than twenty dollars for every such offence.

Shall not stand in any other place.

SECT. 11. No owner, driver, or other person having charge of any hackney carriage, shall stand with such carriage in any place within the city to be employed, other than the stand assigned to such carriage by the mayor and aldermen, under a penalty of not less than two dollars nor more than twenty dollars for each offence.

Shall not stop so as to obstruct.

SECT. 12. No owner, driver, or other person having charge of any hackney carriage, shall stop his carriage abreast of any other carriage in any street within the city, nor stop his carriage in any street, square, lane, alley or public place, so as to obstruct the same, or the sidewalk, flagstone or crossing thereof, under a penalty of not less than two, nor more than twenty dollars for each offence.

SECT. 13. Every owner, driver, or other person having charge of any hackney carriage which has a stand in any street or square, at any railroad depot, steamboat landing, theatre, museum, or other place of public entertainment, shall at all times when driving or waiting for employment, wear a badge on his hat or cap, with the number of his carriage thereon, in brass or plated figures of not less than one inch and a half in size, and so placed that the same may be distinctly seen and read, under a penalty of not less than two, nor more than twenty dollars for each offence.

Driver, &c., shall wear a badge.

SECT. 14. In any street or square, or at any theatre, museum, or other place of public entertainment, where hackney carriages attend for passengers, the mayor, or any person or persons by him authorized, may give directions respecting the standing of such carriages, while waiting for their passengers, and the route they shall go when going to or leaving any such place of entertainment; and if any owner, driver, or other person having the care of any such carriage, shall refuse to obey such order or directions of the mayor, or other person or persons by him authorized, he or they shall be liable to a fine of not less than five, nor more than twenty dollars for each offence.

Mayor may give directions for standing and route.

SECT. 15. The prices, or rates of fare, to be taken by, or paid to the owner, driver, or other person having charge of any hackney carriage, except omnibuses, shall be as follows; that is to say, for carrying a passenger from one place to another within the city proper, or South Boston, or East Boston, twenty-five cents; and to or from South Boston and East Boston, to any other part of the city, thirty-seven and a half cents, exclusive of tolls. For children between three and twelve years of age, if more than one, or if accompanied by an adult, half price only is to be charged for each child; and for children under three years of age, when accompanied by their parents or any adult, no charge is to be made. Every owner, driver, or other person having the charge of any hackney carriage, shall carry

Rates of fare.

with each passenger, in addition to one trunk, a valise, saddle bag, carpet bag, portmanteau, box, bundle, basket, or other article used in travelling, if he be requested so to do, without charge or compensation therefor; but for every additional trunk, or other such article as above named, more than one, he shall be entitled to demand, and receive the sum of five cents.

Carriage not to be driven by a minor, unless, &c.

SECT. 16. No hackney carriage used for conveyance of passengers shall be driven by a minor unless he be specially licensed by the mayor and aldermen, under a penalty of not less than two, nor more than twenty dollars for each offence.

OMNIBUSES.

Time for starting.

SECT. 17. Each license of any omnibus belonging to any line may specify the time that said omnibus shall leave the stand, and no omnibus shall leave the stand designated for it until five minutes shall have elapsed after the departure of the omnibus immediately preceding, under a penalty of not less than two, nor more than twenty dollars for each offence.

Stopping.

SECT. 18. No owner or driver of any omnibus belonging to any line shall stop his omnibus on any part of the route assigned thereto, unless called by, or to leave a passenger, and then for no longer time than may be sufficient for such passenger to take his or her seat, or leave such carriage, under a penalty of not less than two, nor more than twenty dollars for each offence.

Receiving and leaving passengers.

SECT. 19. The driver of every omnibus, when passing through Washington, Court, and Hanover streets, shall receive and leave passengers on his right side of said streets only, under a penalty of not less than two, nor more than twenty dollars for each offence.

Shall not leave the route.

SECT. 20. No owner or driver of any omnibus shall drive his omnibus or permit the same to be driven on any other route or street than that hereinafter designated and established by the mayor and aldermen, under a penalty of not less than ten nor more than twenty dollars for each offence.

SECT 21. *Ordered*, That the following routes be, and the same are hereby designated and established for the different lines of omnibuses running within and into the city of Boston.

Routes established.

SECT. 22. *South Boston Line.* The route for all two horse omnibuses, shall be from South Boston, through Sea, Kneeland, Lincoln, Summer and Washington streets to Cornhill, and return by the same route. For all four horse omnibuses, the route shall be over the South Boston Free Bridge, through Harrison avenue, Rowe, Bedford and Washington streets, to Cornhill, and return by the same route.

South Boston Line.

SECT. 23. *East Boston Line.* Route, from East Boston Ferry, through Commercial, Fleet, Hanover, Tremont and Boylston streets, to the Providence Railroad Depot, and return by the same route.

East Boston Line.

SECT. 24. *Canton Street and Dock Square Line.* Route, from Canton, through Washington street only, to Dock square, and return by the same route.

Canton Street and Dock Square Line.

SECT. 25. *Dover Street and Lowell Railroad Line.* Route, from Dover, through Washington, Court, Green, Leverett, Minot and Lowell streets, to the Lowell Railroad Depot, and return by the same route.

Dover Street and Lowell Railroad Line.

SECT. 26. *Dover Street and Chelsea Ferry Line.* Route, from Dover, through Washington, Court and Hanover streets, to Chelsea Ferry, and return by the same route.

Dover Street and Chelsea Ferry Line.

SECT. 27. *Dover Street and Fitchburg Railroad Line.* Route, from Dover, through Washington, Court, Sudbury, Deacon and Haverhill streets, to the Fitchburg Railroad Depot, and return by the same route.

Dover Street and Fitchburg Railroad Line.

SECT. 28. *Eastern Railroad Omnibus.* Route, through Tremont, Court, State and Commercial streets, to the Eastern Railroad Depot, and return by the same route.

Eastern Railroad Omnibus.

SECT. 29. *Worcester Railroad Omnibuses.* Route, through Portland, Sudbury, Court, State, Washington and Beach streets, to the Worcester Railroad Depot, and return by the same route.

Worcester Railroad Omnibuses.

SECT. 30. *Lowell Railroad Line.* Route, through

Lowell Railroad Line.

Lowell, Merrimac, Portland, Sudbury, Court and State streets, to Kilby square, and return by the same route.

Cambridge Line.

SECT. 31. *Cambridge Line.* Route, through Cambridge, Court and Brattle streets, and return by the same route.

East Cambridge Line.

SECT. 32. *East Cambridge Line.* Route, through Leverett, Green, Court and Brattle streets, and return by the same route.

Charlestown Lines.

SECT. 33. *Charlestown Lines.* Route, through Haverhill, Union and Brattle streets, and return by the same route.

Dorchester Line.

SECT. 34. *Dorchester Line.* Route, through Sea, Summer, Arch and Franklin streets, and return by the same route. The route for Grove Hall omnibus, shall be through Washington and State streets, and return by the same route.

Roxbury Line.

SECT. 35. *Roxbury Line.* Route, from Roxbury, through Washington, Court, Cornhill and Washington streets, to Roxbury.

Roxbury Line, Tremont Road.

SECT. 36. *Roxbury Line, Tremont Road.* Route, from Roxbury, through Washington street or over the Tremont road, to No. 192 Tremont street, and return by the same route.

Jamaica Plain, Brighton and Brookline Lines.

SECT. 37. *Jamaica Plain, Brighton, and Brookline Lines.* Route, through Tremont street or through Park and Beacon streets, and return by the same route.

Chelsea Line.

SECT. 38. *Chelsea Line.* Route, through Haverhill, Union, Hanover and Court streets, to Cornhill, and return by the same route.

TRUCKS, WAGONS, &C.

License for trucks, wagons, &c.

SECT. 39. Every truck, wagon, dray, cart, hand-cart, sleigh, sled or hand-sled, and every other vehicle which shall be used within the city of Boston, for the conveyance from place to place, within the said city, of wood, coal, lumber, stone, brick, sand, gravel, clay, dirt, rubbish, goods, wares, furniture, merchandize, building materials, or article, or thing whatsoever, whether of a like description or not, shall be licensed, as hereinafter provided, and shall have placed upon the outside, and upon each side of the same, the name of the owner, and the number of the license, in plain legible words and figures, of not less than one and one half inches in size, and so that the name may be distinctly seen; and if the owner of any such vehicle, shall use, or suffer the same to be used, or if any other person shall use any such vehicle, without being licensed as hereinafter provided, or without having the name and number so placed as aforesaid, they, or either of them shall be liable to a fine of not less than three dollars, nor more than twenty dollars for each offence.

Mayor and aldermen may license, and revoke.

SECT. 40. The mayor and aldermen will, from time to time, grant licenses to such persons, and upon such terms as they may deem expedient, to have a stand for, to use and to drive, any such vehicle as aforesaid within the city of Boston, and they may revoke such licenses at their discretion; and a record of all licenses so granted, shall be kept by the city marshal.

Fee for license.

City marshal to make quarterly report.

SECT. 41. For every license so granted there shall be paid to the city marshal the sum of one dollar for the use of the city; and the city marshal shall make a quarterly report to the mayor and aldermen, of all sums so received, and shall pay over the same to the city treasurer.

When licenses shall expire.

Shall not be transferred, without, &c.

SECT. 42. All licenses granted as aforesaid, shall expire on the first day of July next after the date thereof, and no license of any vehicle which has a stand in any street, or square, shall be sold, assigned, or transferred, without the consent of the mayor and aldermen, endorsed thereon by the city marshal.

Who shall be liable.

SECT. 43. The person in whose name a license is taken out for any such vehicle, shall, for all the purposes of these orders, be considered as the owner of the same, and liable to all the forfeitures and penalties herein contained, unless upon the sale of any such vehicle, notice be given thereof to the city marshal, and the license delivered up to him.

Neglect to take out license after it is granted.

SECT. 44. Any person who may be licensed as aforesaid, either as owner or driver of any of the before mentioned vehicles, who shall continue to use any such carriage or other vehicle, and shall neglect or refuse to take out his license within thirty days after notice that the same has been granted, shall be liable to a fine of not less than one dollar, and not more than twenty dollars, for each and every day thereafter that he or they shall refuse, or neglect to take out said license.

Truck, &c., shall not be driven by a minor, unless, &c.

SECT. 45. No truck, cart, wagon, or other vehicle, used for any of the purposes mentioned in the 39th section, shall be driven by any minor unless he be specially licensed by the mayor and aldermen as a minor; and if any owner or other person having the care of any such vehicle, shall suffer or permit an unlicensed minor to drive any such vehicle, he or they shall be liable to a fine of not less than two nor more than twenty dollars for each offence.

Number of horses to one truck, &c.

SECT. 46. Not more than two horses shall be harnessed to, and permitted to draw any truck, or sled, in or through any of the public streets, squares, lanes, or alleys of the city, and not more than three horses shall be harnessed to, and permitted to draw any cart, wagon or dray in or through any of the public streets, squares, lanes, or alleys of the city, unless in either of the above cases, for the carriage of any one single article exceeding two and a half tons in weight, and which cannot be divided, under a penalty of not less than five, nor more than twenty dollars: *provided*, that the mayor and aldermen may grant permission upon any special application for that purpose, for more than two horses to draw any truck, or sled, and for more than three horses to draw any cart, wagon, or dray, when they may think it reasonable or necessary: *provided, also*, that four horses or other beasts may, without such special permission, be attached to, and permitted to draw any wagon, employed to transport loads out of the city into the country, or from the country into the city; said four horses or other beasts being yoked in pairs, or so harnessed that two shall travel abreast.

Proviso.

Pace at which horses, &c., shall go. 3 Pick. 462. Thacher's Crim. Cas. 100.

SECT. 47. All drivers, and other persons having the care and ordering of any truck, cart, wagon, sled, or dray, passing in or through the streets, squares or lanes of the city, shall drive their horses or beasts, at a moderate foot pace, and shall not suffer or permit them to go in a gallop, or trot; and such drivers or other persons shall hold the reins in their hands to guide and restrain such horses or beasts, or they shall walk by the head of the shaft, or wheel horse, either holding or keeping within reach of the bridle or halter of the horse or other beast. And any person offending against either of the provisions of this section shall be liable to a fine of not less than five dollars nor more than twenty dollars for each offence.

Length of trucks.

SECT. 48. No truck shall be used in this city, the length whereof, from the end of the shaft to the extreme end of the side, shall be greater than twenty-four feet and six inches, under a penalty of not less than five, nor more than twenty dollars every time such truck is used.

Weight of load.

SECT. 49. No person shall cause to be carried on any truck, or cart, any load the weight whereof shall exceed three tons; or on any wagon, any load the weight whereof shall exceed three tons; excepting the load which may consist of an article which cannot be divided; and any person violating either of the provisions of this section, shall be liable to a fine of not less than ten, nor more than twenty dollars for each offence.

CARRIAGES IN GENERAL.

Carriages shall not remain longer than five minutes without some person, &c. and not longer than twenty minutes in any case.

SECT. 50. No owner, driver, or other person having the care or ordering of any chaise, carryall, hackney carriage, truck, cart, wagon, hand-cart, sleigh, sled, hand-sled, or any other vehicle whatsoever, new or old, finished or unfinished, with or without a horse or horses, or other animal or animals, harnessed thereto, shall suffer the same to remain in any street, square, lane or alley of this city, more than five minutes, without some proper person to take care of the same, or more than twenty minutes in any case; and any person so offending shall be liable to a fine of not less than three or more than twenty dollars for each offence. But this section shall not apply to the carriages of physicians while visiting the sick.

Com. v. Robertson, S. J. C. March T. 1850.

Physicians' carriages excepted.

Bells required in certain cases.

SECT. 51. No carriage or vehicle of any description, whether of burden or pleasure, shall be driven through any part of the city of Boston, during any time that the snow

10

or ice shall be upon, or cover the streets, squares, lanes, or alleys of the said city, unless there shall be three or more bells attached to the horse or horses, or some part of the harness thereof, under a penalty of not less than three dollars, nor more than twenty, for each offence.

Carriages shall not stop so as to obstruct foot passengers, &c.

SECT. 52. No owner, driver, or other person having the care of any truck, cart, wagon, sled, or other vehicle, whether used for burden or pleasure, shall stop or place such vehicle at or near the intersection of any street, lane, or alley, in such manner as to cross the footing or flag stones, or prevent foot passengers from passing the street, lane or alley, in the direction or line of the footway or flag stones, on the side of such street, lane or alley, under a penalty of not less than three, nor more than twenty dollars; and any person who shall have so placed any such vehicle as aforesaid, and shall not immediately, on the request of any foot passenger, cause the same to be removed, or who shall absent himself so that such request cannot be immediately made and complied with, shall be liable to an additional penalty of not less than two, nor more than ten dollars.

Manner of holding reins.

Pace at which horses, &c., shall go. 3 Pick. 462.

SECT. 53. No person shall sit or stand in or upon, or near any carriage, or other vehicle, or on any beast harnessed thereto, with intent to drive the same, unless he or she shall have strong reins, or lines, fastened to the bridle of such beast, and held in his or her hand; nor shall any person suffer, or permit any such beast to run, gallop, trot, pace, or go, at any rate exceeding seven miles to the hour, through any street, lane, square, or alley of the city; and if any person shall violate either of the provisions of this section, he shall be liable to a fine of not less than five dollars nor more than twenty dollars for each offence.

Driver shall remain near, &c.

SECT. 54. Every driver of any truck, wagon, or other vehicle, within the city of Boston, shall remain near to such vehicle while it is unemployed, or standing in the streets, or squares of the city, unless he shall be necessarily absent therefrom, in the course of his duty and business, and shall so keep his horse or horses, and carriage or other vehicle, as that the same shall not obstruct the said streets or squares, or other public passages, in any other manner than is allowed by law, or the ordinance of the city council, or orders of the mayor and aldermen. And no driver of any carriage or other vehicle, while waiting for employment either at any stand which is or may be appointed for such carriages, or other vehicles, respectively, or in the public streets, or squares of the city, shall snap or flourish his whip. And any person who shall violate either of the provisions of this section, shall be liable to a fine of not less than two dollars, nor more than twenty dollars for each offence.

Shall not snap or flourish his whip.

SECT. 55. No truck, cart, or other vehicle, shall be so placed in any street within the city, by the owner, driver, or other person having the care and ordering thereof, as to prevent the passing of any other truck, cart, or carriage of any description, unless it be for a reasonable time, not exceeding six minutes, for the loading or unloading of heavy articles, the weight of which in any several parcel or package, shall not be less than six hundred pounds. And for the loading, or unloading of any dirt, bricks, stone, sand, gravel, or of any articles, whether of the same description or not, the weight of which in any one package shall not be less than five hundred pounds, no truck, cart, wagon, sleigh, sled, or other vehicle, shall be wholly or in part backed or placed across any street, square, lane or alley, or upon the flag stones or crossing of the same, or upon any sidewalk or footway of the same, but shall be placed lengthwise with, and as near as possible to the abutting stone of the sidewalk, or footway; and any owner or driver, or other person having the care of any such vehicle, violating either of the provisions of this section, shall be liable to a fine of not less than five dollars, nor more than twenty dollars, for each offence.

How trucks, &c. shall be placed.

Loading and unloading.

SECT. 56. Every owner, driver, or other person having the care or ordering of any cart, truck, wagon, or sled, or other vehicle, shall place his horse and cart, truck, wagon, or sled, or other vehicle, lengthwise, as near as possible to the post, or abutting stone of the foot or sidewalk of the street in which he shall stand; and no more than one range

Cart, &c. to be placed near sidewalk.

Not more than one range of carts, &c.

of carts, trucks, or other vehicles, shall stand in streets not more than thirty feet wide, and not more than one range on each side, in streets which are of a greater width than thirty feet; and in squares, and other open places they shall be arranged by the said owners, drivers, or other persons, in conformity to the directions of the mayor and aldermen, or of any person by them appointed; and any person who shall violate the provisions of this section, or shall neglect or refuse to obey such directions as aforesaid, shall be liable to a fine of not less than three nor more than twenty dollars.

Horses, &c., not to be fed in streets, &c.

SECT. 57. No owner or driver of any hackney carriage, truck, wagon, dray, cart, sleigh, sled, or any other vehicle whatsoever, with horses or any other beasts harnessed thereto, shall bait or feed any such beast in any street, lane, square or alley of the city, under a penalty of not less than two dollars, nor more than twenty dollars for each offence.

CHELSEA.

STATUTES.

Conditions of the connection between Chelsea and Boston. 1831, 65, § 1.

1. By an act of the legislature, passed June 23, 1831, it was provided, that the connection which by law then subsisted between the city of Boston and the town of Chelsea should continue upon the following conditions, that is to say—First: the said town of Chelsea should, by good and sufficient deeds, assign and release to the said city of Boston, all right, title and interest, in and to all the real

estate and personal estate then belonging, or any time before deemed and taken to belong to the county of Suffolk, and should also relinquish to the said city of Boston, the exclusive care, management, jurisdiction and regulation of the court houses, jails, house of correction, and all other lands, buildings and establishments, deemed county property, or in which the said county of Suffolk claimed, or had claimed or exercised any care, management, jurisdiction or regulation as aforesaid. Secondly: that the said city of Boston should be at liberty to apply, from time to time, to the legislature, for any alterations in the laws establishing and regulating county, municipal or police courts, or respecting the administration of justice, which the said city of Boston should think expedient, without any let, hindrance, interference or claim of right, by the said town of Chelsea, before the legislature or otherwise: *provided*, always, that some court or courts, within the said city of Boston, should have jurisdiction in all matters and things, which, in relation to the town of Chelsea, or the inhabitants thereof, were cognizable by the court of common pleas, or by the court of sessions in the county of Suffolk, before the passing of the "Act to regulate the administration of justice within the county of Suffolk, and for other purposes," passed February 23, 1822.[1] Thirdly: that the said town of Chelsea might, at any time, apply to the legislature to be set off from said county of Suffolk to any other county, without opposition from the said city of Boston.

2. The second section of the same act provided, that the said act should continue and be in force, so far as respects the connection aforesaid, between the said city of Boston and the said town of Chelsea, for the space of twenty years, and thence afterwards until the same should be altered by the legislature, unless the said town of Chelsea should, in the mean time, apply to the legislature, and be set off as aforesaid: *provided, however*, that the rights of property which should be acquired by the said city of Bos-

Duration of the act, provided for. Ibid, § 2.

County property to remain vested in Boston.

---

[1] The act referred to, stat. 1821, c. 109, was repealed by the Revised Statutes.

ton, under this act, should nevertheless remain forever vested in the said city of Boston.

Act to be accepted by the town of Chelsea. Ibid, § 3.

3. By the third section, the act was to take effect, whenever the said town of Chelsea, at any town meeting legally assembled, should accept the same; and from the time of such acceptance, all rights of property of the town of Chelsea, in and to all the estate, real and personal, of the county of Suffolk, should cease and determine and be vested in the said city of Boston. The act was accepted, at a meeting of the inhabitants of the town of Chelsea, duly notified and warned on the 5th of September, 1831.

In Suffolk, county property to belong to the city of Boston. R. S. 14, § 7.

4. By the Revised Statutes, all the real estate and personal estate, in the county of Suffolk, which, on or before the twenty-third day of June, in the year one thousand eight hundred and thirty-one, belonged, or was deemed and taken to belong, to the said county, shall belong to, and be vested in, the city of Boston; and the town of Chelsea shall have no right, title, or interest therein.

Chelsea not to be assessed for county purposes. Ibid, § 34.

5. In the assessment of county taxes, for the county of Suffolk, the town of Chelsea shall not be taxed for county purposes.[1]

CHIMNEYS AND CHIMNEY SWEEPERS.

---

[1] The town of Chelsea was divided by stat. 1846, c. 127, and a portion of the town incorporated into a separate town by the name of North Chelsea.

ORDINANCES OF THE CITY.[1]

Chimneys to be examined and repaired. Dec. 28, 1825.

SECT. 1. The mayor and aldermen, upon complaint made to them, or upon their knowledge and view of any defective chimney, or other fire place within this city, shall, from time to time, take effectual care that the same shall be examined and inspected; and, when in their opinion the safety of the city requires it, shall order the same to be immediately amended or repaired if the same can be properly done; otherwise, to be taken down and demolished. And if the owner or owners of such defective chimney or fire place, shall wilfully neglect or refuse to amend, repair or take down the same, the said owner or owners shall forfeit and pay a sum not less than one, or more than twenty dollars: *provided*, that such owner or owners shall have been served with an order in writing from the mayor and aldermen to amend, repair or take down the said defective chimney or fire place (as the case may be,) duly certified by the city clerk; an attested copy of which order, made and certified by the said city clerk, shall be duly served upon such owner or owners, by any person appointed for that purpose, by the said mayor and aldermen. And the said mayor and aldermen for the time being, shall have full power and authority to order and direct, and they are hereby required to cause such defective chimney or fire place, to be taken down and abated as a common nuisance;—and the owner or owners of such defective chimney or fire place, shall in such case bear, satisfy and pay the whole expense and charge of abating such nuisance, and of taking down and removing such defective chimney or fire place.

Penalty.

Defective chimneys may be abated.

Sweepers of chimneys to be licensed. Ibid.

SECT. 2. The mayor and aldermen are authorized and directed, to appoint and license, from time to time, suitable persons to be sweepers of chimneys in this city, who, together with their apprentices, and others by them employed, shall wear such badges as the mayor and aldermen shall appoint and direct, and whose wages and compensation for

[1] An ordinance for the regulation of chimneys and chimney sweepers, passed Dec. 28, 1825. An ordinance establishing a fire department, &c., passed June 4, 1850, § 26.

their work and service in sweeping chimneys, shall not exceed the rates, which are or may be fixed and appointed by the mayor and aldermen. And if any person who shall not be appointed and licensed as aforesaid, shall presume, either by himself or by his apprentices, or others by him employed, to undertake the sweeping of any chimney in this city, excepting such as are in his own occupation, every such person shall forfeit and pay a sum not less than one dollar, nor more than ten dollars, for every offence of which he shall be duly convicted. And no inhabitant of this city shall employ any person, (excepting his, or her own servant, being in his or her house,) to sweep any of his or her chimneys, within the city, other than one of the chimney sweepers appointed and licensed as aforesaid by the mayor and aldermen; and if any inhabitant of this city shall employ any person, other than the chimney sweepers appointed and licensed as aforesaid, in violation of the provisions of this ordinance, he or they shall forfeit and pay a fine not less than one dollar nor more than ten dollars.

Penalty.

Foul chimneys, how to be examined. Ibid.

SECT. 3. When and so often as complaint is made to the mayor and aldermen, by any chimney sweeper appointed and licensed as aforesaid, or by any inhabitant of the city, against any person or persons, that their chimneys are unsafe by reason of foulness, the mayor and aldermen, or any other person by them empowered, are hereby directed to inspect and view, or order to be inspected and viewed, and to them reported, every such chimney complained of as aforesaid; and if upon such view, inspection and report, the mayor and aldermen shall, either from their own view, or the report of the person appointed to view as aforesaid, judge the same to be unsafe and dangerous to make and keep fire therein by reason of foulness, the said mayor and aldermen shall give notice thereof to the person or persons in the possession or occupancy of the house or tenement to which such chimney or chimneys belong; and every occupier or occupiers of such house or tenement, shall forfeit and pay a sum not less than one dollar, nor more than twenty dollars, for every day in which fire shall be made and kept in such chimney or chimneys

Fires not to be kept in them.

respectively, by such occupier or occupiers, after notice shall have been given them in manner aforesaid, until the same shall be properly and sufficiently swept.

SECT. 4. If any chimney, stove pipe, or flue within the city, shall take or be set on fire, the occupant of the house to which such chimney, stove pipe, or flue appertains, or the person or persons so setting the same on fire, shall forfeit and pay the sum of two dollars; provided, that it shall be lawful for any person to set fire to, and burn his chimney, stove pipe, or flue, between sunrising and noon, if the buildings contiguous are wet with rain or covered with snow; and it shall be the duty of the chief or other engineers to report to the mayor and aldermen the name of every person liable to the penalty provided by this section, in their first returns thereafter.

Penalty for burning chimneys, &c. June 4, 1850.

Proviso.

COMMON AND PUBLIC SQUARES.

ORDINANCE OF THE CITY.[1]

SECT. 1. The mayor and aldermen shall have the care and custody of the common, public squares and public fountains of the city, subject to such ordinances as may

Mayor and aldermen to have the care and custody of the common, public

[1] An ordinance in relation to the common, the public squares and public fountains of the city, passed May 13, 1850.

squares and public fountains. May 13, 1850.

from time to time be adopted by the city council; but no more money shall be expended on the same than is appropriated for that purpose by the city council.

Police officers may remove offenders.

SECT. 2. It shall be lawful for any police officer to remove from the common, or any of the public squares, any person, who is violating any law or ordinance, or is committing any nuisance, or is guilty of any disorderly conduct.

Horses not to be rode on the common.

SECT. 3. No person shall ride, lead or drive any horse in or upon the open grounds of the city, called the common, or in or upon any enclosed public square, unless by permission of the mayor and aldermen; provided, however, that on occasion of military exercise, parade or review, the introduction of any horses on the common, which may be necessary for the purpose of such exercise, parade and review, shall not be deemed an infraction of this ordinance.

Proviso.

Sward, gravel, &c. not to be taken from the common.

SECT. 4. No person shall dig or carry away any of the sward, gravel, sand, turf or earth in or from any part of the common, common lands, or public squares, except by permission of the mayor and aldermen for some public use.

Trees on the common or malls not to be injured, &c. See also R. S. 126, § 42.

SECT. 5. No person, except by permission of the mayor and aldermen, shall climb, break, peel, cut, deface, either by posting up bills of any description or otherwise, remove, injure or destroy any of the trees, growing, or which shall hereafter be planted on the common, or either of the malls adjoining the common, or on the common lands of the city, or in any street or public place of the city.

Filth, &c. not to be placed on the common.

SECT. 6. No person shall, in any manner, carry or cause to be carried into the common, or common lands, or any public square or place of the city, any dead carcass, ordure, filth, dirt, stones, or any offensive matter or substance whatsoever; and no person shall commit any nuisance in the said common, common lands, or any public square or place of the city.

Carpets, where not to be shaken.

SECT. 7. No person shall shake or otherwise cleanse any carpet on any of the common lands, or in any of the public squares or places, streets, lanes, or alleys of the city, except upon the common; and no person shall shake, or otherwise cleanse any carpet upon the said common, within ten rods of either of the malls or either of the public paths, made under the authority of the city government across the same.

SECT. 8. No owner or keeper of any horse or grazing cattle shall suffer the same to go at large, or to feed upon the common, or common lands, public squares, streets, lanes, or alleys of the city, under the penalty hereinafter provided. And any horse or cattle found at large, in said city, not having a keeper, shall be liable to be impounded by any field driver, and detained by him until the payment of fifty cents, together with the cost and charges of impounding and keeping the same.

Cattle, &c. not to go at large.

When to be impounded.

SECT. 9. Any person who shall offend against any of the provisions of this ordinance, shall forfeit and pay for each offence a sum not less than one nor more than twenty dollars, to be recovered by complaint before the justices of the police court.

Penalties.

CONSTABLES.

1. The mayor and aldermen are empowered to appoint annually, such a number of persons as constables as the public service may require; and the said constables, so appointed, shall give bonds to the treasurer, in such sums, and on such conditions, as the said mayor and aldermen shall think proper, for the faithful performance of the duties of their office. By the act of 1802, constables in Boston have the same powers as were by law vested in constables chosen by the towns in this commonwealth. Such constables, in addition to the usual condition of their bonds, shall also be bound to the faithful execution of all warrants committed to them by the treasurer and collector.

Mayor and aldermen to appoint constables. 1802, 7, § 1. 1821, 110, § 13.

Bond.

Powers.

1807, 134, § 3.

Persons injured by breach of bond of constables, may maintain actions in name of treasurer. 1814, 165, § 1. 1821, 110, § 1.

2. When the condition of any bond, given to the treasurer of the city of Boston, by any constable of said city, for the faithful performance of the duties of his office, shall be broken, to the injury of any person, such person may cause a suit to be instituted upon such bond, at his own costs, but in the name of the treasurer of the city of Boston; and the like endorsements shall be made on the writ, and the like proceedings be had thereon, to final judgment and execution, and the like writs of *scire facias*, on such judgment, as may be made and had by a creditor on administration bonds, given to any judge of probate: *provided, however,* that no such suit shall be instituted by any person for his own use, until such person shall have recovered judgment against the constable, his executors or administrators, in an action brought for the malfeasance or misfeasance of the constable, or for non-payment of any moneys collected by the said constable, in that capacity, or a decree of a judge of probate, allowing a claim for any of the causes aforesaid, and such judgment or decree, or so much thereof as shall be unsatisfied, with the interest due thereon, shall be the proportion of the penalty for which execution shall be awarded: *provided, however,* that this act shall not be construed to make any surety in any bond given by the constable as aforesaid, before the passing of this act, liable to any suit, which could not heretofore be legally prosecuted against him.

Proviso.

Proviso.

Copy of bond to be given to persons applying for the same. 1814, 165, § 2.

3. It shall be the duty of the treasurer aforesaid, to deliver an attested copy of any constable's bond to any persons applying and paying for the same, and such attested copy shall be received as evidence in any case: *provided, nevertheless,* that if in any suit, the execution of the bond shall be disputed, the court may order the treasurer to bring the original bond into court.[1]

---

[1] For general provisions respecting constables, see Rev. Stat., c. 15, § 33, 66–80; 1842, c. 37; 1845, c. 70; and 1847, c. 98. See also Taxes.

COURTS.

STATUTES.

1. Duties of the judge of the municipal court to be performed by the court of common pleas.
2. Name, jurisdiction, &c. of said court to continue as heretofore.
3. Times and places of holding the court.
4. How adjourned in the absence of the judge.
5. Jurisdiction of the court.
6. Municipal court to have concurrent jurisdiction with C. C. P. and S. J. C. of proceedings upon recognizances in criminal matters in Suffolk county.
7. May sentence minors to house of reformation in certain cases.
8. Court to issue writs, &c. like C. C. P.
9. Seal and teste of precepts.
10. Seal.
11. Grand jurors to be summoned and empanelled.
12. Proceedings when the grand jury find an indictment for a capital crime.
13. Traverse jurors.
14. Court may grant new trials and allow exceptions. No appeal allowed.
15. How clerk shall be appointed and records kept.
16. Fines, &c. to be paid and accounted for as in C. C. P.
17. Provision for taxing, certifying and paying costs, arising in the municipal court.
18. Clerk to keep and render an account of fees.
19. Salary of clerk.
20. Appointment of justices of police court.
21. Times and place of holding the court.
22. General jurisdiction in criminal cases.
23. Of offences against the by-laws of Boston, except, &c.
24. Jurisdiction of certain assaults.
25. Of larcenies.
26. Of fornication.
27. Appeals allowed.
28. May issue process for witnesses into any county.
29. All warrants in criminal cases to be returnable to the police court.
30. Fees on warrants issued by a justice.
31. Justices of the peace in Boston to be conservators of the peace.
32. Appeal allowed to the municipal court.
33. Attendance, when a case is adjourned.
34. The court to be held also for civil actions.
35. To have exclusive jurisdiction in certain cases.
36. Teste and form of writs.
37. Trustee writs may run into any county.
38. Proceedings to be like those before justices of the peace.
39. Times and place of holding the justices court.
40. Appeal allowed to the C. C. P.
41. Justices to establish general rules of practice. May discharge from prison in certain cases.
42. Senior justice. Seals of the courts.
43. Appointment of the clerk.
44. Clerk to be sworn and to give bond.
45. Duty of the clerk.
46. Same subject.

STATUTES.

MUNICIPAL COURT.

Duties of the judge of the municipal court to be performed by the court of common pleas. 1843, 7, § 1.

1. By the statute of 1843, chapter 7,[1] all the duties, then required by law to be performed by the judge of the municipal court of the city of Boston, shall be performed within and for the county of Suffolk by the justices of the court of common pleas, or by some one of them; *provided, however*, that no one of said justices shall hold more than three monthly terms of said municipal court in succession.

Name, jurisdiction, &c. of said court to continue as heretofore. Ibid, § 3.

2. The name, style, and caption of the said municipal court, and its powers, duties and jurisdiction, shall continue the same as prescribed by law.

Times and places of holding the court. R. S. 86, § 2.

3. The said court shall be held in the city of Boston, on the first Monday of every month, and may be adjourned from time to time, as occasion shall require.

How adjourned in the absence of the judge. Ibid, § 3.

4. If the judge shall be absent, at a time appointed for holding a court, whether at the beginning of a term, or at an adjournment thereof, the clerk shall adjourn the court, either without day, or to such time and place, as the public convenience may in his judgment require, and notice of such adjournment shall be given by proclamation, to be made in the court house by the sheriff or his deputy, and in such other manner as the court may by any general rule direct.

Jurisdiction of the court. Ibid, § 4.

5. The said court shall have original jurisdiction, concurrent with the supreme judicial court, of all crimes,

---

[1] In the case of *Brien v. Commonwealth*, (5 Metc. 508,) it was held, that this statute is not repugnant to the constitution of the commonwealth. Held, also, that the office of judge of the municipal court was virtually abolished.

offences and misdemeanors committed in the county of Suffolk, which are not capital, and of all offences against the by-laws of the city of Boston, and appellate jurisdiction of all offences, which shall be tried and determined before the police court of the city of Boston, or before any justice of the peace for the county of Suffolk.

11 Pick. 28. 6 Pick. 104. 3 Metc. 460.

6. All actions, suits and prosecutions, in the name of the commonwealth, upon recognizances taken in any criminal prosecution or proceeding in the county of Suffolk, may be brought in and before the municipal court of the city of Boston, and said municipal court shall have jurisdiction thereof, concurrent with the court of common pleas and supreme judicial court, in said county, in all cases wherein said court of common pleas and supreme judicial court respectively now have jurisdiction; and all writs for the recovery of the penalties of such recognizances shall be in the forms prescribed by law, and may be sued out in term time or vacation, and shall be served fourteen days before the term at which they are returnable; and said municipal court shall have power and authority to render judgment for the whole, or any part they think proper, of the penal sum of such recognizances respectively, and interest thereon, and issue writs of execution, in form prescribed by law, against the party sued in said actions, and the said writs of execution shall be tested, sealed, directed and served, in the same manner as writs of execution issuing from the court of common pleas of this commonwealth.

Municipal court to have concurrent jurisdiction with C. C. P. and S. J. C., of proceedings upon recognizances in criminal matters in Suffolk county. 1844, 44, § 1.

7. The municipal court has also jurisdiction, concurrent with the police court, to sentence to the house of reformation, in certain cases, minors under the age of sixteen, who live an idle and dissolute life, &c.

May sentence minors to house of reformation, in certain cases. 1847, 208, § 1.

8. The said court shall issue all such writs and processes, and exercise all such powers, as may be necessary or proper for the discharge of their duty, in like manner as may be done by the court of common pleas; and all such writs and processes may run into any county, and shall be obeyed and executed throughout the state.

Court to issue writs, &c. like C. C. P. R. S. 86, § 5. 1843, 7, § 1.

9. All precepts, warrants, venires and processes, issued from said municipal court, shall be tested like similar pro-

Seal and teste of precepts. 1843, 7, § 7.

cesses from the court of common pleas, and shall be under the seal of the municipal court, and signed by its clerk.

Seal. 1844, 44, § 2.

10. The seal of the said municipal court shall in all cases be the same as that of the court of common pleas of this commonwealth.

Grand jurors to be summoned and empanelled. Ibid, § 3. R. S. 136, § 2, repealed, by 1844, 44, § 3. See R. S. 86, § 6.

11. The clerk of the said municipal court, seven days at least, and not more than fourteen days, before each term of the said court, commencing on the first Monday of January, and the first Monday of July, in each year, shall issue a writ of venire facias for twenty-three grand jurors to serve in said court, twenty-two of whom shall be drawn and returned from the city of Boston and one from the town of Chelsea, in said county of Suffolk; and the grand jurors, so returned, shall constitute the grand inquest of the commonwealth for said county, for the term of six months, and until another grand jury is empanelled in their stead.[1]

Proceedings when the grand jury find an indictment for a capital crime. 1844, 44, § 4.

12. If the grand jury, attending at any term of the municipal court, shall find and return to the court any indictment for any crime punishable with death, if the person accused be not in custody, process shall be forthwith issued for the arrest of the party charged with such offence, and the party so charged shall, as soon as may be, be served with a copy of the indictment by the sheriff or his deputy, with an order of court giving notice to the accused, that the indictment will be entered at the supreme judicial court next to be holden in and for said county of Suffolk, or at any intermediate time before the next term when said supreme judicial court shall be in session in said county, and notice of such indictment shall also be forthwith given to the chief or first justice of that court by the clerk of said municipal court; and the said clerk shall transmit and certify the original indictment to the supreme judicial court at the next term thereof, or at any intermediate time when said supreme judicial court shall be in session in said county, where it shall be entered, and the said supreme

Com. v. Webster, S. J. C. March T. 1850.

---

[1] For general provisions respecting the drawing of jurors, and grand jurors, see Rev. Stat. 95, c. 136; stat. 1838, c. 21; 1840, c. 74.

judicial court shall then and there have full cognizance and jurisdiction thereof, and the same proceedings shall be had, as if the said indictment had been found and returned in said supreme judicial court.

13. The traverse jurors of the municipal court shall be drawn and returned from the city of Boston, and from the town of Chelsea, in the manner provided in the ninety-fifth chapter of the Revised Statutes, and writs of venire facias shall be issued for that purpose, returnable at the terms held in January, April, July and October, in each year; and the jurors, so returned at each of those four terms, respectively, shall also serve at the two next succeeding terms.[1]

Traverse jurors. R. S. 86, § 7. Ibid, 95, §§ 34, 35.

14. The said municipal court may grant new trials in the like cases, and upon the same terms and conditions as are provided, in the one hundred and thirty-eighth chapter of the Revised Statutes, for the granting of new trials by the court of common pleas; and exceptions may be taken to any decision or direction of the court in matter of law, in the same manner, and with the same limitations, as are provided in said chapter. But no appeal is allowed to the supreme judicial court.

Court may grant new trials and allow exceptions. Ibid, 86, § 11.

No appeal allowed. Ibid, § 10. 1839, 161.

15. Whenever hereafter a vacancy shall happen in the office of clerk of said municipal court, such vacancy shall be filled by an appointment thereto, to be made by the said judges of the court of common pleas; and the records of the said municipal court are to be kept separate and distinct from those of the court of common pleas.

How clerk shall be appointed, and records kept. 1843, 7, § 2.

16. All fines, forfeitures and costs, accrued or allowed upon any judgment or other proceeding in said court, shall be paid, received and accounted for, in like manner as is provided in the case of criminal prosecutions in the court of common pleas.

Fines, &c. to be paid and accounted for as in C. C. P. R. S. 86, § 9.

17. All costs arising in criminal prosecutions, in the said municipal court, shall be taxed by the prosecuting officer according to law, and the allowance thereof shall be certified by the clerk, under the direction of the court, and

Provision for taxing, certifying and paying costs arising in the municipal court. 1843, 61, § 1.

---

[1] See note on p. 88.

copies thereof transmitted to the county treasurer, as now prescribed by law, and said treasurer shall pay the same upon such certificate and copies.

Clerk to keep and render an account of fees. R. S. 86, § 13.

18. The clerk of the said court shall keep an account of all fees received by him for his official acts and services, under the laws of this commonwealth, excepting fees for such copies as he is not required by law to furnish, and he shall, on the first Wednesday of January, in every year, render to the treasurer of the county of Suffolk his account, on oath, of all fees so received within the year then past.

Salary of clerk. Ibid, § 14.

19. The said clerk shall receive an annual salary of twelve hundred dollars, and in the same proportion for any part of a year, if the fees, for which he is required to account, shall amount to so much; and if, upon rendering his said account, there shall be in his hands any excess above the amount due for his salary, he shall retain for his own use one half of the excess, and shall pay the other half thereof to the said county treasurer, who shall account therefor to the treasurer of the commonwealth.[1]

POLICE COURT.

Appointment of justices of police court. R. S. 87, § 1.

20. The justices of the police court of the city of Boston shall continue to hold their offices according to the tenor of their commissions, and as vacancies occur, others shall be appointed in the manner provided by the constitution, so that there shall be always three justices of the said court.

Times and place of holding the court. Ibid, § 2.

21. The police court shall be held in Boston, for the county of Suffolk, by one or more of the said justices, at nine of the clock in the morning, and at three of the clock in the afternoon, of every day in the year except Lord's days, and days of public thanksgiving and fast.

General jurisdiction in criminal cases. Ibid, § 3. 6 Pick. 104.

22. The said court shall have the same jurisdiction in criminal suits and prosecutions, and in all matters relating

[1] The stat. 1813, c. 178, and Rev. Stat. c. 86, § 12, respecting the salary of the judge of the municipal court, appear to be superseded by stat. 1843, c. 7, § 1, and stat. 1844, c. 44, § 5, which latter section repeals the 6th section of stat. 1843, c. 7.

to treasons, felonies, and other crimes and misdemeanors, committed in the county of Suffolk, and relating to persons found therein, and charged with any of the said offences, and shall have and exercise the same powers in all criminal cases, that are or may be given by law to one or more justices of the peace, or of the peace and quorum in other counties.

See also stat. 1847, 208, cited on p. 8', *ante*; 1840, 79, § 1; 1847, 104; and 1849, 59.

23. The said court shall also have cognizance of all offences against the by-laws of the city of Boston, which are not within the exclusive jurisdiction of some other court.

Of offences against the by-laws of Boston, except, &c. R. S. 87, § 4.

24. The several police courts of this commonwealth shall have concurrent jurisdiction with the municipal court of the city of Boston, and the court of common pleas, of all cases of assault and battery committed upon any constable, police officer, or watchman, while in the discharge of his duty as such officer, except in cases where such assault and battery shall be committed with a dangerous or deadly weapon, or with intent to kill, or when life is endangered. And, for such assault and battery, said police courts may punish by fine, not exceeding thirty dollars, or by imprisonment in the house of correction not more than six months.

Jurisdiction of certain assaults. 1849, 132, § 1.

25. The said police courts shall have concurrent jurisdiction with said municipal court, and court of common pleas, of all larcenies mentioned in the seventeenth section of the one hundred and twenty-sixth chapter of the Revised Statutes, when the money, or other property stolen, shall not be alleged to exceed the value of twenty-five dollars; in all which cases, the punishment shall be by fine not exceeding thirty dollars, or by confinement in the house of correction not more than six months.

Of larcenies. Ibid, § 2.

26. The said police courts shall have concurrent jurisdiction with said municipal court, and court of common pleas, of all cases arising under the fifth section of the one hundred and thirtieth chapter of the Revised Statutes, in which cases the punishment shall be by imprisonment in the county jail not more than three months, or by fine not exceeding thirty dollars.

Of fornication. Ibid, § 3.

Appeals allowed. Ibid, § 4.

27. Any person, convicted under the provisions of the three next preceding sections, may appeal to the municipal court, or court of common pleas, and the appeal shall be allowed on the same terms, and the proceedings therein conducted in all respects, as provided in the one hundred and thirty-eighth chapter of the Revised Statutes respecting appeals from justices of the peace.

May issue process for witnesses into any county. 1838, 147, § 1.

28. The police court in the city of Boston shall have power to issue summons and other process to procure the attendance of witnesses, in the trial and examination of criminal cases, to run into any county, to be served by the sheriff of the county of Suffolk, or of any other county, or either of their deputies, or any constable of the town in which any witness may be.

All warrants in criminal cases to be returnable to the police court. R. S. 87, § 5.

29. All warrants issued by the saidc ourt, or by any justice of the peace in Boston, in any criminal suit or prosecution, shall be made returnable before the said court, and no process returnable before a justice of the peace in the town of Chelsea, except for causes of complaint arising in that town, shall be served in Boston.

Fees on warrants issued by a justice. Ibid, § 6.

30. No fees shall be allowed to any justice of the peace for any warrant issued by him, returnable before said court, unless it shall appear to the court that there was just and reasonable cause for issuing the warrant.

Justices of the peace in Boston to be conservators of the peace. Ibid, § 7.

31. Every justice of the peace in the city of Boston shall, notwithstanding any thing contained in this chapter, have and exercise all the powers and duties of a conservator of the peace, for suppressing all affrays, riots, assaults and batteries, and for arresting all persons concerned therein; and all persons so arrested, whether upon a warrant in writing or otherwise, shall be brought before the said court for examination, to be there dealt with according to law.

Appeal allowed to the municipal court. 1849, 31.

32. Every person, convicted in the county of Suffolk, before any justice of the peace or any police court, may appeal therefrom to the municipal court of the city of Boston, and the appeal shall be entered at the next term of the municipal court, and shall be conducted and disposed of, in

all respects, like appeals in criminal cases from justices of the peace to the court of common pleas in other counties.

33. When any trial or examination, pending before the said court, is adjourned to a future day, as provided in the one hundred and thirty-fifth chapter of the Revised Statutes, the parties and the witnesses shall not be required to attend from day to day, but they shall attend at the time to which the cause is so adjourned, and the recognizances, if any, shall be taken accordingly.[1]

Attendance, when case is adjourned. R. S. 87, § 9.

JUSTICES' COURT.

34. There shall also be a court for the trial of civil actions, to be held by one or more of the justices of the police court, which shall be called the justices' court for the county of Suffolk.

The court to be held also for civil actions. Ibid, § 10.

35. The said justices' court shall have and exercise, exclusively, the same jurisdiction in all civil actions in the county of Suffolk, that is exercised by justices of the peace in other counties.

To have exclusive jurisdiction in certain cases. Ibid, § 11. 3 Pick. 508. 6 Pick. 104. 1 Metc. 148.

36. All writs and processes, issued by the said justices' court, shall bear teste of either of the justices who is not a party thereto, and shall be signed by the clerk, and they shall be, in all other respects, substantially like the writs and processes issued by justices of the peace.

Teste and form of writs. R. S. 87, § 12.

37. When, by a trustee writ, returnable before the justices' court of the county of Suffolk, any person is to be summoned as a trustee, who is liable to be charged as such, and the defendant resides within this commonwealth, but in a county other than that of the trustee, said writ may run into any county, and shall be served on the defendant fourteen days at least before its return day.

Trustee writs may run into any county. 1838, 147, § 3.

38. All the proceedings in the said justices' court, in the hearing, trial and determination of civil actions, and in all matters relating thereto, shall be substantially the same as the proceedings in like cases before jus-

Proceedings to be like those before justices of the peace. R. S. 87, § 13.

---

[1] For provisions in relation to police courts generally, see Rev. Stat. c. 87, §§ 29–46; stat. 1837, c. 157, 217; 1838, c. 147; 1839, c. 157; 1843, c. 22; 1847, c. 208; 1849, c. 137. See also Lunatics.

tices of the peace; and the said justices' court shall have and exercise all such powers as may be necessary or proper for the discharge of their duty, in the same manner as justices of the peace might do in the like cases.

Times and place of holding the justices' court. Ibid, § 14. 6 Pick. 110.

39. The said justices' court shall be held in Boston, on two days in each week, to be fixed and determined by the justices thereof, and as much oftener as occasion shall require, and it may be adjourned to any other time; and all actions therein may be continued to any future day fixed for the sitting of the court.

Appeal allowed to the C. C. P. R. S. 87, § 15.

40. Any party, aggrieved by the judgment of the said justices' court, may appeal therefrom to the court of common pleas for the county of Suffolk, and all the proceedings on such appeal shall be conducted in all respects, as is provided for appeals in civil cases from justices of the peace to the court of common pleas in other counties.

Justices to establish general rules of practice. Ibid, § 16.

May discharge from prison in certain cases.

41. The said justices shall from time to time meet, to establish all necessary rules for the orderly and uniform conducting of the business of both of the said courts, and also to arrange and distribute their duties, so as to equalize the same among themselves, as nearly as may be, and to ensure a prompt and punctual discharge thereof; and on all other occasions requiring the presence of two or more justices; and when so assembled, the said justices may discharge from prison, in the county of Suffolk, any person, who may be there held for no other reason than the non-payment of fine and costs, if it shall appear to them that he is poor and unable to pay the same; provided, that when such person is held under the sentence of any other court, the consent thereto of the judge, or of one of the justices of such other court, shall be first given in writing.

Senior justice. Seals of the courts. Ibid, § 17.

42. The senior justice of said court, for the time being, shall be the first justice of the said police court and justices' court, but each of the said courts shall have a separate and distinct seal.

Appointment of the clerk. Ibid, § 18.

43. The clerk of the said police court and justices' court shall continue to hold his office, according to the tenor of his commission; and upon any vacancy in said office, the governor, with the advice of the council, shall

nominate and appoint one person, to be clerk of both of the said courts, who shall hold his office during the pleasure of the governor and council; and in case of the death or absence of the clerk, the court shall appoint a clerk pro tempore, who shall officiate as such, until the standing clerk shall resume the performance of his duties, or until another shall be appointed by the governor.

44. The clerk shall be sworn to the faithful performance of his duty, and shall give bond to the city of Boston, in such sum as the city council shall order, with a surety or sureties, to the acceptance of the city treasurer, with condition for the faithful performance of the duties of his office.

Clerk to be sworn, and to give bond. Ibid, § 19.

45. The clerk or his assistant shall attend all sessions of both of said courts, and keep a record of all the proceedings of the said police court, and a distinct record of all the proceedings of the said justices' court.

Duty of the clerk. Ibid, § 20.

46. He shall also make out all warrants, writs and processes, which shall be ordered by either of the said courts, and tax all bills of costs, and receive all fines and forfeitures, and all fees, awarded and payable in either of said courts, and all fees for blanks, and for copies in civil and criminal suits; and the amount of all fees received by him for copies shall be indorsed thereon.

Same subject. Ibid, § 21.

47. He shall render to the board of accounts of the city of Boston a quarterly account of all moneys so received by him as clerk, and upon the approval thereof by the board, he shall forthwith pay over the amount due thereon to the city treasurer.

To account for and pay over moneys. Ibid, § 22.

48. He may from time to time appoint one or more assistant clerks, to aid him in the discharge of his duties; but no person shall be so appointed, unless approved by the justices of the said courts.

May appoint assistant clerks. Ibid, § 23.

49. The clerk shall be responsible for the doings of his assistants, and they shall be removable at his pleasure, and shall be sworn to the faithful performance of their duties.

To be responsible for them. Ibid, § 24.

50. Neither of the said justices, nor the said clerk, nor either of his assistants, shall be retained or employed as counsel or attorney in any suit, complaint, or proceeding,

The justices and clerk not to be of counsel or attorney, &c. Ibid, § 25.

in the said police court, or justices' court, nor in any which shall have been heard, examined or tried therein.

Salaries of the justices. Ibid, § 26.

51. The said justices shall severally receive, from the city of Boston, an annual salary, the amount of which shall be from time to time determined by the city council, and shall be paid in quarterly payments, and in the same proportion for any part of a quarter, in full compensation for all their services, except those required of them as members of the board of accounts of the city of Boston.

Salary of the clerk. Ibid, § 27.

52. The said clerk shall also receive from the city an annual salary, the amount of which shall be from time to time determined by the city council, and shall be paid in quarterly payments, and in the same proportion for any part of a quarter, and shall be in full compensation for all his services.

Compensation of assistant clerks. Ibid, § 28.

53. The assistant clerks shall receive from the city such compensation for their services, as shall be ordered by the city council, provided the board of accounts shall certify that their services were necessary.

BOARD OF ACCOUNTS.

Board of accounts for the county of Suffolk. R. S. 14, § 41. 1843, 61, § 2.

54. In the county of Suffolk, the judge of probate and the justices of the police court of said city, shall continue to be the board of accounts; whose duty it shall be to meet, quarter yearly, and as much oftener as may be found necessary, to examine and allow all bills of costs, accounts and charges, arising in the course of proceedings in said municipal and police courts, and in the maintenance and keeping of the prisoners in the jail of the county of Suffolk, and of all other expenses and charges, in keeping said jail and all other places of confinement and punishment, within the city of Boston; and the said board of accounts shall certify all such accounts, charges and expenses, as shall have been allowed by them; and their certificate shall be endorsed on the accounts so allowed, and shall be addressed to the public officer by whom such charges, fees and expenses may by law be payable.

Three of the board to make a quorum.

55. Any three or more, of the members of the board of accounts of the county of Suffolk, shall constitute a quorum

for the performance of their duties; and they shall be entitled, respectively, to receive the sum of three dollars, for each and every day which may be employed by them, in the discharge of their said duties. Their compensation. R. S. 14, § 42.

ORDINANCE OF THE CITY.[1]

SECT. 1. The penalty of the bond to be given by the clerk of the police court, and justices' court, shall be five thousand dollars; the form shall be prescribed by the mayor, with the approbation of the board of aldermen; and the city treasurer shall have the custody of said bond, and be accountable therefor. Penalty of the bond of the clerk of the police and justices' courts. June 17, 1822.

SECT. 2. The bond which is to be taken as aforesaid, shall be in force for one year from the date thereof, and until a new bond is given, and the bond of said clerk shall be renewed annually, in manner as aforesaid. Time for which the bond shall be in force. Ibid.

CRIERS.

ORDINANCE OF THE CITY.[2]

SECT. 1. The mayor and aldermen may from time to time grant licenses to such and so many persons as they Licenses to be granted to common criers. June 10, 1850.

---

[1] An ordinance prescribing the penalty of the bond to be given by the clerk of the police court and justices' court, passed June 17, 1822.

[2] An ordinance to regulate common criers, passed June 10, 1850.

13

may deem expedient, to be common criers in this city; and such licenses shall continue in force until the first day of May next after the date thereof, unless sooner revoked by the mayor and aldermen, and no longer.

Term of license.

Crying without license. Ibid.

SECT. 2. No person shall be a common crier within the city of Boston, or cry any goods, wares or merchandize, lost or found, stolen goods, strays or public sales, in any of the streets, squares, lanes, or market places within the city, unless he shall be licensed as aforesaid.

Criers to keep a list of matters cried, &c. Ibid.

SECT. 3. Every person so licensed shall keep a true and perfect list of all the matters and things by him cried, and the names of the persons, by whom he was employed to cry the same; which list shall be open, and subject to the inspection of the mayor and aldermen, whenever they shall demand the same; and no common crier shall publish or cry any abusive, libellous, profane or obscene matter or thing whatsoever.

Shall not cry libellous matter, &c.

Penalty for violation. Ibid.

SECT. 4. Any person, who shall be guilty of a violation of this ordinance, or any part thereof, shall forfeit and pay, for each offence, a sum not less than one dollar, nor more than twenty dollars.

DEEDS.

ORDINANCE.

1. Mayor authorized to execute deeds, &c.
2. Mayor authorized to discharge and assign mortgages.

ORDINANCE OF THE CITY.[1]

Mayor authorized to execute deeds, &c. Nov. 18, 1833.

SECT. 1. The mayor of the city is authorized and empowered to affix the common seal of the city unto, and to

[1] An ordinance providing for the execution of deeds and leases and discharge of mortgages on behalf of the city, passed November 18, 1833.

sign, seal, execute and deliver, in behalf of the city, all deeds and leases of lands sold or leased by the city, and all deeds, agreements, indentures, or assurances, made and entered into by order of the city council.

Mayor authorized to discharge and assign mortgages. Ibid.

SECT. 2. Whenever any person, having lawful authority to redeem any estate mortgaged to the city, shall make application to the mayor for such purpose, the mayor shall have power, on the payment of the sum of money due on said mortgage, made to the treasurer of the city, to discharge, release, or assign the same without liability or recourse to the city, the assent of the board of aldermen thereto being first had and obtained, and to execute, in behalf of the city, any and all legal instruments that may be necessary for this purpose.

DOGS.

STATUTES.

City council may make by-laws respecting the keeping of dogs. R. S. 58, § 10. 1850, 245. R. S. 2, § 6.

1. The city council of any city in this commonwealth may make such by-laws, concerning the licensing, regulating and restraining of dogs, going at large, as they shall deem expedient, and may affix any penalties, not exceeding ten dollars for any breach thereof; provided, that no such by-law shall extend to any dog, not owned or kept in such city, and that no person shall be obliged to pay more than two dollars, annually, for any license granted under the provisions of this section.[1]

Fees for licenses, to be paid to the treasurer. R. S. 58, § 11. Ibid, 2, § 6.

2. All money received for the several licenses mentioned in the preceding section, in any city, shall be paid to the treasurer for the use of the city.

Dogs, to have collars, with names, &c., of owners. R. S. 58, § 12.

3. Every person, who shall keep or own any dog, shall cause to be constantly kept, about the neck of such dog, a collar, with the name and place of residence of such owner or keeper legibly marked on the same; and any person may kill any dog, being without a collar as aforesaid.[2]

Double damages for injury done by dogs. Ibid, § 13.

4. Every owner or keeper of any dog shall forfeit, to any person injured by such dog, double the amount of the damage sustained by him, to be recovered in an action of trespass, and in such action, the defendant may plead the

---

1 A by-law of a town, made under this section, will be construed to apply only to dogs owned or kept in the town, although, in its terms, it applies to "any person permitting his dog to go at large within the town"; and if it is otherwise valid, it may be enforced against the owner or keeper of a dog within the town. *Commonwealth v. Dow*, (10 Metc. 382.)

2 A by-law of a town imposed a penalty of $10 on any person permitting his dog to go at large in the town, unless the dog should be licensed to go at large, and should wear a collar with the name of the owner or keeper, and the word "licensed" distinctly marked thereon; and the further penalty of $10, if said dog should wear a collar without license. *Held*, that although the latter part of this section might be repugnant to the Rev. Stat. c. 58, §12, and therefore void, yet that the former part was valid, and that the penalty thereby imposed was recoverable of a person who permitted his dog to go at large without being licensed. *Ibid.*

The provision in the Rev. Stat. c. 58, § 12, that any person may kill any dog that is without a collar, does not authorize a person to convert such dog to his own use; and trover by the owner will lie for such conversion. *Cummings v. Perham*, (1 Metc. 555.)

general issue, and give any special matter in evidence, in excuse or justification.

5. Any person may kill any dog, that shall suddenly assault him, while he is peaceably walking or riding, any where out of the enclosure of the owner or keeper of such dog; and any person may kill any dog, that shall be found out of the enclosure or immediate care of its owner or keeper, worrying, wounding or killing any neat cattle, sheep or lambs.

Any person may kill any dog, when, &c.
13 Johns. R. 312.
4 Cowen, 351.
R. S. 58, § 14.

6. If any person shall be assaulted by any dog, in manner as aforesaid, or if any dog shall hereafter be found strolling out of the enclosure or immediate care of its owner or keeper, and if such person shall, at any time within forty-eight hours after such an assault, or the finding of such dog strolling as aforesaid, make oath thereof, before any justice of the peace for the county, or before the clerk of the town or city where the owner of such dog shall dwell, and shall further swear that he suspects such dog to be a dangerous or mischievous dog, and shall give notice thereof to such owner or keeper, by delivering him a certificate of such oath, signed by such justice or clerk, the owner or keeper of such dog shall forthwith kill or confine the same; and if he shall neglect so to do, for the space of twenty-four hours, after notice is given as aforesaid, he shall forfeit the sum of ten dollars, to be recovered to the use of the town or city, on complaint before any justice of the peace, or, in the county of Suffolk, before the police court for said county.

Dangerous dogs, to be confined by owner or killed.
Ibid, § 15.
R. S. 2, § 6.
Ibid.
R. S. 87, § 3.
10 Metc. 382.

7. If, after such notice, such dog shall not be killed or confined, but shall again be found strolling out of the enclosure or immediate care of its owner or keeper, any person may kill such dog; and in any suit brought therefor, the defendant may plead the general issue and give the special matter in evidence.

If owner neglects, after notice, any person may kill his dog.
R. S. 58, § 16.

8. If any dog, after notice given to the owner or keeper, as before provided, shall, by any sudden assault, in manner as aforesaid, wound or cause to be wounded, any person, or shall worry, wound or kill any neat cattle, sheep or lambs, or do any other mischief, the owner or keeper

Owner liable to treble damages, in case, &c.
Ibid, § 17.

shall be liable to pay to the person injured thereby treble damage, to be recovered with costs, by action of debt.

ORDINANCE OF THE CITY.[1]

No dog permitted to go at large without license. June 4, 1850.

SECT. 1. No dog shall be permitted to go at large[2] or loose, in any street, lane, alley, court, or travelled way, or in any unenclosed or public place, in this city, until the owner or keeper of such dog, or the head of the family or the keeper of the house where such dog is kept or harbored, shall have paid to the city clerk two dollars for a license for such dog to go at large.

City clerk shall grant licenses. Fee for same. Ibid.

SECT. 2. The city clerk shall grant a license to any citizen for his or her dog to run at large, on the payment of two dollars; which license shall expire on the first day of February next after the same is given.

Clerk to keep record of same, make quarterly reports, and pay over moneys. Ibid.

SECT. 3. The city clerk shall keep a record of all licenses so granted, with the numbers of the same; and he shall make a report to the mayor and aldermen, once in three months, of all moneys so received; and shall pay over the same to the city treasurer for the use of the city.

Licenses to be numbered. Dogs to wear collars. Ibid.

SECT. 4. Every license so granted shall be numbered, and the person named therein shall cause the same number to be legibly printed or engraved on a collar, to be kept about the neck of the dog intended to be licensed. And no dog shall be considered as licensed, unless the requisition contained in this section be complied with.

City marshal to cause dogs at large, without

SECT. 5. It shall be the duty of the city marshal to cause all dogs to be destroyed which shall be found at

---

[1] An ordinance restraining the going at large of dogs within the city of Boston, passed June 4, 1850.

[2] A dog is "going at large" in a town, if he be loose and following the person who has charge of him, through the streets of the town, at such a distance that he cannot exercise a control over the dog, which will prevent his doing mischief. *Commonwealth v. Dow*, (10 Metc. 382.)

large within the city, without a collar as required by the laws of this commonwealth. collars, to be destroyed. Ibid.

SECT. 6. On complaint being made to the mayor, of any dog within this city which shall, by barking, biting, howling, or in any other way or manner, disturb the quiet of any person or persons whomsoever, the mayor shall issue notice thereof to the person owning, keeping, or permitting such dog to be kept; and in case such person shall neglect to cause such dog to be forthwith removed and kept beyond the limits of the city, or destroyed, he shall forfeit and pay one dollar for every day during which such neglect shall continue after such notice; *provided*, that the justice before whom the complaint respecting such dog shall be heard and tried, shall be satisfied that such dog had in manner aforesaid disturbed the quiet of any person or persons in the said city.

Proceedings in case any dog shall disturb the quiet of any person, by barking, &c.

Proviso. Ibid.

SECT. 7. In case any dog shall be found loose or going at large, contrary to any of the foregoing provisions, the owner or keeper thereof, or the head of the family, or keeper of the house, store, shop, office, or other place where such dog is kept or harbored, shall forfeit and pay a sum not exceeding ten dollars.

Penalty. Ibid.

EAST BOSTON.

STATUTE.

1. In the act to incorporate the East Boston Company, in the city of Boston, passed March 25, 1833, it is provided, that said corporation may purchase, hold and possess, in fee simple or otherwise, all or any part of that

East Boston Company authorized to hold Noddle's Island. 1833, 152, § 2.

island situate in the city of Boston, known by the name of Noddle's Island, with all the flats around the same, and the privileges and appurtenances thereto appertaining, and all rights, easements and water courses therewith used and enjoyed, and to the proprietors of said island belonging; with such personal property as may be necessary for the proper

Proviso. conducting of the affairs of said corporation: *provided*, that the whole real and personal estate of said corporation shall not exceed in value the sum of five hundred thousand dollars: *and provided*, that the lawful owners or proprietors of such estates shall convey the same to said corporation.

Authority to sell, lease, &c., construct dams, docks, wharves and buildings. And said corporation shall also have power to sell and convey, lease, mortgage, or otherwise dispose of said corporate property, or any part thereof, and to manage and improve the same at its will and pleasure, with authority to construct dams, docks, wharves and buildings, and to lay

To lay out streets, &c. out streets and passageways within the limits of said island, as it shall deem expedient.

Corporation shall set apart land for public purposes. Ibid, § 4. 2. Said corporation shall set apart on said island, in such place or places thereon as the mayor and aldermen of the city of Boston may designate, a portion of land, not exceeding in the whole four acres, free of expense to the city, for the purpose of providing proper sites for engine houses, school houses, burial grounds, and for other public purposes: *provided*, that no lot, except the lots for burial grounds, shall contain more than ten thousand feet, without the consent of this corporation: *and provided further*, that said mayor and aldermen shall designate the land so to be taken, within six weeks from the passing of this act.[1]

---

[1] The East Boston Company, by deed dated August 12, 1836, conveyed to the city of Boston a lot of land on Paris street; and by deed dated July 13, 1838, a lot of land on Bennington street, and another on Meridian and Paris streets; in conformity with their act of incorporation. See Suffolk Registry of Deeds, Lib. 409, fol. 89, and Lib. 433, fol. 161.

ELECTIONS.[1]

ORDINANCE OF THE CITY.[2]

SECT. 1. The form of warrants for calling meetings of the citizens of the several wards, shall be as follows, to wit: Form of warrants for ward meetings. Dec. 27, 1826.

L. S. City of Boston.

To either of the constables of the City of Boston.

Greeting:

In the name of the Commonwealth of Massachusetts, you are hereby required, forthwith, to warn the inhabitants of ward No. , qualified as the law directs, to assemble at on the day of at o'clock M. then and there to give in their ballots for

Hereof fail not; and have you there then this warrant, with your doings thereon. Witness Mayor of our said City of Boston the day of in the year of our Lord

By order of the Mayor and Aldermen.

City Clerk.

SECT. 2. All warrants for calling meetings of the citizens of the several wards, which shall be issued by the mayor and aldermen, shall be served by any constable of the city, and returned to the wardens of the several wards in said city, on or before the time of meeting of the citizens of said wards, therein specified. To be served by constables, and returned. Ibid.

---

[1] For general statutes respecting elections, see Rev. Stat. c. 3, 4, 5, 6, 15; stat. 1839, c. 42, 165; 1840, c. 59, 66; 1841, c. 70; 1842, c. 99; 1843, c. 94; 1844, c. 78, 143, 167; 1845, c. 217; 1848, c. 35, 240. See also, City Charter and Amendments, *ante*.

[2] An ordinance prescribing the form of warrants and of the service thereof, passed December 27, 1826.

Form of warrants for general meetings. Ibid.

SECT. 3. The form of warrants for calling meetings of the inhabitants of the said city of Boston, shall be as follows, to wit:

L. S. City of Boston.

To the constables of the City of Boston.

Greeting:

In the name of the Commonwealth of Massachusetts, you are hereby required forthwith to warn the inhabitants of the City of Boston, qualified as the law directs, to assemble at Faneuil Hall, on the day of at o'clock, M. then and there to

Hereof fail not; and have you there then this warrant, with your doings thereon. Witness, Mayor of our City of Boston, the day of in the year of our Lord

By order of the Mayor and Aldermen.

City Clerk.

To be served by constables, and returned. Ibid.

SECT. 4. All warrants which shall be issued by the mayor and aldermen, for calling meetings of the inhabitants of the city, shall be served by any constable of the city, and returned to the mayor and aldermen on or before the meeting of the citizens therein specified.

Time of opening and closing the poll shall be fixed by the mayor and aldermen, and inserted in the warrant. Ibid.

SECT. 5. It shall be the duty of the mayor and aldermen to fix the time when the poll shall close, as well as the time for the opening thereof, in the election of all officers, except ward officers, and insert the same in any warrant and notification to the inhabitants, of such election.

FANEUIL HALL.

ORDINANCE OF THE CITY.[1]

SECT. 1. There shall be appointed annually by the mayor and aldermen a superintendent of Faneuil Hall, whose duty it shall be to supervise and take proper care of said hall and all the rooms over the same and connected therewith, to attend to the admission of visitors, to provide that the said rooms are kept clean and in good order, and to report to the mayor and aldermen all repairs that may be necessary in the same.

Superintendent to be appointed by mayor and aldermen. His general duties. Oct. 14, 1833.

SECT. 2. It shall be the duty of said superintendent to examine at least once in each month and as much oftener as he may deem expedient, the various apartments, comprising the armories, offices and stores connected with said Faneuil Hall, for the purpose of ascertaining any danger that may exist from fire or other causes, and whenever he shall discover any such cause of danger to report the same to the mayor and aldermen.

To examine the apartments once a month. Ibid.

SECT. 3. It shall be the duty of said superintendent to attend to the opening and closing of said hall, at such hours and under such provisions as the mayor and aldermen may direct.

To attend to the opening and closing of the hall. Ibid.

SECT. 4. Said superintendent shall hold his said office during the pleasure of the mayor and aldermen, and in case of a vacancy occurring in said office, the same shall be filled in the manner provided in the first section.

To hold his office during the pleasure of mayor and aldermen. Vacancy. Ibid.

SECT. 5. Said superintendent shall receive such compensation for his services as the city council may from time to time allow.

His salary. Ibid.

---

[1] An ordinance providing for the appointment of a superintendent of Faneuil Hall, passed October 14, 1833.

FANEUIL HALL MARKET.

STATUTE.

Mayor and aldermen authorized to extend Faneuil Hall market. 1823, 148.

1. By an act of the legislature, passed February 21, 1824, the mayor and aldermen were authorized, whenever the city council should declare that the public exigences require that the limits of Faneuil Hall market should be extended in any direction between Ann street on the north, a line drawn from the east end of Faneuil Hall, on the west, the south side of Faneuil Hall, and the lane leading to Green's Wharf on the south, and the harbor on the east, to lay out and widen Faneuil Hall market, within one year from the first day of April, 1824, in such direction within the limits aforesaid, not exceeding one hundred and eighty feet wide, as might be prescribed by the city council: *provided*, that the land taken, by virtue of this act, should

never be used for any other purposes than those described in said act, without the previous consent of the legislature being obtained therefor. The act contained provisions for referring questions of damages for land taken and buildings removed for the purposes thereof; for petitions to the supreme judicial court for indemnity; the appointment of commissioners by the court; and a trial by jury in case either party should be dissatisfied with the award; with special authority for trustees, administrators, &c. to enter into references and take other measures respecting damages; and provisions securing the proceeds to the persons for whom such estates were held in trust.[1]

Provisions respecting damages for land taken, &c.

ORDINANCE OF THE CITY.[2]

SECT. 1. The mayor and aldermen shall annually in the month of June or July, appoint a clerk of Faneuil Hall Market, who shall be removable at their pleasure, and shall receive such compensation for his services as the city council shall annually direct.

Clerk of Faneuil Hall Market. October 26, 1846.

SECT. 2. The clerk of Faneuil Hall Market, shall, whenever authorized by the mayor and aldermen, employ one or more deputies, who shall be approved by the mayor and aldermen, and who shall have power and authority to assist the clerk in the execution of his office, and on any occasion, when said clerk is not present, to officiate for him in his stead, and to perform his duties; but no deputy shall remain in office longer than during the approbation of the mayor and aldermen, and the said clerk shall be re-

His deputies. Ibid.

---

1 The city council, by resolves passed March 11, 1824, declared that the public exigences required such extension; and on July 22, 1824, the mayor and aldermen laid out and widened the said market, "in an easterly direction from said Faneuil Hall to the harbor, between two lines, parallel to the walls of Faneuil Hall aforesaid, and running eastwardly towards the harbor, of which the north line shall be fourteen feet distant from the north side of said hall, and the south line shall be one hundred and eighty feet to the south of said north line." *City Records, vol.* 2, pp. 70, 294.

2 An ordinance for the regulation of Faneuil Hall Market, passed October 26, 1846. An ordinance in addition to an ordinance for the regulation of Faneuil Hall Market, passed May 30, 1850.

sponsible for the conduct of each of his deputies, and such deputies shall receive such compensation for their services as the city council shall annually direct.

Duties of clerk and his deputies. Ibid.

SECT. 3. The clerk of Faneuil Hall Market, and his deputies, shall, under the control of the mayor and aldermen, have the care and superintendence of said market; and it shall be their duty to preserve order in said market, and to execute and carry into effect all the regulations, orders and ordinances, which may be duly made and established from time to time by the city council, or the mayor and aldermen, for the due regulation of the same; and it shall be their duty to enter and prosecute complaints for any violations of said regulations, orders and ordinances.[1]

Limits of the market. May 30, 1850.

SECT. 4. The limits of Faneuil Hall Market, shall include the lower floor, porches and cellars of the building called Faneuil Hall Market, and the streets on each side thereof called North Market street and South Market street, except the northerly sidewalk of North Market street, and the southerly sidewalk of South Market street; and shall also include all those parts of Commercial street and the street lying between the market building and Faneuil Hall, which lie between the inner lines of said sidewalks extended easterly and westerly across said streets.[2]

Clerk, &c., to assign stands for carts, wagons, sleighs, &c. October 26, 1846.

SECT. 5. The said clerk and his deputies, under the direction of the mayor and aldermen, shall have the control of all carts, wagons, sleighs and other vehicles and car-

---

[1] It is not necessary that the clerk of the market before entering a complaint for violation of the regulations of the market, should have the direction of the mayor and aldermen to make such complaint. *Commonwealth v. Rice*, (9 Metc. 253.)

[2] A by-law providing that no inhabitant of the city or any town in the vicinity thereof, not offering for sale the produce of his own farm, &c., shall, without the permission of the clerk of the market, be suffered to occupy any stand for the purpose of vending commodities, in certain streets which by the by-law are a part of the market, was held to be a salutary police regulation, and not void as making a distinction between the inhabitants of the city and its vicinity, and those of distant towns, nor as being uncertain, nor as being in restraint of trade. *Nightingale's case*, (11 Pick., 168.) The city government have an undoubted right to prohibit the occupation of a stand in the streets by any one, or by any one not having a license or permission for that purpose from the clerk of the market. *Ibid*, 171.

riages within the limits of Faneuil Hall Market, and may assign stands within the limits of the said market for the sale of provisions and other articles; and no person shall occupy any stand other than such as may be assigned him, or keep any cart, wagon, sleigh, or other vehicle or carriage, horse, or other beast, within the limits of said market, for any longer space of time, or shall range or locate them in any other manner or form, than such as may be directed by said clerk or either of his deputies; and said clerk and his deputies shall have power and authority to remove from place to place within the limits, (if the owner or possessors thereof neglect or refuse after request so to remove them, or if the owner or possessor be absent therefrom) all such carts, wagons, sleighs, vehicles, and carriages, with their contents remaining therein, and all horses and other beasts, as shall be ranged or formed in any other manner than as directed by said clerk or either of his deputies, and the owner or person having charge of any box, barrel, cask, crate, basket, package, tub, or other vessel, whether empty or not, incumbering any place within the limits of said market house used as passageways either in the said house, or the passageways to and from said house to the middle of the streets, or on the side-walks beyond three feet from the walls of said house, shall, when directed by said clerk or either of his deputies, remove the same with their contents, or cause the same with their contents to be removed without delay, as the said clerk or either of his deputies may direct; and in case of neglect or refusal so to do by such owner or possessor, or the absence of them for more than an hour's time, the owner or possessor thereof, besides being liable for the penalty hereinafter mentioned for violation of this ordinance, shall be liable to pay the expense of such removal by the clerk or either of his deputies, and the keeping of the same, and shall not be entitled to re-delivery or possession of such property so removed by the clerk or either of his deputies, until the expenses of such removal and keeping are paid; and if said expenses are not paid within twenty-four hours after such removal, so much of said property so removed may be sold at

May order the same to be removed.

Penalty for neglect or refusal to remove, when so directed.

public auction, after being advertised for twenty-four hours, as may be necessary to produce the amount in money of said expenses of the removal and keeping, and the cost and charges of the sale and advertising thereof; and the residue of said property shall be subject to the disposal of the owner or person having charge thereof.

Horses, &c. to be taken from the carts, &c. Ibid.

SECT. 6. All horses and other beasts shall be taken from the carts, wagons, sleighs, and other vehicles having provisions or articles of any kind for sale therein, and which shall stand within the limits aforesaid; and the same shall be conducted to a stable, or otherwise removed from said limits, by the owner or driver having charge of the same; and it shall be lawful for the said clerk or either of his deputies, whenever he, or either of them, shall find any cart, wagon, sleigh, vehicle or other carriage, or any ox, horse or other beast, standing or being within the said limits in a manner or in a place not authorized by law and by the ordinances of said city, and not permitted by the consent and direction of said clerk or either of his deputies, or abandoned and left unprotected for more than one hour's time, or found within the limits of the market on any part of the Lord's day or evening, to cause such cart, wagon, sleigh, vehicle or other carriage with its contents therein, and such ox, horse or other beast, to be conducted to some stable or other suitable place; and the owner or person having the care or keeping thereof shall be liable to pay, before the re-delivery thereof to him, the entire cost and expense of the removal and keeping thereof during the time it shall be in said stable, or other suitable place, together with such further sum of money to the city, not exceeding two dollars, for the trouble arising in that behalf, as the said clerk, or either of his deputies shall demand, the same to be paid to, and accounted for by said clerk or his deputies, to said city.

No person to occupy stand without permission of clerk. Ibid. (Repealed May 30, 1850.) 9 Metc. 253.

SECT 7. [No person shall at any time, without the permission of said clerk or either of his deputies, occupy any stand within the limits of said market, with cart, wagon, sleigh, vehicle, carriage, bench, box, basket, barrel, cask, crate, tub, or other vessel or otherwise, for the purpose of vending any articles within the limits of said market, unless he shall, before selling or offering for sale such articles, satisfy the clerk or either of his deputies, upon the request of either of them, by legal proof, or his own certificate in writing, that all the said articles, enumerating them, are the produce of his own farm, or some farm not more distant than three miles from his own dwelling house; and every person occupying any such stand in any of the abovementioned manners, or with any of said carriages or vessels, contrary to the provisions of this ordinance, shall, when directed by the said clerk or either of his deputies, forthwith remove without the limits of said market, and cause his cart, or other carriage, and all his boxes and other vessels, with their contents also, to be removed out of the limits of said market; and if said certificate be false, the signer thereof shall forfeit and pay a penalty not exceeding twenty dollars, and also the said clerk and his deputies shall have power and authority to remove the same in the manner provided in the fifth and sixth sections of this ordinance, or either of them.]

Agents and servants, employed to sell. October 26, 1846.

SECT. 8. When any person occupying any stand in the streets within the limits of said market shall employ any agent or servant to sell in said market any articles for him, or on his account, such servant or agent shall not sell any articles upon account of or for any other person than the person so employing him, nor shall any person occupying a stand as aforesaid, or his servant or agent, be permitted to purchase any provisions or other articles within the limits of said market, for the purpose of selling the same therein again, or exposing the same therein for sale, or permitting any person to sell the same for him therein; nor shall he be permitted to sell within said limits, or expose for sale therein any provisions or other articles for, or on account of, any person not entitled to a stand therein by the terms of this ordinance.

How butter shall be sold. Ibid.

SECT. 9. All butter brought within the limits of said market for sale, shall be sold by weight, and if it is in lumps, each lump shall contain one or more even or integral pounds', half or quarter pound's weight; and the clerk and

15

his deputies shall have power and authority to take and weigh all butter in lumps so exposed for sale in said market, and if found deficient in weight, to destroy the form of said lumps.

Persons guilty of fraud, or convicted of breach of this ordinance, shall not sell for one year, unless, &c. Ibid.

SECT. 10. If any person shall, within the limits of said market, sell, or offer to sell, or exhibit for sale, any article which shall be deficient in the weight or measure for which he sells the same or offers or exhibits the same for sale, or shall practice any fraudulent dealing within said limits, and shall be convicted thereof, or shall be convicted of any breach of this ordinance, or either of the offences enumerated in it, he shall not be permitted to use or hire a stall, or have or occupy a stand within the limits of said market, either as principal, servant or agent, for the purpose of selling or offering for sale any articles in said market, for the term of one year from and after such conviction, unless specially authorized by the mayor and aldermen so to do, after such conviction, and their knowledge of the same.

Stalls to be leased. Ibid.

SECT. 11. The several stalls in said market shall be leased to the respective occupants by written leases, the conditions of which shall be prescribed by the mayor and aldermen; and the rent thereof, together with the rent of the cellars under said stalls, shall be paid to the said clerk of the market, or to such person as the mayor and aldermen shall appoint, and at such times as the mayor and aldermen shall determine; and such lessees shall not underlet the same, or any part of said stalls or cellars, nor permit the same or any part thereof, to be occupied by any other person without the assent of the mayor and aldermen, under the penalty of forfeiting the right to their respective cellars, stalls, and leases.

Lessees shall not permit any offal, &c. to remain. Ibid.

SECT. 12. The said lessees shall not throw, or permit to be thrown, or to remain within the precincts of their respective stalls, any offal, animal substance, scrapings, or any kind of dirt, filth, useless or offensive matter, but shall forthwith remove the same or cause the same to be deposited in some tight vessel, to be approved of by the said clerk or either of his deputies, and to be removed by said lessee as the said clerk or either of his deputies shall direct.

SECT. 13. No person shall throw or sweep any offal, animal or vegetable substance, scrapings or sweepings, damaged salt or pickle, or foul water, from the stalls or cellars into the passageways, or on the side-walks, or into the streets adjoining said market house, at any time during the day or night. Nor shall any person within the limits of said market, sell, or offer to sell or expose for sale, or have in his possession, any meat, fish, bread, vegetables, tallow, skins, pelts, poultry or other articles, which in the opinion of said clerk or either of his deputies, shall be diseased, corrupted, tainted or unwholesome; but such person shall, when directed by said clerk or either of his deputies, forthwith remove all such articles from said limits to such suitable place as the said clerk or either of his deputies shall order; and if such person shall refuse or neglect to comply with such direction, or if the owner or person having charge of such articles be absent for more than one hour's time, the said clerk or either of his deputies shall forthwith remove the same, or cause the same to be removed from said limits to such suitable place as aforesaid, at the expense of such person; and if in the judgment of said clerk or either of his deputies, it shall be necessary for the public health, it shall be their duty to destroy the same; and if any person shall hinder, obstruct or molest said clerk or any of his deputies in the premises, he shall forfeit and pay a sum not exceeding twenty dollars for each offence.

Offal, &c., shall not be thrown into passageways or streets, &c. Ibid.

Tainted meat, &c. shall not be offered for sale. Ibid.

SECT. 14. When the lessee of any stall, or occupant of any cellar in said market house, shall from any cause whatever vacate the same, or shall receive notice from the mayor and aldermen to vacate the same, or shall neglect or refuse to pay his rent for the space of twenty-four hours, or shall neglect or refuse to comply with any regulations established for the good order and cleanliness of the said market house, and its entries, passageways, sidewalks and the streets adjoining said house, the stall or stalls and cellar of such lessee shall thereupon revert to the city and be at the disposal of the mayor and aldermen.

Stalls to revert to mayor and aldermen in certain cases. Ibid.

Sleeping and smoking in market forbidden. Ibid.

SECT. 15. No person shall, within the walls of Faneuil Hall Market House, or on the side-walks of the same, nor within the aforesaid limits of the said market, play at any game, or lie down or sleep, or behave in a disorderly, noisy, or riotous manner: nor shall any person within the limits of said market, smoke, or have in his possession, any lighted pipe or segar. And it shall be the duty of the said clerk and his deputies to prevent idle and disorderly persons, itinerant pedlers, and transient persons selling newspapers, matches or other articles, or making outcries or noises, from frequenting or tarrying in said market house or within the limits of said market, and to cause all such persons so offending to be removed and to be prosecuted.

Idle and disorderly persons, pedlers, &c.

Lord's day. Ibid

SECT. 16. No horse or other beast, and no cart, wagon, sleigh or other vehicle, shall be permitted to stand within the limits of said market on any part of the Lord's day or evening, nor shall any person continue to do business within the limits of said market on any week day after the sunsetting of such day, excepting on Saturdays, and on the evenings immediately preceding Thanksgiving and Christmas days, nor on any evening after the closing of the market house; and if any person shall place or leave any wagon, cart, sleigh or other vehicle, box, barrel, crate, cask or other vessel, empty or otherwise, within the limits of said market on any part of the Lord's day or evening, or any week day after sunset, excepting on Saturdays, and on the evenings immediately preceding Thanksgiving and Christmas days, or on any evening after the closing of the market house, he shall forfeit a penalty not exceeding twenty dollars; and the said clerk or either of his deputies may cause the same to be removed, in the manner provided in the fifth and sixth sections of this ordinance, or either of them.

Evenings of week days, except Saturdays, &c.

Penalty.

Passageways not to be incumbered. Ibid.

SECT. 17. Lessees of stalls and occupants of stands shall not incumber the main passageway or cross passages within the said market house, nor the passageways outside of said house in front of the door ways and leading into the middle of the streets, nor any of the avenues leading to and from the said market, with any casks, barrels, meat, or other articles or incumbrances.

SECT. 18. No person, unless duly authorized by the mayor and aldermen, shall stand in any of the streets, lanes, alleys, squares, or public places of said city, with any cart, wagon, sleigh or other vehicle, horses or other beasts, having meat, poultry, vegetables or other articles of provision for sale; nor be allowed to place any stall, bench, box, basket, barrel, block or table therein, on which to exhibit any such articles for sale.

Standing in streets to sell, without authority, forbidden. Ibid.

SECT. 19. Every person offending against any of the provisions of this ordinance, shall, in addition to the penalties before prescribed, forfeit and pay a sum not less than two dollars, nor more than twenty dollars, to be recovered on complaint before the police court of the city of Boston; but in no case shall all the penalties for one offence exceed the sum of twenty dollars.

Penalties. Ibid.

SECT. 20. The clerk of Faneuil Hall Market, or either of his deputies, may assign stands for all carts, wagons, or vehicles of any description, and places, for the sale of provisions or any other articles whatsoever, in the streets within the limits of the said market, and may demand and receive such rates of charges therefor, as the said clerk may from time to time establish, under the direction of the mayor and aldermen. And every person who shall occupy any stand not so assigned to him, or who shall neglect or refuse to pay the sum demanded for such stand as aforesaid, which he has occupied or may occupy, shall be liable to a penalty of not less than two nor more than twenty dollars; and such person shall, when directed by the said clerk, or either of his deputies, forthwith remove without the limits of the market, and cause his cart, wagon or other vehicle, and all his property, to be also removed, under a further penalty of not less than two dollars nor more than twenty dollars; and the said clerk, or either of his deputies, shall also have power to remove the same forcibly, on the neglect or refusal of such person so to remove as directed.

Clerk may assign stands in the streets within the limits of the market. May 30, 1850.

Penalty for refusal to pay, &c.

Clerk shall pay over moneys received, and make quarterly report. Ibid.

SECT. 21. The said clerk shall pay over all moneys by him received to the city treasurer, and shall make a quarterly report to the mayor and aldermen of all sums so received and paid over.

FINANCE.

STATUTE.

Interest authorized upon accounts current of Boston with banks. 1842, 98.

1. It shall be lawful for the city of Boston to contract with any bank or banks, for the receipt and payment of interest, at a rate not exceeding that established by law, upon an account current of moneys deposited with and drawn from such bank or banks by the said city; any thing con-

tained in the fifty-seventh section of the thirty-sixth chapter of the Revised Statutes, or elsewhere, to the contrary notwithstanding.

ORDINANCE OF THE CITY.[1]

SECT. 1. There shall be appointed in the month of January, annually, by ballot, in each board of the city council, a joint committee of accounts, to consist of two on the part of the board of aldermen, and three on the part of the common council, whose duty it shall be to meet once a month, and as much oftener as they may deem expedient.

Joint committee of accounts. How appointed. Dec. 22, 1825.

SECT. 2. There shall be appointed, in the month of May annually, by concurrent ballot in each board, one able and discreet person, to be styled auditor of accounts; who shall continue in office until removed, or a successor be appointed; who shall receive such compensation for his services as the city council shall authorize and establish, and who shall be removeable at all times, at the pleasure of the city council; who shall be sworn to the faithful discharge of the duties of his office, and give bond with surety or sureties, to be approved by the mayor and aldermen, in the penal sum of five thousand dollars, for the faithful discharge of said duties, the true accounting for and payment over, of all moneys which shall come into his hands, and the delivery over to his successor or to the mayor and aldermen of all the books, accounts, papers and other documents and property, which shall belong to said office; and in case said office should become vacant by death, resignation or otherwise, a successor shall forthwith, and in like manner, be appointed, who shall continue in office until the appointment of a successor.

Auditor of accounts. His appointment. Ibid.

Oath.

Bond.

SECT. 3. No moneys shall be paid out of the city treasury, except in the cases hereinafter provided, unless the expenditures, or the terms of the contract, shall be vouched

No moneys to be paid from city treasury, unless vouched, &c., and drawn for by mayor. Ibid

[1] An ordinance establishing a system of accountability in the expenditures of the city, passed December 22, 1825. An ordinance concerning the public loans and reduction of the city debt, passed March 10, 1834. An ordinance providing for the more regular collection of debts due to the city of Boston, passed February 23, 1835. An ordinance further to provide for a system of accountability in the concerns of the city, passed July 27, 1835. An ordinance in addition, &c., passed December 28, 1840.

by the chairman of the committee of the board under whose authority it has been authorized and made; nor unless the same shall be examined by the auditor, approved by the committee of accounts, and drawn for by the mayor. And it shall be the duty of the mayor to compare such expenditures with the general appropriations made for the various objects, and require the auditor to make an exhibit of the state of such appropriations, monthly, to the city council: *provided*, that in all cases where it is necessary for money to be paid in advance, for contracts made or for work begun, but not completed, the mayor may, upon being satisfied of such necessity, draw upon the city treasurer, for the amount thus necessary to be advanced; which draft shall be paid by the city treasurer, provided the same be countersigned by the auditor; and it shall be the duty of the auditor to countersign all such drafts, not exceeding three hundred dollars, and to charge the same to the proper person, and account; but the said auditor shall not countersign any such draft for any sum exceeding three hundred dollars without the direction of the committee of accounts.

Proviso.

Committee of accounts to direct the manner of keeping the auditor's books, &c., and to pass bills. Ibid.

SECT. 4. It shall be the duty of the committee of accounts to direct the auditor, as to the manner in which the books, records and papers belonging to his department shall be kept, and the mode in which all bills and accounts against the city shall be certified or vouched; and, at least once in every month, to examine, and if they see fit, to pass all bills and accounts against the city, which shall be certified by the auditor.

Auditor. His duty as to keeping books, and making communications to city council. Ibid.

SECT. 5. It shall be the duty of the auditor to keep in a neat methodical style and manner, a complete set of books, under the direction of the committee of accounts; wherein shall be stated among other things, the appropriation for each distinct object of expenditure, to the end that whenever the appropriations for the specific objects shall have been expended, he shall immediately communicate the same to the city council, that they may be apprised of the fact; and either make a further appropriation, or withhold further expenditure for such object or objects as they may deem expedient: the auditor shall also receive all bills and accounts from persons having demands against the city; examine them in detail; cast up the same; and have them filed and entered in books, in such manner and form as the committee of accounts shall order and direct. And when the auditor shall have any doubt concerning the correctness of any such bill or account presented against the city, he shall not enter the same in a book until he shall have exhibited the same, with his objections, to the committee of accounts at their next meeting, for their consideration and final decision. And it shall also be the duty of the auditor to render any other services, from time to time, as the city council, or the committee of accounts shall direct.

Receiving, examining and casting bills, &c.

To render other services, when required.

SECT. 6. The city treasurer shall make up his annual accounts to the thirtieth of April; and the financial year shall begin on the first day of May, and end on the thirtieth day of April in each year.

City treasurer, when to make up his accounts. Commencement of the financial year. Ibid.

SECT. 7. There shall be annually appointed a joint committee of finance, to consist of the mayor on the part of the board of mayor and aldermen, and seven members of the common council to be chosen by that board, whose duty it shall be, under the direction of the city council, to negotiate all loans made on account of the city, whether on behalf of the committee on the reduction of the city debt, hereinafter mentioned, or for any other purpose, and to consider and report on all subjects relating to the finances of the city.

Joint committee of finance.

Their appointment and duty. March 10, 1834.

SECT. 8. The mayor, the president of the common council, and the chairman of the joint committee of finance on the part of the common council, shall be a committee, to be called the committee on the reduction of the city debt, whose duty it shall be to cause all moneys passed to their credit in the books of the auditor of accounts, to be applied to the purchase or payment of the capital of the debt of the city, in the manner they may from time to time deem expedient, and it shall be the duty of the auditor and of the treasurer of the city, to conform to all orders in writing, in

Committee on the reduction of the city debt. Ibid.

this respect, which shall be made and signed by all the members of said committee.

City debt. What moneys to be applied annually to the reduction thereof. Ibid.

SECT. 9. All balances of money, remaining in the treasury at the end of any financial year; all receipts in money on account of the sale of real estate of any description, now belonging, or which may hereafter belong to the city; all receipts on account of the principal sum of any bond or note now owned, or which may hereafter be owned by the city; and also of the annual city tax, in every future year, a sum that shall not be less than three per centum of the amount of the principal of the city debt, and not less than fifty thousand dollars in each year, shall be and the same hereby is appropriated to the payment or the purchase of the capital of the city debt.

Dec. 28, 1840.

Auditor to pass such moneys to the credit of the committee, &c. March 10, 1834.

SECT. 10. It shall be the duty of the auditor, annually, to pass to the credit of the committee on the reduction of the city debt, all receipts in money, the proceeds of either of the sources before mentioned, and the said amount out of the annual tax, and the sums so passed to the credit of said committee shall be drawn from the treasury of the city for the payment of the purchase of the capital of the city debt, in the manner before mentioned, and in no other mode and for no other purpose whatsoever.

Committee authorized to lend to treasurer, sums not immediately wanted. Ibid.

SECT. 11. The committee on the reduction of the city debt are hereby authorized, to lend on interest to the treasurer of the city any amount so passed to their credit as aforesaid, which may not be immediately wanted for the purchase or redemption of said debt.

Debts due the city to be put in hands of city solicitor for suit. Feb. 23, 1835.

SECT. 12. In all cases where specific provision is not now made, either by the laws of the commonwealth or by the ordinances of the city for the collection of debts due to the city, whether for the principal or interest of any note or bond, or arising from any assessment, contract or account, or in any other manner whatsoever, if the party owing such debt shall not, within sixty days after demand made, pay the same, such claim of the city shall be placed by the treasurer or the auditor of accounts, as the case may be, in the hands of the city solicitor, who shall forthwith put the same in suit: *provided, however*, that where, in the judgment of the mayor and aldermen, the interests of the city require, they may direct any debt due to the city to be put in suit at any time after the same may become due.

City officers to pay over moneys to the treasurer. July 27, 1835. June 25, 1849.

SECT. 13. It shall be the duty of the city clerk, the auditor of accounts, the city marshal, the weighers of hay, and the city registrar, respectively, to pay over to the city treasurer, as often at least as once in three months, all moneys which they shall receive belonging to the city, and all other officers authorized to collect such moneys shall pay the same over to said treasurer, as soon as they may be collected.

To lay statement before city council. Ibid.

SECT. 14. It shall be the duty of the city clerk, the auditor of accounts, the city marshal, the weighers of hay, and the city registrar, respectively, as early as may be in the months of February, May, August and November, in every year, to lay before the city council a statement of the whole amount of moneys which shall have been received at their respective offices, during the three preceding months; specifying in detail the sums received from each source of income. They shall also report the amounts, if any, which remain due to the city, and unpaid, and generally, any other information which they may possess, in relation to the said statement.

Auditor to lay before city council schedules of leases. July 27, 1835.

SECT. 15. It shall be the duty of the auditor of accounts to lay before the city council annually, in the month of May, a schedule of all the leases of the city property, specifying severally the names of the lessees, the rates of rent, and the periods when the leases will terminate. He shall also, in the month of February annually, lay before said council, an estimate of the amount of money necessary to be raised for the ensuing year, under the respective heads of appropriation, and shall, on or before the first day of July annually, make and lay before said council, a statement of all the receipts and expenditures of the past financial year, giving in detail, the amount of appropriation and expenditure for each specific object, the receipt from each source of income, and the operations of the committee on the reduction of the city debt; the whole to be arranged,

Estimates of money to be raised.

Statement of receipts and expenditures

as far as practicable, to conform to the accounts of the city and county treasurer, so that their coincidence may be apparent; and said statement shall be accompanied by a schedule of the property belonging to the city, and also by an exhibit shewing the debts due by the city, the rates of interest thereon, and the years in which the same will become due. The auditor shall also open an account with the treasurer of the city, wherein said treasurer shall be charged with the whole amount of taxes placed in his hands for collection, also the whole amount, in detail, of all bonds, notes, mortgages, leases, rents, interest, and other sums receivable, in order that the value and description of all personal property belonging to the city may be at any time known at the office of the auditor.

Account with the treasurer.

Joint committee to audit treasurer's accounts. Ibid.

SECT. 16. There shall be annually appointed in the month of May a joint committee, to consist of two on the part of the board of aldermen and three on the part of the common council, whose duty it shall be to examine, audit and settle the accounts of the city and county treasurer for the preceding financial year; and said committee shall not only compare said accounts with the vouchers thereof, but shall ascertain whether all sums due to the city have been collected and accounted for; they shall also examine the notes, bonds, and other securities, belonging to the city, and make a full and particular report of their proceedings to the city council.

FIRE.

STATUTES.

1. City council may establish a fire department. May make provisions respecting the same. Appointment of engine-men, &c., to be made by mayor and aldermen.
2. Powers, &c., of city council may be exercised by means of any board, &c.

3. Engineers, &c., to have the powers and duties of firewards. To examine places where shavings, &c., are collected, &c. Ordinances may be made, &c.
4. Exemptions of members of fire department.
5. City council may appropriate money for relief of members injured, &c.
6. Engineers shall attend at fires.
7. Engineers, &c., may order buildings to be pulled down, &c.
8. Engineers, &c., may command assistance.
9. Engineers may give orders to engine-men, and others, &c.
10. Owners of buildings, &c., pulled down, to be indemnified, except, &c.
11. Embezzling, &c., of property, at a fire, to be deemed larceny.
12. Penalty for injuring fire engines.
13. Engineers may require and compel assistance. Penalty for disobeying.
14. Penalty for making bonfires.
15. Penalty for false alarms of fire. Prosecutions shall be made before police court.
16. Penalty for roasting cocoa, except in licensed buildings.
17. Manner in which tar kettles and other boilers shall be constructed. Penalty.
18. Penalty for carrying fire through the streets, &c., smoking pipes, cigars, &c.
19. Penalty for having lighted pipe, cigar, candle, &c., in any ropewalk, barn, &c.
20. Recovery of penalties. Duty of engineers to prosecute.
21. Power to regulate the keeping of gun cotton, and other like substances.
22. City council, &c., may make rules in relation to storage and sale of camphene.

ORDINANCE.

1. Fire department shall consist of engineers, engine-men, hydrant-men, and hook and ladder men.
2. Chief and other engineers to be chosen annually.
3. May be removed by city council. Mayor and aldermen may discharge officers or members of companies.
4. Certificates to be received by engineers.
5. Organization of board of engineers. Secretary. Rules and regulations. Powers of the board. Absences to be reported.
6. Duty of engineers at fires.
7. Case of fire in adjoining towns.
8. Powers of the chief engineer.
9. In case of his absence, the next in rank shall execute his duties.
10. Engine, hydrant, and hook and ladder companies.
11. Members to be of full age, citizens, and voters.
12. Term of service. Condition of being entitled to pay.
13. Foreman, assistant foreman, and clerk. Meeting for choice of officers.
14. Officers chosen shall be notified of their election.
15. Certificate of appointment, in case of approval by mayor and aldermen. Otherwise, a new election. Neglect or refusal to elect.
16. Officers receiving certificates, shall serve until discharged, &c.
17. Duties of foremen.
18. Duty of officers and members of companies in case of fire.
19. Suction hose-men and leading hose-men.
20. Steward.
21. Caps, badges, and insignia.
22. Members guilty of neglect or refusal of duty, &c., shall be dismissed. Additional penalty.

STATUTES.

City council may establish a fire department. 1850, 262, § 1. (Adopted by the city council. June 4, 1850.)

1. The city council of the city of Boston may establish a fire department for said city, to consist of so many engineers and other officers, and so many engine-men and other members, as the city council, by ordinance, shall from time to time prescribe; and said city council shall have authority to make such provisions in regard to the time and mode of appointment, and the occasion and mode of removal of either such officers or members, to make such requisitions in respect to their qualifications and period of service, to define their office and duties, to fix and pay such compensation for their services, and, in general, to make such regulations in regard to their conduct and government, and to the management and conduct of fires, and persons attending at fires, subject to the penalties provided for the breach of the city by-laws, as they shall deem expedient: *provided*, that the appointment of engine-men, hose-men and hook-and-ladder-men shall be made by the mayor and aldermen exclusively.

May make provisions respecting the same.

Appointment of engine-men, &c., to be made by mayor and aldermen.

Powers, &c., of city council may be exercised by means of any board, &c. Ibid, § 2.

2. The powers and duties mentioned in the preceding section, or any of them, may be exercised and carried into effect by the said city council, in any manner which they

may prescribe, and through the agency of any persons, or any board or boards, to whom they may delegate the same.

3. The engineers or other officers of the department, so appointed as aforesaid, shall have the same authority, in regard to the prevention and extinguishment of fires, and the performance of the other offices and duties now incumbent upon fire-wards, as are now conferred upon fire-wards by the Revised Statutes, or the special acts relating to the city of Boston, now in force. They shall also have authority, in compliance with any ordinance of said city, to make an examination of places where shavings and other combustible materials are collected or deposited, and to require the removal of such materials, or the adoption of suitable safe-guards against fire. And said city council are hereby authorized to make suitable ordinances upon this latter subject matter, under the penalties enacted in the city charter.

Engineers, &c., to have the powers and duties of firewards. Ibid, § 3.

To examine places where shavings, &c., are collected, &c.

Ordinances may be made, &c.

4. All officers and members of the fire department shall be exempted from military duty, or from serving as jurors or constables, during the time of their employment in said department.

Exemptions of members of fire department. Ibid, § 4. R. S. 18, § 17; and 95, § 3.

5. The city council aforesaid are hereby authorized, whenever, and as often as they shall deem it expedient, to appropriate any sum or sums of money, in the way that may be judged by said council most advisable, for the relief or indemnity of any officer or member of the fire department, who may sustain corporal injury, or contract sickness in the discharge of his duty, or consequent thereon.[1]

City council may appropriate money for relief of members injured, &c. 1850, 262, § 5.

6. When a fire shall break out it shall be the duty of the engineers immediately to repair to the place of such fire, and to carry with them a suitable staff or badge of their office.

Engineers shall attend fires. R. S. 18, § 3. 1850, 262, § 3.

7. The engineers who shall be present at the place in immediate danger from any fire, or any three of them, or in their absence, two or more of the civil officers, present, or, in their absence, two or more of the chief military officers of the city present, shall have power, to direct the

Engineers, &c., may order buildings to be pulled down, &c. R. S. 18, § 4. 1850, 262, § 3. R. S. 2, § 6, clause 17.

[1] The stat. of 1850, c. 262, repealed stat. 1822, c. 52; 1819, c. 104; 1825, c. 52; 1826, c. 97; 1828, c. 123; and 1831, c. 52.

pulling down or demolishing of any such house or building, as they shall judge necessary to be pulled down or demolished, in order to prevent the further spreading of the fire.

Engineers, &c., may command assistance. R. S. 18, § 5. 1850, 262, § 3.

8. During the continuance of any fire, the said engineers or other officers, respectively, may require assistance for extinguishing the same, and for removing any furniture, goods or merchandize from any building on fire or in danger thereof; and may appoint guards to secure the same; and may also require assistance, for pulling down or demolishing any house or building, when they shall judge it necessary; and may suppress all tumults and disorders at such fire.

Engineers may give orders to engine-men, and others, &c. R. S. 18, § 6. 1850, 262, § 3.

9. The said engineers, or other officers, shall have authority to direct and appoint the stations and operations of the engine-men, with their engines, and of all other persons, for the purpose of extinguishing the fire; and if any person shall refuse or neglect to obey any such orders, he shall forfeit, for each offence, a sum not exceeding ten dollars.

Owners of buildings, &c., pulled down, to be indemnified, except, &c. R. S. 18, § 7. 1850, 262, § 3.

10. In case the pulling down or demolishing of any house or building, by directions of the engineers or other officers aforesaid, shall be the means of stopping the said fire; or if the fire shall stop before it come to the same, then every owner of such house or building shall be entitled to recover a reasonable compensation therefor from the town; but when the building, so pulled down or demolished, shall be that in which the fire first begun and broke out, the owner thereof shall receive no compensation therefor.

Embezzling, &c., of property, at a fire, to be deemed larceny. R. S. 18, § 8. 1850, 262, § 3.

11. In any such case of fire, if any person shall purloin, embezzle, convey away, or conceal any furniture, goods or chattels, merchandize or effects of the inhabitants, whose houses or buildings shall be on fire or endangered thereby, and shall not, within two days, restore or give notice thereof to the owner, if known, or, if unknown, to one of the engineers, the person so offending shall be deemed guilty of larceny and be punished therefor, as is provided in such case in the one hundred and twenty-sixth chapter of the Revised Statutes.

12. If any person shall wantonly or maliciously break or injure any fire engine, or the apparatus thereto belonging, he shall be punished by a fine not exceeding five hundred dollars, or by imprisonment not exceeding two years, and be further ordered to recognize, with sufficient surety or sureties, for his good behavior, during such term of time as the court shall order.

Penalty for injuring fire engines. R. S. 18, § 23.

13. It shall be lawful for any one or more of the engineers aforesaid to require and compel the assistance of all or any of the inhabitants of the city; and any other persons, who shall be present as spectators of any fire; and in any suit or prosecution therefor, it shall be lawful for them to plead the general issue, and give the statute in evidence; and if any person shall disobey the lawful and reasonable command of any engineer or engineers, to aid in extinguishing such fire, or in rescuing property from destruction thereby, such person, so offending, shall be liable to a fine not exceeding twenty dollars, to be recovered in manner provided in the twentieth section.

Engineers may require and compel assistance. 1817, 171, § 13. 1821, 110, § 1. 1850, 262, § 3.

Penalty for disobeying.

See § 20, *post.*

14. If any person shall be concerned in causing or making a bonfire, in any town in the commonwealth, within ten rods of any house or building, he shall be punished, on conviction before any court proper to try the same, by a fine not exceeding twenty dollars, or by imprisonment not exceeding one month.

Penalty for making bonfires. 1837, 177, § 1. See R. S. 2, § 6, clause 17.

15. If any person, without reasonable cause, shall, by outcry, or the ringing of bells, or otherwise, make or circulate, or cause to be made or circulated, in any town in the commonwealth, any false alarm of fire, he shall be punished, on conviction, as mentioned in the preceding section, by a fine not exceeding fifty dollars; *provided, however*, that all proceedings under this act within the city of Boston, shall be had on complaint before the police court of said city, saving always the right of appeal to the municipal court of the city of Boston, as in other cases.

Penalty for false alarms of fire. 1837, 177, § 2.

Prosecutions shall be made before police court.

16. If any person or persons shall, within the city of Boston, roast, or cause to be roasted, any cocoa, for the purpose of manufacturing the same into chocolate, in any building whatever, excepting such as may or shall be li-

Penalty for roasting cocoa, except in licensed buildings. 1817, 171, § 6. 1821, 110, § 1. 1850, 262, § 3.

censed for that purpose by the major part of the engineers of the city aforesaid, he, she or they, shall forfeit and pay for every such offence, a sum not exceeding five hundred dollars, nor less than two hundred dollars.

Manner in which tar kettles and other boilers shall be constructed. 1817, 171, § 9. 1821, 110, § 1.

17. Every tar kettle, which shall be made use of in the city for the purpose of boiling tar, for the use of any ropewalk, and every kettle, boiler, or copper, for the use of any caulker, graver, ship carpenter, tallow chandler, soap boiler, painter or other like artificer, shall be so fixed as to prevent all communication whatsoever between the contents of such kettle, boiler or copper, and the fire. And the fire-place under every such tar or other kettle, boiler or copper, shall be constructed with an arch built over the same, and secured by an iron door, in such manner as to enclose the fire therein; and every person who shall erect any tar kettle or other kettle, boiler or copper, or use the same for any or either of the purposes aforesaid, contrary to the provisions of this act, shall for every such offence, forfeit and pay a sum not exceeding three hundred dollars, nor less than fifty dollars, according to the degree and aggravation of the same.

Penalty.

Penalty for carrying fire through the streets, &c., smoking pipes, segars, &c. 1817, 171, § 10. 1821, 110, § 1. 1850, 262, § 3.

18. Every person who shall carry any fire through the streets, lanes, or on any wharves in the city, except in some covered vessel, or who shall kindle a fire in any of the places aforesaid, without the permission therefor in writing, of one or more of the engineers aforesaid, or shall smoke or have in his or her possession, any lighted pipe or segar, in any street, lane or passageway, or on any wharf in said city, shall forfeit and pay for each and every offence the sum of two dollars, to be recovered of the person so offending, or of his parent, guardian, master or mistress.

Penalty for having lighted pipe, segar, candle, &c., in any ropewalk, barn, &c. 1817, 171, § 11. 1821, 110, § 1. 12 Metc. 231.

19. If any person shall have in his or her possession, in any ropewalk, or in any barn or stable within the city, any fire, lighted pipe or segar, lighted candle, or lamp, except such candle or lamp is kept in a secure lantern, the person so offending shall forfeit and pay for each offence, a sum not exceeding one hundred dollars nor less than twenty dollars.

20. All and any of the penalties which are given in and by the thirteenth, and the four preceding sections, may be recovered by indictment, information or complaint in any court proper to try the same; and in such indictment, information or complaint, it shall not be necessary to set forth any more of said sections, than so much thereof as relates to, and is necessary, truly and substantially to describe the offence alleged to have been committed. And it shall be the duty of each and every one of said engineers, and they and each of them are hereby required, to inquire after all offences which shall come to their knowledge, and which shall be committed against the true intent and meaning of said sections, and shall cause the same to be duly prosecuted.

Recovery of penalties. 1817, 171, § 12.

Duty of engineers to prosecute. Ibid. 1850, 262, § 3.

21. By an act passed March 6, 1847, the inhabitants of any town, and the government of any city in this commonwealth, may order that no gun-cotton, or other substance prepared, like it, for explosion, shall be kept within the limits of such town or city, excepting under the regulations and penalties that were then applicable by law to gunpowder; and if it shall be considered necessary for public safety, they may restrict the quantity to be so kept to one fifth of the weight of gunpowder allowed by law in each case provided for.

Power to regulate the keeping of gun-cotton, and other like substances. 1847, 51.

22. The inhabitants of any town, and the city council of any city, in this commonwealth, may make and adopt such rules and regulations in relation to the storage and sale, within the limits of such town or city, of camphene, or any similar explosive or inflammable fluid, as they may deem reasonable, and may annex penalties to any breach of such rules and regulations, not exceeding twenty dollars for any one offence.[1]

City council, &c., may make rules in relation to storage and sale of camphene. 1850, 165.

---

[1] For other provisions respecting fire, not applicable to Boston, see R. S. c. 18, §§ 1, 2, 9—22, c. 58, §§ 5–9; 1839, c. 138; 1844, c. 152; 1845, c. 237.

For the incorporation of the Charitable Association of the Boston Fire Department, and a subsequent act respecting the same, see 1829, c. 44, and 1838, c. 131.

See also Buildings, Furnaces for Glass, Gunpowder, and Steam Engines and Furnaces.

ORDINANCE OF THE CITY.[1]

FIRE DEPARTMENT.

Fire department shall consist of engineers, engine-men, hydrant-men and hook and ladder men. June 4, 1850.

SECT. 1. The fire department shall consist of a chief engineer, of nine other engineers, and of as many engine-men, hydrant-men, and hook and ladder men, to be divided into companies, as the number of engines and the number and quantity of other fire apparatus belonging to the city shall from time to time require.

Chief, and other engineers to be chosen annually. Ibid.

SECT. 2. There shall be chosen, annually, in the months of January or February, a chief engineer and nine other engineers, who shall hold their offices one year and until others are chosen in their places; provided, however, that no assistant engineer shall hold over in case five of the new board are elected; and in all cases of holding over, preference shall be given to seniority of age.

May be removed by city council. Ibid.

SECT. 3. The city council may, by a concurrent vote, at any time, remove from office the chief engineer, or any of the other engineers; and the mayor and aldermen may at any time discharge any or all of the officers or members of either of said companies.

Mayor and aldermen may discharge officers or members of companies.

Certificates to be received by engineers. Ibid.

SECT. 4. Each engineer shall, upon his appointment, receive a written or printed certificate or warrant in the words following, viz: "This certifies that A. B. is appointed an engineer (or chief engineer) of the fire department of the city of Boston, and is entitled to all the immunities belonging to said office.

Given under my hand this day of A. D. 18

Mayor.

City Clerk."

And the respective rank of the engineers shall be determined by the mayor and aldermen.

Organization of board of engineers. Ibid.

SECT. 5. The engineers so chosen, shall meet and organize themselves into a board of engineers, a majority of whom shall form a quorum, and of which, in the absence of

---

[1] An ordinance establishing a fire department, and providing for preventing and extinguishing fires, passed June 4, 1850.

the chief engineer, the senior engineer present shall be presiding officer; and they may appoint such secretary or other officers, and make such rules and regulations for their own government, as they may see fit, and such secretary shall receive such compensation as the city council may deem expedient. They shall have the superintendence and control of all the engine and other houses used for the purposes of the fire department, and of all furniture and apparatus thereto belonging, and of the engines and all other fire apparatus belonging to the city, and over the officers and members of the several companies attached to the fire department, and over all persons present at fires, and they may make such rules and regulations for the better government, discipline and good order of the department, and for the extinguishment of fires, as they may from time to time think expedient, the same not being repugnant to the laws of this commonwealth, or to any ordinance of the city, and being subject to the approbation of the mayor and aldermen. The assistant engineers shall report their absences from fires to the chief engineer, with the reasons therefor, who shall keep a record of the same, and make a report thereof, stating all the facts, to the city council, every year prior to the election of engineers. In the absence of the chief engineer, the clerk shall make said record and report.

Secretary.

Rules and regulations.

Powers of the board.

Absences to be reported.

SECT. 6. It shall be the duty of said engineers, whenever a fire shall break out in the city, immediately to repair to the place of such fire, and to carry with them a suitable staff or badge of their office; to take proper measures that the several engines and other apparatus be arranged in the most advantageous situations, and duly worked for the effectual extinguishment of the fire; to require and compel assistance from all persons, as well members of the fire department as others, in extinguishing the fire, removing furniture, goods, or other merchandize from any building on fire, or in danger thereof, and to appoint guards to secure the same; and also in pulling down or demolishing any house or building if occasion require, and further to suppress all tumults and disorders. It shall also

Duty of engineers at fires. Ibid.

be their duty to cause order to be preserved in going to, working at, or returning from fires, and at all other times when companies attached to the department are on duty.

Case of fire in adjoining towns. Ibid.

SECT. 7. Whenever any fire occurs in either of the adjoining towns, it shall be the duty of only such and so many of said engineers to repair to such towns, as shall have been previously designated for such purpose by the board of engineers.

Powers of the chief engineer. Ibid.

SECT. 8. The chief engineer shall have the sole command at fires over all the other engineers, all members of the fire department, and all other persons who may be present at fires, and shall direct all proper measures for the extinguishment of fires, protection of property, preservation of order, and observance of the laws, ordinances and regulations respecting fire; and it shall be the duty of said chief engineer to examine into the condition of the engines and all other fire apparatus, and of the engine and other houses belonging to the city and used for the purposes of the fire department, and of the companies attached to the said department, as often as circumstances may render it expedient, or whenever directed so to do by the mayor and aldermen, or by the committee of the board of aldermen on the fire department, and annually to report the same to the mayor and aldermen, and oftener if thereunto requested; also, to cause a full description of the same, together with the names of the officers and members of the fire department, to be published annually in such manner as the mayor and aldermen shall direct; and whenever the engines or other fire apparatus, engine or other houses used by the fire department, require alterations, additions, or repairs, the chief engineer, under the direction of the board of aldermen or of the committee on the fire department shall cause the same to be made; and it shall be moreover the duty of the chief engineer to receive and transmit to the board of aldermen all returns of officers, members and fire apparatus, made by the respective companies as hereinafter prescribed, and all other communications relating to the affairs of the fire department; to keep fair and exact rolls of the respective companies, specifying the time of admission and discharge, and the age of each member; to report in writing to the city clerk, who shall keep a record of the same, once in each year, or oftener if directed so to do by the mayor and aldermen, all accidents by fire which may happen within the city, with the causes thereof as well as can be ascertained, and the number and description of the buildings destroyed or injured, together with the names of the owners or occupants.

SECT. 9. In case of the absence of the chief engineer, the engineer next in rank who may be present, shall execute the duties of his office, with full powers.

In his absence, the next in rank shall execute his duties. Ibid.

SECT. 10. As many engine, hydrant, and hook and ladder companies shall from time to time be formed by the mayor and aldermen, as they shall deem expedient, and each of said companies shall consist of as many men as said mayor and aldermen may appoint.

Engine, hydrant, and hook and ladder companies. Ibid.

SECT. 11. No person under twenty-one years of age shall be employed as a member of the fire department; nor shall any person be so employed who is not a citizen of the United States, and a legal voter in the city of Boston.

Members to be of full age, citizens and voters. Ibid.

SECT. 12. The terms of service for the members of the fire department shall commence on the first day of the month, and shall continue for periods of six months each. And no member shall be entitled to pay unless he serves the whole of said period of six months, and in the same company in which he enters, except in cases of sickness, death, or removal from the city.

Term of service. Ibid.

Condition of being entitled to pay.

SECT. 13. Each of the companies formed and appointed by the mayor and aldermen, shall have a foreman, an assistant foreman and a clerk, and these officers shall be chosen by the written votes of their respective companies, at a meeting specially held for that purpose, of which meeting and purpose the members shall be notified by the clerk, at least three days previous thereto; and if there be no clerk, the commanding officer of said company for the time being, if there be one, may issue his order in writing to any member of the company to perform that duty until one shall be elected; and if the person so notified shall wilfully refuse or neglect so to do, he shall forfeit and pay a sum

Foreman, assistant foreman and clerk. Ibid.

Meeting for choice of officers.

not exceeding twenty dollars, and shall, in addition thereto, be dismissed from the department; and if there be no commanding officer, the acting chief engineer shall issue the order as aforesaid, and shall likewise designate and detail some one of the board of engineers to preside at said meeting.

Officers chosen shall be notified of their election. Ibid.

SECT. 14. Whenever it shall appear, that any person has a majority of the written votes of the electors, at a meeting notified as mentioned in the preceding section, and at which there shall be a majority of the whole company present, the presiding officer shall forthwith inform him of the fact, and shall make return of every election, or refusal to elect, to the chief engineer; and said return shall be transmitted by said chief engineer to the mayor and aldermen.

Certificate of appointment, in case of approval by mayor and aldermen. Ibid.

SECT. 15. If the persons so receiving the votes of the company shall be approved by the mayor and aldermen for the respective offices to which they shall have been elected, they shall receive a certificate of appointment signed by the mayor, and shall thereby be invested with all the authority and subject to all the duty required by the laws, the city ordinances, and the rules and regulations of the fire department; and in case the persons are not approved by the mayor and aldermen, the mayor shall issue his order to the chief engineer to have a new election held in the manner heretofore expressed; and if the members of the company shall then neglect or refuse to elect some person or persons to fill the vacant offices whom the mayor and aldermen shall approve, the mayor and aldermen shall appoint some suitable person or persons to the same. If the members of any company shall neglect or refuse to elect any officer, they may be disbanded by the mayor and aldermen.

Otherwise a new election.

Neglect or refusal to elect.

Officers receiving certificates, shall serve until discharged, &c. Ibid.

SECT. 16. Whenever any person shall have received his certificate of appointment to any office as aforesaid, he shall perform all the duties thereof until discharged therefrom, either by death or resignation, or by order of the mayor and aldermen, in which case the mayor shall direct the chief engineer to cause a meeting to be held, as heretofore provided, to fill the vacancy.

SECT. 17. It shall be the duty of the foremen to see that the several engines and apparatus committed to their care, and the several buildings in which the same are deposited, and all things in or belonging to the same, are kept neat, clean, and in order for immediate use; it shall also be their duty to preserve order and discipline at all times in their respective companies, and require and enforce a strict compliance with the city ordinances, the rules and regulations of the department, and the orders of the engineers. They shall also keep or cause to be kept by the clerk of their respective companies, fair and exact rolls, specifying the time of admission, discharge and age of each member, and accounts of all city property intrusted to the care of the several members, in a book provided for that purpose by the city, which rolls or record books are always to be subject to the order of the board of engineers and the mayor and aldermen. They shall also make or cause to be made to the chief engineer, true and accurate returns of all the members, with their ages, and the apparatus entrusted to their care, whenever called upon so to do.

Duties of foremen. Ibid.

SECT. 18. It shall be the duty of the officers and members of the several engine, hydrant, and hook and ladder companies, whenever a fire shall break out in the city, to repair forthwith to their respective engines, hose, hook and ladder carriages, and other apparatus, and to convey them in as orderly a manner as may be, to or near the place where the fire may be, in conformity with the directions of the chief or other engineers; to exert themselves in the most orderly manner possible, in working and managing the said engines, hose, hooks and ladders, and other apparatus; and in performing any duty that they may be called upon to do, by any engineer; and upon permission of the chief or other engineer, shall in an orderly and quiet manner return said engines, hose, hook and ladder carriages, and other apparatus, to their respective places of deposit. *Provided*, that in the absence of all the engineers such

Duty of officers and members of companies, in case of fire. Ibid.

direction and permission may be given by their respective foremen.

Suction hose men and leading hose men. Ibid.

SECT. 19. The board of engineers shall appoint two or more suction hose men, and three or more leading hose men, for each engine company, on the nomination of the company, and the men thus appointed shall hold their station for six months, unless sooner removed by the mayor and aldermen, and until others are appointed in their place.

Steward. Ibid.

SECT. 20. The said engineers shall also appoint a steward to each company, who shall hold his office in like manner for not less than six months. It shall be his duty to keep clean the house, the engine, hose, or other apparatus which may belong to the company, to clear the snow from the side-walk connected with the house in winter, and generally to see that the engine and apparatus are ready for immediate use.

Caps, badges, and insignia. Ibid.

SECT. 21. The engineers and members of the several companies regularly appointed, shall wear such caps, badges, or insignia, as the mayor and aldermen shall from time to time direct, to be furnished at the expense of the city, and no other person or persons shall be permitted to wear the same, except under such restrictions and regulations as the mayor and aldermen may direct.

Members guilty of neglect or refusal of duty, &c., shall be dismissed. Ibid.

SECT. 22. If any member of either of the several companies shall wilfully neglect or refuse to perform his duty, or shall be guilty of disorderly conduct, or disobedience to the officers or to any engineer, he shall for such offence be dismissed from the department, and shall in addition, be liable to a penalty of not less than five nor more than twenty dollars for each offence.

Additional penalty.

Engineers shall report such neglect or refusal. Ibid.

SECT. 23. It shall be the duty of the chief engineer, or other engineers, to report to the mayor and aldermen, the name of every person not a member of either of said companies, who shall, contrary to law, refuse or neglect to obey any orders of any engineer, given at any fire.

Duty of constables and police officers, in case of fire. Ibid.

SECT. 24. It shall be the duty of such of the constables or police officers of the city, as may be selected by the engineers for that service, to repair with their staves or such other badges of office as the mayor and aldermen shall direct, on the alarm of fire, immediately to the place where the fire may be, and there to use their best skill and power under the direction of the chief engineer or city marshal, for the preservation of the public peace, the prevention of theft, and destruction of property, and the removal of all suspected persons; for which service the constables or police officers shall receive such compensation as shall be in each case ordered by the mayor and aldermen.

Duty of watchmen, in case of fire. Ibid.

SECT. 25. Immediately on the alarm of fire, during the night, it shall be the duty of the respective watchmen to give notice thereof within their respective districts, by springing their rattles, crying "fire," or ringing a bell, and mentioning the street or direction where it may be; and if any watchman shall neglect so to do, he shall forfeit and pay two dollars; and if it shall happen that a chimney only shall be on fire, either by night or day, the bell shall not be rung, but only when a building is proclaimed to be on fire.

Power of engineers to pull down buildings when necessary. Ibid.

SECT. 26. Whenever it shall be adjudged, at any fire, by any three or more of the engineers, of whom the chief engineer, if present, shall be one, to be necessary, in order to prevent the further spreading of the fire, to pull down or otherwise demolish any building, the same may be done by their joint order.

Duty of chief and other engineers to examine places where shavings, &c., are deposited, and to order their removal. Ibid.

SECT. 27. It shall be the duty of the chief and other engineers to inquire for and examine into all shops and other places, where shavings or other such combustible materials may be collected and deposited, and at all times to be vigilant in taking care of the removal of the same, whenever in the opinion of any two of them the same may be dangerous to the security of the city from fires, and to direct the tenant or occupant of said shops or other places to remove the same; and, in case of such tenant's or occupant's neglect or refusal so to do, to cause the same to be removed at the expense of such tenant or occupant; who shall in addition be liable to a penalty not exceeding twenty dollars for such neglect or refusal; and any person who shall obstruct the said engineers or any of them in carrying out the provisions of this section, shall also be liable to a penalty not exceeding twenty dollars. It shall also be

Penalty for neglect or refusal to remove the same.

Engineers to prosecute, &c.

the duty of said engineers to take cognizance of and to cause prosecution to be instituted in all cases of infraction of the laws relative to the erection of wooden buildings, or of any other laws or ordinances for the prevention of fire within the limits of the city.

Duties of engineers respecting gunpowder. Ibid.

SECT. 28. The power of making and establishing rules and regulations for the transportation and keeping of gunpowder within the city of Boston, and of granting licenses for the keeping and sale thereof in the city, according to the provisions of an act entitled "an act further regulating the storage, safe keeping, and transportation of gunpowder in the city of Boston," and of any other act or acts on the same subject, shall be exercised and performed by the chief and other engineers, and the power and duty of seizing any gunpowder kept or being within the city or the harbor thereof contrary to the provisions of the said act or acts, shall be exercised and performed by the said engineers or any of them; and in case of any seizure being made by any engineer other than the chief, he shall forthwith report to the chief engineer, who shall cause said gunpowder to be libelled and prosecuted in the manner prescribed in the said acts, and all the other powers and duties granted or enjoined in and by the said act or acts, shall be performed by the said chief or one of the other engineers.

Moneys received for fines, &c., to be paid into city treasury, unless, &c. Ibid.

SECT. 29. All moneys received for fines, forfeitures and penalties, arising under this ordinance and the laws of this commonwealth, regulating the storage and transportation of gunpowder, the erection of buildings within the city of Boston, and the prevention and extinguishment of fire, unless by such laws otherwise specially provided, shall be paid into the treasury of the city, to be applied in such way as is provided in the acts of this commonwealth.

Certificate of seven years' service, and badge. Ibid.

SECT. 30. Every member of the fire department of the city of Boston, who shall have served according to law for seven successive years, shall be entitled to receive a certificate thereof, signed by the mayor of said city, and all persons who shall receive said certificate as aforesaid, shall be entitled to wear the badge of the department, and to do duty therein, under such organization and management as the mayor and aldermen may determine.

Compensation. Ibid.

SECT. 31. There shall be paid annually to each member of the department such sum as the city council may from time to time determine, and in case of the sickness or absence from the city of any member, for forty-eight hours or more, he shall provide a substitute, whose name he shall return to the clerk of his company.

Substitute to be provided in case of sickness or absence.

Members shall not assemble in engine houses, &c., except, &c. Ibid.

SECT. 32. The members of the several companies shall not assemble in the houses intrusted to their care, except for the purpose of taking the engine or apparatus, on an alarm of fire, and of returning the same to the house, and taking the necessary care of said apparatus after its return; and except for the business meetings of the companies.

GENERAL PROVISIONS.[1]

Penalty for firing any gun, &c. within the city. July 22, 1850.

SECT. 33. No person shall fire or discharge any gun, fowling piece, or fire arms, within the limits of the city of Boston, under a penalty for every such offence of not less than one dollar, nor more than twenty dollars; *provided*, however, that this section shall not apply to the use of such weapons at any military exercise or review, or in the lawful defence of the person, family, or property of any citizen.

Proviso.

Penalty for having or selling rockets, &c. without license. Ibid. See R. S. 58, §§ 5, 6.

SECT. 34. If any person shall have in his possession, with intent to sell, or shall offer for sale, or shall sell, or give away any of the fire works called rockets, crackers, squibs, or serpents, without the license of the mayor and aldermen, he shall for every such offence forfeit a sum not exceeding ten dollars.

Penalty for having or setting fire to rockets, &c. Ibid.

SECT 35. If any person shall have in his possession, with intent to set fire to, or shall set fire to, any rocket, cracker, squib, or serpent, or shall throw any lighted rocket, cracker, squib, or serpent within the city, without the license of the mayor and aldermen, he shall, for every offence, forfeit a sum not exceeding ten dollars.

---

[1] An ordinance in relation to fire-arms, fire-works, bonfires and brick kilns, passed July 22, 1850.

Penalty for making any bonfires, &c. Ibid. July 22, 1850.

SECT. 36. If any person shall make any bonfire, or other fire in any of the streets, squares, commons, lanes, or alleys, or on any wharf within the city, without the license of the mayor and aldermen, he shall be punished by a fine not exceeding twenty dollars.

Penalty for erecting, making or firing any brick-kiln, &c. Ibid.

SECT. 37. No person shall erect, make, or fire, or cause to be erected, made, or fired within any part of the city, any brick-kiln or lime-kiln, without the license of the mayor and aldermen, under a penalty of not less than one dollar, nor more than twenty dollars, and a like sum for every week he shall continue such kiln, after notice to remove the same.

FUEL.

Committee of city council shall make contracts for fuel. May 8, 1843. Feb. 9, 1846.

SECT. 1. All contracts for wood, bark, coal and other fuel, for the use of the city, in each and every of its respective branches and departments, as well for the use of the public schools and primary schools, as all other public buildings and offices, excepting the several institutions at South Boston, shall be made by a committee of the city council, whose duty it shall be to advertise in the public newspapers, in which the city ordinances are printed, for sealed proposals for furnishing the same, at least one week previously to making any contract for the same, and the proposals shall contain the terms for which each particular description of fuel will be furnished, separately and dis-

Shall advertise for sealed proposals.

[1] An ordinance regulating the purchase of fuel for the use of the city, passed May 8, 1843.

tinctly; and such proposals being considered, shall be accepted, or rejected, according to the terms, as may be deemed advisable by said committee; and the contract so made, shall provide for the delivery of the same at such different times and in such places as may be required by the superintendent of public buildings during the year; and such contract shall be made annually, between the months of May and September.

SECT. 2. All fuel of every description which shall be contracted for, shall, previously to the delivery thereof, be weighed or measured by a weigher or measurer appointed for that purpose by the city; and it shall be the duty of the superintendent of public buildings to attend to the delivery and reception of the same, and to give certificates therefor, as the same is delivered, to the end that the proper quantity and quality may be ascertained to have been received by the committee; and it shall be the duty of the chairman of said committee to certify the bills of the same previously to the payment thereof.

Fuel shall be weighed or measured. May 8, 1843.

Superintendent of public buildings shall attend to delivery, &c.

FURNACES FOR GLASS.

STATUTE.

1. Furnaces for making glass must be licensed.
2. Unlicensed furnace shall be deemed a common nuisance.
3. Not to be in force until adopted by city council, &c.
4. Shall take effect from and after its passage.

1. No furnace for the making of glass shall be hereafter erected or put up for use in any city or town in this commonwealth, unless a license therefor shall be first granted in the manner provided in the first section of the one hundred and ninety-seventh chapter of the acts of the legislature, passed in the year one thousand eight hundred

Furnaces for making glass must be licensed. 1846, 96, § 1.

and forty-five, and such license shall be applied for, granted and recorded in the manner provided in said act.[1]

Unlicensed furnace shall be deemed a common nuisance. Ibid, § 2.

2. Any such furnace hereafter erected, without such license, shall be deemed and taken to be a common nuisance, without any other proof than proof of its use, and may be abated and removed in the manner provided in said act.

Not to be in force until adopted by city council, &c. Ibid, § 3.

3. This act shall not be in force in any town or city, unless the same shall be adopted in the manner provided in tenth section of the act aforesaid.[2]

Ibid, § 4.

4. This act shall be in force from and after its passage.[3]

GUNPOWDER.

STATUTES.

1. Taking loaded arms into houses prohibited, under penalty of ten pounds.
2. Loaded arms in houses may be seized by engineers. To be sold at public auction if adjudged to be forfeited upon their complaint.
3. Appeals in such prosecutions.
4. Powder, how much may be kept by any United States or state officer, and where.
5. Powder kept contrary to above provision, may be seized by engineers and sold.
6. Gunpowder exceeding one pound, not to be kept within two hundred yards of any wharf, or on the main land. Forfeiture.
7. No gunpowder to be sold within the city without license from engineers. Form of license to contain rules and regulations. Time in which it shall continue in force. Engineers may rescind same. Fees for license.
8. Engineers may establish rules and regulations.
9. Gunpowder in Boston contrary to the provisions of law, may be seized and libelled. Service of copy and summons. Costs. Adjudication. Service may be made in any county.
10. Penalty for hindering engineers, or attempting to rescue powder. Duty of all citizens to assist the engineers.
11. Engineers may enter and examine stores, &c., of those li-

---

[1] See Steam Engines and Furnaces, § 1.

[2] This act was adopted by the City Council of Boston, January 25, 1847.

[3] For Furnaces for the melting of iron, see Steam Engines and Furnaces.

1. If any person shall take into any dwelling-house, stable, barn, out-house, ware-house, store, shop or other building within the city of Boston, any cannon, swivel, mortar, howitzer, cohorn, or fire arm, loaded with or having gunpowder in the same, or shall receive into any dwelling house, stable, barn, out-house, store, ware-house, shop, or other building within said city, any bomb, grenade, or other iron shell, charged with, or having gunpowder in the same, such person shall forfeit and pay the sum of ten pounds, to be recovered at the suit of the engineers, in an action of debt before any court proper to try the same; one moiety thereof, to the use of said engineers, and the other moiety to the support of the poor of said city.

Taking loaded arms into houses prohibited, under penalty of ten pounds. 1782, 46, § 1. 1821, 110, § 1. 1850, 262, § 3.

2. All cannons, swivels, mortars, howitzers, cohorns, fire-arms, bombs, grenades, and iron shells of any kind, that shall be found in any dwelling-house, out-house, stable, barn, store, ware-house, shop or other building, charged with or having in them any gunpowder, shall be liable to be seized by either of the engineers of said city; and upon complaint made by the said engineers to the court of common pleas, of such cannon, swivels, mortars, or howitzers, being so found, the court shall proceed to try the merits of such complaint by a jury; and if the jury shall find such complaint supported, such cannon, swivel, mortar or howitzer, shall be adjudged forfeit, and sold at public auction, and one half of the proceeds thereof shall be disposed of to the engineers, and the other half to the use of the poor of the city of Boston. And when any fire arms, or any bomb, grenade,

Loaded arms in houses may be seized by engineers. 1782, 46, § 2. 1821, 110, § 1. 1850, 262, § 3.

To be sold at public auction if adjudged forfeit upon their complaint. See R. S. 86, § 4.

or other shell, shall be found in any house, out-house, barn, stable, store, ware-house, shop or other building, so charged, or having gunpowder in the same, the same shall be liable to be seized in manner aforesaid; and on complaint thereof, made and supported before a justice of the peace, shall be sold and disposed of, as is above provided for cannon.

Appeals. 1782, 46, § 3. But see 1839, ch. 161.

3. Appeals were provided for in prosecutions under the two preceding sections, as was usual in other cases.

Powder, how much may be kept by any United States or state officer, and where. 1813, 143, § 1. 1821, 110, § 1. 1850, 262, § 3.

4. No commissary, or any other officer or officers, or any person or persons, in the service of the United States, or acting in the department of commissary or quarter master general of this commonwealth, shall be permitted to have, keep, or possess within the city of Boston, a greater quantity of gunpowder than four hundred pounds; and the powder so had and possessed within the said city shall be kept in a place approved of by the engineers of the said city, either under ground in a vault, or in a stone or brick building secured against explosion by fire.

Powder kept contrary to above provision, may be seized by engineers and sold. 1813, 143, § 2. 1821, 110, § 1. 1850, 262, § 3.

5. Any gunpowder which shall be found in the possession of, or which may be had or kept within the city of Boston, by any officer or officers, or any person or persons whatsoever, acting in behalf or under the authority of the United States, or by any agent or servant of such officers or persons; and all gunpowder possessed, had or kept, by any officer of the commissary or quarter master general's departments of the state of Massachusetts, or persons acting under the authority of these departments, contrary to the provisions of the preceding section, may be seized by any two or more of the engineers of the city of Boston, and the same may be libelled and condemned and sold, and the proceeds thereof distributed, as is by law provided for the forfeiture of gunpowder in other cases within said city.

Gunpowder exceeding one pound, not to be kept within two hundred yards of any wharf, or on the main land. 1833, 151, § 1.

6. No person, except on military duty in the public service of the United States, or of this commonwealth, shall keep, have or possess, in any building, or in any place, or in any carriage, or on any wharf, or on board of any ship, or other vessel, within two hundred yards of any wharf, or of the main land, in the city of Boston, gunpowder in any quantity exceeding one pound, in any way or manner, other

than by this and the eight following sections, and by the rules and regulations hereinafter mentioned, may be permitted and allowed. And all gunpowder, had, kept or possessed, contrary to the provisions of said sections, and of such rules and regulations, shall be forfeited, and liable to be seized and proceeded against in the manner hereinafter provided.

Forfeiture.

7. It shall not be lawful for any person or persons to sell any gunpowder, which may, at the time, be within the city of Boston, in any quantity, without first having obtained from the engineers of said city, a license, signed by the chief engineer, or by the secretary of the board of engineers, on which shall be written, or printed, a copy of the rules and regulations by them established, relative to keeping, selling and transporting gunpowder within said city, and every such license shall be in force for one year from the date thereof, unless annulled by the board of engineers, and no longer; but such license may, prior to the expiration of that term, be renewed by the chief engineer or the said secretary, from year to year, by endorsement thereon: *provided always*, that the board of engineers may rescind any such license, if in their opinion the person or persons have disobeyed the law, or infringed any rules and regulations established by said board of engineers. And every person who shall receive a license to sell gunpowder as aforesaid, shall pay for the same the sum of *five dollars*, and for the renewal thereof, the sum of *one dollar*, which sums shall be paid to the board of engineers, for their use, for the purpose of defraying the expenses of carrying these enactments into execution.

No gunpowder to be sold within the city, without license from engineers. Ibid, § 2.

Form of license to contain rules and regulations.

Time in which it shall continue in force.

Engineers may rescind same.

Fees for license

8. The board of engineers of the city of Boston may establish rules and regulations, from time to time, relative to the times and places at which gunpowder may be brought to or carried from said city by land or water, the times when and the manner in which the same may be transported through said city, to direct and regulate the kind of carriages and boats, in which the same may be so brought to, carried from and through said city, and to direct the manner in which gunpowder may be kept by

Engineers may establish rules and regulations. Ibid, § 3. Thacher's Crim. Cases, 14.

licensed dealers, and other persons, and to direct and require all such precautions as may appear to them needful and salutary to guard against danger in the keeping and transportation of gunpowder.

Gunpowder in Boston contrary to the provisions of law may be seized and libelled. 1833, 151, § 5. 1 Metc. 225, 232. Thacher's Crim. Cases, 14, 596.

9. All gunpowder, which shall be kept, had or possessed within the city of Boston, or brought into or transported through the same, contrary to the provisions of said sections,[1] and to the rules and regulations made as aforesaid, may be seized and taken into custody by any one or more of the engineers of said city, and the same shall, within twenty days next after the seizure thereof, be libelled, by filing in the office of the clerk of the municipal court of the city of Boston, a libel, stating the time, place and cause of such seizure, a copy of which libel, or the substance thereof, together with a summons or notice, which such clerk is hereby authorized to issue, shall be served on the person or persons, in whose custody or possession such gunpowder shall have been seized, if such person be an inhabitant of this commonwealth, by delivering a copy thereof to such person or persons, or leaving such a copy at his, her, or their usual place of abode, fourteen days at least before the sitting of the court at which the same is to be heard, that such person or persons may appear and shew cause why the gunpowder so seized and taken should not be adjudged forfeit. And if the gunpowder so seized shall be adjudged forfeit, the person or persons, in whose custody or possession the same was seized, or the occupant or tenant of the place wherein the same was so seized, shall pay all costs of prosecution, and execution shall be issued therefor: *provided*, that it appear to the court that such person or persons had notice of such prosecution by service as aforesaid; and in case the person or persons in whose custody or possession such gunpowder may be seized, shall be unknown to the engineer or engineers making such seizure, or in case such gunpowder, at the time of seizure, may not be in the custody or possession of any person, or if it shall appear by

Service of copy and summons.

Costs.

Adjudication.

---

[1] That is. sections 6, 7, 8, 9, 10, 11, 12, 13 and 14, in the text.

the return of the officer that such person cannot be found, or has no place of abode in this commonwealth, then said court shall and may proceed to adjudication thereon. And such libel or summons, and also such writ of execution for costs, shall and may be served and executed in any county in this commonwealth, and by any officer competent to execute civil process in like cases.

Service may be made in any county.

10. Any person or persons, who shall rescue, or attempt to rescue, any gunpowder seized as aforesaid, or shall aid or assist therein, or who shall counsel and advise, or procure the same to be done, or who shall molest, hinder or obstruct any engineer in such seizure, or in conveying gunpowder so seized to a place of safety, shall forfeit and pay a fine for each offence of not less than one hundred dollars, and not exceeding five hundred dollars, to be sued for and recovered by action of the case, by any person or persons who shall sue for the same, in any court proper to try the same; and it is hereby made the duty of all persons to aid and assist such engineer or engineers in executing the duties hereby required.

Penalty for hindering engineers or attempting to rescue powder. Ibid, § 6.

Duty of all citizens to assist the engineers.

11. The said engineers, or any of them, may enter the store or place of any person or persons licensed to sell gunpowder, to examine and ascertain if the laws, rules and regulations relating thereto are strictly observed; and on an alarm of fire, may cause the powder there deposited to be removed, or destroyed, as the case may require; and it shall be lawful for any one or more of the engineers of said city to enter any dwelling house or other place in the city of Boston, to search for gunpowder, first having obtained from a justice of the police court in said city a search warrant therefor, which warrant the justices of said court are hereby authorized to issue, upon the complaint of such engineer or engineers, supported by his or their oath.

Engineers may enter and examine stores, &c., of those licensed, to ascertain if their rules, &c., are observed

Power in case of fire. Ibid, § 7.

Search warrant.

12. Any person who shall suffer injury by the explosion of any gunpowder, had, kept, or transported within the city of Boston, contrary to the provisions of said sections,[1] and of the rules and regulations established as aforesaid, may

Persons injured by gunpowder kept contrary to law, may have an action for damages. Ibid, § 8.

---

[1] That is, sections 6, 7, 8, 9, 10, 11, 12, 13, and 14, in the text.

have an action of the case in any court proper to try the same, against the owner or owners of such gunpowder, or against any other person or persons who may have had the possession or custody of such gunpowder, at the time of the explosion thereof, to recover reasonable damages for the injury thus sustained.

Engineers to publish their rules and regulations in newspapers. Ibid, § 9.

13. It shall be the duty of the engineers of the city of Boston, to cause all such rules and regulations as they may make and establish, by virtue of the authority given as aforesaid, to be published in two or more newspapers printed in the city of Boston, and to cause such publication to be continued three weeks successively, for the information and government of all persons concerned.

How fines, &c., may be recovered. Ibid, § 10.

14. All fines, penalties and forfeitures, which may arise and accrue under the eight preceding sections, shall and may be prosecuted for and recovered, either in the manner therein specially provided, or by indictment, complaint, or information in any court proper to try the same. And said act shall be taken and deemed to be a public act, of which all courts, magistrates and citizens are bound to take notice as such; and in any libel, action, indictment, information, or complaint upon said act, it shall not be necessary to set forth any more of the same than so much thereof as relates to, and may be necessary truly and substantially to describe the offence alleged to have been committed.[1]

Not necessary to set forth more of the act than is necessary to describe the offence.

Penalty for keeping or selling gunpowder, contrary to law. 1837, 99, § 1. 1 Metc. 225. Ibid, 232. Thacher's Crim. Cases, 14. Ibid, 596.

15. Any person who shall keep, have or possess any gunpowder within the city of Boston, contrary to the provisions of the nine preceding sections, or to the rules and regulations of the board of engineers therein mentioned, or who shall sell any gunpowder in said city without having a license therefor, or contrary to such license, or the rules

[1] The statute of 1833, c. 151, referred to in § 14, in the text, contained, in § 12, a general repeal of acts and parts of acts inconsistent therewith, which apparently repeals stat. 1792, c. 7; 1801, c. 20; 1803, c. 120; 1807, c. 137; 1816, c. 26; and 1820, c. 47.

It also provided, that all rules and regulations, made and established by the engineers, under and by virtue of the provisions of former acts, should continue to have the same force and effect, until altered or annulled by the said engineers, as if this act had not been passed.

and regulations aforesaid, shall forfeit a sum not less than one hundred dollars, and not exceeding five hundred dollars, for each offence; and if any gunpowder, kept contrary to the said provisions, or to such license, or to the rules and regulations aforesaid, shall explode in any building, or on board of any ship or other vessel, or in any place in said city, the occupant, tenant or owner of which has not then a license to keep and sell gunpowder therein, such occupant, tenant or owner shall forfeit a sum not less than one hundred dollars, and not exceeding one thousand dollars for each offence.

How fines shall be appropriated. 1837, 99, § 1. § 2.

16. The several fines, penalties and forfeitures, mentioned in the ten preceding sections, shall enure to the sole use of the board of engineers of the fire department of said city of Boston: *provided, however*, that whenever, on the trial of any prosecution under the said sections, any one or more of the said engineers shall be sworn and examined as a witness on behalf of the prosecution, a record thereof shall be made in court, and in such case, the fine, penalty, or forfeiture shall enure to the use of the poor of the city of Boston, to be paid over to the overseers of the poor thereof.[1]

Proviso.

When gunpowder less than ten quarter casks is seized, a libel or complaint may be filed in the police court. 1841, 58, § 1.

17. Whenever any quantity less than ten quarter-casks of gunpowder shall be seized and taken into custody by any one or more of the engineers of the fire department of the city of Boston, a libel or complaint may be filed in the clerk's office of the police court of said city of Boston, and the said police court of said city shall have jurisdiction thereof; and the like proceedings thereon (excepting a trial by jury,) shall be had in said court as are provided for by the fifth section of the act passed on the twenty-fifth day of March, in the year one thousand eight hundred and thirty-three,[2] in the like cases of seizures and proceedings before the municipal court;—saving always to any party aggrieved by any final judgment of said police court, the right of appeal and trial by jury in said municipal court.

---

[1] The 3d section of stat. 1837, c. 99, repealed the 4th and 11th sections of stat. 1833, c. 151.

[2] That is, the ninth section above.

Fines may be sued for by chief engineer, or one or more engineers, &c. Ibid, § 2.

18. All fines, penalties and forfeitures imposed by the twelve preceding sections, may be sued for and recovered by the chief engineer, or any one or more of the engineers of the fire department of the said city of Boston, or by any person thereto authorized by a vote of the board of engineers of the said fire department.[1]

HARBOR.

---

[1] For general provisions respecting gunpowder, see R. S. c. 28, § 92–94, c. 58, §§ 7, 8, 9. For powers of the board of engineers to make rules and regulations for gunpowder, see Fire, *ante*, page 140.

ISLANDS.

1. Concurrent jurisdiction has been ceded to the United States, by the Commonwealth of Massachusetts, over the following places, viz: the light-house on Light-House Island in the harbor of Boston; the beacon on the spit of sand near the light-house; the islands called Castle Island and Governor's Island; the place called Half Way Rock, in Boston Bay, for a beacon; a tract of land for a light-house on Long Island Head; the place called Nix's Mate, for a beacon; George's Island and Lovell's Island; Minot's

Concurrent jurisdiction of certain places ceded to the U. S. States. Light-house on Light-house Island. R. S. 1, § 2. 1790, 4. Beacon. Ibid. Castle Island and Governor's Island. 1798, 13. 1807, 125. 1846, 16. R. S. 1, § 2. Half Way Rock. Long Island Head. 1819, 69. R. S. 1, § 2. Nix's Mate. 1832, 41. 1834, 39. R. S. 1, § 2. George's Island. Lovell's Island. 1846, 16. Minot's Rock, or Ledge. 1847, 109.

Part of Great Brewster. 1849, 45.

Rock, or Ledge, in Massachusetts Bay; and a portion of the island called Great Brewster, for the purpose of the erection and maintenance thereon of a sea wall, for the preservation of said island.

Rainsford Island conveyed in trust, for a hospital. Suffolk Records of Deeds, Lib. 53, fol. 162.

2. Rainsford Island was conveyed by deed, by John Loring and others, December 7, 1736, to the treasurer and receiver general of the Province of Massachusetts Bay, "in trust for the use of the Governor, Council and Assembly of his Majesty's Province of the Massachusetts Bay and their successors forever, to be used and improved for an hospital for the said province."

Hospital on Rainsford Island to be under the care of the mayor and aldermen of Boston. Rev. Stat. 11, § 4.

3. By the Revised Statutes it is provided that the hospital establishment on Rainsford Island, the island itself, and all property thereon, belonging to or connected with the said hospital establishment, shall be under the sole care of the mayor and aldermen of Boston; who shall appoint all such officers and servants as they shall deem necessary, prescribe their respective duties, and establish their compensation.

Mayor and aldermen to render an account annually. Ibid, § 5.

4. The said mayor and aldermen shall, annually in the month of January, file in the office of the secretary of the commonwealth, an exact account of the state of the property of the commonwealth belonging to, or connected with, the said hospital establishment, and also of all money expended thereon, in the course of the preceding year.[1]

The governor authorized to release to the city of Boston the commonwealth's title to Rainsford Island. Resolves, 1846, 138.

5. A resolve was passed, April 16, 1846, that his excellency the governor, by and with the advice and consent of the council, be authorized and requested to inquire into and ascertain the title of the commonwealth to Rainsford Island, in the harbor of Boston, and to the State Arsenal, in the city of Boston, and that the governor, by and with the advice and consent of the council, have power to release unto the city of Boston, all the right and title of the com-

---

[1] By stat. 1839, c. 79, a new provision was made respecting the accounts of expenses on Rainsford Island, but that statute was repealed by stat. 1840, c. 88. By stat. 1841, c. 96, several new provisions were enacted, and the above sections of the Revised Statutes were repealed, but the 4th section contained a provision, that the act should take effect, if the city council of Boston should accept the same, within sixty days after its passage; and it does not appear that they ever did accept it. See Records of City of Boston, vol. 19, pp. 50 and 61.

monwealth to said island and arsenal, upon such terms and considerations, as, in their judgment, the interests of the commonwealth may require.

No earth or stones to be taken from Bird Island, without license. 1818, 4. 1821, 110, § 13.

6. No earth or stones shall be taken from the island, called Bird Island, in Boston harbor, in the county of Suffolk, without license first had and obtained of the mayor and aldermen of the city of Boston, for that purpose, in writing, by the person taking the same, specifying the quantity allowed to be removed, and the object of removing it. And every person, who, without permission obtained as aforesaid, shall remove any earth or stones from the said island, in any boat, or in any ship or vessel whatsoever, shall forfeit and pay for each offence, the sum of twenty dollars to the use of the said city, to be recovered by the mayor and aldermen of the said city, by an action of debt in any court proper to try the same.

Penalty

Ibid, § 1, 13.

Penalty for carrying away earth, gravel, &c., from islands in the harbor. 1834, 168, § 1.

7. If any person shall wilfully carry away, from any island within the harbor of Boston, or from any beach adjacent thereto, any earth, gravel, stone, or other material composing such island or beach, without the consent of the owner thereof, the person or persons so offending shall forfeit and pay, for each offence, to the use of the commonwealth, a sum not exceeding one hundred dollars, nor less than five dollars, to be recovered by indictment in any court competent to try the same; *provided*, that this act shall not be construed to prevent the taking of shell fish from such islands and beaches.[1]

---

[1] The act of 1845, ch. 117, imposed a penalty on any person who should take, carry away or remove any stones, gravel or sand, from beaches in the town of Chelsea. In the case of *Commonwealth v. Tewksbury*, (11 Metc. 55) it was held that this act was passed for the purpose of protecting the harbor of Boston, and extended as well to the owners of the soil as to strangers; but that it was not such a taking of private property and appropriating it to public uses, within the meaning of the Declaration of Rights, art. 10, as to render it unconstitutional and void, although no compensation was therein provided for the owners. By the act of 1846, ch. 206, the first mentioned act was repealed as to part of said Tewksbury's beaches in Chelsea, and $500 were ordered to be paid him out of the treasury of the commonwealth, "as an indemnity for the loss suffered by him under the operation of said act, by reason of being unnecessarily debarred from the use of his land, for the purpose, as was intended, of securing the harbor of Boston." See also act of 1847, c. 168.

Penalty for building a fire on Spectacle Island. Ibid, § 2.

8. If any person shall wilfully build a fire on Spectacle Island, in the harbor aforesaid, without the consent of the owner or owners thereof such person shall suffer the like forfeiture, and to be recovered and appropriated in like manner as is provided in the preceding section.

HARBOR LINES.

Line in the harbor from Free bridge to Warren bridge established. 1837, 229, § 1.

9. By an act passed April 19, 1837, the line described in the following section, from the Free Bridge in the harbor of Boston to Warren Bridge in said harbor, was established as one of the lines in said harbor, beyond which no wharf or pier should ever be extended into and over the tide water of the commonwealth.[1]

Description of the line. Ibid, § 2.

10. The said line begins at the east end of the north abutment of the Free Bridge, and runs straight to the southerly corner of Brown's wharf; thence, by the end of the same, and of Wright's four wharves, fronting on the channel, to the east corner of Wright's northeast wharf; thence, on a straight line, to the south corner of Wales's wharf, and by the end to the east angle of the same; thence from this last point straight to the south corner of Arch wharf; the line then follows the end of the last and Otis's wharf to the east corner of the last; the direction is then straight to the southeast angle of Foster's south wharf; then straight to the south corner of Rowe's wharf. From this point in a straight direction to the south corner of Long wharf; thence straight to the south angle of the advanced part of the said wharf, and by the end of the same to the east corner thereof; thence the line is straight to the east end of Union wharf. From the last point straight to the southeast corner of Battery wharf. Here the three next lines commence to advance further into deep water than the following wharves, to the west corner of Gray's, and are thus drawn through the southeast angle of Battery

This portion of the line fixed by 1850, 216.

[1] A building which extends into the harbor of Boston, beyond the commissioners' line established under the acts of 1837, ch. 229, and 1840, ch. 35, and which is also below low water mark, and an obstruction to the navigation, is a public nuisance, notwithstanding it was erected previous to the passing of those acts. *Garey v. Ellis*, (1 Cushing's R. 306.)

and the west corner of Gray's wharf; a circular arc is struck, with a radius of twelve hundred feet, and three equal chords of four hundred and seventy feet are drawn upon this arc: then from Battery wharf the line is northerly four hundred and seventy feet, forming an angle of twenty-seven degrees and fifteen minutes with the chord of the said arc. From the end of the last the line is also four hundred and seventy feet long, and parallel with the said chord. From the end of the last mentioned line the line is four hundred and seventy feet to the west corner of Gray's wharf, forming the same angle with the chord of the whole arc as that from Battery wharf. From Gray's the line is straight to the north corner of Vinal's wharf. The line then passes along the end of this and Brown's wharf to the west corner of the last; thence straight crossing Charles River Bridge to the northeast corner of Trull's wharf; thence the line is straight to the south abutment of Warren Bridge. Which said line thus described is part of the line reported by commissioners appointed under the resolve, passed the fifth of March, in the year one thousand eight hundred and thirty-five, to survey the harbor of Boston, and by said commissioners drawn and defined on plans by them taken, and deposited in the library, excepting that the line herein described and intended, varies from the line of said commissioners by crossing Charles River Bridge in a straight line from Brown's wharf to Trull's wharf, as above expressed.

11. It was prescribed by the said act, that no wharf, pier or building, or incumbrance of any kind should ever be extended beyond the said line into or over the tide water in said harbor.

Wharves, &c., not to be extended beyond the line. 1837, 229, § 3. 1850, 216, § 2.

12. It was also prescribed that no person should enlarge or extend any wharf or pier, which was then erected on the inner side of said line, further towards the said line than such wharf or pier then stood, or than the same might have been lawfully enlarged or extended before the passing of the said act, without leave first obtained from the legislature.

No wharf, &c., to be extended towards the line without leave. 1837, 229, § 4. 1850, 216, § 3.

No wharf, &c., to be erected or extended in the harbor. 1837, 229, § 5.

13. No person shall in any other part of the said harbor of Boston, belonging to the commonwealth, erect or cause to be erected any wharf or pier, or begin to erect any wharf or pier therein, or place any stones, wood or other materials in said harbor, or dig down or remove any of the land covered with water at low tide, in said harbor, with intent to erect any wharf or pier therein, or to enlarge or extend any wharf or pier now erected; *provided, however*, that nothing herein contained shall be construed to restrain or control the lawful rights of the owners of any lands or flats in said harbor.

Penalty. Ibid, § 6.

14. Every person offending against the provisions of the five preceding sections, shall be deemed guilty of a misdemeanor, and shall be liable to be prosecuted therefor, by indictment or information in any court of competent jurisdiction, and on conviction shall be punished by a fine not less than one thousand dollars, nor more than five thousand dollars, for every offence, and any erection or obstruction which shall be made, contrary to the provisions and intent of said five preceding sections, shall be liable to be removed and abated as a public nuisance, in the manner heretofore provided for the removal and abatement of nuisances on the public highways.

Erection may be abated as a nuisance.

Additional lines established. 1840, 35, § 1.

15. By an act passed March 17, 1840, the lines described in the four following sections were established as the lines of the channel of the harbor of Boston, beyond which no wharf or pier should ever be extended into and over the tide water of the commonwealth.

Lines between South Boston free bridge and the old South Boston bridge. Ibid, § 2.

16. The line between South Boston free bridge and the old South Boston bridge on the north side of the channel, begins at the east end of the north abutment of the South Boston free bridge, and runs westerly to the east corner of Wright's wharf, at the westerly side of said bridge, being forty-six feet from the west end of said abutment; thence westerly till it meets the northeasterly corner of the first wharf belonging to the South Cove Corporation; thence southerly by the ends of the wharves of said corporation, as now built, to Heath's wharf, and by the end of Heath's wharf to the southerly corner thereof: thence southerly to

South Boston old bridge, by a line drawn at right angles with said bridge, from a point two hundred and ninety-three feet westerly, from the westerly side of the draw of said bridge. The line on the south side of the channel begins on the north side of South Boston old bridge, at a point one hundred and seventeen feet easterly from the westerly side of the draw in said bridge, and four hundred and seventy-four feet westerly from the range line of the westerly side of the brick building standing at the corner, on the easterly side of First street and northerly side of Fourth street, and four hundred and thirty feet from the face of the east stone abutment of said bridge: thence running northerly to the southwesterly corner of Alger's wharf; thence by the end of said wharf to the northerly corner of the same; thence northeasterly to the wharf belonging to the South Boston Iron Company, thence to the end of George C. Thacher's large wharf, and by the same to the northwest corner of said Thacher's small wharf; and thence easterly by said small wharf, sixty-four feet to South Boston free bridge, at a point forty-three feet northerly, from the south stone abutment of said bridge; thence southerly by the westerly side of said bridge forty-three feet to the said abutment; thence easterly by said abutment to the east end of the same: the said line then extends five hundred and twenty feet straight, so as to form an angle with said bridge of seventy-five degrees: from this point, the line is straight in a northerly direction, in such position, that, if it is continued straight, it shall not approach within six hundred feet of Arch wharf.

Lines between Warren bridge, (Boston side,) and Mill Dam. Ibid, § 3.

17. The line between the Warren Bridge and the Boston and Roxbury Mill Dam, on the Boston side of the channel, begins at the easterly end of the south abutment of Warren Bridge, and runs by the face of said abutment, to the west angle of the same. From this the line is straight to the northern angle of the solid part of the Boston and Lowell Railroad ground; the line then continues in the same direction, running westerly, till it meets the north-easterly side of the bridge of the Boston and Lowell Railroad Corporation, at a point sixty-five feet from the

south stone abutment of said bridge; thence straight to the westerly side of Canal bridge, at the southerly side of the pier wharf on which the gymnasium stood, being at a point one hundred and six feet southerly, from the southerly side of the draw in said Canal bridge; thence to the north easterly corner of the solid wharf, belonging to the Charles River Wharf Company, and by the end of said wharf to the westerly corner of the same; thence to a ledge of rocks, off against the end of Taylor's wharf, at a point, one hundred and eighty feet from said wharf, and four hundred and sixty-nine feet from a brick house standing at the corner on the northwesterly side of Brighton street, and northerly side of Poplar street; thence straight to the southwesterly corner of the pier wharf situate on the southerly side of West Boston bridge, crossing the westerly side of said bridge, at a point fourteen feet easterly, from the draw in said bridge, and one hundred and eighty-eight feet westerly, from a brick building standing at the corner, on the easterly side of Charles street, and southerly side of Cambridge street; thence, the line is straight, in a direction, to a point on the northerly side of the Boston and Roxbury Mill Dam, which point is eight hundred feet westerly from a brick building standing at the corner, on the easterly side of Charles street, and northerly side of Beacon street, and one hundred and twenty-five feet westerly, from the sea wall at the easterly end of said Mill Dam, and keeping in that direction till it intersects a line drawn parallel with, and two hundred feet from the northerly side of said dam[1]; thence westerly by said parallel line to the west end of said dam.

Lines on the Charlestown side of the harbor. Ibid, § 4.

18. The line on the Charlestown side of the harbor begins at the southwest corner of the most westerly navy yard wharf in Charlestown, and running southwesterly about one thousand six hundred and fifteen feet, to a timber pier of Charles river bridge, which is three hundred and forty feet northerly, from the draw in said bridge, and five hundred and ninety two feet southerly, from the southerly corner of a brick store, on the northerly side of Water

[1] This part of the line was altered by stat. 1841, c. 60, and further altered by stat. 1850, c. 317. See pp. 163, 170, *post*.

street, at the junction of Main and Water streets; thence on the same course to a point, one hundred feet from the west side of Charles river bridge, being in all one thousand seven hundred and thirty-five feet; thence northwesterly, about five hundred and twenty feet, crossing Warren bridge, to the southwest corner of Thompson's wharf, which corner is three hundred and thirty-eight feet from the southwest rail of the Charlestown Branch Railroad, and two hundred and seventy-eight feet from the sea wall built by the Charlestown Land and Wharf Company; thence northwesterly, about five hundred and fifteen feet to the southeast corner of the wharf belonging to the Charlestown Land and Wharf Company, nearly opposite a passage way; thence northwesterly, about nine hundred and twenty feet, to a point in range with the east side of Fifth street, being two hundred and eighty-four feet westerly, from the sea wall, measured on a line in range with said east side of Fifth street; thence, northwesterly, about five hundred and ninety feet, to a point fifteen feet from the south corner of wharf B, occupied by Charles Gould, as a lime wharf, which point is three hundred and twelve feet from the sea wall of the Charlestown Land and Wharf Company; thence northwesterly, about four hundred feet, to Prison Point bridge, at a point which is eighty-six feet easterly, from the east side of the draw in said bridge, and three hundred twenty-three feet southwesterly from the sea wall, measuring along the southeasterly side of said Prison Point bridge.

Lines on East Boston side of the harbor. Ibid, § 5.

19. The line on the East Boston side of the harbor, commences at a point on the East Boston flats, on the northerly side of Bird Island channel, which point is denoted by the letter A on the plan of the harbor, and is situated on a line, in range with the southerly side of Sumner street, in said East Boston, and at the distance of eight hundred feet from the intersection of the east side of Jeffries street and southerly side of Sumner street; thence running westerly from said point, about one thousand feet, to the point B, situated in the division line between the upland lots numbered sixty and sixty-one, produced five hundred and seventy-five feet from the south side of Mar-

ginal street, or about eight hundred and eighty feet in said line from the south side of Sumner street; thence, again, westerly, on a straight line, about two thousand feet, to the point C, in range with the division line between the water lots of Peter Dunbar, and Fettyplace and Lamson, at the distance of one thousand one hundred feet from the southwesterly side of Marginal street, and one thousand six hundred and ninety feet from the southwesterly side of Sumner street; thence northwesterly by a line, parallel to the southwesterly side of Sumner street, nine hundred and eighty feet to the point D, in the range of the easterly boundary line of the water lot of the Eastern Railroad Company, and one thousand six hundred and ninety feet from Sumner street; thence the line runs straight, a northerly course, about two thousand six hundred feet, to the point E, situated at the distance of five hundred and ten feet from the point F, which point F is situate in the division line between the water lots of Samuel Aspinwall, and Pratt and Cushing; the said point F being one hundred and seventy feet northeasterly, from the southwesterly side of Sumner street, in the northwesterly side of a street forty feet wide, on which street said Samuel Aspinwall, and Pratt and Cushing are bounded, southeasterly; the line from E to F (being five hundred and ten feet in length,) makes a right angle with the line D E; from the point E the line is an arc of a circle, described from the centre F, with a radius of five hundred and ten feet, to the point G in the division line between the water lots of said Aspinwall, and Pratt and Cushing; thence from the point G the line runs straight four hundred and seventy-eight feet, to the point H in the southwesterly division line of the water lot of the East Boston Timber Company, and in the range line of the northeast side of Maverick street, at the distance of seven hundred and fifty-six feet from the west side of Border street. From the point H the line continues straight about five hundred and seventy feet, to the point I, in the northerly division line of flats or water lots of the East Boston Timber Company, at the distance of eight hundred and forty-five feet, from the west side of Border street. From the point I, the line continues northerly, a straight course, about three thousand three hundred feet to the point K, fixed at the distance of one thousand one hundred and seventy feet from the intersection of the easterly side of Meridian street, and southerly side of Eagle street, measured on a right line, running northwesterly from said intersection, at an angle of one hundred and forty-six degrees and thirty-nine minutes with said Eagle street.

20. The same act prescribed that no wharf, pier, building, or incumbrance of any kind, should ever be extended beyond the said line into or over the tide water in said harbor, nor should any wharf or pier which was then erected on the inner side of said line, extend further towards the said line than such wharf or pier then stood, or than the same might have been lawfully enlarged or extended before the passing of the said act, without leave being first obtained from the legislature.

No wharf, &c., to be extended beyond the line, nor further towards the line, without, &c. Ibid, § 6.

21. Every person or corporation offending against the provisions of the six preceding sections, shall be deemed guilty of a misdemeanor, and shall be liable to be prosecuted therefor, by indictment or information, in any court of competent jurisdiction; and, on conviction, shall be punished by a fine not less than one thousand dollars nor more than five thousand dollars, for every offence; and any erection or obstruction which shall be made contrary to the provisions and intent of this section and the six preceding sections, shall be liable to be removed and abated as a public nuisance, in the manner heretofore provided for the removal and abatement of nuisances on the public highway.

Penalty. Ibid, § 7.

Erection may be abated as a nuisance.

22. By an act passed March 6, 1841, the line of that part of the harbor of Boston, lying between West Boston bridge and the Boston and Roxbury mill dam, which was established by the act of March seventeenth, one thousand eight hundred and forty, was altered in part, and ordered thereafter to run as follows; that is to say, beginning at the southwesterly corner of the pier wharf situate on the southerly side of West Boston bridge, and thence running southerly

Alteration of line between West Boston Bridge and the Boston and Roxbury Mill Dam. 1841, 60. See p. 160, *ante*.

to a point in the line heretofore established by the act last aforesaid; which point is eight hundred feet distant from the corner of said pier; and from the said last mentioned point rnnning again southerly, but more westerly, in a direction to a point on the northerly side of said Boston and Roxbury mill dam, which point is ten hundred and eighty-six feet distant from a brick building standing at the corner on the easterly side of Charles street, and northerly side of Beacon street, until it comes to a line running parallel with said mill dam, and two hundred feet distant from the northerly side thereof, then uniting with a line established by said last mentioned act.[1]

Additional lines established. 1847, 278, § 1.

23. By an act passed April 26, 1847, the lines described in the three following sections, were established as lines of the channel of the harbor of Boston beyond which no wharf or pier should ever be extended into and over the tide-water of the Commonwealth.

First line. Ibid, § 2

24. The first line is drawn from the southerly end of the island built by the Boston and Maine Railroad Company, between the channels of Charles River and Miller's River to the southerly corner of the northwesterly abutment of Canal (or Cragie's) bridge. The second line is drawn straight from the face of the said abutment of Canal Bridge, through a point on the northerly side of West Boston Bridge, two thousand feet from the easterly side of the draw in said bridge, to a point two thousand feet northerly from the harbor line heretofore established on the northerly side of the Boston and Roxbury Mill Dam. The next line is drawn from this last point westerly, parallel to said Mill Dam, and two thousand feet from said harbor line, to the northern shore of Charles River near its mouth.

Second line.

Third line.

Fourth line. Ibid, § 3.

25. The fourth line is in Miller's River, and is drawn from the south corner of the aforesaid Boston and Maine Railroad Company's island northerly, along the westerly side of the same, and thence in the same straight line to

---

[1] This part of the line was further altered by stat. 1850, c. 317. See p. 170, *post*.

the northerly side of the old channel. The fifth line is drawn from the point where the fourth line meets the northerly side of the said channel, northwesterly, northerly and northeasterly, along the sea-wall recently built by the Charlestown Branch Railroad Company, to the westerly projection of the State Prison Yard. The sixth line is parallel to the fourth line, and two hundred feet westerly. It extends from the channel of Charles River to the south side of the channel of Miller's River. The seventh line is drawn from the north end of the sixth, as just described, to a point on the north side of Prison Point Bridge, five hundred feet westerly of the centre line of the Boston and Maine Railroad. The eighth line is drawn from the northern extremity of the seventh to a point opposite the west end of the Fitchburg Railroad Bridge, and distant from the same three hundred feet. The ninth line is drawn from the last mentioned point to the northerly corner of the southeasterly abutment of the Boston and Lowell Railroad Bridge over Miller's River.

Fifth line. Sixth line. Seventh line. Eighth line. Ninth line.

26. The tenth line is in South Bay, and is drawn from a point on the south side of the South Free Bridge, (one hundred and fifty feet southeasterly of the southeasterly side of the draw,) in a southerly direction, parallel to the Dorchester Turnpike three thousand feet. The eleventh line is on the westerly side of the channel, and is drawn from the southerly corner of Miller and Nason's wharf, southerly, in a direction at right angles with the South Bridge, across the same, to a point twelve hundred and fifty feet distant therefrom. The twelfth line is drawn from the last mentioned point to the westerly side of the artificial channel of Roxbury Creek, one thousand feet southeasterly from Harrison Avenue, opposite the South Burying ground.

Tenth line. Ibid, § 4. Eleventh line. Twelfth line.

The said lines, thus described, are the lines reported by commissioners under the resolve passed the twenty-second day of March, in the year one thousand eight hundred and forty-five, "authorizing the survey of South Bay, Charles and Mystic Rivers," and by said commissioners drawn and defined on plans by them taken and deposited in the library of the commonwealth.

Being the lines reported by commissioners.

No wharf, &c., to be extended beyond said lines, or further towards them. Ibid, § 5.

27. It was prescribed by the said act, that no wharf, pier, building or incumbrance of any kind, should thereafter be extended beyond the said lines or either of them, into or over the tide water in said harbor; nor should any wharf or pier, which was then erected on the inner side of either of said lines, be extended farther towards the said line, than such wharf or pier then stood, or than the same might have been lawfully enlarged or extended before the passing of the said act, without leave being first obtained from the legislature.

Penalties. Ibid, § 6.

28. Every person offending against the provisions of the five preceding sections, shall be deemed guilty of a misdemeanor, and shall be liable to be prosecuted therefor, by indictment or information, in any court of competent jurisdiction; and on conviction, shall be punished by a fine not less than one thousand dollars, nor more than five thousand dollars, for every offence; and any erection or obstruction which shall be made contrary to the provisions and intent of the said last mentioned sections, shall be liable to be removed and abated as a public nuisance, in the manner heretofore provided for the removal and abatement of nuisances on the public highway.

Erections to be abated as nuisances.

Lines in Chelsea Creek established. 1849, 204, § 1.

29. In that part of the harbor of Boston, lying between East Boston and Chelsea, and known as Chelsea Creek, the lines described in the following section, which are the same lines reported by the commissioners, authorized by a resolve of the general court, passed on the tenth day of May, in the year one thousand eight hundred and forty-eight, "to define, upon a plan or plans, such lines," in said part of said harbor, "as they shall think expedient to establish, beyond which no wharves or other structure shall be extended into and over the tide waters of the commonwealth," and by them drawn and defined upon certain plans taken by them, and deposited in the library, were established, by an act passed on the second day of May, one thousand eight hundred and forty-nine, as the lines beyond which no wharf or pier should ever thereafter be extended into or over the tide water of said part of said harbor.

30. The line on the East Boston side of said creek, commences at a point on the westerly side of East Boston, which point is the northerly terminus of the commissioners' line, heretofore established around East Boston, said point being denoted by the letter A on said plans; thence running northeasterly from said point, about five hundred and thirty-eight feet, to a point marked B, fixed at the distance of nine hundred and fifty-six feet from the intersection of the easterly line of Meridian street, and the northerly line of Condor street, measuring, in a right line, northwesterly from said intersection, at an angle of one hundred and forty degrees with the northerly side of said Condor street; thence again northeasterly, about nine hundred and ninety-six feet, to a point marked C, situate eleven hundred and forty-seven feet from the northerly side of Condor street, measuring northerly, and at right angles thereto, and from a point one hundred and eighteen feet and nine inches easterly from the intersection of the easterly line of Meridian street, and northerly line of Condor street; thence easterly about four hundred and five feet, to a point marked D, situate one thousand and seventy-two feet from the northerly side of Condor street, measuring northerly, and at right angles thereto, from a point in said side of said street, nineteen hundred and twenty feet westerly from the intersection therewith of the easterly side of Knox street; thence again easterly, about seven hundred and fifty-three feet, to a point marked E, situate eight hundred and forty-two feet from the northerly side of Condor street, measuring northerly, and at right angles thereto, from a point in said side of said street twelve hundred feet westerly from the intersection therewith of the easterly side of Knox street; thence again, easterly, about thirteen hundred and fifteen feet, to a point marked F, being the northwesterly corner of the westerly pier of the Glendon Rolling Mill Company's Wharf, said corner being at the distance of eight hundred and sixty feet from the northerly side of Eagle street, measuring northerly, and at right angles thereto; thence again, easterly, by the face of the two piers of said wharf, about two hundred and seventy-two

Line on East Boston side. Ibid, § 2.

feet, to the point marked G, being the northeasterly corner of the easterly pier of said wharf; thence again, easterly, about four hundred and sixty feet to a point marked H, situate eight hundred and fourteen feet from the northerly side of Eagle street, measuring northerly, and at right angles thereto, from a point in said side of said street, four hundred and sixty feet westerly from the intersection therewith of the westerly side of Chelsea street; thence northeasterly about four hundred and fifteen feet to a point marked I, situate six hundred and eighty-five feet from the westerly side of Chelsea street, measuring northwesterly, and at right angles thereto, from a point in said side of said street, six hundred and eighty-five feet northerly from the intersection therewith of the northerly side of Eagle street; thence northeasterly again, about one thousand and fifteen feet, to a point marked K, on the west side of Chelsea Free Bridge, said point being one hundred and fifty-eight feet, northerly, from the face of the south abutment of said bridge.

Line on Chelsea side.

The line on the Chelsea side of said creek commences at a point on the west side of Chelsea Free Bridge, situate two hundred and two feet southerly, from the intersection of the same with the southerly line of Marginal street, in the town of Chelsea, said point being marked L on the plan; thence running southwesterly about nine hundred and fifty-five feet to a point marked M, situate three hundred and six feet from the south line of Marginal street, measuring southerly, and at right angles thereto, from a point in said side of said street, fifteen feet easterly from the first bend therein, west of Chelsea Free Bridge, aforesaid; thence again, southwesterly, about three hundred and seventeen feet to a point marked N, situate three hundred and ninety-four feet from the southerly side of Marginal street, measuring southerly, and at right angles thereto, from a point in said side of said street, sixty feet westerly from the aforementioned bend therein; thence westerly, about three hundred and eighty-six feet, to a point marked O, situate four hundred and fifty-five feet from the southerly side of Marginal street, measuring southerly and at right angles thereto, from a point in said side of said street, four hundred and forty feet westerly from the aforementioned bend therein; thence again, westerly, about two hundred and ten feet, to a point marked P, being the southwesterly corner of the Glendon Rolling Mills Company's Pier on the Chelsea Flats, situate in the division line of the Winnisimmet Company's water lots, numbered 21 and 22, and four hundred and sixty-five feet from the southerly side of Marginal street, measuring southerly and at right angles thereto; thence again westerly, about thirteen hundred and thirty feet, to a point marked Q, situate in the division line between Austin and Carruth's wharves, and two hundred and forty-eight feet from the southerly side Marginal street, measuring southerly and at right angles thereto; thence again, westerly, about seven hundred and forty feet, to a point marked R, situate in the line of the southerly side of Hawes's wharf continued and three hundred feet from the southerly side of Marginal street, measuring southerly and at right angles thereto; thence again, westerly, about six hundred and thirty-three feet, to a point marked S, situate four hundred and five feet from the southerly side of Marginal street, measuring southerly, in the line of the easterly side of the Winnisimmet Company's solid wharf; thence southwesterly about four hundred and eighty-five feet, to a point marked T, being the southeasterly corner of the small pier of the Winnisimmet Company, on the easterly side of their ferry slip; thence again southwesterly, about sixty feet, to a point marked U, being the southerly extremity of the easterly line of spring piling of the aforesaid ferry slip; thence westerly across the mouth of said slip about one hundred and twelve feet to a point marked V, being the southerly extremity of the westerly line of the spring piling of said ferry slip, and situate two hundred and twenty feet southwesterly from the intersection of the Winnisimmet Company's existing sea-wall, on the westerly side of the aforesaid ferry slip, with the continuation of the west side of Winnisimmet street, measuring in the line of said continuation; thence southwesterly about eight hundred feet to a dolphin driven into the flats and marked W, situate eight hundred feet from the easterly side of Chelsea Toll Bridge, measuring easterly, and at right angles thereto, from a point in said side of said bridge four hundred and ten feet south of the north abutment of said bridge.

No wharf, &c., shall be extended beyond said lines. Ibid, § 3.

31. The same act prescribed, that no wharf, pier, or structure, of any kind, should ever thereafter be extended beyond said lines, into or over the tide water in said part of said harbor.

Penalty. Ibid, § 4.

32. Every person offending against the provisions of the three preceding sections, shall be deemed guilty of a misdemeanor, and shall be liable to be prosecuted therefor, by indictment or information, in any court of competent jurisdiction, and on conviction, shall be punished by a fine not less than one hundred dollars, nor more than one thousand dollars, for every offence; and any erection or obstruction which shall be made contrary to the provisions and intent of this act, shall be liable to be removed and abated as a public nuisance, in the manner by law provided for the removal and abatement of nuisances on the public highways.

Erection may be abated, as a nuisance.

Line between West Boston Bridge and Boston and Roxbury Mill Dam further altered. 1850, 317. § 1. See pp. 159, 160, 163, *ante*.

33. By an act passed May 3, 1850, the line of that part of the harbor of Boston, lying between West Boston Bridge and the Boston and Roxbury Mill Dam, which was established by an act passed on the seventeenth day of March, one thousand eight hundred and forty, and altered by an act passed on the sixth day of March, one thousand eight hundred and forty-one, was further altered and directed after May 3, 1850, to run as follows, that is to say, beginning at the southwesterly corner of the pier wharf situate on the southerly side of West Boston Bridge, thence running southwesterly, in a straight line, in a direction to a point on the northerly side of said Boston and Roxbury Mill Dam, which point is ten hundred and eighty-six feet distant from a brick building standing at the corner, on the easterly side of Charles street and northerly side of Beacon street, until it comes to a line running parallel with said Mill Dam, and two hundred feet distant from the northerly side thereof; then uniting with a line established by said

act passed on the seventeenth day of March, one thousand eight hundred and forty.

34. By the same act it was prescribed that no wharf, pier, building, or incumbrance of any kind, should, after said third day of May, eighteen hundred and fifty, be extended beyond said line established in the preceding section, into or over the tide-water in said harbor.

No wharf, &c., to be extended beyond said line. Ibid, § 2.

35. The proprietors of the wharves and flats lying between West Boston Bridge and the Boston and Roxbury Mill Dam, were thereby authorized to extend their wharves and the lines of their respective flats to the said last mentioned line, in a direction at right angles thereto, provided that no person's legal rights shall be infringed thereby.

Proprietors authorized to extend wharves, &c., to said line, provided, &c. Ibid, § 3.

36. The three preceding sections are to take effect, only if and on condition that the proprietors of said wharves and flats shall cause a good and substantial sea-wall to be built and maintained on said last mentioned line through its whole length.

Act, not to take effect unless a sea wall is built. Ibid, § 4.

HARBOR REGULATIONS.

37. No vessel which shall cast anchor in the harbor of Boston, between India wharf and Gray's wharf, shall anchor within five hundred feet of the line described in the second section of an act entitled "An Act to preserve the harbor of Boston, and to prevent encroachments therein," passed on the nineteenth day of April, in the year one thousand eight hundred and thirty-seven; and no vessel which shall cast anchor between the easterly side of Lamson's wharf and the easterly side of Tuttle's wharf, at East Boston, shall anchor within five hundred feet of the line described in the fifth section of "An Act concerning the harbor of Boston," passed the seventeenth day of March, in the year one thousand eight hundred and forty, unless for the purpose of hauling in as soon as practicable, to some wharf in said harbor, or unless compelled to do so by reason of stress of weather, or unavoidable casualty; and, for every offence against either of the foregoing provisions in this section, after having been notified thereof by the harbor-master, who may be appointed as hereinafter men-

No vessel to anchor except within certain limits. 1847, 234, § 2.

See p. 156, *ante.*

See p. 158, *ante.*

Exception.

Penalty.

tioned, or by any party aggrieved, the master, commander, or owners of such vessel, shall be subject to a penalty not exceeding twenty-five dollars.

Trim of vessels at wharves. Ibid, § 2. See 1848, 314, § 3; also, p. 174, § 46, *post*, for additional provisions.

38. The master, commander, or owners of every vessel, shall, as soon as practicable after having hauled to the end of any wharf that extends to the channel in said harbor, cause her lower yards to be cockbilled, and her jib-boom to be rigged in, so that the said jib-boom may not annoy any other vessel or vessels going in or out of the adjoining docks; and the lower yards and jib-boom shall be kept so arranged while such vessel lies at the end of the wharf as aforesaid, and until she is preparing immediately to leave her berth; and for every offence against any of the provisions in this section, the master, commander or owners, or either of them, of such vessel, shall be subject to a penalty not exceeding ten dollars.

Penalty.

Penalty for throwing stones, &c., into the harbor. Ibid, § 3. See 1848, 314, § 2; also, p. 174, § 45, *post*.

39. No person shall throw or deposit in said harbor, or any part thereof, any stones, gravel, ballast, cinders, ashes, dirt, mud, or other substances, which may in any respect, tend to injure the navigation thereof; and whoever shall offend against the provisions of this section shall be subject to a penalty not exceeding fifty dollars.

Regulation of warps and lines. Ibid, § 4.

40. No warp or line shall be passed across the mouth of any slip, for the purpose of hauling a vessel by said slip, before the vessel shall be within one hundred feet of said slip, if the owners or occupants thereof object, unless the harbor-master, who may be appointed as hereinafter mentioned, shall have decided it to be necessary: and for every offence against this provision, the master, commander, or owners of such vessel, shall be subjected to a penalty not exceeding five dollars.

Penalty.

City council may appoint a harbor-master. Ibid, § 5.

41. The city council of the city of Boston may, if they shall deem it expedient, annually appoint, by concurrent ballot in each board, a harbor-master for the port of Boston, who shall hold his office for one year, and until another shall be appointed in his place, or until he shall be removed by said city council; and before entering upon his office, he shall give bond to the said city, with sufficient sureties, to the satisfaction of the mayor and aldermen, in the penal

Bond.

sum of two thousand dollars, conditioned for the faithful discharge of the duties of said office; and in case of the sickness or disability of the said harbor-master, he may appoint a deputy, subject to the approval of said mayor and aldermen, to perform his duties during such sickness or disability; and said harbor-master shall be allowed and paid quarterly, out of the city treasury, such salary for his services, as said city council shall, from time to time, establish.

He may appoint a deputy, in case, &c.

Compensation.

42. It shall be the duty of the said harbor-master to enforce the execution of the several provisions of this section and the five preceding sections, and of all other laws of the commonwealth relating, in any way, to said harbor; and to prosecute all violations of such laws and ordinances, and to take all lawful measures to prevent the doing of any act by which the flow of the tides, or the force, direction, or depth of the current into, out of, or through the said harbor may, in any degree, be injuriously affected. And said harbor-master shall also have authority, so to regulate the anchorage of vessels that, as far as may be practicable, ferry-boats may pass unobstructed, and the channel shall be kept clear, from the wharves to Castle Island.

His duties and authority. Ibid, § 6.

43. All the several penalties mentioned in the six preceding sections may be recovered by complaint before the police court of the city of Boston, or by indictment, for the use of the said city.

Recovery of penalties. Ibid, § 7.

44. The harbor-master authorized to be appointed, by section forty-one, shall have authority to regulate the anchorage of all vessels in the upper harbor of Boston, and, when necessary, to order the removal of such vessels, and to cause the same to be removed in obedience to such order, at the expense of the master or owners thereof; and if any person shall obstruct said harbor-master in the performance of any of his duties, as prescribed by this, the seven preceding, or the three succeeding sections, or shall neglect or refuse to obey any lawful order made by said harbor-master, he shall be liable to a penalty, not exceeding fifty dollars, for each offence, to be recovered by indictment, for the use of the city of Boston.

Harbor-master's further authority. 1848, 314, §. 1.

Penalty for obstructing him in the performance of his duties, or for neglect to obey his orders.

How to be recovered.

Master or owners of vessel also liable to penalty for throwing stones, &c., in harbor. Ibid, § 2.

45. Whenever any person on board of any vessel, shall violate the provisions of the thirty-ninth section, the master or owners of said vessel shall be liable to the penalty prescribed in said last mentioned section, as well as the person so offending.

All yards of vessel to be cock-billed, &c., while vessel is at wharf. Ibid, § 3.

46. The provisions of the thirty-eighth section shall apply to all the yards of vessels as well as the lower yards, any thing in said last mentioned section to the contrary notwithstanding.

Vessels in harbor to keep an anchor watch, and light. Ibid, § 4.

47. All vessels at anchor in the harbor of Boston shall keep an anchor watch at all times, and shall keep a clear and distinct light, suspended at least six feet above the deck, during the night; and whenever the provisions of this section shall be violated on board any vessel, the master or owners shall be liable to a penalty of not more than twenty dollars, to be recovered in the manner provided in section forty-three, and shall be held liable to pay all damages that may be occasioned by such violation.

Penalty. How to be recovered.

No ashes, &c., to be thrown into the harbor. 1837, 229, § 7.

48. No ashes, cinders, or other rubbish, or materials of any description shall be put or thrown out of any steamboat in the harbor of Boston above fort Independence, under a penalty of ten dollars for each offence.[1]

ORDINANCE OF THE CITY.[2]

Joint standing committee on the preservation of the harbor. Their duties. Nov. 12, 1846.

There shall be appointed, annually, a joint standing committee of the city council, consisting of two members of the board of mayor and aldermen, and three members of the common council, whose duty it shall be to suggest such measures, and do and perform such acts, as may by them from time to time be deemed necessary for the pre-

---

[1] For further provisions as to Boston Harbor, see resolves of 1850, ch. 27 and 111.

[2] An ordinance relating to the preservation of Boston Harbor, passed November 12, 1846.

servation of Boston harbor and the security of the rights and interests of the city therein; provided no expense shall be incurred exceeding the appropriation previously made by the city council for these purposes.

HAWKERS AND PEDLERS.

1. From and after the first day of July next, every hawker, pedler, or petty chapman, or other person, going from town to town, or from place to place, or from dwelling-house to dwelling-house, in the same town, either on foot, or with one or more horses, or otherwise carrying for sale, or exposing to sale, any goods, wares or merchandise, or taking a residence in any town for that purpose, for a less time than one year, except as provided in the second section, or under a license, granted as hereinafter provided,

Hawkers, pedlers, petty chapmen, and other itinerant dealers, to be licensed. 1846, 244, § 1.

shall forfeit a sum not exceeding two hundred dollars for every offence; and nothing contained in this section shall be construed to restrain sales at public auction, according to law.

Articles enumerated, which may be sold by hawkers, &c., without license.

2. Any person may go about, as aforesaid, selling and exposing to sale, any fruits and provisions whatever, live animals, brooms, agricultural implements, fuel, newspapers, books, or pamphlets, agricultural products of the United States, the products of his own labor or any labor of his own family; but the sale of jewelry, wines, spirituous liquors, playing cards, indigo, and feathers, as aforesaid, is hereby prohibited: *provided*, if the city council of any city shall authorize the mayor and aldermen of such city, or the inhabitants of any town shall authorize the selectmen of such town, to restrain the sale, by minors, of any goods, wares, or merchandise, the sale of which in the manner aforesaid, is permitted in this section, such mayor and aldermen, or selectmen, while such authority remains in force, may exercise in the premises, all the powers they are by law authorized to exercise in relation to theatrical exhibitions and public shows; and any violation of such restraint, when the same shall be imposed by the regulations of said mayor and aldermen, or said selectmen, or any sale of the articles in question, without a license, where the same shall be required in exercise of the authority above granted, shall subject the persons guilty of the same to a penalty not exceeding ten dollars for every offence: *provided, further*, that no such restraint imposed, or license granted, shall remain in force beyond the term of office of those by whom the same was imposed or granted.

Power of cities and towns to restrain such sales. Ibid, § 2.

Licenses to be granted by the secretary of the commonwealth, upon the certificate of selectmen or mayors, as to the citizenship, residence, and good repute of the applicants. Ibid, § 3.

3. The secretary of the commonwealth may grant a license to go about selling and exposing to sale, any goods, wares or merchandise, not prohibited in the second section, to any applicant, who shall file in his office, a certificate, signed by a majority of the selectmen of any town, or the mayor of any city, in the commonwealth, which certificate shall state that, to the best knowledge and belief of such mayor or selectmen, the applicant therein named, is a citizen of the United States, and resides in such city or town,

and is in good repute for morals and integrity. And the mayor or selectmen as aforesaid, before granting such certificate, shall require every such applicant to make oath that he is the person named therein, that he is a citizen of the United States, and is a resident of such city or town, which oath shall be certified by a justice of the peace, and accompany the certificate.

Extent of such licenses, sums to be paid to the treasurers of towns or cities therein mentioned, and powers conferred thereby. Ibid, § 4.

4. The secretary of the commonwealth shall cause to be inserted, in every license, the names of such cities and towns as the applicant shall select, with the sum to be paid to the respective treasurers thereof, annexed, and shall receive from the applicant one dollar for each city or town so inserted; and every person so licensed, is hereby authorized to sell, as aforesaid, any goods, wares or merchandise, not prohibited in the second section, in any city or town mentioned in his license, upon first tendering to the treasurer thereof, the sum stated to be due; and the treasurer of such city or town shall make a certificate on the face of the license, stating the sum so received. No license granted under this act shall be pleaded in bar to any complaint against the person licensed, if it be proved that he exposed to sale in any county, city or town, mentioned in such license, any article not permitted or prohibited in the second section, prior to tendering to the treasurer thereof the sum required by this act, or in any county, city or town, not mentioned in such license: *provided*, that this act shall not be construed to require any person so licensed, to pay the sum due to the treasurer of any county, city or town, before he is prepared to trade therein.

Sums payable for such licenses. Ibid, § 5.

5. Every person licensed under the foregoing sections, in addition to the sum payable to the secretary of the commonwealth, shall pay to the treasurer of each city or town, mentioned in his license, the sums following:—For every town containing not more than one thousand inhabitants, according to the United States census, next preceding the date of any license, three dollars. For every town containing more than one thousand and not more than two thousand inhabitants, six dollars. For every town containing more than two thousand and not more than three

thousand inhabitants, eight dollars. For every town containing more than three thousand and not more than four thousand inhabitants, ten dollars. And for every town containing more than four thousand inhabitants, the sum shall be increased, in addition to ten dollars, one dollar for every one thousand inhabitants, over four thousand contained therein: *provided*, that the sum to be paid to the treasurer of any city or town shall, in no case, exceed twenty-five dollars.

Dates and terms of licenses granted. Records of licenses, how and by whom to be made. Ibid, § 6.

6. Every license granted under these provisions before the first day of January, A. D., 1847, shall bear date on the first day of July, A. D., 1846, and shall continue in force till the first day of January aforesaid, and no longer; and the amount to be paid therefor shall be one half of any sums herein provided to be paid for a similar license for a year, and every license granted after the aforesaid first day of January, shall bear date on the first day of January of the year in which it is granted, and shall continue in force one year and no longer; and it shall not be lawful for any person to sell under any such license, except the person licensed therein or named in a transfer of the same, as hereinafter provided. The secretary of the commonwealth shall keep a record of all licenses granted, with the number of each, the name and residence of the person licensed, and the counties, cities and towns, mentioned therein, and also of all special state licenses. The treasurers of the counties, cities and towns, shall severally keep records of all licenses upon which the sums provided in this act have been paid, with the number of each, the name and residence of the persons licensed, and the sums received thereon, and all such records shall be open for public inspection.

Special state and county licenses, how, and upon what terms, to be granted. Ibid, § 7.

7. In addition to the licenses authorized in the foregoing sections, the secretary of the commonwealth, upon the conditions required in the third section, may grant special state licenses, upon payment, by the applicant, of one hundred dollars for each license; and the person so licensed, shall be authorized to expose to sale any goods, wares or merchandise, not prohibited in this act, in any city or town in this commonwealth; and may also grant, as aforesaid,

special county licenses, upon payment, by the applicant, of one dollar for each county mentioned therein; and the person so licensed, shall be authorized to expose to sale, to any person within said counties, any tin, britannia, glass or wooden wares, of the manufactures of the United States, or any other goods, wares or merchandise, manufactured by himself, or his employer, and not prohibited in this act, upon tendering to the treasurer of each county mentioned in said license, respectively, the sums following:—For Suffolk, Essex, Middlesex and Worcester, each four dollars. For Norfolk, Berkshire, Hampden, Bristol and Plymouth, each three dollars. For Franklin, Hampshire and Barnstable, each two dollars. For Nantucket, one dollar; for Dukes, one dollar. And the county treasurers, respectively, upon the receipt of any sum, as aforesaid, shall certify thereto on the face of the license, stating the amount so received.

8. All sums paid to the secretary of the commonwealth under this act, shall be for the use of the commonwealth; and all sums paid to the treasurer of any county, city or town, shall be for the use of the county, city or town, so receiving the same. Any license granted under this act, upon proceedings had by the applicant, as provided in the third section, may be transferred by the secretary of the commonwealth; and the person to whom such license is transferred, shall be liable, in all respects, as if he were the person originally licensed.

Sums paid for licenses, to belong to the state, or to the county, city, or town, receiving the same. Ibid, § 8.

9. Every person licensed as herein provided, shall post his name, residence, and the number of his license, in a conspicuous manner, upon his parcels or vehicle, and whenever such license is demanded of him, by any selectman or justice of the peace, he shall forthwith exhibit it, and if he neglect or refuse to do so, shall be subject to the same penalty as if he were without a license, and this act, or a synopsis thereof, shall be printed on every license.

Name, residence, and number of license to be borne on the vehicle, &c. License to be exhibited, to selectmen, &c., when demanded. Ibid, § 9.

10. The license of any person who shall be convicted of a violation of any provision of this act, shall be void. Any person who shall counterfeit or forge a license, or who shall have a counterfeited or forged license in his posses-

Penalties for violations of this act. Ibid, § 10.

sion, with the intent to utter or use the same as true, knowing it to be false and counterfeit, or who shall attempt to sell under a license which has expired, or is forfeited, or which was not granted to him, and has not been transferred to him, shall forfeit a sum not exceeding one thousand dollars.[1]

HAY AND HAY SCALES.

STATUTES.

Weighers of hay to be appointed. R. S. 28, § 95.

1. The mayor and aldermen may from time to time appoint, for a term not exceeding one year, some person or persons to have the superintendence of the hay scales

---

[1] The act of 1846, c. 244, § 11, repealed Rev. Stat. c. 35. §§ 7 and 8.

belonging to the city, who shall weigh hay offered for sale in the city, and any other article offered to be weighed.

2. The persons so appointed shall conform to all such rules and regulations, as shall be established by the city council, concerning the said hay scales, and the compensation or fees for weighing hay and other articles.

Shall conform to rules to be established by city council. Ibid, § 96.

3. The city council may remove any weigher of hay, and fill any vacancy that may occur from death or otherwise.

City council may remove weighers, &c. Ibid, § 97.

4. If any person, not appointed as aforesaid, shall set up any hay scales in the city, for the purpose of weighing hay, or other articles, he shall forfeit the sum of twenty dollars a month, so long as the same shall be continued, to be recovered by an action of debt, and appropriated to the use of the city.[1]

Penalty for setting up scales, without authority. Ibid, § 98.

5. All pressed hay, which shall be offered for sale in this commonwealth, shall be branded upon the crate enclosing it, with the first letter of the christian name and the whole of the surname of the person packing and screwing, or otherwise pressing said hay, and with the name of the town and state where said hay shall be pressed.

How crates of pressed hay shall be branded. 1836, 240, § 1.

6. All pressed hay, which shall be offered for sale without being branded as aforesaid, shall be forfeited, one half to the person or persons prosecuting therefor, and the other half to the use of the city or town where said hay shall be so offered for sale.

Forfeiture, and to whose use, of hay offered for sale without the required brand. Ibid, § 2.

7. All forfeitures, incurred under the two preceding sections, may be recovered, with costs of suit, by action, bill, plaint or information, before any justice of the peace, or other court proper to try the same.

Mode of recovering such forfeiture. Ibid, § 3.

8. The mayor and aldermen of each city in this commonwealth, in which bale or bundle hay is sold, may, on the petition of ten or more legal voters of such city, annually

Mayor and aldermen may, on petition, appoint inspectors of bale or bundle hay. 1847, 246, § 1.

---

[1] This section of the Revised Statutes contains a provision, that this and the three preceding sections shall not apply to any town, which shall not adopt the same, and shall cease to operate in such town, when the town shall so determine. This provision does not seem applicable to the city of Boston, but the city council have deemed it expedient to adopt these sections expressly. See p. 184, *post*, § 8.

appoint one or more persons as inspectors of bale or bundle hay, who shall be sworn to the faithful discharge of the duties of their office.

May remove inspectors, and fill vacancies. Ibid, § 2.

9. Said mayor and aldermen may remove any inspector so appointed, and fill any vacancy that may occur from death or otherwise.

Duties of inspectors. Ibid, § 3.

10. It shall be the duty of the inspector to inspect and weigh all bale or bundle hay, within the limits of the city, or ward for which he may be appointed, when requested so to do by the owner or vendor of such hay.

How inspected hay shall be branded. Ibid, § 4.

11. All bales or bundles of hay so inspected, which are found to be sweet, of good quality, and free from damage or any improper mixture, shall be branded or marked *No.* 1. All bales or bundles which are found to be sweet, and free from damage or any improper mixture, but consisting of hay of a secondary quality, shall be branded or marked *No.* 2. All bales or bundles which are found to be wet, or in any way damaged, or which shall contain any straw or other substances not valuable as hay, shall be branded or marked *bad.* Each bale or bundle so inspected shall also be branded or marked with the first letter of the christian name, and the whole of the surname, of the inspector, and the name of the city or town for which he is inspector, together with the month and year when inspected; and also the net weight of the bundle.

Inspectors to furnish themselves with scales, &c. Ibid, § 5.

12. Each inspector shall furnish himself with proper scales, weights, seals, and other suitable instruments for the purposes aforesaid.

Fees, how fixed, and by whom paid. Ibid, § 6.

13. The fees for inspecting, weighing, and marking, as provided for in the five preceding sections, shall be fixed by the respective officers having the power of appointment, and shall be paid by the employer of the inspector.

Penalty for selling without inspection, &c. Ibid, § 7.

14. Any person who shall sell any bale or bundle hay, in any city or town in this commonwealth, where an inspector is appointed, as required by the six preceding sections, which has not been inspected and weighed as therein provided, shall forfeit, for each bale or bundle so sold, two dollars, to be recovered in any court proper to try the same, one half to the complainant, and the other half to

the city or town in which such sale shall have been made: *provided*, that no inspection under this act shall be made, where the vendor and vendee shall certify, in writing, to the inspector, that they object to an inspection. Proviso.

ORDINANCE OF THE CITY.[1]

SECT. 1. The mayor and aldermen shall appoint suitable places in the streets or squares of the city, as stands for the sale of hay and straw. Stands for sale of hay and straw. Aug. 20, 1850.

SECT. 2. The owner or driver of any wagon, cart, sled, or other carriage, containing hay or straw for sale, who shall stand for the sale of such hay or straw, in any other street, square or place whatsoever, than one of those so appointed by the mayor and aldermen, shall be liable to a penalty not exceeding twenty dollars. Penalty for standing in any other place for sale of hay or straw. Ibid.

SECT. 3. The mayor and aldermen shall establish, from time to time, a sufficient number of public scales for the weighing of hay and other articles, and cause the same to be erected, and furnished with decimal weights, which shall be used in all cases; and shall appoint suitable persons to have the superintendence of the same, and to weigh hay and other articles, according to law. Scales to be established, &c. Ibid. Weighers appointed.

SECT. 4. The persons so appointed shall attend personally at the scales which may be assigned to them respectively, every day through the year, Sundays, public fasts, thanksgivings, and the anniversary of American Independence, excepted, from sunrise to sunset, (with liberty to close their respective offices from seven to eight o'clock in the forenoon during the months of April, May, June, July, August, and September, and from eight to nine o'clock during the other six months, and from one to two o'clock in the afternoon, through the whole year;) shall deliver to the driver of every load of hay or straw weighed, a certifi- Duties of weighers.

---

[1] An ordinance relating to the weighing of hay and other articles, passed August 20, 1850.

cate in such form as is hereinafter provided; and shall keep an account of all hay and other articles which shall be weighed at said scales, in books to be furnished by the mayor and aldermen, which shall be always open to their inspection, and when filled, shall be deposited with the city clerk.

Form of weighers' accounts and certificates. Ibid.

SECT. 5. The accounts to be kept by said weighers, and the certificates to be given to the drivers of loads, as mentioned in the preceding section, shall specify the name of the owner or driver, the town from which the load shall have been driven, the weight and tare, the amount of fees received, and the date of the certificate.

Fees for weighing. Ibid.

SECT 6. The fees, for weighing hay and other articles, to be received by the said weighers, and by them paid over to the city treasurer, as provided by the city ordinances, shall be as follows, to wit: one cent and a half for every hundred pounds of hay or straw, one half of a cent for every hundred pounds of anthracite or other coal, and one cent for every hundred pounds of all other articles; *provided*, that the fee for weighing any article other than hay or straw shall never be less than ten cents. The cart or vehicle containing the same, and other tare, shall be weighed without any charge. And no fees shall be taken for any weighing done on account of the city.

Compensation of weighers. Ibid.

SECT. 7. The said weighers shall receive such compensation as the city council may, from time to time, determine.

R. S. 28, § 95–98, adopted.

SECT. 8. The ninety-fifth, ninety-sixth, ninety-seventh, and ninety-eighth sections of the twenty-eighth chapter of the Revised Statutes, are hereby adopted.

HEALTH.

STATUTES.

1. Powers formerly vested in the board of health for Boston, transferred to the city council.
2. Powers formerly vested in boards of health of towns, now vested in city councils of cities.
3. How such powers and duties may be exercised. Either branch of council, or any committee, may be board of health.
4. Nuisances, how and by whom to be removed. Penalty.
5. Order to remove nuisance, how to be served.
6. Proceedings when order is not complied with. Expenses, by whom paid.
7. How expenses shall be recovered.
8. Fines, &c., to whom to enure, and how recovered.
9. Physician to the board of health.
10. Compensation of physician, &c.
11. Board of health, to make regulations as to nuisances, &c.
12. May make provision as to infected articles.
13. May make regulations as to interments, &c.
14. Notice of their regulations to be published.
15. Board to examine into nuisances, &c.
16. When a party is convicted of a nuisance, the court may order it removed at his expense.
17. Court of common pleas, &c., may issue injunctions in cases of nuisance.
8. How board of health may make compulsory examination of premises, when refused, &c.
19. Board may grant permits for the removal of nuisances, infected articles or sick persons.
20. If the infected person cannot be removed, provision to be made for him, &c.
21. Persons may be stationed on the borders of other states, to examine, &c.
22. Any two justices may issue warrants to remove sick persons.
23. One justice may issue warrant to secure infected articles.
24. Justices may impress houses and stores, &c., for safe keeping of goods, &c.
25. Officers may break open houses, shops, &c., and command aid.
26. Expenses to be paid by owners of goods.
27. Town shall make compensation for houses, &c., or services impressed.
28. Board of health may remove the occupants of any cellar, &c., occupied as a dwelling house, which is unfit for the purpose, and a cause of nuisance, &c.
29. Removal of prisoners attacked with diseases in jail.
30. Return of removal to be made to the court. Such removal shall not be an escape.
31. Towns may establish a quarantine ground.
32. Two or more towns may establish common quarantine ground.
33. Board of health may establish the quarantine of vessels.
34. Quarantine regulations to extend to all persons, &c.

ORDINANCE.

STATUTES.

1. By the seventeenth section of the act establishing the city of Boston, all the power and authority by law vested in the board of health for the town of Boston, at the time of the passage of the said act, relative to the quarantine of vessels, and relative to every other subject whatsoever, was transferred to, and vested in the city council, to be carried into execution by the appointment of health commissioners,

Powers formerly vested in the board of health of Boston, transferred to the city council. 1821, 110, § 17.

or in such other manner as the health, cleanliness, comfort, and order of the said city might in their judgment require, subject to such alterations as the legislature might from time to time adopt.[1]

Powers formerly vested in boards of health of towns, now vested in city councils of cities. 1849, 211, § 1.

2. By the act of May 2, 1849, it was provided that all the powers vested in, and the duties prescribed to boards of health of towns, by the general laws, should be vested in, and prescribed to city councils of cities, in case no special provision to the contrary was made in such laws themselves, or in the special laws applicable to any particular city.

How such powers and duties may be exercised. Ibid, § 2.

3. The powers and duties above named, may be exercised and carried into effect by city councils, in any manner which they may prescribe, or through the agency of any persons to whom they may delegate the same, notwithstanding a personal exercise of the same, collectively or individually, is prescribed in the instance of towns, as above referred to. And city councils are authorized to constitute either branch, or any committee of their number, whether joint or separate, the board of health for all, or for particular purposes, within their own cities.

Either branch of council, or any committee, may be board of health.

Nuisances, how and by whom to be removed. Ibid, § 3. 7 Pick. 76. Penalty.

4. Whenever any nuisance, source of filth, or cause of sickness, shall be found on private property, within any city, the board of health, or health officer, shall order the owner, or occupant thereof, to remove the same, at his own expense, within twenty-four hours, or such other time as they shall deem reasonable, after notice served, as provided in the succeeding section; and if the owner, or occupant,

---

[1] It is not only the right but the duty of the city government of Boston, so far as they may be able, to remove every nuisance which may endanger the health of the citizens. And they have necessarily the power of deciding in what manner this shall be done, and their decision is conclusive, unless they transcend the powers conferred on them by the city charter. Police regulations to direct the use of private property so as to prevent its being pernicious to the citizens at large, are not void although they may in some measure interfere with private rights without providing for compensation. The property of a private individual may be appropriated to public use in connexion with measures of municipal regulation, and in such case compensation must be provided for, or the appropriation will be unconstitutional and void. *Baker v. City of Boston*, (12 Pick. Rep. 184.)

shall neglect so to do, he shall forfeit a sum not exceeding twenty dollars, for every day during which he shall knowingly permit such nuisance or cause of sickness to remain, after the time prescribed, as aforesaid, for the removal thereof.

5. The order mentioned in the last section shall be communicated by a written notice, served personally upon the owner or occupant, or their authorized agent, by any person competent to serve a notice in a civil suit; or such notice may be left at the owner, occupant, or agent's last and usual place of abode, if the same be known, and is within the state; and if the owner or agent's residence is unknown, or without the state, the premises being unoccupied, then such notice may be served by posting up the same on the premises, and by advertising in one or more public newspapers, in such manner, and for such length of time, as the board of health, or health officer, shall deem expedient.

Order to remove nuisances, how to be served. 1849, 211, § 4.

6. If the owner or occupant shall not comply with the order above mentioned, the board of health may cause the said nuisance, source of filth, or cause of sickness, to be removed, and all expenses, incurred thereby, shall be paid by the said owner or occupant, or by such other person as shall have caused or permitted the same, if such owner or occupant, or such other person, shall have had actual notice from the board of health of the existence of said nuisance, source of filth, or cause of sickness.

Proceedings when order is not complied with. Ibid, § 5.

Expenses, by whom paid.

7. All expenses incurred by any town or city in the removal of nuisances, or for the preservation of the public health, and which are recoverable of any private person or corporation, by virtue of any provisions of law, may be sued for and recovered in an action of debt before any court having jurisdiction of the amount claimed.

How expenses shall be recovered. Ibid. § 6.

8. All fines and forfeitures incurred under the general laws, or the special laws applicable to any town or city, or the ordinances, by-laws and regulations of any town or city, relating to health, shall enure to the use of such town or city; and may be recovered by complaint, in the name of the treasurer, before any justice of the peace of the county,

Fines, &c., to whom to enure, and how recovered. Ibid, § 7. Com. v. Fahey, S. J. C. March T. 1850.

or police court of the city, in which the offence may have been committed.[1]

Physician to the board of health. R. S. 21, § 3.

9. Every board of health may appoint a physician to the board, who shall hold his office during their pleasure.

Compensation of physician, &c. Ibid, § 4.

10. The board of health shall establish the salary or other compensation of such physician, and shall regulate all fees and charges of every person employed by them in the execution of the health laws and of their own regulations.

Board of health, to make regulations as to nuisances, &c. Ibid, § 5.

11. The board of health shall make such regulations respecting nuisances, sources of filth, and causes of sickness, within their respective towns,[2] and on board of any vessels in their harbors, as they shall judge necessary for the public health and safety; and if any person shall violate any such regulation, he shall forfeit a sum not exceeding one hundred dollars.

May make provision as to infected articles. Ibid § 6.

12. The said board shall also make such regulations, as they may judge necessary for the public health and safety, respecting any articles which are capable of containing or conveying any infection or contagion, or of creating any sickness, when such articles shall be brought into or conveyed from their town, or into or from any vessel; and if any person shall violate any such regulations, he shall forfeit a sum not exceeding one hundred dollars.

May make regulations as to interments, &c. Ibid, § 7.

13. The said board shall also make all regulations, which they may judge necessary for the interment of the dead, and respecting burying grounds in their towns.

Notice of their regulations to be published. Ibid, § 8.

14. Notice shall be given, by the board of health, of all regulations made by them, by publishing the same in some newspaper of their town, or, where there is no such newspaper, by posting them up in some public place of the town; and such notice of said regulations shall be deemed legal notice to all persons.

---

[1] The 8th section of stat. 1849, c. 211, repealed the 10th, 11th, and 46th sections of Rev. Stat. c. 21, and so much of stat. 1816, c. 44, as is inconsistent with the provisions above given.

[2] The word "town" in the Revised Statutes may be construed to include cities. R. S. 2, § 6, clause 17. See also stat. 1849, c. 211, § 1, *ante*, p. 188, § 2.

15. The board of health shall examine into all nuisances, sources of filth, and causes of sickness, that may, in their opinion, be injurious to the health of the inhabitants within their town, or in any vessel within the harbor of such town, and the same shall destroy, remove or prevent, as the case may require.[1]

Board to examine into nuisances, &c. Ibid, § 9. 7 Pick. 76.

16. When any person shall be convicted, on an indictment for a common nuisance, that may be injurious to the public health, the court may, in their discretion, order it to be removed or destroyed, at the expense of the defendant, under the direction of the board of health of the town, where the nuisance is found; and the form of the warrant to the sheriff, or other officer, may be varied accordingly.

When a party is convicted of a nuisance, the court may order it removed at his expense. R. S. 21, § 12.

17. The court of common pleas, or any one of the justices thereof, in term time or vacation, may, in all cases, either before or pending a prosecution for a common nuisance affecting the public health, issue an injunction to stay or prevent the same, until the matter shall be decided by a jury or otherwise; and may issue all such other writs and processes, and make all such orders and decrees, according to the course of proceedings in chancery, as may be necessary or proper to enforce such injunction; and may dissolve the same, when the court or any one of the said justices shall think it proper.

Court of common pleas, &c., may issue injunctions, in cases of nuisance. Ibid, § 13.

18. Whenever the board of health shall think it necessary, for the preservation of the lives or health of the inhabitants, to enter any land, building or vessel, within their town, for the purpose of examining into, and destroying, removing or preventing any nuisance, source of filth, or cause of sickness, and shall be refused such entry, any member of the board may make complaint, under oath, to any justice of the peace of his county, stating the facts of the case, so far as he has knowledge thereof, and such justice may thereupon issue a warrant, directed to the sheriff or either of his deputies, or to any constable of such town, commanding them to take sufficient aid, and, being accom-

How board of health may make compulsory examination of premises, when refused, &c. Ibid, § 14.

---

[1] The 10th and 11th sections of the 21st chapter of the Revised Statutes were repealed by stat. 1849, c. 211, § 8.

panied by any two or more members of said board of health, between the hours of sunrise and sunset, to repair to the place where such nuisance, source of filth or cause of sickness complained of, may be, and the same to destroy, remove or prevent, under the directions of such members of the board of health.

Board may grant permits for the removal of nuisances, infected articles, or sick persons. Ibid, § 15.

19. The board of health may grant permits for the removal of any nuisance, infected article or sick person, within the limits of their town, when they shall think it safe and proper so to do.[1]

If the infected person cannot be removed, provision to be made for him, &c. Ibid, § 17. 1838, 158. See § 39, p. 197, *post*.

20. When any person, coming from abroad, or residing in any town within this state, shall be infected, or shall lately before have been infected, with the plague, or other sickness, other than small pox, dangerous to the public health, and the infected person cannot be removed, without danger to his health, the board of health shall make provision for him, as directed in the sixteenth section of the twenty-first chapter of the Revised Statutes,[2] in the house in which he may be; and, in such case, they may cause the persons in the neighborhood to be removed, and may take such other measures, as they shall judge necessary, for the safety of the inhabitants.

Persons may be stationed on borders of other states, to examine, &c. R. S. 21, § 18.

21. The board of health of any town near to, or bordering upon, either of the neighboring states, may appoint, by writing under their hands, suitable persons to attend at any places, by which travellers may pass from infected places in other states; and the persons, so appointed, may examine such passengers, as they may suspect of bringing with them any infection, which may be dangerous to the public

---

[1] The 16th section of the 21st chapter of the Revised Statutes was repealed by stat. 1837, c. 244, § 3.

[2] The section here referred to, which was repealed by stat. 1837, c. 244, § 3, provided, that, in case of such infection, the board of health "shall make effectual provision, in the manner in which they shall judge best, for the safety of the inhabitants, by removing such sick or infected person to a separate house, if it can be done without danger to his health, and by providing nurses, and other assistance and necessaries, which shall be at the charge of the person himself, his parents or master, if able, otherwise at the charge of the town to which he belongs; and, in case such person is not an inhabitant of any town, then at the charge of the commonwealth."

health, and, if need be, may restrain them from travelling, until licensed thereto by the board of health of the town, to which such person may come; and any passenger, coming from such infected place, who shall, without license as aforesaid, travel within this state, unless it be to return by the most direct way to the state from whence he came, after he shall be cautioned to depart by the persons appointed as aforesaid, shall forfeit a sum not exceeding one hundred dollars.

Any two justices may issue warrants to remove sick persons. Ibid, § 19.

22. Any two justices of the peace may, if need be, make out a warrant, directed to the sheriff of the county, or his deputy, or to any constable, requiring them, under the direction of the board of health, to remove any person, infected with contagious sickness, or to impress and take up convenient houses, lodging, nurses, attendants, and other necessaries for the accommodation, safety and relief of the sick.

One justice may issue warrant to secure infected articles. Ibid, § 20.

23. Whenever, on the application of the board of health, it shall be made to appear to any justice of the peace, that there is just cause to suspect that any baggage, clothing or goods, of any kind, found within the town, are infected with the plague or any other disease, which may be dangerous to the public health, such justice of the peace shall, by warrant, directed to the sheriff or his deputy, or to any constable, require him to impress so many men, as said justice shall judge necessary, to secure such baggage, clothing or other goods, and to post said men as a guard over the house or place, where such baggage, clothing or other goods shall be lodged; which guard shall take effectual care to prevent any persons removing or coming near to such baggage, clothing or other goods, until due inquiry be made into the circumstances thereof.

Justices may impress houses and stores, &c., for safe keeping of goods, &c. Ibid, § 21.

24. The said justice may also, by the same warrant, if it shall appear to him necessary, require the said officers, under the direction of said board of health, to impress and take up convenient houses or stores, for the safe keeping of such baggage, clothing or other goods; and the board of health may cause them to be removed to such houses or stores, or to be otherwise detained, until they shall, in

the opinion of the said board of health, be freed from infection.

Officers may break open houses, shops, &c., and command aid. Ibid, § 22.

25. The said officers, in the execution of such warrant, shall, if need be, break open any house, shop, or other place mentioned in said warrant, where such baggage, clothing, or other goods, shall be; and they may require such aid, as shall be necessary to effect the execution of the warrant; and all persons shall, at the command of either of the said officers, under a penalty not exceeding ten dollars, assist in the execution of the warrant.

Expenses to be paid by owners of goods. Ibid, § 23.

26. The charges of securing such baggage, clothing or other goods, and of transporting and purifying the same, shall be paid by the owners thereof, at such rates and prices, as shall be determined by the board of health.

Town shall make compensation for houses, &c., or services impressed. Ibid, § 24.

27. Whenever the sheriff or other officer shall impress or take up any houses, stores, lodging, or other necessaries, or shall impress any men, as provided by law, the several parties interested shall he entitled to a just compensation therefor, to be paid by the town, in which such persons or property shall have been so impressed.

Board of health may remove the occupants of any cellar, &c., occupied as a dwelling-house, which is unfit for the purpose, and a cause of nuisance, &c. 1850, 108.

28. Whenever the board of health of any city or town shall be satisfied, upon due examination, that any cellar, room, tenement, or building, occupied as a dwelling place, within such city or town, is unfit for that purpose, and a cause of nuisance or sickness, either to the occupants or to the public, such board of health may issue a notice in writing, to such persons, or any of them, requiring them to remove from, or quit such cellar, room, tenement, or building, within such time as the said board of health may deem reasonable. And if the person or persons so notified, or any of them, shall neglect or refuse so to remove and quit, within the time mentioned, it shall be lawful for such board of health to remove them forcibly, and to close up such cellar, room, tenement, or building, and the same shall not be again occupied as a dwelling place, without the consent in writing, of the board of health, under a penalty of not less than ten, nor more than fifty dollars, to be recovered by indictment of the owner or owners, if they shall have knowingly permitted the same to be so occupied.

29. Whenever any person, confined in any common jail, house of correction, or work house, shall be attacked with any disease which, in the opinion of the physician of the board of health, or of such other physician as they may consult, shall be considered dangerous to the safety and health of the other prisoners, or of the inhabitants of the town, the board of health shall, by their order in writing, direct the removal of such person to some hospital, or other place of safety, there to be provided for and securely kept, so as to prevent his escape, until their further order; and if such person shall recover from the disease, he shall be returned to the said prison or other place of confinement. **Removal of prisoners attacked with diseases in jail.** R. S. 21, § 25.

30. If the person so removed shall have been committed by order of any court, or under any judicial process, the order for his removal, or a copy thereof, attested by the presiding member of said board of health, shall be returned by him, with the doings thereon, into the office of the clerk of the court, from which the process was issued for committing such prisoner; and no prisoner, removed as aforesaid, shall be considered as having thereby committed an escape. **Return of removal to be made to the court.** Ibid, § 26. **Such removal shall not be an escape.**

QUARANTINE.

31. Any town[1] may establish a quarantine ground, in any suitable place, either within or without its own limits; provided, that, if such place shall be without its limits, the assent of the town, within whose limits it may be established, shall be obtained therefor. **Towns may establish a quarantine ground.** Ibid, § 27.

32. Any two or more towns may, at their joint expense, establish a quarantine ground for their common use, in any suitable place, either within or without their own limits; provided, that if such place shall be without their limits, they shall obtain the assent of the town, within whose limits such place may be. **Two or more towns may establish common quarantine ground.** Ibid, § 28.

33. The board of health in each seaport town may, from time to time, establish the quarantine, to be performed by all vessels arriving within the harbor of such town; and **Board of health may establish the quarantine of vessels.** Ibid, § 29.

[1] See note to § 11, *ante*.

may make such quarantine regulations, as they shall judge necessary for the health and safety of the inhabitants.

Quarantine regulations to extend to all persons, &c. Ibid, § 30.

34. The quarantine regulations, so established, shall extend to all persons, and all goods and effects, arriving in such vessels, and to all persons, who may visit or go on board the same.

To be binding on all persons after public notice. Ibid, § 31. See § 14, *ante*, p. 190.

35. The quarantine regulations aforesaid, after notice thereof shall have been given, in the manner above provided, shall be observed by all persons; and any person who shall violate any such quarantine regulation, shall forfeit a sum not less than five dollars, nor more than five hundred dollars.

Vessels to be ordered to quarantine ground. R. S. 21, § 32.

36. The board of health, in each seaport town, may, at all times, cause any vessel arriving in such port, when such vessel or the cargo thereof shall in their opinion be foul or infected, so as to endanger the public health, to be removed to the quarantine ground, and be thoroughly purified, at the expense of the owners, consignees, or persons in possession of the same; and they may also cause all persons, arriving in or going on board of such infected vessel, or handling such infected cargo, to be removed to any hospital under the care of said board of health, there to remain under their orders.

Penalty if master, seamen, &c., refuse to make answer on oath, &c. Ibid, § 33.

37. If any master, seaman or passenger, belonging to any vessel, on board of which any infection may then be, or may have lately been, or suspected to have been, or which may have been [*at*], or which may have come from, any port where any infectious distemper prevails, that may endanger the public health, shall refuse to make answer on oath to such questions, as may be asked him, relating to such infection or distemper, by the board of health of the town, to which such vessel may come, (which oath any member of said board may administer,) such master, seaman or passenger so refusing, shall forfeit a sum not exceeding two hundred dollars; and, in case he be not able to pay said sum, he shall suffer six months' imprisonment.

Quarantine expenses to be paid by such person or owner. Ibid, § 34.

38. All expenses, incurred on account of any person, vessel or goods, under any quarantine regulations, shall be paid by such person, or the owner of such vessel or goods, respectively.

DANGEROUS DISEASES.

39. Whenever any person coming from abroad or residing in any town in this state, shall be infected, or shall lately before have been infected, with the plague, or other sickness dangerous to the public health, except the small pox, the board of health of said town shall make effectual provision in the manner which they shall judge best for the safety of the inhabitants, by removing such sick or infected person to a separate house or otherwise, and by providing nurses and other assistance and necessaries; which shall all be at the charge of the person himself, his parents or master, if able, otherwise at the charge of the town to which he belongs; and in case such person is not at inhabitant of any town in this state, then at the charge of the commonwealth.

Board of health to provide for safety of inhabitants, when persons are infected with dangerous sickness. 1837, 244, § 1. 1848, 119, § 1.

40. When any disease dangerous to the public health, other than the small pox, shall break out in any town, the board of health thereof shall immediately provide such hospital or place of reception for the sick and infected as they shall judge best for their accommodation, and the safety of the inhabitants, and such hospitals and places of reception shall be subject to the regulations of the said board of health, in the same manner as is provided in the case of established hospitals, in the succeeding sections, and the said board of health may cause such sick and infected person to be removed to such hospital or places of reception, unless the condition of the sick or infected person be such as not to admit of his removal without danger to his health, in which case the house or place where such person shall remain shall be considered as a hospital to every purpose aforesaid; and all persons residing in or in any way concerned with the same, shall be subject to the regulations of said board of health, as before provided.

Board to provide hospitals immediately, when any dangerous disease breaks out unexpectedly. 1837, 244, § 2. 1848, 119, § 1.

41. The inhabitants of any town may establish, within the same town, and be constantly provided with, one or more hospitals for the reception of persons, having the small pox, or other disease, which may be dangerous to the public health.

Hospitals for the small pox, &c., may be provided by towns. R. S. 21, § 35.

To be under the orders of the board of health. Ibid, § 36.

42. All such hospitals shall be subject to the orders and regulations of the board of health, or a committee of such town appointed for that purpose.

Not to be established within 100 rods of houses in adjoining town, unless, &c. Ibid, § 37.

43. No such hospital shall be established, within one hundred rods of any inhabited dwelling house, situated in any adjoining town, without the consent of such adjoining town.[1]

Physician and others, in hospitals, to be subject to board of health. Ibid, § 39.

44. When any hospital shall be so established, the physician, the persons inoculated or sick therein, the nurses, attendants, and all persons, who shall approach or come within the limits of the same, and all such furniture and other articles, as shall be used or brought there, shall be subject to such regulations, as may be made by the board of health, or the committee appointed for that purpose.[2]

Selectmen and board of health shall give notice of dangerous disease by red flags, &c. Ibid, 21, § 41. 1838, 158.

45. When any disease dangerous to the public health, other than the small pox, is found to exist in any town, the selectmen and board of health shall use all possible care to prevent the spreading of the infection, and to give public notice of infected places to travellers, by displaying red flags at proper distances, and by all other means, which in their judgment shall be most effectual for the common safety.

Penalty on physicians and others, for violating regulations. R. S. 21, § 42. 1838, 158.

46. If any physician or other person, in any of the hospitals or places of reception before mentioned, or who shall attend, approach or be concerned with the same, shall violate any of the regulations lawfully made in relation thereto, either with respect to himself, or his or any other person's property, the person so offending shall, for each offence, forfeit a sum not less than ten nor more than one hundred dollars.

Every householder to give notice of small pox, &c., in his family. R. S. 21, § 43. 1838, 158. 1840, 39.

47. When any householder shall know that any person within his family is taken sick of the small pox, or any other disease dangerous to the public health, he shall immediately give notice thereof to the selectmen or board of health of the

---

[1] The 38th section of the 21st chapter of the Revised Statutes was in effect repealed by stat. 1838, c. 158.

[2] The 40th section of R. S. c. 21, was repealed by stat. 1837, c. 244, § 3. See also 1838, c. 158.

town in which he dwells; and if he shall refuse or neglect to give such notice, he shall forfeit a sum not exceeding one hundred dollars.[1]

Penalty on physicians, for not giving notice of small pox, &c. R. S. 21, § 44. 1838, 158. 1840, 39.

48. When any physician shall know that any person, whom he is called to visit, is infected with the small pox, or any other disease dangerous to the public health, such physician shall immediately give notice thereof to the selectmen, or board of health of the town in which the diseased person may be; and every physician, who shall refuse or neglect to give such notice, shall forfeit for each offence a sum not less than fifty nor more than one hundred dollars.

Towns may provide for inoculation of its inhabitants, and defray expenses. Ibid, § 45.

49. Each town may, at any meeting, make suitable provision for the inoculation of the inhabitants with the cow pox, under the direction of the board of health of each town, or of a committee chosen for that purpose; and they shall raise all necessary sums of money, to defray the expenses of such inoculation, in the same manner as other town charges are paid.[2]

OFFENSIVE TRADES.

Mayor and aldermen to assign places for offensive trades. Ibid, § 47.

50. The mayor and aldermen of the city of Boston, when they shall judge it necessary, shall, from time to time, assign certain places for the exercising of any trade or employment, offensive to the inhabitants, or dangerous to the public health; and they shall forbid the exercise of either of them in places not so assigned; and all such assignments shall be entered in the records of the city; and they may be revoked, when the city officers shall think proper.

If such place become a nuisance, court of common pleas may revoke, &c. Ibid, § 48.

51. When any place or building so assigned shall become a nuisance, by reason of offensive smells or exhalations proceeding from the same, or shall become otherwise hurtful or dangerous to the neighborhood or to travellers, and the same shall be made to appear, on a trial before the court of common pleas for the county, upon a complaint

---

[1] The stat. 1838, c. 158, repealed so much of R. S. c. 21, §§ 16, 17, 38, 40, 41, 42, 43 and 44, as relates to the small pox; but stat. 1840, c. 39, repealed so much of stat. 1838, c. 158, as related to said 43d and 44th sections.

[2] Section 46 of R. S. c. 21, was repealed by stat. 1849, c. 211, § 8.

made by the board of health or by any other person, the said court may revoke such assignment, and prohibit the further use of such place or building, for the exercise of either of the aforesaid trades or employments, and may cause such nuisances to be removed or prevented.

Action for damages from nuisances. Ibid, § 49. Shaw v. Cummiskey, 7 Pick. 76.

52. Any person, injured either in his comfort or the enjoyment of his estate, by any such nuisance, may have an action on the case, for the damage sustained thereby; in which action, the defendant may plead the general issue and give any special matter in evidence.

GENERAL PROVISIONS.

Selling corrupt or unwholesome provisions, without notice. R. S. 131, § 1.

53. If any person shall knowingly sell any kind of diseased, corrupted, or unwholesome provisions, whether for meat or drink, without making the same fully known to the buyer, he shall be punished by imprisonment in the county jail, not more than six months, or by fine not exceeding two hundred dollars.

Adulterating food or liquors. Ibid, § 2.

54. If any person shall fraudulently adulterate, for the purpose of sale, any substance intended for food, or any wine, spirits, malt liquor or other liquor, intended for drinking, with any substance injurious to health, he shall be punished by imprisonment in the county jail, not more than one year, or by fine not exceeding three hundred dollars, and the articles so adulterated shall be forfeited and destroyed.

Adulterating drugs or medicines. Ibid, § 3.

55. If any person shall fraudulently adulterate, for the purpose of sale, any drug or medicine, in such a manner as to render the same injurious to health, he shall be punished by imprisonment in the county jail, not more than one year, or by fine not exceeding four hundred dollars, and such adulterated drugs and medicines shall be forfeited and destroyed.

Violation of sepulture. R. S. 130, § 19.

56. If any person, not being authorized by the board of health, overseers of the poor, directors of any work house, or selectmen of any town, or by the directors of the house of industry, overseers of the poor, or mayor and aldermen of the city of Boston, shall wilfully dig up, disinter, remove or convey away any human body, or the remains thereof,

or shall knowingly aid in such disinterment, removal or conveying away, every such offender, and every person accessory thereto, either before or after the fact, shall be punished by imprisonment in the state prison, not more than one year, or in the county jail, not more than two years, or by fine not exceeding two thousand dollars.

Penalty for selling tainted fish for food. R. S. 28, § 90.

57. If any person shall sell within this state, or shall export therefrom, any tainted or damaged fish, unless with the intent that the same shall be used for some other purpose than as food, he shall forfeit the sum of ten dollars for every hundred pounds of such fish, and in the same proportion for any other quantity thereof; and upon any trial in such case, the burden of proof shall be upon the defendant, to show for what purpose such fish was so exported or sold.

Board of health authorized to cover flats in the Mill Dam empty basin with water. 1814, 39, § 5.

58. The board of health of the city of Boston is authorized and empowered to cause the flats, on the westerly side of Boston, within the empty basin, between the Boston and Roxbury Mill Dam and Boston Neck, or any portion of them, to be kept constantly covered with water, if in the opinion of said board, it shall be necessary to the health of the inhabitants of said city; and for that purpose to cause a dam of a suitable height, at their discretion, to be placed and kept at the sluice gate or gates in the principal dam of said empty basin, in order to retain the water therein, at the sole expense of the Boston and Roxbury Mill Corporation.

City authorized to establish a cemetery in any town, and to make rules, &c., with consent of such towns. 1849, 150. 16 Pick., 121.

59. The city of Boston is authorized to purchase and hold land, for a public cemetery, in any town in this commonwealth, and to make and establish all suitable rules, orders, and regulations, for the interment of the dead therein, to the same extent that the said city of Boston is now authorized to make such rules, orders, and regulations, for the interment of the dead within the limits of the said city; *provided*, that the consent of any town, in which the said cemetery is proposed to be located, shall first be obtained for the purpose.[1]

---

[1] Certain provisions in relation to health, which were formerly in force in the city of Boston, but which appear to have been in effect repealed by late enactments, are inserted in the Appendix.

ORDINANCE OF THE CITY.[1]

Mayor and aldermen shall constitute the board of health. Aug. 20, 1850.

SECT. 1. The mayor and aldermen shall constitute the board of health of the city, for all purposes, and shall exercise all the powers vested in, and shall perform all the duties prescribed to, the city council as a board of health; subject only to any limitations and restrictions contained in the ordinances, regulations and orders of the city council.

Execution of health laws and ordinances committed to city marshal. Ibid.

SECT. 2. The execution of the laws and ordinances relating to the subject of internal health, shall be under the superintendence of the city marshal and his deputies; and it shall be their duty, and they and each of them shall have power, to enforce all laws, ordinances, regulations and orders, relating to causes of sickness, nuisances and sources of filth, existing within the city, except as is otherwise provided in this ordinance; subject always to the direction, authority and control of the mayor and aldermen.

Consulting physicians. Ibid.

Their duties.

SECT. 3. In the month of May or June, annually, there shall be appointed, by concurrent vote of the city council, five consulting physicians, whose duty it shall be, in case of an alarm of any contagious or other dangerous disease, occurring in the city or neighborhood, to give to the mayor or either board of the city council all such professional advice and information as they may request, with a view to the prevention of such disease, and, at all convenient times when requested, to aid and assist them with their counsel and advice in all matters that relate to the preservation of the health of the inhabitants.

Owners, &c., of dwelling-houses, &c., shall furnish them with suitable drains and privies. Ibid.

SECT. 4. The owner, agent, occupant, or other person having the care of any tenement used as a dwelling-house, or of any other building with which there is a privy connected and used, shall furnish the same with a sufficient drain under ground to carry off the waste water, and also with a suitable privy, the vault of which shall be sunk under ground and built in the manner hereinafter prescribed, and of a capacity proportionate to the number of inhabitants of such tenement, or of those having occasion

---

[1] An ordinance relating to the public health, passed August 20, 1850.

to use such privy. Any such owner, agent, occupant or other person, who shall neglect to comply with the provisions of this section, shall be liable to a penalty for each and every week during which such offence shall continue. Penalty.

SECT. 5. All vaults or privies shall be so constructed that the inside of the same shall be at least two feet distant from the line of every adjoining lot, unless the owner of said adjoining lot shall otherwise agree and consent; and also from every street, lane, alley, court, square, or public place, or public or private passage way. Every vault shall be made tight, so that the contents thereof cannot escape therefrom, except as is provided in the following section. How vaults and privies shall be constructed. Ibid.

SECT. 6. The superintendent of sewers, under the direction of the mayor and aldermen, is authorized to permit, under such restrictions, and on the payment of such sum, not exceeding twenty dollars, as they shall deem expedient, the construction of sufficient passage ways or conduits under ground, for the purpose of conveying the contents of any of the vaults aforesaid into any common sewer or drain. Vaults may be connected with common sewers, by permission of superintendent of sewers. Ibid.

SECT. 7. If the mayor and aldermen shall at any time be satisfied that any tenement, used as a dwelling-house, or any such other building as is mentioned in the fourth section, is not provided with a suitable privy, and vault and drain, or either of them as aforesaid, they may give notice in writing to the owner, agent, occupant, or other person having the care thereof, or, in case neither the owner, agent, or person having the care thereof, is an inhabitant of the city, public notice in two newspapers printed in Boston, requiring such owner, agent, occupant or other person, within such time as they shall appoint, to cause a proper and sufficient privy and vault and drain, or either of them, to be constructed for such tenement or other building; and in case of neglect or refusal to obey such notice, the mayor and aldermen shall have power to cause such privy and vault and drain to be made for such tenement or other building, the expense of which shall be paid by such owner, agent, occupant or other person; and in case any such drain, vault, or privy is constructed as aforesaid for Proceedings, where a suitable privy, vault and drain, is not constructed. Ibid.

the use of more than one house, then the owner, agent, occupant, or other person having the charge of each of such houses, shall be liable to pay a proportional part of such expense.

Offensive vaults, privies and drains, shall be cleansed. Ibid.

SECT. 8. Whenever any vault, privy or drain, shall become offensive or obstructed, the same shall be cleansed and made free; and the owner, agent, occupant, or other person having charge of the land, in which any vault or privy or drain may be situated, the state and condition of which shall be in violation of the provisions of this ordinance, shall remove, cleanse, alter, amend, or repair the same, within a reasonable time after notice in writing to that effect, given by the mayor, any alderman, or the city marshal. In case of neglect or refusal, for the space of five days, the mayor and aldermen shall cause the same to be removed, cleansed, altered, amended or repaired, as they may deem expedient, at the expense of the owner, agent, occupant, or other person as aforesaid, and such owner, agent, occupant or other person, shall also be liable to a penalty.

Regulations as to cleansing vaults and privies. Ibid.

SECT. 9. No vault or privy shall be emptied, without a permit from the city marshal, or his deputy; nor in any other mode, or at any other time, than he shall direct and appoint; conformable to such regulations and contracts as the mayor and aldermen from time to time shall make on the subject, and always at the expense of the owner, agent, occupant, or other person having charge of the tenement in which such vault is situated.

Applications for cleansing vaults. Ibid.

SECT. 10. A book shall be kept in the office of the city marshal, in which shall be entered all applications for opening and cleansing vaults; and the same shall receive attention in the several wards in the order in which they are made.

What sums shall be paid therefor.

The mayor and aldermen shall from time to time determine the sum to be paid by persons who shall make such applications between the fifteenth day of September and the first day of March; and all persons making such application between the first day of March and the first day of June, shall be charged and shall pay double the amount so determined; and all persons making such application between the first day of June and the fifteenth day of September, shall be charged and shall pay at least three times the amount so determined.

SECT. 11. No vault shall be opened between the first day of June and the fifteenth day of September, in each year; unless, on inspection caused to be made, the city marshal or his deputy shall be satisfied of the necessity of the same, for the health or comfort of the inhabitants. In such case, no more of the contents shall be taken away, than they or either of them shall deem to be absolutely necessary for present safety and relief, and such precautions shall be used relative to the preventing of any offensive effluvia, as they, or either of them shall direct, at the expense of the owner, agent, occupant, or other person having charge of the premises.

Further regulations. Ibid.

SECT. 12. All waste water shall be conveyed through sufficient drains under ground, to a common sewer, or to such reservoir, sunk under ground, as shall be approved by the superintendent of sewers. And no person shall suffer any waste or stagnant water to remain in any cellar or upon any lot or vacant ground by him owned or occupied.

Waste water. Ibid.

SECT. 13. Whenever, upon due examination, it shall appear to the mayor and aldermen, that the number of persons occupying any tenement or building in the city is so great as to be the cause of nuisance and sickness, and the source of filth; or that any tenements or buildings are not furnished with vaults constructed according to the provisions of this ordinance, and sufficient privies, and drains under ground, for waste water, they may thereupon issue their notice, in writing, to such persons or any of them, requiring them to remove from and quit such tenement or building within such time as the mayor and aldermen shall deem reasonable. And if the person or persons so notified, or any of them, shall neglect or refuse to remove from and quit such tenement or building within the time mentioned in such notice, the mayor and aldermen are hereby authorized and empowered thereupon forcibly to remove them; and such person or persons shall further be liable to a penalty for such neglect or refusal.

Mayor and aldermen may remove persons from tenements, where too numerous, or unprovided with vaults, &c. Ibid.

House offal, how to be kept. Ibid.

SECT. 14. All house offal, whether consisting of animal or vegetable substance, shall be deposited in convenient vessels, and kept in some convenient place, to be taken away by the city scavengers, which shall be done not less than twice in each week.

Manner of its removal. Ibid.

SECT. 15. No person shall remove or carry, in, along, or through, any of the streets, squares, courts, lanes, avenues, places, or alleys, of the city of Boston, any house dirt, or house offal, or any refuse substances, either animal or vegetable, from any of the dwelling-houses or other places in the city, unless such person so removing or carrying the same, and the mode in which the same shall be removed or carried, shall have been expressly licensed by the mayor and aldermen, upon such terms and conditions as they shall deem the health and interest of the city require.[1]

No filth shall be thrown out into streets, &c. Ibid.

SECT. 16. No person, without the license of the mayor and aldermen, shall throw into, or leave in or upon, any street, court, square, lane, alley, wharf, public square, public enclosure, vacant lot, or any pond or body of water within the limits of the city, any dead animal, dirt, sawdust, soot, ashes, cinders, shavings, hair, shreds, manure, oyster, clam or lobster shells, waste water, rubbish or filth of any kind, or any refuse animal or vegetable matter whatsoever. Nor shall any person throw into, or leave in or upon any dock, flats or tide water within the jurisdiction of the city, any dead animal or other foul or offensive matter, except as provided in the nineteenth section of this ordinance.

Penalty. Ibid.

SECT. 17. If any of the substances, in the preceding section mentioned, shall be thrown or carried from any house, warehouse, shop, cellar, yard, or other place, or left in any of the places specified in the preceding section, the owner of such house, warehouse, shop, cellar,

---

[1] A by-law of Boston, prohibiting any person not duly licensed therefor by the mayor and aldermen from removing the house dirt and offal from the city, is valid, and binds a stranger coming within the city. *Vandine's case*, (6 Pick. Rep. 187.)

yard, or other place, as aforesaid, as well as the occupant thereof, and the person who actually threw, carried or left the same, or who caused the same to be thrown, carried or left, shall severally be held liable for such violation of this ordinance; and all such substances shall be removed from the place where they have been so thrown or left as aforesaid, by such owner or occupant, within two hours after personal notice in writing to that effect, given by the mayor, any alderman, or the city marshal; or such removal shall be made under the direction of either of the officers just named, and the expense thereof borne by such owner or occupant.

Filth, &c., may be removed by order of mayor and aldermen. Ibid.

SECT. 18. All dirt, saw dust, soot, ashes, cinders, shavings, hair, shreds, manure, oyster, clam or lobster shells, waste water, or any animal or vegetable substance, rubbish or filth of any kind, in any house, warehouse, cellar, yard, unaccepted street, or other place, which the mayor and aldermen shall deem injurious to the health of the city, shall be removed by the owner, or occupant, of such house, warehouse, cellar, yard, unaccepted street, or other place, where the same shall be found, within twenty-four hours, or such other time as the mayor and aldermen shall deem reasonable, after notice in writing to that effect, served personally upon the owner, or occupant, or their authorized agent, by any person competent to serve a notice in a civil suit, or left at the owner, occupant or agent's last and usual place of abode, if the same be known and be within the state; or such removal shall be made under the direction of the mayor and aldermen, and the expense thereof borne by such owner or occupant, and in addition, they or either of them shall be liable to a penalty.

Sale and keeping of fish regulated. Ibid.

SECT. 19. No person shall bring into the city for sale, nor shall sell, nor offer for sale, any halibut, cod, haddock, or mackerel, until the same shall have been cleansed of their entrails and refuse parts; and such entrails and refuse parts shall be thrown overboard, below low water mark; and shall never be kept beyond the flowing of the tide next after such fish are so cleansed; and until so thrown overboard, they shall be kept, in a safe manner, on board the vessels or boats in which the fish were brought. And no person shall sell and deliver, from any stall, fish box, cart, or other place, any fish of any kind, except flounders, smelts, and other small fish, salmon and shad, until the same shall have been cleansed of their entrails and refuse parts; and such entrails and refuse parts shall be kept in some tight vessel until the same shall be thrown into the sea below low water mark, which shall be done within twenty-four hours after the fish shall have been so cleansed. And no person shall sell, or offer for sale in the city, fish of any kind, unless the same be kept in covered stalls, fish boxes or other houses, which shall always be clean and in good order, or in clean covered carts or boxes, well secured from the rays of the sun.

Fish, &c., not be sold, &c., in certain streets, except, &c. Ibid.

SECT. 20. No person shall sell, or offer for sale, in the street, any fish, lobsters, oysters, or shell-fish of any kind, in Market square, Merchants row, South Market street, North Market street, or the street running from Long wharf to Clinton street, or in that part of Washington street between Hayward place and Kneeland street, those parts of Kneeland, Beach and Essex streets, between Front and Washington streets, nor in those parts of Boylston and Eliot streets between Tremont and Washington streets, except by permission of the mayor and aldermen, and on such conditions as they shall order.

Vegetables to be divested of parts not used for food. Ibid.

SECT. 21. No person shall bring into the city, or have in his possession for sale, or shall sell or offer for sale within the city, any vegetables whatever, (excepting green peas in the pods, and green corn in the inner husks,) which have not previously been divested of such parts or appendages as are not commonly used for food; and no person shall have such parts or appendages in his possession, in any public or private market, or in any store, shop or other place, or in any cart or vehicle in said city, used or occupied for the sale of vegetables or other articles of food.

Swine and goats not to be kept without license. Ibid.

SECT. 22. No swine or goats shall be kept within the limits of the city, without the license of the mayor and aldermen, and only in such place and manner as they shall direct.

SECT. 23. The owners and occupants of livery and other stables within the city, shall not wash or clean their carriages or horses, or cause them to be washed or cleaned, in the streets or public ways, nor otherwise encumber the same; they shall keep their stables and stable yards clean, and shall not permit more than two cart loads of manure to accumulate and remain in or near the same, at any one time between the first day of May and the first day of November; nor shall they, within that period, remove any manure, nor cause or suffer the same to be removed, except between the hour of twelve at night and two hours after sunrise.

Horses and carriages not to be washed in streets, &c. Ibid.

SECT. 24. No person shall land on any wharf or other place, or shall otherwise bring into the city, any decayed or damaged grain, rice, coffee, fruit, potatoes, or other vegetable product, without a permit therefor from the mayor and aldermen, and in such manner as they shall direct.

Damaged grain, &c., not to be landed without a permit. Ibid.

CITY PHYSICIAN.

SECT. 25. There shall be chosen annually in the month of May, and whenever a vacancy occurs, by concurrent vote of the two branches of the city council, a city physician, who shall hold his office until a successor is appointed or he is removed. He shall be removable at the pleasure of the city council, and shall receive such compensation as the said council may from time to time determine.

City physician. Ibid.

SECT. 26. The said physician shall examine into all nuisances, sources of filth and causes of sickness, which may be on board of any vessel at any wharf within the harbor of Boston, or which may have been landed from any vessel on any wharf, or other place, when notified of the same; and, under the direction of the mayor and aldermen, shall cause the same to be removed or destroyed.

He shall examine into nuisances, &c. Ibid.

SECT. 27. There shall be provided by the city council a suitable apartment for the city physician, free of expense to him; at which place he shall attend, at such times as the mayor and aldermen may direct; and he shall vaccinate, without charge, any inhabitant of Boston, not previously vaccinated, who may apply for that purpose; he shall also give certificates of vaccination to such children as have

His apartment. Ibid.

He shall vaccinate inhabitants who apply, &c.

been vaccinated and shall require such certificates for admission to the public schools: *provided*, that no person shall be entitled to the benefits of this section, who shall wilfully neglect or refuse to return to the office of the city physician, when requested by him, for the purpose of enabling him to ascertain the effect of the vaccination, or to renew the necessary supply of virus for the use of said office.

Proviso.

To keep and supply vaccine virus. Ibid.

SECT. 28. The said city physician shall always have on hand, as far as is practicable, a sufficient quantity of vaccine virus, and he shall supply the physicians of the city institutions, and the dispensary, with the same, without expense to them.

To attend cases of disease in jail. Ibid.

SECT. 29. The said city physician shall attend upon all cases of disease in the jail of the county of Suffolk, and shall perform all the professional services required at said jail.

To examine cases of disease, when called upon by mayor and aldermen, &c. Ibid.

SECT. 30. The said city physician shall examine all cases of disease, within the city, and inquire into all sources of danger to the public health, whenever he shall be called upon by the board of mayor and aldermen, or the overseers of the poor, and shall give his professional services and advice therein without charge.

To keep record of cases of small pox, &c. Ibid.

SECT. 31. The city physician shall keep a record of all cases of small pox, or other malignant diseases, attended by him under this ordinance, and shall make such reports thereof to the mayor and aldermen, as they may from time to time direct.

To keep record of doings of his office. Ibid.

SECT. 32. The said city physician shall also keep a correct record of all the doings of his office, and shall make a regular return thereof to the city council, as often as once in three months.

Harbor master shall report to city physician vessels having hides, &c. Ibid.

SECT. 33. Whenever any vessel shall arrive in the harbor of Boston, between the first day of April and the fifteenth day of November in any year, having on board any hides, hide cuttings, skins, rags, or fruit, it shall be the duty of the harbor master to give immediate notice thereof to the city physician.

Master of such vessel shall give notice to harbor

SECT. 34. It shall be the duty of every master and consignee of any vessel, arriving within the time fixed in the preceding section, and containing the articles therein named, or any of them, to give immediate notice of the arrival of such vessel to the harbor master or the city physician.

master or city physician. Ibid.

PORT PHYSICIAN.

SECT. 35. There shall be chosen annually in the month of May, and whenever a vacancy occurs, by concurrent vote of the two branches of the city council, a port physician, who shall hold his office until a successor is appointed or he is removed. He shall be removable at the pleasure of the city council, and shall receive such compensation as the said council may from time to time determine.

Port physician. Ibid.

SECT. 36. The said port physician shall reside at Deer Island, which is hereby made and declared to be the place of quarantine for the port of Boston. He shall be superintendent of the quarantine hospital, and physician to all the city establishments which are or may be located upon said island, and which shall not be otherwise provided for. He shall also perform all such services as may be required of him by the city council or the mayor and aldermen in relation to quarantine.

To reside at Deer Island and superintend quarantine hospital, &c. Ibid.

SECT. 37. The said port physician shall keep a record of all cases of small pox, or other malignant diseases, attended by him under this ordinance, and shall make such reports thereof to the mayor and aldermen, as they may from time to time direct.

To keep record of cases of small pox, &c. Ibid.

SECT. 38. The said port physician shall also keep a correct record of his other doings, and shall make a regular return thereof to the city council, as often as once in three months.

To keep record of his other doings. Ibid.

INTERMENT OF THE DEAD.

SECT. 39. The department relative to the interment of the dead is placed under the superintendence of the city registrar, whose duty it shall be, and he shall have power, to carry into execution all laws, ordinances, regulations and orders relating to the interment of the dead, subject al-

Interment of dead shall be under superintendence of city registrar. Ibid.

ways to the direction, authority and control of the mayor and aldermen.

He shall have care of burying grounds. Ibid.

SECT. 40. The said registrar shall have the care and custody of all the burying grounds in the city, and it shall be his duty to keep the same in good repair, and secured from trespassers, and to prevent any and all nuisances therein.

May give licenses for burials, &c. Ibid.

SECT. 41. The said registrar is authorized to give licenses for burials, and the removal of dead bodies from the city, and to point out the place, depth, width and range of all graves to be dug in the several burying grounds, and to declare the limits in such grounds, within which no grave shall be dug, which in his judgment would be dangerous to the public health.

Dead bodies shall not be buried without license. Ibid. 16 Pick., 121.

SECT. 42. No person shall bury or inter, or cause to be buried or interred, any dead body, without having first obtained a license so to do from the city registrar, nor in violation of any direction or order of the said registrar, given in accordance with the preceding section.

Graves shall be three feet deep. Aug. 20, 1850.

SECT. 43. No person shall inter, or cause to be interred any dead body in a grave which shall be less than three feet deep from the surface of the ground surrounding the grave to the top of the coffin.

Registrar shall provide funeral cars, &c. Ibid.

SECT. 44. The said registrar shall provide all funeral cars used in the city, and shall have the care and custody of the same. He shall cause them to be kept clean and in good repair, and shall permit no person to use the same except funeral undertakers, appointed by the mayor and aldermen, as provided in the following section.

Funeral undertakers. Ibid.

SECT. 45. In the month of January, annually, the mayor and aldermen shall appoint, for a period of one year, such a number of funeral undertakers as they may deem expedient, who shall be responsible for the decent, orderly and faithful management of the funerals undertaken by them, and for a strict compliance with the ordinances of the city in this behalf.

Porters.

Each undertaker may employ porters, of a discreet and sober character, to assist him, and shall be accountable for their conduct; and said undertakers and porters shall always be removable at the pleasure of the mayor and aldermen.

No other person shall undertake funeral. 16 Pick., 121.

No person not appointed as aforesaid, shall undertake the management of any funeral.

SECT. 46. No person shall bury or inter, or cause to be buried or interred, any dead body at any other time of the day than between sun-rising and sun-setting, except when otherwise ordered by the city registrar. No bell shall be tolled in the city of Boston, at any funeral, without a special permit therefor from the mayor. The corpse of every person of ten years of age and upward, shall be conveyed to the grave or tomb in a funeral car, to be drawn by not more than two horses; *provided, however*, that, on extraordinary occasions, permission may be obtained from the mayor and aldermen, on application for that purpose, to dispense with any of the provisions of this section.

Time for burials. Aug. 20, 1850. **Tolling of bell.** **Funeral car.**

SECT. 47. No graves shall be opened or dug in any of the burying grounds in the city, excepting at East Boston and South Boston, unless by permission of the mayor and aldermen, or the city registrar.

No grave to be dug without permission. Ibid.

SECT. 48. No person shall remove, or cause to be removed from the city, any dead body, for interment, without having first obtained the license of the city registrar.

No dead body to be removed from city without license. Ibid.

SECT. 49. No person shall remove any dead body, or the remains of any such body, from any of the graves or tombs in this city, or shall disturb, break up or remove any dead body in any tomb or grave, without the license of the city registrar.

No dead body to be disturbed without license. Ibid.

SECT. 50. No grave or tomb shall be opened, from the first day of June to the first day of October, except for the purpose of interring the dead, without the special permission of the mayor and aldermen, or the city registrar.

No grave, &c., to be opened, except, &c., without permission. Ibid.

SECT. 51. The following fees shall be paid for services in the execution of this ordinance, to wit: to the city, fifty cents for every child under the age of ten years, and one dollar for every person of the age of ten years or upwards, buried, and twenty-five cents per mile for any distance that a funeral car may be sent out of the city, which, together with the fees for graves and tombs, are to be collected by the undertaker in each and every case, from the families of the persons interred. The undertakers shall be entitled to receive the following fees, and no more, namely:—for digging a grave eight feet deep, and covering the same, two

Burial fees. Ibid.

dollars and fifty cents; for digging a grave six feet six inches deep, one dollar and fifty cents; for digging a grave five feet deep, one dollar and twenty-five cents; and for one four feet deep, one dollar. For opening and closing a tomb, seventy-five cents. For attendance and service at the house of a person deceased, in collecting and returning chairs, and other service, one dollar. For every family notified by request, five cents. For tolling a bell by special permission, fifty cents. For placing a corpse in a coffin, when requested, and removing the same down stairs, one dollar. For the use of one horse in the car, and leader, one dollar and fifty cents; and for each additional horse, seventy-five cents; and twenty-five cents each mile in addition for every horse attached to the car, when the same is sent out of the city. For carrying a corpse from the house to the car, and from the car to the grave, tomb or vault, and placing the same therein, and closing the same, including the assistance of the funeral porters, three dollars; and the same fees shall be allowed and paid in all cases of removing a corpse from any public vault, and reburying or entombing the same, as are allowed and paid for burying or entombing a corpse in any grave, vault or tomb, as aforesaid. For the burial of children, under ten years of age, to wit: for digging a grave three and a half feet deep, seventy-five cents; for service at the house, one dollar; for tolling a bell by special permission, fifty cents; for carrying the corpse to the carriage, and from the carriage to the place of deposit, one dollar; and for the use of a pall, twenty-five cents. And when a corpse shall be carried into a church for a funeral service, the undertaker may make an additional charge of two dollars; and when the ground shall be frozen, the charge for digging graves may be augmented, at the discretion of the city registrar. And it shall be the duty of the several undertakers to pay over, monthly, to the city registrar, the fees received by them on account of the city, provided for and established in this section.

Mayor and aldermen may make regula-

SECT. 52. The mayor and aldermen are authorized to make and adopt any regulations in relation to the interment of the dead which they may deem expedient, not inconsistent with the foregoing provisions. tions in relation to interment. Ibid.

SECT. 53. Every person offending against any of the provisions of this ordinance, in relation to which a penalty is not prescribed by the laws of the commonwealth, shall forfeit and pay a sum not less than five dollars, nor more than twenty dollars, for each offence. Penalty for offences against this ordinance. Ibid.

HOUSE OF CORRECTION.

House of correction for Suffolk. 1824, 28, § 2.

1. The house of correction within the city of Boston shall be the house of correction for the county of Suffolk.[1]

---

[1] The stat. 1824, c. 28, contained several other provisions respecting the house of correction, all of which, however, although not expressly repealed, appear to be superseded by stat. 1834, c. 151, and by Rev. Stat. c.

2. There shall be erected, or otherwise provided, by the county commissioners, in their respective counties, and by the mayor and aldermen in the city of Boston, at the charge of the said counties and city respectively, a fit and convenient house or houses of correction, where not already provided, with convenient yards and work-shops, and other suitable accommodations, adjoining or appurtenant thereto, for the safe keeping, correcting, governing and employing of all rogues, vagabonds and common beggars, all lewd, vicious, idle and disorderly persons, and all other offenders who may be committed thereto in due course of law.

House of correction to be erected or provided. R. S. 143, § 2.

3. The yards of such houses of correction shall be of sufficient extent for the convenient employment of the persons confined therein, and shall be enclosed by fences of sufficient height and strength to prevent escapes, and also to prevent all access to, or communication with, any persons confined therein, by persons without. Until such house of correction shall be provided, the jail in any county, or a part thereof, may be used for that purpose; but every jail so used shall be provided with a sufficient yard, which shall be enclosed in the manner directed in this section.

Extent and enclosure of yards. Ibid, § 3.

Jails to be used, until house of correction is provided.

4. The commissioners in their respective counties, and the city council, in the city of Boston, shall appoint a suitable person to be master of each house of correction, and to hold his office during their pleasure; and they shall also establish such rules and orders,[1] not repugnant to the laws of the commonwealth, as they shall deem necessary, for restraining, governing and punishing the persons there confined.

Master to be appointed. Ibid, § 4.

Rules to be established.

5. Any police court or justice of the peace, and also the court of common pleas and municipal court, may com-

Vagabonds, &c., shall be committed to such house. Ibid, § 5.

143, §§ 2, 4, 11, 13, 14, 16. The act of 1825, c. 182, § 7, provided, that the city council might, at their discretion, establish within the city, two or more houses of correction, to be houses of correction for the county of Suffolk; and that it should be lawful for the mayor and aldermen to transfer persons held under sentence in either of said houses, to any other of said houses, when in their opinion, the health, moral improvement, or beneficial employment of such persons would be promoted thereby.

[1] The rules and orders adopted by the city council, October 23, 1843, are inserted in the appendix.

mit to the house of correction, to be there kept and governed according to law, and to the rules and orders thereof, all rogues and vagabonds, and all idle and dissolute persons, who go about begging; all persons who use any juggling, or unlawful games or plays; common pipers and fiddlers; stubborn children, runaways, common drunkards, common night walkers, pilferers, and all lewd, wanton, and lascivious persons, in speech or behavior; common railers and brawlers, and persons who neglect their calling or employment, misspend what they earn, and do not provide for themselves, or for the support of their families; all persons, who shall sell any spiritous or fermented liquor without license, in the open air, in any booth or other temporary building, in any house, shop, room or apartment, used for the purpose of tippling or gaming, or in which tippling or gaming is allowed, or which is used for the resort of loose, lascivious, wanton, or dissolute persons; all persons who shall be convicted of stealing money or goods, not exceeding the value of five dollars, and all other idle and disorderly persons, upon conviction, in the manner hereafter provided, of any of the offences aforesaid.

Manner of commitment. Ibid, § 6.

6. When any person shall be accused of any offence, or of any disorderly conduct, mentioned in the preceding section, or shall be liable, by virtue of any law of this commonwealth, to be committed, for any cause, to the house of correction of the county, or to the house of industry or workhouse established in any town, complaint shall be made in writing, under oath, to a justice of the peace for the county, or to a police court for the town where the offence shall be committed, and such magistrate shall thereupon cause the person complained of to be brought before himself, or before some other magistrate, by warrant, and upon conviction of the offence set forth in such complaint, such person may be sentenced to be committed to the house of correction for the county, or to the house of industry or workhouse, within the city or town, there to be kept at work for a term not exceeding six months; and the master, keeper, director or overseer of such house, shall receive all persons who shall be so committed, and set them to work, if they be able, and

employ and govern them, while they remain in his custody, in the manner required by law, and prescribed by the rules and orders established for that purpose.

Appointment of overseers. Ibid, § 11.

7. The commissioners, in their respective counties, and the city council of Boston, may appoint two or more, not exceeding five, suitable and discreet persons of the county or city, to be overseers of the house of correction therein, who shall see that the rules established for the management of the house of correction, and the government of the persons confined therein, are strictly observed; the overseers shall examine all accounts of the master, relating to the earnings of the prisoners, and all the expenses of the institution, and they shall keep a register, fairly written, of all their official proceedings.

Their duties.

Overseers to make contracts for work. Ibid, § 12.

8. The overseers of each house of correction may make contracts, for work to be done in the house, with any person who may be disposed to supply materials to be there wrought; they may also make contracts for letting out to hire, during the day time, any of the persons there confined, to employers living near enough, in their opinion, to the house of correction, for the said overseers, or the master of the said house, to have the general inspection of the conduct of the persons so let out to hire, and of the treatment they receive. The overseers shall receive such reasonable compensation, as may be allowed by the commissioners, or city council, respectively, who may remove any overseer, and fill all vacancies.

Their compensation. Removal. Vacancies.

Prisoners supposed to be reformed may be discharged. Ibid, § 13. See *ante*, § 5.

9. Whenever it shall appear to the overseers or directors of any house of correction, house of industry or workhouse, that any person there confined, on a conviction before any justice of the peace, of either of the offences mentioned in the fifth section above, except stealing money or goods not exceeding the value of five dollars, has reformed, and is willing and desirous to return to an orderly course of life, they may, in their discretion, by a written order, discharge such person from confinement; and if such person shall have been committed by the court of common pleas, the municipal court of the city of Boston, or any police court, he may be discharged by said courts, respectively, upon

the recommendation of the overseers or directors; and if a person so discharged shall afterwards be convicted of any of the said offences, committed after the former conviction, either in the same or a different county, he may be sentenced by the magistrate or court, before whom the second conviction is had, to hard labor in the house of correction, house of industry, or workhouse, for a term not exceeding one year.

Their sentence if again convicted.

Materials for work. R. S. 143, § 14.

10. The commissioners in the several counties, and the overseers of the house of correction in Boston, shall cause to be provided, at the expense of the city, and of the respective counties, suitable materials and implements, sufficient to keep at work all the persons committed to the house of correction, according to law, and may, from time to time, establish such rules as they shall think needful, for the employment and government of the persons so committed, for the procuring and preservation of such materials and implements, and for the keeping and settling of all accounts of the costs and other expenses of procuring the same, and of all labor performed by each of the persons so committed; they shall also determine, from time to time, what sum the master shall receive, for the board of the persons so committed to his custody, and the master shall receive such further compensation for his services, in addition to the price allowed him for the board of those who are so committed, as the commissioners in their counties, and the city council in Boston, shall deem just and reasonable.

Compensation of master.

Master's claim for keeping, &c., how allowed and paid. Ibid, § 15.

11. The overseers of each house of correction shall, on the application of the master or keeper thereof, twice in each year, and oftener if they shall think necessary, examine and audit his accounts for the care and expense of supporting and employing the persons committed to his custody; they shall certify what sum is due for the supporting and employing of each of the said persons, after deducting the net profit, if any, of his labor; if any of the said persons shall refuse or neglect to pay the sum, so certified by the overseers to be due, for the space of fourteen days after demand in writing by such master or keeper, he may commence his action at law, by a general indebita-

tus assumpsit, and recover against such person the sum found to be justly due, which shall be deemed to be his [his] own proper debt; but the defendant in such action may prove on the trial, that the whole sum, allowed and certified by the overseers, was not justly due, and he may tender, or bring into court, such sum of money as he shall admit to be due to the plaintiff in such action, as in other cases.

12. Whenever the said overseers shall certify that any sum is due as aforesaid, for supporting and employing in the house of correction any person who has not sufficient estate to pay the same, and such person shall have a parent, master, or kindred, liable by law to maintain him, the said master or keeper may demand and recover such sum as may be justly due, of the person or persons so liable; if such pauper have no parent, master, or kindred, liable by law to maintain him, the same may be demanded and recovered of the town wherein he shall have his lawful settlement,[1] and upon refusal or neglect to make payment, for the space of thirty days after the same shall have been demanded, in writing, of the parent, master or kindred, or of any member of the city council of the city, or any overseer of the poor of the town respectively liable by law therefor, the said master or keeper, at any time within two years after his account shall have been so certified, and not afterwards, may commence and maintain his action at law for the same, against the party so liable, in the same form of action, and subject to the same defence, which are prescribed and allowed in the preceding section; provided, that the city of Boston shall be entitled to the same remedies for maintaining any person in the house of correction in said city, which are provided for the masters or keepers of houses of correction.[2]

Master may demand and recover such sum as may be due. Ibid, § 16. 20 Pick., 112. 22 Pick., 211.

Proviso as to Boston.

13. Any person, convicted of an offence, punishable wholly or in part by imprisonment in the county jail, may be

Courts may sentence to jail or house of correction. R. S. 143, § 17.

[1] But not exceeding one dollar per week. See 1843, c. 66, § 3, i. e. § 27, *post*.

[2] The provisions of this section are modified by stat. 1839, c. 146, § 2, c. 156, and 1843, c. 66. See §§ 23–27, pp. 224, 225, *post*.

sentenced to suffer such imprisonment in the house of correction, instead of the jail, or to suffer solitary imprisonment and be confined at hard labor, either in the jail or the house of correction.

Same subject. Ibid, § 18.

14. If any boy, under the age of sixteen years, shall be convicted of an offence, which is punishable by imprisonment in the state prison, such convict not having been before sentenced to imprisonment in the state prison in this state, or in any state prison or penitentiary within the United States, the court, if sentence of solitary imprisonment and confinement at hard labor, for a term not exceeding three years, is awarded against such convict, and also when the sentence of confinement, at hard labor, for any term of time, is awarded against a female convict of whatever age, shall order such sentence to be executed, either in the house of correction or in the county jail, and not in the state prison; but the provisions of this and the preceding section shall not prevent the courts in the city of Boston, from sentencing such convicts to confinement in any place, in which juvenile offenders may be by law confined.

Certain convicts in Boston may be sent to the house of reformation.

Sentence of certain convicts not before sentenced. Ibid, § 19.

15. When the punishment of solitary imprisonment, and confinement at hard labor for a term not exceeding three years, shall be awarded by the court against any convict, who has not been before sentenced to the like punishment, by any court in this state, or within the United States, such sentence may be executed, either in the house of correction, or in the county jail, or in the state prison.

Sentence to solitary confinement and hard labor, in jails, &c , how and where to be executed. Ibid, § 20.

16. When any convict shall be sentenced to solitary imprisonment and hard labor, in any house of correction or jail, the master or keeper thereof shall execute such sentence of solitary imprisonment, by confining the convict in one of the cells, if there be any in such house of correction or jail, and if there be none, then in the most retired and solitary part of such house or jail; and, during the time of solitary imprisonment, such convict shall be fed with bread and water only, unless other food shall be necessary for the preservation of his health: No intercourse shall be allowed with any convict in solitary imprisonment, except for the conveyance of food, and other necessary purposes, unless

some minister of the gospel shall be disposed to visit him, in the manner hereafter provided.

17. As soon as the term of solitary imprisonment shall have expired, the master or keeper shall furnish the convict with tools and materials, or with other means, to work in any suitable manner, in which he can be usefully or profitably employed, either in the said house of correction or jail, or within the close yard thereof; such convict may, if necessary, be confined by a log and chain, or in such other manner as shall prevent his escape, without unnecessarily inflicting bodily pain, or interrupting his labor; the overseers of the house of correction, or, when such punishment is inflicted in the jail, the sheriff of the county, shall oversee the execution of all such sentences.

How convict shall be kept at work, and confined. Ibid, § 21.

18. If any convict shall be refractory, or, during the time for which he is sentenced to hard labor, shall refuse or neglect, without reasonable cause, to labor in any suitable manner, when required, such convict, so long as he shall continue to be refractory, or shall refuse or neglect to labor, shall be kept in solitary confinement, and fed with bread and water only, in the manner before provided.

Punishment of prisoners refusing to work, &c. Ibid, § 22.

19. The commissioners, and the mayor and aldermen of the city of Boston, may order such sums of money, as may from time to time be necessary, to be advanced out of the treasuries of their respective counties, to the master of the house of correction, or keeper of the jail, for the purpose of providing such tools and materials, and such other things, as may be required for the employment, restraint, and safe keeping of the convicts.

Advancement of money for tools and materials. Ibid, § 23.

20. All money, so advanced, shall be by such master or keeper appropriated, under the direction of the officers, by whose order the same was advanced, and he shall account to them for the expenditure of the same.

Such money and proceeds of labor to be accounted for. Ibid, § 24. 1839, 146, § 1.

21. Such master or keeper shall cause the articles, manufactured by the prisoners in his custody, or the produce of their labor, to be disposed of to the best advantage, and accounts to be kept of the proceeds of the same; all such accounts shall be presented to and settled by the

How articles manufactured, &c., shall be disposed of. R. S. 143, § 25. See R. S. 143, § 24, and 1839, 146, § 1.

said officers, semiannually, and as much oftener as they shall think necessary; such master or keeper shall pay into the treasury of the county, at such times as the said officers shall direct, the amount of sales, and other proceeds of the labor and earnings of the prisoners in his custody, or the balance thereof.[1]

Expense of supporting convicts, how paid. R. S. 143, § 27.

22. All charges and expenses of safe keeping, maintaining, and employing convicts, who have been sentenced to imprisonment in the county jail or house of correction, except such part thereof as may be reimbursed by their labor, and also the expense of the safe keeping of all persons, charged with offences and committed for trial, shall be paid from the county treasury, the accounts of the keeper or master being first settled and allowed by the commissioners of such county, and in the county of Suffolk, by the board of accounts; but not more than one dollar per week shall be paid by the Commonwealth, for the support of any such person, and no allowance from the county treasury shall be made to any keeper or master, for the support of any prisoner, committed to such jail or house of correction, by virtue of the provisions contained in the fifth and sixth sections of the one hundred and forty-third chapter of the Revised Statutes,[2] when such prisoner shall be of sufficient ability to support himself, or shall have either parent, master or kindred, who are able, and obliged by law to maintain him, or when such prisoner shall have a legal settlement within this state.[3]

What expense may be recovered of towns, or prisoner's kindred. 1839, 146, § 2.

23. No master or keeper of any house of correction shall have a right to demand and recover of any city or town in which any person sentenced to such house of correction has a lawful settlement, or of any kindred of such person liable by law to maintain him, any further or greater

---

[1] Section 26, of the 143d chapter of the Revised Statutes, was repealed by stat. 1839, c. 146, § 1.

[2] That is, §§ 5 and 6, in the text, pp. 217–219, *ante*.

[3] The provisions of this section have been since modified by stat 1839, c. 156, and 1843, c. 66. See sections 23–27, pp. 224, 225, *post*.

sum than the amount of the personal expenses of the maintenance of such person during his confinement therein, deducting therefrom such sum as he may have earned by his personal labor: *provided*, that this section shall not apply to any claim which the master or keeper of the house of correction in the city of Boston may have upon said city, for expenses incurred in said house of correction. Proviso.

24. No allowance shall be made by the commonwealth for the maintenance and support of any prisoner in any jail or house of correction, after the first day of July, 1839; but the expense of maintaining and supporting all such prisoners as have no legal settlement in this commonwealth, shall be borne by the county in which such jail or house of correction is established. No allowance to be made by the commonwealth, after July 1, 1839. 1839, 156.

25. Whenever any person shall be committed to the house of correction in any county for any offence mentioned in the fifth section of the one hundred and forty-third chapter of the Revised Statutes,[1] and the person so committed shall have a legal settlement in any town in this commonwealth, it shall be the duty of the master, keeper, or overseers of such house of correction, immediately to notify the selectmen of such town in writing, by mail or otherwise, of such commitment. Notice to be given to selectmen, when vagabonds, &c., who have a settlement in any town, are committed to house of correction. 1843, 66, § 1.

26. Whenever any person shall be committed to any house of correction in this commonwealth for any offence not mentioned in the fifth section of the one hundred and forty-third chapter of the Revised Statutes,[1] the expense of his safe keeping, support and maintenance, shall not be recoverable against any town in this commonwealth, but shall be paid in the manner provided by law. Towns not held to support persons committed to house of correction, for offences not mentioned in R. S. 143, § 5. 1843, 66, § 2.

27. Not more than one dollar per week shall be recoverable of, or demanded against, any town for the safe keeping, support and maintenance, of any person committed to any house of correction. Towns not liable for more than $1 a week for support of prisoners in house of correction. Ibid, § 3.

28. The commissioners for the several counties, and in the county of Suffolk, the judge of probate, and the justices of the police court, shall be inspectors of the prisons in the Inspectors of prisons. R. S. 143, § 28. 1843, 61, § 2.

---

[1] That is, § 5, in the text, pp. 217, 218, *ante*.

Their duties. said counties, respectively, and shall, by themselves or their committee, visit and inspect the jails, houses of correction, and all other places of confinement or imprisonment, within their respective jurisdictions, and shall fully examine into every thing relating to the government, discipline and police thereof; and the keeper of each jail, and master of each house of correction, shall make returns, at least twice in each year, to the said inspectors, at such time and in such form as they shall direct, setting forth the names, ages, and residence, if known, of all persons who are or have been in custody, since the last return, the cause of their imprisonment, and the manner in which they have been treated and employed, the punishments inflicted, if any, and the names of all persons, who have died, escaped, been pardoned or discharged, with all other circumstances, required by the inspectors.

Keepers, masters, &c., to make returns.

Duties of inspectors. R.S. 143, §§ 29, 30.

29. The said inspectors in the county of Suffolk shall, by a committee of not less than three of their members, visit, and inspect twice in each year, once in June or July, and once in December, the jail, the house of correction, and all other places of imprisonment and confinement, established by law in the city of Boston; and such committee shall, as soon as may be after each inspection, make and subscribe a detailed report to the said mayor and aldermen, in relation to the prisons in the city of Boston, stating the condition of each prison, as to health, cleanliness and discipline, at the time of inspection; the number of persons confined there within the six months next preceding, or since the last inspection, and for what causes; the manner in which convicts, if any, have been employed; the number of persons usually confined in one room; the distinction, if any, usually observed in the treatment of the different classes of persons detained in such prisons; the punishments which have been inflicted; the evils or defects, if any, in the construction, discipline or management, of such prisons; the names of the prisoners, who have died, escaped, been pardoned or discharged; and whether any of the provisions of law, in relation to such prisons, have been

To make reports.

violated or neglected, with the causes, if known, of such violation and neglect.[1]

30. Whenever the said inspectors, or any of them, shall visit any of the said prisons, either for the purpose of inspection, or any other cause, the sheriff, master, keeper, or other officer, having charge thereof, shall admit the said inspectors, when required, into every apartment of such prison, exhibit all books, precepts, documents, accounts and papers, which may be required, relating to the concerns of the prison, or to the detention or confinement of any person therein, and afford to the inspectors, or their committee, such aid as may be requested, in the performance of any part of their duties; the inspectors or their committee may examine, on oath, to be administered by one of them, either by interrogatories in writing, to be answered in writing and subscribed, or otherwise, as they may direct, any officer, keeper or other person, in relation to the concerns or management of any prison; they may also converse with any of the prisoners, apart and without the presence of any officer or keeper.

Powers of inspectors. Ibid, § 31.

31. If it shall appear to the inspectors in any county, from the report of their committee or otherwise, that any of the provisions of law, in relation to prisons, have been violated or neglected, in their county, they shall forthwith give notice thereof to the county or district attorney.

Shall give notice of violations of law, &c. Ibid, § 32.

32. Said inspectors shall cause to be transmitted to the governor, on or before the second Wednesday of January, in each year, authentic copies of any information, by them given to the county or district attorney, in relation to any violation or neglect of the law respecting prisons, with such further statements and suggestions, as may, in their opinion, require the attention of the government.

Inspectors to transmit to the governor, copies of any such information. Ibid, § 33. 1840, 15, § 3.

33. No sheriff, jailer, master of a house of correction, or other officer or under keeper of any prison, shall, under

Spirit and strong drink prohibited, unless, &c. R. S. 143, § 34.

---

[1] The 29th section of the 143d chapter of the Revised Statutes, was so amended by stat. 1845, c. 221, that the county commissioners, by a committee of not less than two of their number, shall, twice in each year, visit and inspect all the prisons in their county, provided the interval between the visits and inspections of said prisons shall not exceed eight months.

any pretence, give, sell or deliver, or knowingly suffer to be given, sold, or delivered, to any person committed to jail for debt, and supported at the charge of the creditor, or to any prisoner in confinement upon conviction or charge of any offence, any spiritous liquor, or mixed liquor, part of which is spiritous, or any wine, cider, or strong beer, unless the attending physician of the prison shall certify in writing, that the health of such prisoner requires it, in which case he shall be allowed the quantity prescribed, and no more.

Classification and separation of prisoners. Ibid, § 35.

34. Male and female prisoners shall not be put or kept in the same room, in any jail or house of correction; nor, unless the crowded state of the jail or house of correction shall require it, shall any two prisoners, other than debtors, be allowed to occupy the same room, except for work: every jailer shall keep all persons committed for debt, separate from felons, convicts and persons confined upon a charge of felony or other infamous offence, and shall prevent all conversation between prisoners in different apartments. All minors, in prison upon conviction or charge of an offence, shall be kept separate from those, who are notorious offenders, or who have been convicted of any felony or other infamous crime: no person, committed on charge of an offence, shall be confined with a convict, nor shall any prisoner, charged with or convicted of an offence not infamous, be confined with one charged with or convicted of an infamous crime, except while at labor, or when assembled for moral or religious instruction, at which times no communication shall be allowed between prisoners of different classes.

Penalties for neglect of duty, by sheriff, jailer, &c. Ibid, § 36.

35. If any sheriff, jailer, or master of any house of correction, shall give, sell or deliver, to any prisoner in his custody, or shall willingly or negligently suffer any such prisoner to have or drink any spiritous, fermented or other strong or mixed liquor, prohibited by the thirty-third section, or shall place or keep together prisoners of different sexes, or different classes, in his custody, contrary to the provisions of the preceding section, he shall in each case forfeit for the first offence, the sum of twenty-five dollars,

and for any such offence committed after the first conviction, fifty dollars, to the use of the county; and such officer shall, on such second conviction, be further sentenced to be removed from office, and to be incapable of holding the office of sheriff, deputy sheriff or jailer, or master or keeper of any prison, for the term of five years.

Penalty for furnishing, or attempting to furnish, spirits to prisoners. Ibid, § 37.

36. If any person shall give, sell or deliver, to any person committed to prison for debt, and supported at the charge of the creditor, or to any prisoner, in confinement upon conviction or charge of any offence, any spiritous or other liquors, as mentioned in the said thirty-third section, or shall have in his possession, within the precincts of any jail or house of correction, or other like place of confinement, mentioned in the one hundred and forty-third chapter of the Revised Statutes, any such liquors, with intent to convey or deliver the same to any person or prisoner confined therein, he shall be punished by fine, not exceeding fifty dollars, or by imprisonment in the county jail or house of correction, not more than two months; and no jailer, or master, or keeper of any house of correction, house of industry or work-house, shall be licensed to sell any strong or mixed liquors, as a retailer or otherwise.

Regulations concerning health and cleanliness of jail, and house of correction. Ibid, § 38.

37. The keeper of each jail, and the master of every house of correction, shall see that the same is constantly kept in as cleanly and healthful a condition as may be, and shall cause the whole interior thereof, including the floors, to be thoroughly whitewashed with lime, at least twice in each year; and the walls and floors of each room, while any person shall be confined therein, between the first of May and the first of November, shall be so whitewashed, once in each month, at the expense of the county: no permanent vault shall be used in any apartment, or part of any jail or house of correction, and where any such vault now exists, the same shall be securely closed up; every room, which is occupied by a prisoner, in any such prison, shall be furnished with a suitable bucket, with a cover made to shut tight, for the necessary accommodation of such prisoner; and such bucket, when used, shall be emptied daily, and shall be constantly kept in good order.

Personal cleanliness of prisoners. Ibid, § 39.

38. Such keeper and master, shall see that strict attention is constantly paid to the personal cleanliness of all the prisoners in their custody, as far as may be, and shall cause the shirt of each prisoner to be washed, and the prisoner himself to be shaved, once at least in each week: each prisoner shall be furnished daily with as much clean water, as he shall have occasion for, either as drink, or for the purpose of personal cleanliness, and with a clean towel once a week: no clothes shall be washed, or hung out wet, in any room which is occupied by a prisoner during the night: all the prisoners, not in solitary confinement, shall be served, three times each day, with wholesome food, which shall be well cooked, in good order, and in sufficient quantity.

Food.

Each prisoner shall have a weekly bath, unless, &c. 1848, 324, § 1.

39. Each prisoner, who may be confined in any of the prisons of the commonwealth, shall have a weekly bath of cold or tepid water, which shall be applied to the whole surface of the body; unless, by reason of the sickness of such prisoner, such bath shall be hurtful or dangerous.

Ventilation. Ibid, § 2.

40. The state-prison, and the houses of correction, shall, within six months after May 10th, 1848, be ventilated in a suitable and efficient manner.

Instruction in reading and writing. Ibid, § 3.

41. The warden and inspectors of the state-prison, the county commissioners of each county, the mayor and aldermen of the city of Boston, with the sheriffs of each county, respectively, are hereby authorized to furnish, at the expense of said counties, suitable instructions in reading and writing, for one hour each evening, (except Sundays,) to all such prisoners as may be benefited by such instruction, and desirous to receive the same.

Prisoners to have bibles. R. S. 143, § 40.

May be visited by ministers.

42. The said keeper or master shall provide, at the expense of the county, for each prisoner under his charge, who may be able and desirous to read, a copy of the bible or of the new testament, to be used by such prisoner, at proper seasons, during his confinement; and any minister of the gospel, disposed to aid in reforming the prisoners, and instructing them in their moral and religious duties, shall have access to them, at seasonable times, either while

in solitary imprisonment, or when not required to be employed in labor.

43. The county commissioners of the several counties in this commonwealth are authorized, at their discretion, and at the expense of their respective counties, to provide moral and religious instruction for the prisoners confined in the jails and houses of correction of their respective counties.

County commissioners authorized to provide moral and religious instruction. 1848, 29, § 1.

44. The inspectors of prisons in the several counties, shall cause to be transmitted, in their annual returns to the governor, a statement of the expense incurred in carrying the preceding section into effect in their respective counties.

Inspectors shall return a statement of the expense. Ibid, § 2.

45. If any disease shall break out in any jail or other prison, which, in the opinion of the inspectors of such prison, may endanger the lives or health of the prisoners, to such a degree as to render their removal necessary, the said inspectors may designate, in writing, some suitable place within the same county, or any prison in a contiguous county, as a place of confinement for such prisoners; and such designation, being filed with the clerk of the court of common pleas for the county, shall be a sufficient authority for the sheriff, jailer, master or keeper, to remove all the prisoners in his custody to the place designated, and there to confine them, until they can be safely returned to the place whence they were removed; and any place, to which the prisoners shall be so removed, shall, during their imprisonment therein, be deemed a prison of the county in which they were originally confined, but they shall be under the care, government and direction of the officers of the county in which they are confined.

Removal of prisoners, in case of pestilence. R. S. 143, § 41.

46. If any jail or other prison, or any building near thereto, shall be on fire, and the prisoners shall be exposed to danger by such fire, the sheriff, jailer, or other person having charge of such prison, in his discretion, may remove such prisoners to a place of safety, and there confine them, so long as may be necessary to avoid such danger; and such removal and confinement shall not be deemed an escape of such prisoners.

Removal, in case of danger from fire. Ibid, § 42.

Removal of prisoners to different jails, in the same county. Ibid, § 43.

47. In any county, in which there are several jails, the sheriff may cause the prisoners in his custody, to be confined in either of such jails, and may, at his discretion, remove them from one jail to another, within his county, for their health or safe keeping, or for the purpose of their more convenient appearance at any court.

Supply of fuel, &c., and allowance therefor. Ibid, § 44.

48. The keeper of each jail, and the master of each house of correction, shall furnish, at the expense of the county, necessary fuel, bedding and clothing, for all prisoners who are in custody upon charge or conviction of any offence against the commonwealth, and the necessary charges therefor shall be allowed, in the manner following; the said keeper or master shall present to the commissioners for the county, or, in the county of Suffolk to the board of accounts, a full account of all charges, by him incurred for fuel, bedding and clothing for such prisoners, and also for necessary furniture, for the said prison; and the said commissioners, or board of accounts, shall make a reasonable allowance therefor, which shall be paid to the said keeper or master out of the county treasury.

Jailer, &c., to obey orders for furnishing specific rations, under penalty. Ibid, § 45.

49. Whenever the commissioners of any county, or the mayor and aldermen of the city of Boston, shall direct specific rations or articles of food, soap, fuel, or other necessaries, to be furnished to the prisoners in any jail or house of correction, the keeper or master thereof shall conform to such direction; and if he shall neglect or refuse to furnish the same, he shall be subject to the same penalties, for a first and a second offence, which are prescribed by the thirty-fifth section, above, for the offences therein mentioned.

Restraint and punishment of refractory prisoners. Ibid, § 46.

50. If any person, confined in any jail or house of correction, upon any conviction or charge of an offence against the commonwealth, shall be refractory or disorderly, or shall wilfully or wantonly destroy or injure any article of bedding, or other furniture, or a window, door, or any other part of such prison, the sheriff of the county, and the overseers of the house of correction, respectively, after due inquiry, may cause such person to be kept in solitary confinement, not more than ten days for any one offence; and

during such solitary confinement, he shall be fed with bread and water only, unless other food shall be necessary for the preservation of his health.

51. If any person, committed to jail on mesne process or on execution, or for any other cause, than those mentioned in the preceding section, shall be guilty of either of the offences therein specified, and be thereof convicted before a justice of the peace for the county, or a police court, on complaint of the keeper thereof, he shall be punished by solitary imprisonment, as directed in the preceding section, not more than ten days for any one offence; such offender shall also be liable for double the amount of the damage done to the jail, furniture or other property, to be recovered with costs of suit, in an action of trespass, which may be brought by the sheriff or county treasurer, in the name and to the use of the county.

Same subject. Ibid, § 47.

Recovery for damage done.

52. Nothing contained in the two preceding sections shall be construed to take from any sheriff, jailer, or master of any house of correction, any part of the authority, with which he was before invested by the law, to preserve order and enforce strict discipline among all the prisoners in his custody.

Sheriff's and keeper's authority. Ibid, § 48.

53. If any person, lawfully imprisoned in any jail or house of correction, under sentence of confinement at hard labor, shall break such prison and escape, he shall be punished by imprisonment in the state prison or county jail not more than three years, in addition to the unexpired portion of the term for which he was originally sentenced.

Punishment of prisoners for escaping. Ibid, § 49.

54. If any person, lawfully imprisoned in any jail, house of correction, or house of industry, for any cause not mentioned in the preceding section, shall break such prison and escape, he shall be punished by imprisonment, either in the state prison, the county jail or house of correction, not more than one year, in addition to the unexpired portion of the term for which he was originally sentenced.

Same subject. Ibid, § 50.

55. If any person, lawfully imprisoned for any cause in any prison or place of confinement established by law, other than the state prison, shall forcibly break the same, with intent to escape, or shall by any force or violence attempt

Punishment for attempting to escape. Ibid, § 51.

to escape therefrom, although no escape be effected, he shall be punished by imprisonment in the county jail or house of correction, not more than one year, in addition to any term for which he was held in prison, at the time of such breaking or attempt to escape.

Secretary to prepare and transmit blank forms of returns. 1840, 15, § 1.

56. It shall be the duty of the secretary of the commonwealth, annually, under the direction of the governor and council, to prepare a blank form of return concerning jails and houses of correction as they shall exist on the first day of November, and the individuals who shall have been confined therein within the year ending on that day, with such inquiries concerning the same as may be considered proper and expedient; and the secretary shall transmit said blanks to the sheriffs, and to the overseers of the houses of correction in the several counties, in the month of September.

Sheriffs and overseers of houses of correction, to make true yearly returns. Ibid, § 2.

57. The sheriffs and the overseers of the houses of correction of the several counties shall annually, on or before the fifteenth day of November, transmit to the secretary of the commonwealth true answers to the inquiries contained in the blanks aforesaid; and the secretary shall prepare an abstract therefrom, and shall submit the same, in a printed form, to the legislature, at the ensuing session thereof.

Secretary to amend form of return, so as to give information respecting insane and idiotic persons. 1849, 74, § 1.

58. It shall be the duty of the secretary of the commonwealth to amend the blank form of return, required by the two preceding sections, so that accurate information shall be obtained in relation to such insane and idiotic persons as are under the charge of the keepers of jails, or houses of correction, or other county receptacles for these purposes, in the following particulars, viz: the number, name, age, birthplace, duration of insanity, duration of confinement, means of support, place of confinement, specifying whether in jails, houses of correction, or in buildings specially provided for the purpose, cause of commitment, by whom committed, whether previously subjected to any curative treatment and at what place, their present condition, whether they are furnished with employment, under whose care they are now placed, and if any of them are under the superintendence of convicts.

59. The secretary shall embody these returns in such manner as he shall deem advisable. Same subject. Ibid, § 2.

60. No city or town shall, hereafter, erect or maintain an almshouse, or house of correction, within the limits of any other city or town, unless the consent of the inhabitants of the city or town, within which such almshouse or house of correction is proposed to be erected or maintained, shall have been first obtained, at a legal meeting of the inhabitants of said town or city.[1] No city or town shall erect an alms-house or house of correction within another city or town, without consent of the latter. 1848, 291, § 1.

HOUSE OF INDUSTRY.[2]

[1] For further provisions respecting houses of correction generally, and offences punishable by confinement therein, see Rev. Stat. c. 143, 1837, c. 157, 217; 1840, c. 15; 1842, c. 59; 1846, c. 11; 1847, c. 160; and 1848, c. 276. For provisions respecting insane convicts, see 1836, c. 223; 1842, c. 100; 1844, c. 120; and Lunatics. For provisions respecting jails, see R. S. c. 143, 145; act of amendment, § 19; 1836, c. 223; 1837, c. 157, 217; 1839, c. 156; 1840, c. 15; 1842, c. 59, 100; 1845, c. 221; 1846, c. 11, 78, 88; 1847, c. 160, 165; 1848, c. 29, 276, 324. See also House of Reformation.

[2] Some account of the origin and history of the House of Industry may be found in the appendix.

Directors of the house of industry to be chosen. 1833, 126, § 1.

1. The city council of the city of Boston are empowered, whenever they deem it expedient, to appoint, by concurrent ballot in each board, a sufficient number of persons, not exceeding twelve, a majority of whom shall constitute a quorum for the transaction of business, to be directors of the house of industry in the said city, who shall hold their office for the term of one year, and until others are appointed in their place; and said city council are further empowered, in like manner, to fill all vacancies which may occur in said board of directors, during the year for which it is appointed. And said directors may appoint a superintendent, and any other officers necessary for the government of said house, and shall have all the powers, and be subject to all the duties prescribed to said board by virtue of the several acts to which this is in addition.[1]

Vacancies, to be filled.

Superintendent and other officers.

Powers of the directors as to the house. 1822, 56, § 2.

2. The act of 1822, ch. 56, § 2, provided that the directors of the house of industry shall have and exercise the like authority and power, in using, regulating and governing said house of industry, as are had and exercised by overseers of the poor within this commonwealth, and may

[1] This section appears to supersede the 1st section of stat. 1822, c. 56, in relation to the number of directors, and the time of choosing.

send such persons to said house, and for such purposes, as overseers of the poor are by law authorized to do. [1]

3. The directors of the house of industry in the city of Boston shall have and exercise all the powers and perform all the duties relative to paupers, and the binding out of children and other persons committed to said house of industry for support, as the overseers of the poor of the several towns in this commonwealth have and exercise, in relation to paupers and the binding out of children, and other persons, under and by virtue of the several laws of this commonwealth; and all acts of said directors shall impose the same duties, liabilities and obligations, in all judicial tribunals, on the city of Boston aforesaid, and on the several towns and individuals of this commonwealth, as the same acts would impose, if done and performed in the same manner by the overseers of the poor of the several towns in this commonwealth. [2]

Powers and duties of the directors as to binding out children. 18.6, c. 111. R. S. 80, § 27.

4. The said directors shall, in the month of April, in every year, make report in writing to the city council of the persons who shall have been resident in said house of industry, during the next preceding twelve months, and the manner in which such persons shall have been employed during their residence therein; and the said directors shall also render to the city council in the month of April, annually, an account of all moneys received and paid on account of the said house.

Directors to make annual reports. 1822, 56, § 4.

5. All rules and orders for the governing and managing said house of industry, shall, within two months after the same shall have been made, be submitted to the city council; and such rules and orders shall be in force until repealed or altered by the said directors, or until disapproved of by vote of the said city council.

Rules to be submitted to city council. Ibid, § 5.

6. No rules or orders shall be established for the governing and managing said house of industry, by the direc-

Five directors may establish rules. Ibid, § 6.

---

1 The 3d section of the stat. of 1822, c. 56, relates to powers given by stat. 1787, c. 54; which statute was repealed by the stat. of 1834, c. 151, and the latter statute was also repealed by the Revised Statutes. See also R. S. 143, § 5, and 1837, 217.

2 See §§ 8–29, pp. 238–242, *post*, for provisions in relation to apprentices.

tors thereof, unless at a meeting at which five or more of said directors are present.[1]

Remedies for recovering expenses of the support of paupers. 1824, 28, § 1.

7. By an act passed June 12, 1824, it was provided that the city of Boston should be entitled to the same remedies in order to recover the expenses of supporting any poor person maintained in the house of industry of said city, that towns in this commonwealth were entitled to for the recovery of the expenses of persons, for whom support or relief was provided by overseers of the poor, or under their direction.[2]

APPRENTICES.

Overseers of the poor may bind children of paupers, and pauper children. R. S. 80, § 6. 2 Pick. 451. 16 Pick. 44. 19 Pick. 358. 7 Greenl. 457. 4 N. Hamp. R. 139.

8. The overseers of the poor may bind, as apprentices or servants, the minor children of any poor person, who has become actually chargeable to their town, as having a lawful settlement therein, or who is supported there, in whole or in part, at the charge of the commonwealth, and also all minor children, who are themselves chargeable to the town, as having a lawful settlement therein, or as poor persons supported by the commonwealth.[3]

Until what age, and upon what terms. R. S. 80, § 7. 5 Pick. 250.

9. Such children, whether under or above the age of fourteen years, may be bound, females to the age of eighteen years, or to the time of their marriage within that age, and males to the age of twenty-one years; and provision shall be made in the contract, for teaching such children to read, write and cypher, and for such other instruction, benefit and allowance, either within or at the end of the term, as the overseers may think reasonable.

---

[1] This section would not seem to be in force, in case the city council should choose such a number of directors, that a less number than five would constitute a quorum, under stat. 1833, c. 126, § 1. See § 1.

[2] For general provisions respecting workhouses, almshouses, overseers of the poor, and paupers, see R. S. c. 16, 45, 46, 143; stat. 1837, c. 54, 194, 217; 1841, c. 116; 1844, c. 146; 1846, c. 88; 1848, c. 247, 291; 1849, c. 66, 74, 151. See House of Correction, Paupers and Overseers of the Poor.

[3] The powers hereby given to overseers of the poor, are given to the directors of the house of industry in Boston, or such other officers as have the care or charge of the poor in said city. See § 29, *post*, p. 242. See, also, § 3, *ante*, p. 237.

10. No minor shall be so bound by the overseers, unless by an indenture of two parts, sealed and delivered by the overseers and by the master, one part of which shall be deposited with the town clerk, and be safely kept by him for the use of the minor.

By indenture of two parts; one to be kept for the minor. R. S. 80, § 8.

11. All considerations, of money or other things, paid or allowed by the master, upon any contract of service or apprenticeship, made in pursuance of this chapter, shall be paid or secured to the sole use of the minor thereby bound.

Money, &c., paid by any master, to be for the use of the apprentice. Ibid, § 9.

12. Parents and guardians, and selectmen and overseers, shall inquire into the treatment of all children, bound by them respectively, or with their approbation, and of all who shall have been bound by their predecessors in office, and defend them from all cruelty, neglect, and breach of contract, on the part of their masters.

Parents, selectmen, &c., to inquire into the treatment of children. Ibid, § 10.

13. In case of any such misconduct or neglect of the master, a complaint may be filed by the parents, guardian, selectmen, or overseers, in the court of common pleas for the county in which the master resides, setting forth the facts and circumstances of the case, and the court, after having duly notified the master, shall proceed to hear and determine the cause, with or without a jury, as the allegations of the parties may require.

May file a complaint for misconduct of the master in C. C. P. Ibid, § 11.

14. After a full hearing of the parties, or of the complainants alone, if the master shall neglect to appear, the court may render a judgment or decree, that the minor be discharged from his apprenticeship or service, and for the costs of the suit against the master, and may award execution accordingly, and the minor may be thereupon bound out anew.

The court may thereupon discharge the apprentice, &c. Ibid, § 12.

15. If the complaint shall not be maintained, the court shall award costs for the master against the complainants, and shall issue execution accordingly; excepting, that in case of such a complaint by selectmen or overseers, the court shall not award costs against them, unless it shall appear that the complaint was made without any just or reasonable cause.

May award costs for the master. Ibid, § 13.

16. Every master shall moreover be liable, whether such complaint shall have been filed or not, to an action on the

Master also liable to an action on the indenture. Ibid, § 14.

indenture, for the breach of any covenant on his part therein contained; and all damages recovered in such action, after deducting the necessary charges in prosecuting the same, shall be the property of the minor, and may be applied and appropriated to his use, by the person who shall recover the same, and the residue, if any, shall be paid to the minor, if a male, at his age of twenty-one years, and if a female, at her age of eighteen years, or at the time of her marriage within that age.

By whom such action may be brought. Ibid, § 15.

17. Such action may be brought, either by the parent, or his executors or administrators, or by the guardian, or any one who shall succeed him in that trust, or by the overseers or their successors in that office, or it may be brought in the name of the minor, by his guardian or next friend, as the case shall require, or by himself, after the expiration of the term of apprenticeship or service.

Proceedings therein, when brought by the overseers. Ibid, § 16.

18. If the action is brought by the overseers, it shall not abate by the death of any of them, or by their being succeeded in office, but shall proceed in the names of the original plaintiffs, or the survivor of them, or the executors or administrators of the survivor; and the money recovered therein shall be deposited in the town treasury, to be applied and disposed of as provided in the sixteenth section.

Limitation of such action by the apprentice. Ibid, § 17.

19. No such action shall be maintained by the apprentice or servant, unless it be commenced during the term of apprenticeship or service, or within two years after the expiration thereof.

In case of judgment for the plaintiff, the court may discharge the apprentice. Ibid, § 18.

20. If judgment in such action, by whomsoever brought, shall be rendered for the plaintiff, in the court of common pleas, or the supreme judicial court, the court may also, upon the motion of the plaintiff, discharge the minor from his apprenticeship or service, if it shall not have been already done in the manner before provided, and the minor may be thereupon bound out anew.

Apprentice absconding may be arrested, and returned, or imprisoned. Ibid, § 19.

21. If any apprentice or servant, bound as aforesaid, shall unlawfully depart from the service of his master, any justice of the peace, upon complaint on oath made to him by the master, or by any one in his behalf, may issue his warrant to apprehend the apprentice or servant, and bring

him before the said justice; and if the complaint shall be supported, the justice may order the offender to be returned to his master, or may commit him to the common jail or house of correction, there to remain for a term not exceeding twenty days, unless sooner discharged by his master.

22. The justice's warrant, when directed to any officer or other person by name, shall authorize him to convey the offender to the place of residence of the master, although it may be in any other county in the state. Proceedings in such case. Ibid, § 20.

23. All the costs, incurred in any such process against a servant or apprentice, shall be paid, in the first instance, by the complainant; and if the complaint shall be supported, the amount of the costs may be recovered by the master, in an action on the indenture, if the same were executed by a parent or guardian, and if recovered against a guardian, the amount paid by him in such action may be charged by him in his guardianship account; and if the indenture were executed by overseers of the poor, or by the minor with the approbation of the selectmen, the amount of such costs may be recovered in action against the minor, after he shall arrive at full age. Costs therein, of whom recoverable. Ibid, § 21.

24. If any such apprentice or servant shall be guilty of any gross misbehavior, or refusal to do his duty, or wilful neglect thereof, his master may file his complaint in the court of common pleas, for the county in which he resides, setting forth the facts and circumstances of the case, and the court, after having duly notified the apprentice or servant, and all persons who have covenanted on his behalf, and also the selectmen, who shall have approved of the indentures, or their successors in that office, shall proceed to hear and determine the cause, with or without a jury, as the allegations of the parties may require. Master may file a complaint for misconduct of the apprentice, and proceedings thereon. Ibid § 22. 2 Pick. 451

25. After a full hearing of the parties, or of the complainant alone, if the adverse parties shall neglect to appear, the court may render a judgment or decree, that the master be discharged from the contract of apprenticeship or service, and for the costs of the suit; such costs to be recovered of the parent or guardian of the minor, if there be any who executed the indenture, and execution therefor to be issued Master may be thereupon discharged from the contract. R. S. 80, § 23.

accordingly; and if there be no parent or guardian liable for such costs, the amount thereof may be recovered in an action against the minor, after he shall arrive at full age; and any minor discharged as aforesaid, may be bound out anew.

Apprenticeship discharged by the death of the master. Ibid, § 24.

26. No indenture of apprenticeship or service, made in pursuance of the eightieth chapter of the Revised Statutes,[1] shall bind the minor after the death of his master, but the apprenticeship or service shall be thenceforth discharged, and the minor may be bound out anew.

Minor may be bound to a mistress, to whom all the foregoing provisions shall apply. Ibid, § 25.

27. Any indenture of apprenticeship or service, made in pursuance of said eightieth chapter, by or in behalf of a minor, may be made either with a woman or a man, and all the foregoing provisions shall apply as well to mistresses as to masters.

Common law right not affected. Ibid, § 27. 7 Mass. 147. 1 Mason, 78. 8 Johns. R. 328. 3 B. & A. 584. 1 Ashm. 267.

28. Nothing contained in said eightieth chapter shall prevent or affect the right of a father, by the common law, to assign or contract for, the services of his children for the term of their minority, or of any part thereof.

Provisions as to city of Boston. R. S. 80, § 27.

29. Everything, which is prescribed in the preceding twenty-one sections to be done by the selectmen of any town, shall and may be done by the mayor and aldermen of the city of Boston; and everything, prescribed to be done by the overseers of the poor of any town, shall and may be done by the overseers of the poor of the said city, or by the directors of the house of industry therein, or by such other officers as shall have the care and charge of the poor in said city.

HOUSE OF REFORMATION.

STATUTES.

1. City council may erect or use buildings in the city, for juvenile offenders.
2. Children convicted of criminal offences may be received by directors.
3. Appeal from judgment of the police court, under the second section, to the municipal court.
4. Children leading an idle or dissolute life, &c., may be sentenced to the house of reformation. To be kept, &c., till of age.

---

[1] That is, the chapter containing §§ 8—29 in the text.

1. By the act of 1825, c. 182, § 1, passed March 4, 1826, the city council of the city of Boston were authorized to erect a building in said city, for the reception, instruction, employment and reformation of such juvenile offenders, as are hereinafter named; or to use for these purposes the house of industry, or correction, at South Boston, or any other house or building belonging to said city, that the city council might appropriate to these uses.

City council may erect or use buildings in the city for juvenile offenders. 1825, 182, § 1.

2. The directors of the said house of industry, or such other persons as said city council shall appoint directors of said house, for the employment and reformation of juvenile offenders, shall have power, at their discretion, to receive and take into said house all such children who shall be convicted of criminal offences or taken up and committed under and by virtue of an act of this commonwealth, "for suppressing and punishing of rogues, vagabonds, common beggars, and other idle, disorderly and lewd persons,"[1] and who may, in the judgment of any justice of the supreme judicial court, sitting within and for the county of Suffolk, or of the judge of the municipal court of the city of Boston, or of any justice of the police court within and for the city of Boston, be proper objects therefor; and upon the conviction or commitment aforesaid, of any child, in the judgment

Children convicted of criminal offences may be received by directors. Ibid, § 2.

[1] The act here cited, i. e. stat. 1787, c. 54, was repealed by stat. 1834, c. 151, § 22 and the latter statute was itself repealed by the Revised Statutes. Most of the provisions of the former in relation to the punishment of the class of offences named therein, are incorporated in Rev. Stat. 143, § 5. See House of Correction, pp. 217, 218, § 5, *ante*.

of such judge or justice a proper object for the said house of employment and reformation, the said judge or justice, previously to declaring the sentence of the law on such child, shall cause notice to be given to the directors of the said house; and in case the said directors shall declare their assent to the admission of such child into said house, the said judge or justice shall sentence him or her to be committed to said house of employment and reformation, subject to the control of the directors thereof, in conformity with the provisions of the succeeding sections.

Appeal from judgment of the police court, under the second section, to the municipal court. 1829, c. 18.

3. Any party aggrieved by the sentence of the police court, or any justice thereof, passed pursuant to the second section, may appeal from such sentence, to the next municipal court in the said city, whose judgment shall be final, as in other cases of appeals from the judgment of justices of the peace, to the courts of common pleas, in criminal cases; the party appealing recognizing with sufficient surety or sureties, to the satisfaction of the justice of the police court, by whom the sentence is passed, to enter and prosecute such appeal, and in the mean time to keep the peace, and be of good behavior.

Children leading an idle or dissolute life, &c., may be sentenced to house of reformation. 1825, 182, § 3.

4. Any justice or judge of either of the said courts respectively, on the application of the mayor, or of any alderman of the city of Boston, or of any director of the house of industry, or house of reformation, or of any overseer of the poor, of said city, shall have power to sentence to said house of employment and reformation all children who live an idle or dissolute life, whose parents are dead, or if living, from drunkenness, or other vices, neglect to provide any suitable employment, or exercise any salutary control over said children. And the persons thus committed, shall be kept, governed and disposed of, as hereinafter provided, the males till they are of the age of twenty-one years, and the females of eighteen years.[1]

To be kept, &c., till of age.

---

[1] All of this section except the last sentence, was substantially re-enacted by stat. 1847, c. 208, § 1. See § 10, p. 248, *post.*

5. The directors of said house of industry, or such other persons as said city council shall appoint directors of the institution, authorized by the first section, may receive the persons sentenced and committed as aforesaid, into said institution; and they shall have power to place the persons committed to their care, the males until they arrive at the age of twenty-one years, and the females until they arrive at the age of eighteen years, at such employments, and to cause them to be instructed in such branches of useful knowledge, as shall be suitable to their years and capacity; and they shall have power to bind out said minors as apprentices or servants, until they arrive at the ages aforesaid, to such persons, and at such places, to learn such arts, trades, and employments, as in their judgment will be most for the reformation, amendment, and future benefit and advantage of such minors. And the provisions of an act, entitled "an act providing for the relief and support, employment and removal of the poor, and for repealing all former laws made for these purposes," passed the twenty-sixth day of February, in the year of our Lord one thousand seven hundred and ninety-four, contained in the fourth, fifth and sixth sections thereof, so far as they relate to binding out children as servants or apprentices, are adopted as a part hereof; and the said directors shall have all the powers, and be subject to all the duties, of the overseers of the poor, as set forth in the sections aforesaid, of the act aforesaid; and the master or mistress, servant and apprentice, bound out as aforesaid, shall have all the rights and privileges, and be subject to all the duties, set forth in the sections aforesaid, of the act aforesaid.[1]

Directors to employ and instruct children. Ibid, § 4.

Shall have power to bind out.

To have powers, &c., of the overseers of the poor.

---

[1] The sections of the act referred to, (stat. 1793, c. 59, which was repealed by the Revised Statutes,) are as follows:—

SECT. 4. *And be it further enacted*, That said overseers be and they hereby are empowered, from time to time, to bind out, by deed indented or poll, as apprentices, to be instructed and employed in any lawful art, trade, or mystery, or as servants to be employed in any lawful work or labor, any male or female children, whose parents are lawfully settled in and become actually chargeable to their town or district; also, whose parents, so settled, shall be thought by said overseers to be unable to maintain them

Overseers authorized to bind out poor children.

Court may discharge, on recommendation of directors. Ibid, § 5.

6. Whenever said directors, overseers, or managers, shall deem it expedient to discharge any minor, committed to their charge as aforesaid, and not bound out as a servant or apprentice, and shall recommend the same in writing to the court by whom such minor was committed, said court

---

Proviso.

(whether they receive alms, or are so chargeable or not,) *Provided*, They be not assessed to any town or district charges, and also all such who, or whose parents residing in their town or district, are supported there at the charge of the commonwealth, or whose parents are unable to support them as aforesaid, to any citizen of this commonwealth; that is to say, male children till they come to the age of twenty-one years, and females till they come to the age of eighteen, or are married; which binding shall be as valid and effectual in law as if such children had been of the full age of twenty-one years, and had, by a like deed, bound themselves, or their parents had been consenting thereto: Provision to be made in such deed for the instructing of male children, so bound out, to read, write and cypher, and of females to read and write, and for such other instruction, benefit and allowance, either within or at the end of the term, as to the overseers may seem fit and reasonable.

Provision for instruction of children that are bound out.

Duty of overseers respecting such children.

SECT 5. *And be it further enacted*, That it shall be the duty of said overseers, to inquire into the usage of children already legally bound out, or that may be bound out by force of this act, and to defend them from injuries. And upon complaint by such overseers, made to the court of common pleas in the county where their town or district is, or where the child may be bound, against the master of any such child, for abuse, ill treatment or neglect, said court (having duly notified the party complained of) may proceed to hear the complaint, and if the same be supported, and the cause shall be judged sufficient, may liberate and discharge such child from his or her master, with costs, for which execution may be awarded; otherwise the complaint shall be dismissed, but without costs, unless it appear groundless and without probable cause, in which case costs shall be allowed the respondent.

Court C. Pleas authorized to discharge such children from their master, in case, &c.

Apprentices discharged, may be bound anew. Overseers may recover damages for breach of covenants in the deed.

And any apprentice or servant, so discharged, or whose master shall decease, may be bound out anew for the remainder of the term, in manner aforesaid. And such overseers may also have remedy, by action on such deed, against any person liable thereby, for recovery of damages for breaches of any of the covenants therein contained, which, when recovered, shall be placed in the town or district treasury, deducting reasonable charges, and disposed of by the overseers, at their discretion, for the benefit and relief of such apprentice or servant within the term; the remainder, if any, to be paid him at the expiration thereof; and the court before which such cause shall be tried originally, and on the appeal, may also, upon the plaintiff's request, if they see cause, liberate and discharge such apprentice or servant from his master, if it hath not then been already done in the method before directed by this act. And such apprentice or servant shall have like remedy when their term is expired, for damages for the causes aforesaid, other than such (if any) for which damages may have been re-

Apprentices may also have action on the deed.

shall have power to discharge him or her from the imprisonment or custody aforesaid.

7. The said judge or either of the said justices, on the application of either of the persons mentioned in the fourth section, shall have power to order the transfer of any child committed to the common jail, or the house of correction,

Children already committed to house of correction may be transferred to house for juvenile offenders. Ibid, § 6.

---

covered as aforesaid, by action upon such deed to be delivered them for that purpose, and on which no endorsement shall be necessary: *Provided*, Such action be commenced within two years after the expiration of the term; and where such deed shall have before been put in suit, an attested copy from the proper office may be used and have the same force as the original. And no action brought by overseers shall abate by the death of some of them, or by their being succeeded in office, pending the action, but it shall proceed in the names of the original plaintiffs or the survivors of them.

Proviso.

And in case of elopement, any such apprentice or servant may be apprehended by any justice of the peace of the county, where he is bound or where he may be found, upon the complaint of the master, or any other on his behalf, and returned to his master by any person to whom the warrant may be directed, or may be first sent to the house of correction at the justice's discretion. And every person enticing any such apprentice or servant to elope from his master, or harboring him, knowing him to have eloped, shall be liable to the master's action for all damages sustained thereby. And the court of common pleas, either in the county where the overseers binding, or the master of any apprentice or servant bound, live, may also, upon complaint of such master, for gross misbehavior, discharge such apprentice or servant from his apprenticeship or service, after due notice to such overseers, and hearing thereupon.

In case of elopement, apprentices may be apprehended.

Persons enticing to elope, liable to action of the master.

Common pleas may discharge apprentices for misbehavior.

SECT. 6. *And be it further enacted*, That said overseers shall have power to set to work, or bind out to service by deed, as aforesaid, for a term not exceeding one whole year at a time, all such persons residing and lawfully settled in their respective towns or districts, or who have no such settlement within this commonwealth, married, or unmarried, upwards of twenty-one years of age, as are able of body, but have no visible means of support, who live idly, and use and exercise no ordinary or daily lawful trade or business to get their living by; and also all persons who are liable by any law to be sent to the house of correction, upon such terms and conditions as they shall think proper. *Provided, always*, That any person thinking him or herself aggrieved by the doings of said overseers, in the premises, may apply, by complaint, to the court of common pleas in the county where they are bound, or where the overseers who bound them dwell, for relief; which court, after due notice to the overseers and to their masters, shall have power, after due hearing and examination, if they find sufficient cause, to liberate and discharge the party complaining from his or her master, and to release him or her from the care of the overseers, otherwise to dismiss the complaint, and to give costs to either party or not, as the court may think reasonable.

Overseers authorized respecting persons of age.

Proviso, that court may revise overseers' doings.

and inmates of the same, on March 4, 1826, to the said house for the employment and reformation of juvenile offenders, to be received, kept, or bound out by the directors thereof, in conformity with the foregoing provisions.

Separate branch for females may be established. 1843, 22, § 1.

8. The city of Boston is authorized to establish, in any building or buildings, or part of any building, used by said city, as a house of industry, or for any other purpose, a separate branch or branches of said house of reformation and employment, for females, or for the separate classification of such females.

Children leading an idle or dissolute life, &c., may be sentenced to house of reformation. 1847, 208, § 1.

9. The municipal or police court of said city, upon the complaint, under oath, of the mayor or any alderman thereof, or of any of the directors of the house of industry, or of the said house of reformation and employment, or of the overseers of the poor of said city, that any minor, under the age of sixteen years, lives an idle and dissolute life, and that his parents are dead, or, if living, do, from vice or any other cause, neglect to provide suitable employment for, or to exercise salutary control over such minor, shall have power, upon conviction thereof, to sentence such minor to such house of reformation and employment, to be kept and governed according to law.

Right of appeal saved. Ibid, § 2. 1843, 22, § 3.

10. Nothing in the two preceding sections is to be construed to take away the right of appeal from the police court to the municipal court.[1]

ORDINANCE OF THE CITY.[2]

Directors of house of industry appointed directors of house of reformation. City Records, vol. 19, p. 172.

SECT. 1. The directors of the house of industry are hereby appointed directors of the house of reformation, with authority to take such steps as may be necessary to

---

[1] See the acts respecting the State Reform School, 1847, c. 165, and 1850, c. 112.

[2] The house of reformation was originally established in a portion of the building occupied as a house of correction, and was under the care of the directors of the house of industry until 1833, when a separate board was chosen. In 1841 a committee was appointed, of which Mr. Chapman,

unite the same with the Boylston Asylum, now under their charge, and henceforward to use the building for the new institution, which shall be called the Boylston School and House of Reformation, but shall be a part of the house of industry, and which is hereby declared to be also the institution for the reception, instruction, employment, and reformation of juvenile offenders, under the act passed March 4th, 1826. House of reformation united with Boylston Asylum.

SECT. 2. The said directors shall have all the rights and powers of the directors of the house of reformation, as to all children who have been heretofore indented from the said house, and as to protecting the rights, and superintending the welfare of said children, and enforcing the provisions of said indentures. Rights and powers of directors. Ibid.

INTELLIGENCE OFFICES.

STATUTE.

1. No person shall establish or keep an intelligence office, without a license, under penalty.
2. Mayor and aldermen may grant and revoke licenses for establishing and keeping intelligence offices.

1. No person shall hereafter establish or keep any intelligence office, for the purpose of obtaining places of employment for male or female family domestics, servants, or other laborers, except seamen, or for procuring or giving No person shall establish or keep an intelligence office, without a license, under penalty. 1848, 270, § 1.

---

the mayor, was chairman, "with instructions to consider the whole subject of the house of reformation, and whether any change is expedient in the law establishing said institution, and to report by ordinance or otherwise." This committee reported, among other things, that it was expedient to place this institution under the charge of the directors of the house of industry; and they reported two orders to that effect, which were adopted June 28, 1841, and are inserted above. See City Documents of 1841, Nos. 6 and 14. See also City Records, vol. 4, pp. 24, 46, 52, 112, (b), 148, 149, 200, 223, 333; vol. 10, pp. 145, 147, 480; vol. 11, pp. 127, 149, 250, 324; vol. 12, p. 283; vol. 19, p. 172.

information concerning such places for or to such domestics, servants, or laborers, or for the purpose of procuring, for employers, domestics, servants, or other laborers, except seamen, or procuring or giving information concerning such domestics, servants, or laborers, for or to employers, without a license as hereinafter provided, under a penalty of not less than ten dollars for each and every day such office shall be so kept, to be recovered, by complaint, in any court of competent jurisdiction.

Mayor and aldermen may grant and revoke licenses. Ibid, § 2.

Fee.

2. The mayor and aldermen of any city, may grant licenses, for the term of one year, to suitable persons, for the foregoing purposes, and may revoke and annul the same whenever they may deem it expedient; and they shall be entitled to have and recover, for each and every license so granted, the sum of one dollar and no more.

LAMPS.

Mayor and aldermen empowered to set up lamps, and make rules respecting the same. 1825, 3, § 1.

1. It shall be lawful for the mayor and aldermen of the city of Boston for the time being, to cause to be set up and affixed, such and so many lamps in the streets and other places in the said city, for the purpose of lighting the same, as they may determine to be convenient and necessary. And the said mayor and aldermen are empowered to make all necessary contracts, rules, orders, and regulations, respecting the said lamps, and the lighting and keeping the same in repair, and the regulation and preservation of the same, as they may deem most for the benefit of said city.

Penalties for wilfully break-

2. Whoever shall wilfully, maliciously, carelessly or wantonly break, throw down, extinguish, or otherwise in-

jure any of the said lamps, or the posts, irons, or other furniture to the same belonging, shall upon conviction thereof, forfeit and pay a sum not less than ten dollars nor more than thirty dollars for each lamp so broken or damnified, and the like sum for each post or the iron or other furniture so broken or damaged, and costs of prosecution; which fines and forfeitures shall enure, the one moiety thereof to the use of the commonwealth, and the other moiety to the use of the person who shall prosecute for the same.[1]

ing or injuring the same, &c. Ibid, § 2. 1823, 113, §§ 1, 2.

3. Every person who shall wilfully or maliciously extinguish any lamp, or break, destroy or remove any lamp, or any lamp post, or any railing or posts, erected on any bridge, sidewalk, street, highway, court or passage, shall be punished by imprisonment in the county jail, not more than six months, or by fine not exceeding fifty dollars.[2]

Penalty for the same, under the Revised Statutes. R. S. 126, § 43.

LEATHER.

STATUTES.

1. Deputy inspectors of sole leather to be appointed, and to give bond.
2. Inspector general to make annual returns.
3. Sole leather not to be sold until inspected, weighed and sealed, except, &c.
4. Penalty for buying or selling sole leather, not inspected.
5. Inspector to inspect sole leather offered for inspection, except, &c.
6. Deputy inspector to inspect on application, &c.
7. Sole leather to be weighed and stamped.

---

1 The stat. of 1825, c. 3, provided for the same penalties mentioned in stat. 1823, c. 113, to be recovered and appropriated in the same manner. The statute last mentioned was repealed by the Revised Statutes. The 3d section of stat. 1825, c. 3, repealed an old act, passed June 29, 1773; 3 Sp. Laws, App. 27.

2 Whether this section is applicable to Boston and operates as a repeal of the preceding section, (stat. 1825, c. 3, § 2,)—*quære.*

Deputy inspectors of sole leather to be appointed, and to give bond. R. S. 28, § 121.

1. The inspector general of sole leather[1] shall appoint one or more deputy inspectors; and in the city of Boston, they shall be appointed upon the application of the mayor and aldermen, and in any town on application of the selectmen thereof; and the said inspector general shall be answerable for the doings of his deputies, and shall take a bond, with sufficient sureties, from each of them to himself and his successors in office, in a penal sum not exceeding three hundred dollars.

Inspector general to make annual returns. Ibid, § 122.

2. The inspector general of sole leather shall annually, in the month of January, make a return, to the secretary of the commonwealth, of the number and weight of all the sides of sole leather, inspected by him and his deputies during the year, ending on the first day of that month; and in such return, he shall designate the quantity of each quality of leather so inspected, and the quantity of sole leather manufactured out of the state, so far as the same can be ascertained.

Sole leather not to be sold until inspected, weighed and sealed, except, &c. Ibid, § 123.

3. No sole leather, made of the hides of neat cattle, except such as shall have been previously inspected and sealed by one of the inspectors of this state, or by some inspector lawfully appointed for that purpose in some other of the United States, shall be sold to any person, for any purpose whatsoever, within any town in which there is an inspector, whether such sole leather is manufactured within

[1] The inspector general of sole leather is appointed by the governor, with the advice and consent of the council, and holds his office for five years unless sooner removed. He is required to give bonds, with sufficient sureties, to the treasurer of the commonwealth, in the penal sum of three thousand dollars. See Rev. Stat. c. 28, §§ 1, 2, 3, 4, 120.

this state or brought into the same from any place whatsoever, until the same shall have been inspected, weighed and sealed, by one of the inspectors of such town[1] within this state.

Penalty for buying or selling sole leather not inspected. Ibid, § 124.

4. If any person shall, within any town,[1] for which an inspector has been appointed, buy or sell any sole leather, which shall not have been inspected as aforesaid, he shall forfeit one dollar for each side of leather so bought or sold, to be recovered to the use of the town where the offence shall have been committed.

Inspector to inspect sole leather offered for inspection, except, &c. Ibid, § 125.

5. Every inspector, whenever requested, shall inspect, within the town for which he is appointed, all sole leather offered for his inspection; provided, however, that when there shall be less than thirty sides of leather to be inspected, and the distance shall be more than one mile from his place of residence, he may either require such sole leather to be brought to him for inspection, or may demand and shall be entitled to receive at the rate of ten cents for each mile, which he shall travel in such case, to be computed both in going from and returning to his place of residence.

Deputy inspector to inspect on application, &c. Ibid, § 126.

6. Each deputy inspector, who is appointed for any one town in a county, shall, upon application made to him, inspect sole leather in any other town of the same county, when there is no inspector for such other town; and he shall also, upon the like application, inspect sole leather in any town of any adjoining county, when there is no inspector appointed in such adjoining county.

Sole leather, how weighed and stamped. Ibid, § 127.

7. Each inspector shall furnish himself with proper scales, weights and seals, for the purpose aforesaid; and shall weigh each side of sole leather which he shall inspect, and shall impress thereon his name, and the name of the place for which he is inspector, at full length, and also the weight thereof; and on all sole leather, which he shall find manufactured of good hides, in the best manner, he shall impress the word *best*, and on all manufactured of good hides, in a merchantable manner, the word *good*, and on all

---

[1] In the construction of statutes, the word "town" may be construed to include all cities, &c. Rev. Stat. c. 2, § 6, clause 17.

manufactured of damaged hides, in a merchantable manner, the word *damaged*, and on all sole leather not belonging to any of the qualities aforesaid, the word *bad*.

Penalty for counterfeiting, &c., inspectors' marks. Ibid, § 128.

8. If any person shall counterfeit, alter or deface, such marks on any side of sole leather, so inspected, he shall for each offence forfeit the sum of twenty-five dollars, to the use of the town where the offence shall have been committed.

Fees. Ibid, § 129.

9. The inspector general and each deputy inspector shall be paid for inspecting, weighing and sealing each side of sole leather, the sum of two cents, which shall be paid by the purchaser; and the inspector general may receive, from each of his deputies, two mills for each side of sole leather, which such deputy may inspect, weigh and seal as aforesaid.

Penalty when weight varies five per cent. Ibid, § 130.

10. If any side of sole leather shall, when dried in a merchantable manner, so vary as to weigh five per cent. more or less than the weight marked thereon by the inspector, who inspected the same, he shall be subject to the payment of the whole variation, at a fair valuation, to be recovered, in an action of the case, by the party injured thereby.

Manufacturers may stamp their articles. Ibid, § 131.

11. Each manufacturer of leather, or of boots, half boots, shoes, pumps, sandals, slippers or over-shoes, shall have the exclusive right of stamping said articles, by him manufactured, with the first letter of his christian name, and the whole of his surname at large, and the name of the town or place of his abode; and such stamping shall be considered as a warranty that the article stamped is merchantable, and made of good materials and well manufactured; and none of the said articles shall be considered as merchantable, unless stamped as aforesaid.

Such stamp a warranty.

Penalty for fraudulently stamping. Ibid, § 132.

12. Any person, who shall fraudulently stamp, or aid and abet in fraudulently stamping, either of the articles enumerated in the preceding section, with the name or stamp of any other person, shall be punished either by fine, not exceeding one hundred dollars, or imprisonment, not exceeding six months, or both.

Measurers of upper leather to be appointed by

13. The mayor and aldermen of the several cities, and the selectmen of the several towns in this commonwealth,

shall, annually, in the month of April, when thereto requested by two or more citizens of said cities or towns, appoint one or more persons as measurers of upper leather, who shall be sworn to the faithful discharge of their duty. mayor and aldermen. 1841, 119, § 1.

14. It shall be the duty of said measurers, appointed, as aforesaid, to go, whenever requested, to any place within the town or city for which they are appointed measurers, to measure and seal any number of sides of upper leather, made of the hides of neat cattle, buffalo or other animal, usually heretofore sold by measure, except such as shall have been previously measured and sealed by one of the measurers of the same town or city, or of some other town or city in this state, or by some person lawfully appointed for that purpose, in some other of the United States. To attend to measuring and sealing upper leather. Ibid, § 2.

15. Each measurer shall furnish himself with proper racks or measures, for the purpose of ascertaining the number of square feet in each side of upper leather which he shall be requested to measure, and also suitable seals, and shall impress thereon his name, and the name of the place for which he is a measurer, at full length, and also the measure thereof in square feet, as low as a quarter. To procure measures and seals for the purpose, &c. Ibid § 3.

16. If any person shall counterfeit, wilfully alter, or deface such marks on any side of upper leather so measured, he shall, for each offence, forfeit the sum of twenty-five dollars, one half to the use of the complainant, and one half to the use of the town where such offence shall have been committed. Penalty for counterfeiting, &c., measurers' marks. Ibid, § 4.

17. Every measurer shall be paid for measuring and sealing each side of upper leather, the sum of one cent, which shall be paid by the person who shall have requested him to measure and seal the same. Fees of measurer, and how paid. Ibid, § 5.

LIBRARY.

STATUTE.

City of Boston authorized to establish a public library.

City of Boston authorized to establish a public library. 1848, 52.

By the act of 1848, c. 52, the city of Boston is authorized to establish and maintain a public library, for the use of the inhabitants of the said city; and the city council of the said city may, from time to time, make such rules and regulations, for the care and maintenance thereof, as they may deem proper; *provided, however*, that no appropriations for the said library shall exceed the sum of five thousand dollars, in any one year.[1]

LICENSED HOUSES.

STATUTE.

1. Innholders' and retailers' licenses may be granted by commissioners, and the mayor and aldermen, &c. Licenses shall specify place, and shall protect no other.
2. Victuallers' licenses, in Boston.
3. All licenses to expire on the first of April.
4. Fee for licenses.
5. Licenses to sell wine, &c., may be granted without fee.
6. The mayor and aldermen, &c., shall forbid innholders, &c., selling to spendthrifts.
7. Such prohibition to be renewed, if no reform is effected. Penalty for transgressing such prohibition.
8. Same subject.
9. Licensed houses in Boston.
10. License may authorize the keeping of an inn, &c., without authority to sell liquor.
11. Licenses may be granted for the sale of intoxicating liquors, for mechanical and medicinal purposes only.

---

[1] The second section of this act contained a provision that it should be null and void unless it should be accepted by the city council within sixty days after its passage. The act was passed March 18, 1848. It was accepted April 3, 1848. See City Records, vol. 26, p. 125.

For general provisions concerning libraries and lyceums, see R. S. c. 41, and 1846, c. 94.

1. The commissioners, in the several counties, may license, for the towns in their respective counties, as many persons to be innholders, or retailers therein, as they shall think the public good may require; and the mayor and aldermen of the city of Boston may, in like manner, license innholders and retailers, in the said city; and the court of common pleas in the county of Suffolk may, in like manner, license innholders and retailers in the town of Chelsea; and every license, either to an innholder or retailer, shall contain a specification of the street, lane, alley, or other place, and the number of the building, or some other particular description thereof, where such licensed person shall exercise his employment; and the license shall not protect any such person from the penalties, provided in the forty-seventh chapter of the Revised Statutes, for exercising his employment in any other place, than that which is specified in the license.

Innholders' and retailers' licenses may be granted by commissioners, and the mayor and aldermen, &c. R. S. 47, § 17.

Licenses shall specify place, and shall protect no other.

2. The mayor and aldermen of the city of Boston may license, for the said city, as many persons to be common victuallers, as they shall think the public good may require;[1] and every such license shall contain such a specification or description, as is mentioned in the preceding section, of the street, or other place, and of the building, where the licensed person shall exercise his employment; and the license shall not protect him from the penalties, provided in said forty-seventh chapter, for exercising it in any other place.

Victuallers' licenses in Boston. Ibid, § 18.

3. All licenses to any innholder, retailer, or common victualler, shall expire on the first day of April, in each year; but any license may be granted or renewed, at any time during the preceding month of March, to take effect from the said first day of April; and after that day, they may be granted for the remainder of the year, whenever the officers authorized to grant the same shall deem it expedient.

All licenses to expire on the first of April. Ibid, § 19.

4. Every person who shall be licensed as before provided, shall pay therefor to the clerk of the city of Boston,

Fee for licenses Ibid, § 20.

[1] See House of Correction, p. 229, § 36, *ante*.

the clerk of the court of common pleas for the county of Suffolk, or to the clerk of the commissioners of the respective counties so licensing said person, one dollar, which shall be paid by said clerks to the treasurers of their respective counties, for the use of said counties; and such person shall also pay twenty cents to the use of the said clerks respectively; and no other fee or excise whatever shall be taken from any person, applying for or receiving a license, under the provisions of the said chapter.

Licenses to sell wine, &c., may be granted without fee. Ibid, § 21.

5. Any license to an innholder, retailer, or common victualler, may be so framed as to authorize the licensed person to sell wine, beer, ale, cider, or any other fermented liquor, and not to authorize him to sell brandy, rum, or any other spiritous liquor; and no excise or fee shall be required for such a license.

The mayor and aldermen, &c., shall forbid innholders, &c., selling to spendthrifts. Ibid, § 14.

6. When any person shall, by excessive drinking of spiritous liquors, so misspend, waste or lessen his estate, as thereby either to expose himself or his family to want or indigent circumstances, or the town to which he belongs to expense, for the maintenance of him or his family, or shall so habitually indulge himself in the use of spiritous liquors, as thereby greatly to injure his health or endanger the loss thereof, the selectmen of the town, in which such spendthrift lives, shall, in writing under their hands, forbid all licensed innholders, common victuallers and retailers of the same town, to sell to him any spiritous or strong liquors aforesaid, for the space of one year; and they may in like manner forbid the selling of any such liquors to the said spendthrift, by the said licensed persons of any other town to which the spendthrift may resort for the same; and the city clerk of the city of Boston shall, under the direction of the mayor and aldermen thereof, issue a like prohibition, as to any such spendthrift living in the said city.

Such prohibition, to be renewed, if no reform is effected. Ibid, § 15.

Penalty for transgressing such prohibition.

7. The said mayor and aldermen, and said selectmen, shall, in the same manner, from year to year, renew such prohibition, as to all such persons as have not in their opinion reformed within the year; and if any innholder, common victualler or retailer, shall, during any such prohibition,

sell to any such prohibited person, any such spiritous liquor, he shall forfeit for each offence twenty dollars.

8. When the said mayor and aldermen, or selectmen, in execution of the foregoing provisions, shall have prohibited the sale of spiritous liquors to any such spendthrift, if any person shall, with a knowledge of said prohibition, give, sell, purchase, or procure for and in behalf of such prohibited person, or for his use, any such spiritous liquors, he shall forfeit for each offence twenty dollars.

Same subject. Ibid, § 16.

9. The mayor and aldermen of the city of Boston shall exercise and perform all the powers and duties of county commissioners, relating to licensed houses in the said city, as is prescribed in the forty-seventh chapter of the Revised Statutes.

Licensed houses in Boston. R. S. 84, § 8.

10. Any license to an innholder or common victualler may be so framed as to authorize the licensed person to keep an inn or victualling house, without authority to sell any intoxicating liquor, and no excise or fee shall be required for such license: *provided*, that nothing contained in this, or the nine preceding sections, shall be so construed as to require the county commissioners to grant any licenses when, in their opinion, the public good does not require them to be granted.

License may authorize the keeping of an inn, &c., without authority to sell liquor. 1837, 242, § 2.

11. The county commissioners, in the several counties, upon the recommendation of the selectmen of the towns in which such persons may reside, and the mayor and aldermen of the several cities, may authorize, by license, for a period of time not exceeding one year, and revocable at their pleasure, as many persons as they shall think the public good may require, to sell, in the towns or cities where they reside, intoxicating liquors in a less quantity than twenty-eight gallons, and that delivered and carried away all at one time, for mechanical and medicinal purposes only.[1]

Licenses may be granted for the sale of intoxicating liquors, for mechanical and medicinal purposes only. 1850, 232, § 2.

---

[1] For general laws respecting the sale of spiritous liquors, see R. S. c. 47; 1837, c. 242; 1840, c. 1; 1844, c. 102, 160; and 1850, c. 232.

LUMBER.

STATUTE.

Ordinances may be established respecting survey of lumber.

ORDINANCE.

1. Surveyor general of lumber to be appointed. Shall give bond.
2. May appoint deputy surveyors. Their duties. Proviso.
3. There shall be four sorts of pine boards and planks.
4. Two sorts of pine joists.
5. Two sorts of spruce, hemlock, and juniper boards, plank and joists.
6. Two sorts of ash, maple, and other hard wood, &c.
7. Two sorts of other timber.
8. One sort of mahogany and cedar. Manner of surveying the same.
9. Hewn timber. Sawed timber. Contents, how to be marked. Deduction. Lumber to be sold according to these marks. How surveys shall be made.
10. Fees; to be paid by the purchaser.
11. How collected and paid over.
12. Surveyor general to make annual returns.
13. Penalty for conniving at fraud. For neglect of duty.
14. Penalty for selling or purchasing lumber not surveyed, except, &c.

STATUTE.

City government may establish ordinances respecting survey of lumber. R. S. 28, § 155. 9 Greenl. 54.

In the city of Boston, the city government may establish any ordinances and regulations, with suitable penalties, respecting the appointment of surveyors and the survey and admeasurement of boards, plank, timber, and lumber of every description, brought by water into said city for sale, as they may from time to time determine to be expedient.

ORDINANCE OF THE CITY.[1]

Surveyor general of lumber to be appointed. July 25, 1842.

SECT. 1. There shall be a surveyor general of lumber, for the city of Boston, who shall be well skilled in the surveying and admeasurement of lumber, to be appointed in the month of February annually, by concurrent vote of the city council, who shall hold his office for one year, and

---

[1] An ordinance regulating the survey and admeasurement of lumber brought into the city of Boston by water, for sale, passed July 25, 1842; and an ordinance in addition thereto, passed December 31, 1847.

until a successor be chosen, unless sooner removed. And before he shall enter on the duties of his office, he shall give bond, with sufficient sureties, to the mayor and aldermen, in the sum of two thousand dollars, for the faithful discharge of his duty, and he shall be sworn faithfully to perform the same. Shall give bond.

SECT. 2. The said surveyor general of lumber shall have power to appoint such a number of competent and discreet deputy surveyors of lumber, clapboards and shingles, as he shall judge sufficient, not, however, less than twelve, nor more than twenty-two; out of which number he shall appoint one or more deputy surveyors, whose sole and especial duty it shall be to survey oak, and other hard wood commonly used in ship building; and also one or more deputy surveyors, whose sole and special duty it shall be to survey mahogany, ash, cedar, and other ornamental wood and lumber; and said surveyor general shall be answerable for his deputies, and shall take bond from them respectively for the faithful discharge of their duty, and they shall be sworn faithfully to perform the same, and they shall be removable at the pleasure of said surveyor general. And it shall be the duty of said surveyor general and his deputies to survey and admeasure all lumber brought into the city of Boston by water, for sale, according to the provisions of this ordinance: *provided*, that no person shall be appointed or continued in office as a deputy surveyor, who is employed by any dealer in the kind of lumber which he is appointed to survey, except in the duties of his office, or who is himself a dealer in that kind of lumber. May appoint deputy surveyors. Ibid, Dec. 1847. July 25, 1842. Their duties. Proviso.

SECT. 3. In the survey of pine boards and planks, there shall be four sorts; the first sort shall be denominated number one, and shall include boards not less than one inch thick, straight-grained, and free from rot, sap, knots and shakes. The second sort shall be denominated number two, and shall include boards not less than one inch thick, free from rot and large knots, and suitable for planing; provided that such boards as are clear, but are deficient in thickness as aforesaid, shall be received as number two by making such allowance for the deficiency in There shall be four sorts of pine boards and planks. Ibid.

thickness as may be required to make them equal to one inch thick. The third sort shall be denominated number three, and shall include boards not less than seven-eighths of an inch thick, nearly free from rot, and nearly square-edged, and suitable for covering buildings. The fourth sort shall be denominated number four, and shall include all boards and plank of every description, not being within the other three denominations.

Two sorts of pine joists. Ibid.

SECT. 4. In the survey of pine joists, there shall be two sorts; the first sort shall be denominated number one, and shall include all joists that are sound and square-edged; the second sort shall be denominated number two, and include all other descriptions.

Two sorts of spruce, hemlock, and juniper boards, plank and joists. Ibid.

SECT. 5. In the survey of spruce, hemlock, and juniper boards, plank and joists, there shall be two sorts; the first sort shall be denominated number one, and shall include all boards, plank and joists that are sound and square-edged. The second sort shall be denominated number two, and shall include all other descriptions.

Two sorts of ash, maple, and other hard wood, &c. Ibid.

SECT. 6. In the survey of ash, maple, and other hard wood, and ornamental boards, plank, and joists, there shall be two sorts. The first sort shall be denominated number one, and shall include all boards, plank, and joists, that are sound and free from shakes. The second sort shall be denominated number two, and shall include all other descriptions.

Two sorts of timber, except mahogany and cedar. Ibid.

SECT. 7. In the survey of timber, except mahogany and cedar, there shall be two sorts. The first sort shall be denominated number one, and shall include all timber that is sound, straight, square-edged, and in lengths or joints not less than sixteen feet in length, due allowance being made for sap. The second sort shall be denominated number two, and shall include timber of all other descriptions.

One sort of mahogany and cedar. Manner of surveying the same. Ibid.

SECT. 8. In the survey of mahogany and cedar, there shall be but one sort. And it shall be the duty of the surveyor general of lumber, and of his deputies, who are specially appointed to survey mahogany and cedar, to number all the mahogany and cedar logs or sticks, contained in each lot or cargo, in regular numerical order, and to mark the number of each log or stick upon the same, in legible characters. And the said surveyor shall, to the best of his ability, ascertain the whole number of feet, board measure, in each and every log or stick, and what quantity thereof is merchantable, and what is refuse. And said surveyor shall thereupon issue a certificate, or survey bill, of said survey, in which shall be stated the number of each log or stick, and the whole number of feet contained in the same, and specifying the number of feet which is merchantable and refuse.

SECT. 9. All hewn timber six inches square and upwards, except timber called scab, shall be surveyed and sold as ton timber, at and after the rate of forty cubic feet to a ton. All sawed timber shall be surveyed and sold by board measure. In the survey of boards, planks, joists and sawed timber, the contents of the same shall be truly marked thereon, in plain and legible numbers, and all other marks shall be erased. And on the second and third sorts of boards and planks, the numbers two and three shall be in like manner marked thereon respectively. Allowance and deduction shall be made for splits, not exceeding in any case one half the extent of the splits. All boards, planks, joists, and sawed timber, shall be received and sold according to the contents thereof as fixed and marked under the aforesaid regulations; but all surveys shall be made under the direction of the surveyor general, by his deputies; and application shall be made, by all persons requiring surveys, to the surveyor general, who shall in each and every case notify and direct his deputies in rotation.

Hewn timber. Ibid.

Sawed timber.

Contents, how to be marked.

Deduction for splits.

Lumber to be sold according to these marks.

How surveys shall be made.

SECT. 10. The fees for surveying and marking according to the foregoing provisions of this ordinance, and to be paid by the purchaser, shall be as follows, viz:—for pine, spruce, hemlock, and juniper boards, planks, joists, and sawed timber, twenty-four cents for every thousand feet, board measure; for pine, spruce, hemlock and juniper timber, twelve cents for every ton; for oak timber, twenty-four cents for every ton; for ash, maple, and other hard wood, and ornamental boards, plank and joists, forty cents for every thousand feet, board measure; for Cuba, St. Do-

Fees; to be paid by the purchaser. Ibid.

mingo and other branch or hard mahogany, one dollar for every thousand feet, board measure; and for mahogany from the bay of Honduras, and for cedar, seventy-five cents for every thousand feet, board measure.

How collected and paid over. Ibid.

SECT. 11. The deputy surveyors shall collect the fees, specified in the tenth section, as often as once in three months, and when collected shall pay over to the surveyor general, to his own use, ten cents for every hundred cents so collected and received by them.

Surveyor general to make annual returns. Ibid.

SECT. 12. It shall be the duty of the surveyor general annually, on the first Monday of February, to make a true return to the city council, of all lumber surveyed by his deputies, specifying the various kinds and qualities, and by whom surveyed, and the amount of all fees received by him and his deputies, pursuant to this ordinance.

Penalty for conniving at fraud. Ibid.

SECT. 13. If the said surveyor general, or either of his deputies, shall be guilty of, or connive at any fraud or deceit, in surveying, marking or numbering, the contents of any boards, plank, joists or timber, he shall forfeit and pay for every offence, a sum not less than ten dollars, nor more than twenty dollars. And if the surveyor general or his deputies, on due notice and request, shall unreasonably neglect or refuse to perform the duties enjoined by this ordinance, he shall forfeit and pay for every such offence, a sum not less than ten dollars nor more than twenty dollars; one half of the aforesaid forfeitures to be recovered by him or them who shall sue for the same to his or their use; and the other half to the use of the city of Boston, before any court of competent jurisdiction.

For neglect of duty.

Penalty for selling or purchasing lumber not surveyed, except, &c. Ibid.

SECT. 14. It shall not be lawful for any person within the city of Boston, to sell or to purchase any boards, plank, joists or timber, brought by water into said city, unless they shall be surveyed, marked and numbered, conformably to the provisions of this ordinance, except only such as are, *bona fide*, intended to be exported, and shall be actually shipped for the purpose of such exportation within one year after the same shall have been sold and delivered to the person first purchasing or receiving the same in said city. And every person who may sell or purchase any boards, plank, joists or timber, not surveyed, marked or numbered as herein is provided, subject only to the foregoing exceptions, shall forfeit and pay for all boards, plank, joists and timber so sold and purchased, double the amount of fees due for the services herein prescribed for the surveyor general and his deputies, to be sued for and recovered in any court of competent jurisdiction, by the surveyor general, or his deputy, one half thereof to the use of the person who shall sue for the same, and the other half to the use of the city of Boston.[1]

LUNATICS.

STATUTES.

1. Boston lunatic hospital to be erected.
2. Superintendent.
3. Ordinances respecting hospital may be passed.
4. Inspectors of prisons to be inspectors of hospital.
5. Amount to be allowed for support of persons confined. Fees.
6. Insane persons confined in house of correction, &c., and patients removed from state lunatic hospital, shall be confined in Boston lunatic hospital.
7. Boston police court may commit to Boston lunatic hospital in certain cases. Appeal to municipal court.
8. Notice of intended application to police court shall be first given to mayor, &c.
9. Mayor and aldermen may discharge from confinement. May provide for custody of lunatic in other places. Expense, how reimbursed.
10. Trustees of state lunatic hospital may remove lunatics, when necessary to accommodate others.
11. Remedies for recovering expenses of support of lunatic so removed.
12. A town that pays for support of lunatics, may recover the expense, of the town in which they have settlement.

ORDINANCE.

1. Board of visitors.
2. Rules and regulations to be submitted to city council.
3. Superintendent.
4. His duties.
5. Subordinate officers. Rules.
6. Superintendent to make annual report.

---

[1] For general laws respecting the survey of lumber, see R. S. c. 28, § 141–155.

34

STATUTES.

Boston lunatic hospital to be erected. 1839, 131, § 1.

1. The city council of the city of Boston are hereby authorized to erect and maintain a hospital, for the reception of insane persons not furiously mad; and provision shall be made for the comfortable support of all persons confined therein.

Superintendent. Ibid, § 2.

2. The said city council shall appoint a superintendent, who shall be a physician, and constantly reside at said hospital.

Ordinances respecting hospital may be passed. Ibid, § 3.

3. The said council shall have power to pass such ordinances as they may deem expedient for conducting, in a proper manner, the business of the institution, and for appointing such other officers as, in their opinion, may be necessary.

Inspectors of prisons to be inspectors of hospital. Ibid, § 4.

4. The inspectors of prisons for the county of Suffolk shall be inspectors of said hospital, and shall perform the like duties in relation to it that they are now by law required to perform in relation to the prisons in said county.[1]

Amount to be allowed for support of persons confined. Ibid, § 5.

5. [Whenever it shall be made to appear, on application in writing to the judge of the municipal court in the city of Boston, that any person is insane, not being furiously mad, the said judge is hereby authorized to order the confinement of such person in the said hospital: provided, that upon the request of such person, the question of his sanity shall be tried by a jury in said court.] Such sum per week shall be allowed and paid, for the support of every such person confined as aforesaid, as the mayor and aldermen of the city of Boston shall direct; and if, in any case, there shall be no parent, kindred, master, guardian, town or city, obliged by law to maintain the person so confined, and if he have no means of supporting himself, the same sum shall be paid out of the treasury of the commonwealth, for his support, as may be allowed for other lunatic or insane state paupers, [and any person, committed as aforesaid by said judge, may at any time be discharged, when, in his opinion, such discharge would be for the benefit of the per-

---

[1] See House of Correction, § 28–32, p. 225, 227, *ante*.

son so confined, or when, in his opinion, such person would be comfortably supported by any parent, kindred, friends, master or guardian, or by any town or city in which such person may have a legal settlement ;] and the [said] judge, jury and other officers, and all witnesses, shall receive the same fees and compensation for services performed and for attendance and travel, as are allowed by law for like services in criminal proceedings, to be taxed, allowed and paid in the same manner. [1]]

Fees.

6. All insane persons who are confined in the house of correction or the house of industry in said city, or may hereafter be subject to confinement therein, and all lunatics, idiots, and other patients, who shall be removed from the state lunatic hospital at Worcester, to the city of Boston, by the trustees thereof, by virtue of the fourteenth and fifteenth sections of the forty-eighth chapter of the Revised Statutes, shall hereafter be confined in the said Boston lunatic hospital. [2]

Insane persons confined in house of correction, &c., and patients removed from state lunatic hospital, shall be confined in Boston lunatic hospital. Ibid, § 6.

7. Whenever it shall be made to appear, on application in writing to the police court of the city of Boston, that any person is insane, not being furiously mad, and is either chargeable or likely to become chargeable to the city or the state, or being furiously mad, has his legal settlement in and is chargeable to said city, the said police court are hereby authorized to order the confinement of such person in the said Boston lunatic hospital, saving to the person complained against, the right to appeal from such order to the municipal court of the city of Boston, as is now allowed from other judgments of said police court by law. And upon his appeal, the question of his sanity shall, upon his request therefor, be tried by a jury in said court. If on such appeal it shall be made to appear that such person is

Boston police court may commit to Boston lunatic hospital, in certain cases. 1840, 79, § 1.

Appeal to municipal court.

---

[1] So much of the act, of which this section, forms a part, as relates to the commitment of persons to the Boston Lunátic Hospital, by the judge of the municipal court of the city of Boston, and to their discharge therefrom by him, was repealed by stat. 1840, c. 79, § 4.

[2] See the fifteenth section referred to, *post*, § 10, p. 269. The 7th section of stat. 1839, c. 131, was in effect repealed by stat. 1840, c. 79, § 3. See § 9, *post.*

insane as aforesaid, and is or is likely to be chargeable as aforesaid, the said municipal court shall affirm the judgment of the said police court, with additional costs, and issue a warrant for his commitment according to law; otherwise such person shall be discharged.

Notice of intended application to police court shall be first given to mayor, &c. Ibid, § 2.

8. Any person who shall apply for the commitment of any lunatic, under the provisions of the preceding section, shall first give notice in writing to the mayor of the city of Boston, of his intention to make such application, and satisfactory evidence that such notice has been given shall be produced to the said police court, at the time of making such application. And the said police court may order any further notice of such application to be given to the person complained of, or to any other person or persons in his behalf, as they shall deem to be necessary or reasonable.

Mayor and aldermen may discharge from confinement. Ibid, § 3.

9. Any person committed to said hospital by either of the courts as aforesaid, and any person who may be confined in said hospital, upon his removal from the state lunatic hospital, as provided in the sixth section, may at any time be discharged therefrom by the mayor and aldermen of the said city of Boston, whenever the cause of confinement shall have ceased to exist, or when in the opinion of the said mayor and aldermen such discharge would be for the benefit of the person so confined, or when in their opinion such person would be comfortably supported by any parent, kindred, friends, master or guardian, or by any town or city in which such person may have a legal settlement. And said mayor and aldermen, whenever in their opinion, such lunatic or insane person can in such manner be more comfortably provided for, and the safety of the public will not be endangered thereby, may provide for his custody and support in other places than in said hospital, the said lunatic or insane person still continuing subject to the order and direction of the said mayor and aldermen; or, said mayor and aldermen may deliver him to the custody and care of any city or town in which he may have a legal settlement. The expense of so providing for such lunatic or insane person, shall be reimbursed in the same manner, and recovered by the same remedies, as are pro-

May provide for custody of lunatic in other places.

Expense of same, how reimbursed.

vided in the sixteenth section of the forty-eighth chapter of the Revised Statutes:[1] *provided*, that in no case shall the sum charged for such provision exceed two dollars and fifty cents per week.

Trustees of state lunatic hospital may remove lunatics, when necessary to accommodate others. R. S. 48, § 15.

10. If, at any time, the lunatics in the state lunatic hospital at Worcester shall be so numerous, that they cannot all be suitably accommodated therein, and in the opinion of the trustees, it shall be proper that some of them should be removed therefrom, the trustees may remove, to the jails or houses of correction in the respective counties, from which such lunatics were sent, so many of them as may be necessary, in order to afford suitable accommodation for the remainder of them; and the keepers of the jails and houses of correction in the said counties shall receive the lunatics so removed; and a certificate, under the hands of three or more of the trustees, shall be their sufficient warrant therefor; and in making selections among the lunatics for such removal, the trustees shall, in all cases, when other circumstances are equal, select foreigners before citizens, and among citizens, they shall select those, who, in their opinion, are least susceptible of improvement at the hospital; and the lunatics so removed shall be subject to the order and direction of the commissioners of said counties, respectively.[2]

Remedies for recovering expenses of support of lunatic so removed. Ibid, § 16. 18 Pick. 379.

11. For reimbursing any expenses, incurred by the city of Boston, for the support of any lunatic, removed as is provided in the preceding section, the said city, if such lunatic had any legal settlement in this state, shall have the like remedy against the town or city, where his settlement is, as towns have against each other, to recover the expenses of supporting paupers, and subject to the like conditions and limitations; and if the said lunatic has not a legal settlement in this state, the said city of Boston may recover the said expenses, in an action for money laid out and expended, in the name of the treasurer, against the said lu-

---

[1] See *post*, § 11.

[2] See *ante*, § 6, p. 267, for confinement of persons so removed in Boston Lunatic Hospital.

natic, his executors and administrators; and if he shall have no estate to satisfy the execution in such suit, and shall not have a legal settlement in this state, the said city shall be indemnified by the commonwealth.

A town that pays for support of lunatics, may recover the expense, of town in which they have settlement. 1841, 77.

12. Whenever any lunatic or insane person shall be committed to the state lunatic hospital, at Worcester, from any town wherein he has not a legal settlement, and such town shall pay the expense of his support at said hospital, such town may recover from the town in which he has a legal settlement the full amount of all the expense so paid to said hospital.[1]

ORDINANCE OF THE CITY.[2]

Board of visitors. March 13, 1845.

SECT. 1. There shall be chosen by the city council, annually, in the month of January or February, seven persons, including one alderman and one member of the common council, who shall be a board of visitors of the Boston lunatic hospital, who shall hold their offices until others are chosen in their places, and who shall have all the powers and perform all the duties prescribed to the board of visitors of the said hospital, by the succeeding sections.

Rules and regulations to be submitted to the city council.

SECT. 2. All rules and regulations which shall be made by the said board of visitors, for the employment, compensation and discharge of the subordinate officers, attendants, and domestics, and for the government and management of the said hospital, shall, within one month after the same shall have been made, be submitted to the city council, and such rules and regulations shall be in force until repealed

---

1 For other provisions respecting the State Lunatic Hospital at Worcester, and general laws respecting lunatics, see R. S. c. 48; 1836, c. 223; 1837, c. 228; 1838, c. 31, 73; 1839, c. 149; 1842, c. 96, 100; 1843, c. 65; 1844, 120, 146; 1848, c. 320; 1849, c. 68, 74; 1850, c. 150. See also House of Correction.

2 An ordinance relating to the Boston Lunatic Hospital, passed October 3, 1842, and two ordinances in addition thereto, passed March 13, 1845, and June 4, 1846.

by said board of visitors, or until disapproved of by vote of the said city council.

SECT. 3. There shall be annually chosen by concurrent vote of the city council, in the month of September or October, a superintendent; he shall hold his office until another is chosen in his place; he shall be removable at the pleasure of the city council, and receive such salary as the said council may fix and determine, and in case of a vacancy in said office, the said council may at any time proceed forthwith to fill the same. **Superintendent. October 3, 1842.**

SECT. 4. The superintendent, under the direction of the board of visitors, shall have the control of all departments of the hospital, and of all subordinate officers, attendants and domestics, and of the patients, and the charge of the grounds, buildings and appurtenances. **His duties. Ibid.**

SECT. 5. The board of visitors shall determine what subordinate officers, attendants and domestics are necessary, and prescribe such rules for their employment, compensation and discharge, as they shall think proper. They shall have power to make such rules and regulations for the government and management of the hospital, as they may deem expedient, not inconsistent with this ordinance or the laws of the commonwealth. **Subordinate officers. Ibid.** **Rules.**

SECT. 6. The superintendent of the Boston lunatic hospital shall, in the month of December annually, report to the board of visitors of said institution, upon such matters as they may direct in reference to the general state of the hospital, and condition of the inmates during the preceding year, ending on the thirtieth day of November; and said board of visitors shall communicate said report, with such further information as they may deem important, to the city council forthwith. **Superintendent to make annual report. June 4, 1846.**

MARSHAL.

ORDINANCE OF THE CITY.[1]

Appointment of city marshal. Sept. 12, 1850. Tenure of office.

SECT. 1. There shall be appointed, by the mayor and aldermen, annually, in the month of May or June, and whenever a vacancy occurs, a city marshal, who shall hold his office one year from the time of his appointment, unless removed as is hereinafter provided.

To be constable. Ibid. To be sworn and give bond. Rank.

SECT. 2. The said city marshal shall also be appointed a constable of the city, and shall take the oath and give bond according to law. He shall have precedence and control over all other constables and police officers, whenever engaged in the same service, and whenever directed thereto by the mayor and aldermen.

Additional bond. Ibid.

SECT. 3. The said city marshal, in addition to the bond mentioned in the preceding section, shall give a bond, with sureties, to be approved by the mayor and aldermen, in the sum of one thousand dollars, for the faithful performance of the duties of his office.

Deputies. Ibid.

SECT. 4. The said city marshal, whenever authorized by the mayor and aldermen, may appoint one or more deputies, to be approved by the mayor and aldermen, who shall also be appointed special police officers. They shall assist the city marshal in the duties of his office, and may act for him on all proper occasions, in his absence; and he shall be responsible for their conduct.

---

[1] An ordinance providing for the appointment of a city marshal, and fixing his duties, passed September 12, 1850.

SECT. 5. The said city marshal and his deputies shall receive such compensation as the city council may from time to time determine, and they or either of them may be removed from office at any time by the mayor and aldermen.

Compensation. Ibid.

May be removed.

SECT. 6. The said city marshal shall attend at his office daily, by himself or his deputy or deputies, at all hours, day and night, including Sundays, for the purpose of receiving all complaints of the inhabitants, respecting offences committed against the laws, the ordinances of the city, and orders of the mayor and aldermen, and shall be vigilant in detecting any such offences. He shall institute prosecutions against all offenders against such laws, ordinances and orders, without unnecessary delay, and shall attend to the trial of the same, and shall take proper measures for the conviction of such offenders, whenever the same are discovered by him or brought to his notice.

Marshal to attend at his office to receive complaints, &c. Ibid.

Duty as to prosecutions of offenders.

SECT. 7. The said city marshal shall keep a correct record of all the doings of his office, and shall make a regular report thereof to the city council, as often as once in three months, and at such other times as they shall require.

To keep record. Ibid.

To make report.

SECT. 8. The said city marshal shall take notice of all nuisances, impediments, and obstructions in the streets, lanes, alleys, courts, public places and squares of the city, and shall remove the same, or take all proper measures in relation thereto according to law, under the direction of the mayor and aldermen.

Duty as to obstructions in streets. Ibid.

SECT. 9. The said city marshal shall enforce and carry into effect, to the utmost of his power, all and every of the ordinances of the city and orders of the mayor and aldermen which shall be in force; he shall obey and execute all the commands and orders of the mayor and aldermen, in relation to any matter or thing in which the city may be in any wise concerned or interested; and shall comply with all such regulations, as may at any time be prescribed by the mayor and aldermen.

To enforce ordinances of the city and orders of mayor and aldermen. Ibid.

OFFICERS AND OFFICE HOURS.

ORDINANCE OF THE CITY.[1]

Time and mode of choosing certain officers. Sept. 9, 1850.

SECT. 1. The following city officers shall be chosen annually, in the month of January or February, by concurrent vote of the two branches of the city council, to wit: surveyors of highways, fence viewers, cullers of hoops and staves, field drivers, pound keepers, and inspectors of lime.

Certain provisions to be directory merely. Ibid.

SECT. 2. Whenever any ordinance shall provide for the election of any city officer, at or within a time specified, such provision shall be considered as directory; and an election after the expiration of such time shall be valid.

Committee on public buildings to assign, &c., offices and rooms. Ibid.

SECT. 3. It shall be the duty of the committee on public buildings, under the direction of the mayor and aldermen, to assign and furnish in a proper manner suitable offices and rooms in the public buildings, or to procure the same elsewhere at the expense of the city, for the various city officers.

Office hours of treasurer. Ibid.

SECT. 4. The office hours of the city treasurer shall be from nine of the clock in the forenoon until two of the clock in the afternoon.

Of city clerk, auditor and registrar. Ibid.

SECT. 5. The office hours of the city clerk, the auditor of accounts, and the city registrar, shall be, from the first day of April to the first day of October, from eight of the clock in the forenoon until two of the clock in the afternoon, and from three and one half of the clock in the afternoon until six of the clock in the afternoon; and the remainder of the year, from nine of the clock in the forenoon until two of the clock

---

[1] An ordinance in relation to city officers and office hours, passed Sept. 9, 1850.

in the afternoon, and from three and one half of the clock until five of the clock in the afternoon.

Of assessors. Ibid.

SECT. 6. The office hours of the assessors shall be the same as those appointed in the next preceding section, except for such portion of the year as they may be necessarily absent, for the purpose of appraising the real and personal property, and obtaining the number of polls, for taxation.

Officers to attend at other times, if required. Ibid.

SECT. 7. Each of the officers before named shall attend the duties of their several offices at such other times as the mayor and aldermen may deem the interest of the city to require.

Duties of city clerk. Ibid.

SECT. 8. The city clerk, under the direction and control of the mayor and aldermen, shall have the care and custody of the city records, and of all documents, maps, plans and papers, respecting the care and custody of which no other provision is made. He shall attend and keep the records at all meetings of the city council.

ORDINANCES, AND BY-LAWS.[1]

STATUTES, &c.

1. By-laws may be annulled by general court.
2. Power of city council of Boston to make by-laws. Provisoes.
3. City councils of all cities shall have power to make by-laws respecting peace, good order, and internal police.
4. In complaints, &c., upon by-

---

[1] All by-laws must be reasonable or they are void. Whether a by-law be reasonable or not is for the court to determine, and evidence to the jury on that question is inadmissable. *Commonwealth v. Worcester*, (3 Pick. 462.) The mayor and aldermen of Boston have no power to suspend a by-law of the city, nor to authorize a violation of it. *Ibid.* By the Revised Statutes, c. 15, § 15, it is provided that all by-laws made by any town shall be published in one or more newspapers printed in the county where such town is situated. The by-laws made by any town are binding upon all persons coming within the limits thereof, as well as upon the inhabitants of such

STATUTES, &c.

By-laws may be annulled by general court. Const. of Mass. Amend. Art. 2.

1. It is provided, by the constitution of the commonwealth, that all by-laws, by municipal or city governments, erected and constituted by the general court, shall be subject, at all times, to be annulled by the general court.

Power of city council to make by-laws. 1821, 110, § 15.

2. The city charter, § 15, provides, that the city council shall have power to make all such needful and salutary by-laws, as towns by the laws of this commonwealth have power to make and establish, and to annex penalties, not exceeding twenty dollars, for the breach thereof, which by-laws shall take effect and be in force from and after the times therein respectively limited, without the sanction or confirmation of any court, or other authority whatsoever; *provided*, that such by-laws shall not be repugnant to the constitution and laws of this commonwealth: *and provided also*, that the same shall be liable to be annulled by the legislature thereof.

Provisoes.

City councils of cities shall have power to make by-laws respecting peace, good

3. The act of 1847, c. 262, provides that the city council of any city shall have power and authority to make all by-laws, not inconsistent with the laws of the common-

---

town, *Ibid*, § 14. See also *Vandine's case*, (6 Pick. 187.) A by-law may be good in part, and void for the rest. *Rogers v. Jones*, (1 Wend. (N. Y.) 260.) See *Austin v. Murray*, (16 Pick. 121.) *Commonwealth v. Dorr*, (10 Metc. 382.) By-laws cannot be made to operate retrospectively, *Howard v Savannah*, (Charlt. (Geo.) Rep. 173.) A by-law of a town or corporation, imposing penalties for particular offences, seems not to be void merely because a general law of the state imposes penalties for the same offences. *Rogers v. Jones*, (1 Wend. (N. Y.) Rep. 237.) See 1 Bay, 382.

wealth, that may be necessary to preserve the peace, good order, and internal police of the city, and may annex suitable penalties, not exceeding twenty dollars for any one breach thereof, to be recovered by complaint before any police court in such city, or any justice of the peace in a city where no police court is established: *provided*, that nothing herein contained shall be construed to affect the provisions of an act entitled "An act to prevent obstructions in the streets of cities, and to regulate hackney coaches and other vehicles," passed in the year eighteen hundred and forty-seven.[1]

order, and internal police. 1847, 262. 1 Cush. 493. 3 Pick. 462. 1 Metc. 130, 135.

4. In any complaint, prosecution, or other process, founded upon the by-laws of any town or city, no part of such by-law shall be required to be recited or set forth, but the offence may be described therein with the degree of certainty required in prosecutions upon public statutes; *provided*, that nothing herein contained shall affect the degree or kind of evidence required at the trial of the existence of such by-law.[2]

In complaints, &c., upon by-laws, no part of such by-law shall be required to be recited. 1846, 62. 3 Pick. 462. 5 Pick. 44.

5. The police court of the city of Boston has cognizance of all offences against the by-laws of the city of Boston, which are not within the exclusive jurisdiction of some other court.

Police court shall have cognizance of offences against the by-laws of the city, except, &c. R. S. 87, § 4.

6. The municipal court of the city of Boston has also original jurisdiction, concurrent with the supreme judicial court, of all crimes, offences and misdemeanors committed in the county of Suffolk, which are not capital, and of all offences against the by-laws of the city of Boston; and appellate jurisdiction of all offences, which shall be tried and determined before the police court of the city of Boston, or before any justice of the peace for the county of Suffolk.

Jurisdiction of municipal court. R. S. 86, § 4.

7. By an act passed June 17, 1817, making certain provisions respecting weights and measures, "and for the more easy recovery of fines and penalties within the town of Boston," it was provided, that, all fines, forfeitures, and penalties accruing within said Boston, under the said act, or for

How fines, &c., shall be recovered and appropriated. 1817, 50, § 3. But see p. 189, § 8, *ante*.

[1] See the statute referred to, 1847, c. 224, on p. 63, *ante*.

[2] See also actions, § 7, p. 24, *ante*, as to prosecutions founded on special acts of the legislature.

the breach of any by-law which was then in force, or which might thereafter be duly enacted and made, might be recovered by indictment, information or complaint, in the name of the commonwealth, in any court competent to try the same; and that all fines so recovered and paid, should be appropriated to the uses for which the same were then by law ordered to be applied.[1]

Person committed for non-payment of fine, &c., shall not be confined more than ten days. Ibid, § 4.

8. The same act also provided, that when any person, who, upon a conviction before a justice of the peace, for any offence mentioned therein, or for the breach of any by-law of the town of Boston, should be sentenced to pay a fine, and should not appeal from said judgment, or if upon claiming an appeal, should fail to recognize as therein provided, and upon not paying the fines and cost so assessed upon him, should be committed to prison, there to remain until he or she should pay such fines and cost, or be otherwise discharged according to law; such persons should not be holden in prison for a longer term than ten days; and at the expiration of that term, the keeper of the said gaol was authorized to release such person from confinement.[2]

ORDINANCE OF THE CITY.[3]

Enacting style of city ordinances. Sept. 16, 1850.

SECT. 1. All by-laws of the city shall be denominated ordinances, and the enacting style shall be, "Be it or-

---

[1] This provision was not repealed by the incorporation of the city. The city charter did not annul the rights and privileges of the town of Boston. It only conferred on the then existing corporation a new name with additional powers. *Commonwealth v. Worcester*, (3 Pick. 474.) A right of appeal was also reserved, in this statute which is no longer applicable; different provisions having since been made upon the subject. See Courts, pp. 85–93, *ante*. For special provisions as to public health, see p. 189, § 8, *ante*. See also Rev. Stat. c. 118, § 42, and c. 133, § 14.

[2] Whether this provision is repealed by subsequent enactments,—*quære*. See Rev. Stat. c. 87, § 16, (*ante*, p. 94, § 41); *Ibid*, c. 145, § 3; stat. 1842, c. 59; 1850, c. 185.

[3] An ordinance in relation to the ordinances and by-laws of the city, passed Sept. 16, 1850.

dained by the mayor, aldermen and common council of the city of Boston, in city council assembled, as follows."

SECT. 2. All ordinances of the city shall be recorded at length by the city clerk in a book to be kept for that purpose, previous to which they shall be examined by a joint standing committee of the city council on ordinances, who shall certify on the backs of the originals that they are rightly and truly enrolled.

Ordinances to be examined, enrolled and recorded. Ibid.

SECT. 3. The ordinances of the city council, and the orders of the mayor and aldermen, shall be published and promulgated by inserting the same two weeks successively in the newspapers published in the city of Boston, wherein are printed the laws of the commonwealth for the time being, and in such other of the newspapers published and printed within the city, as the city council may designate; but this and the second section are directory merely, and a failure to comply with the same shall not affect the validity of any order or ordinance.

Ordinances, and the orders of mayor and aldermen, to be published. Ibid.

This provision to be directory merely.

SECT. 4. All fines and penalties for the violation of any of the ordinances of the city council, or any of the orders of the mayor and aldermen, when recovered, shall enure to the use of the city, and shall be paid into the city treasury, except in those cases where it may be otherwise provided by the acts of the legislature, or the ordinances of the city.

Fines to enure to the use of the city, except, &c. Ibid.

SECT. 5. This ordinance shall take effect on the first day of January, in the year one thousand eight hundred and fifty-one.

When this ordinance shall take effect. Ibid.

OVERSEERS OF THE POOR.[1]

STATUTES.

1. Incorporation of the Overseers of the Poor.
2. Moneys and estates given, devised, &c., for the use of the poor, vested in said corporation. Proviso, that they shall not hold more than £60,000.
3. Shall have perpetual succession. May hold real estate not exceeding £500 by the year.
4. Shall have a common seal, and may make by-laws, &c.
5. Instruments made and acts done shall be binding.
6. Incorporation of the trustees of John Boylston's charitable donations.
7. Bequests, &c., made by John Boylston, vested in said corporation.
8. Said corporation to have perpetual succession, and to hold real and personal estate.
9. Shall have a common seal, and may make by-laws, &c.
10. Instruments and acts shall be binding.
11. Corporation authorized to bind out poor persons, &c.
12. Power of surrendering indigent boys to the Boston Asylum for Indigent Boys, shall be exercised by the overseers of the poor.

Incorporation of the Overseers of the Poor. 1772, Apr. 23 and 25, § 1. 22 Pick. 122.

1. By an act passed in 1772, after reciting that many charitably disposed persons have given and bequeathed considerable sums of money and other interest and estate to the poor of the town of Boston, and their use, and many other persons were well inclined to make charitable donations to the same good purpose, but the overseers of the poor of the same town not being incorporated, the good

[1] The city charter provided for the choice of overseers of the poor and prescribed their duties, (*ante*, p. 17, § xxvii.) But by subsequent acts of the legislature a large portion of their powers has been transferred to the directors of the house of industry, who now perform in Boston most of the duties imposed upon overseers of the poor in the various towns by the general laws. The overseers of the poor, in practice, furnish "out door relief," and may send paupers to the house of industry. When received there, they come under the charge of the directors of that institution. The overseers of the poor in the town of Boston were regularly incorporated for certain charitable purposes in 1772, and it has been judicially held that the provision in the city charter, just mentioned, was a continuance of the corporation so created in 1772, and not a dissolution or suspension of it. *Overseers of the Poor of Boston v. Sears*, (22 Pick. 122.) See House of Industry, and the account in the Appendix of the origin of this institution. See also House of Reformation and Paupers.

intentions of those who had made, and those who inclined to make such charitable donations, had been either wholly frustrated or not carried into full effect, it was enacted, that the overseers for the time being of the poor of the town of Boston in the county of Suffolk and province of the Massachusetts Bay, be created, made erected, and incorporated into a body politic by the name of the Overseers of the Poor of the Town of Boston in the Province of the Massachusetts Bay in New England, and that they and their successors in said office have perpetual succession by said name.

Money and estates given, devised, &c., for the use of the poor, vested in said corporation. Ibid, § 2.

2. By the same act, all and singular sum and sums of money, interest and estate, real or personal, of what name or nature soever theretofore given, or at any time thereafter to be given, granted, bequeathed, or devised by any way or means whatsoever to the poor of the town or to their use, not exceeding the sums and value in the said act aforementioned, were to all intents and purposes vested in the same overseers and their said successors in their said corporate capacity; and they were enabled in the same capacity to receive, manage, lease, let and dispose the same according to best discretion, to and for the use and benefit of the poor of the said town. Provided always, that the said overseers shall not be able to receive or be capable of having or holding any moneys or personal estate of any kind or nature whatsoever, at any time above and beyond the sum and amount of sixty thousand pounds lawful money of this province, accounting and reckoning the whole moneys and value of all the personal estate, personal securities and choses in action, which they shall own or be vested withal in their corporate capacity together, and that all gifts and bequests of money or personal estate of any kind made to the said corporation, or which by the tenor of this act they might take or be vested with, shall be utterly void at all times hereafter when their whole stock in moneys, personal securities, or choses in action and personal estate which the said corporation shall have, own, and be vested with the property of, shall, taken reckoned together, amount to the said sum of sixty thousand pounds.

Proviso, that they shall not hold more than £60,000.

Shall have perpetual succession. Ibid, § 3.

3. It was further enacted, that the said overseers and their successors in said office, by the name aforesaid, have a perpetual succession by that name, to sue or be impleaded by its said corporate name to purchase lands and hold them not exceeding the sum of five hundred pounds, lawful money, by the year, and to manage, lease, bargain, and sell or otherwise dispose of all or any part thereof, and do all acts as natural persons may, as from time to time the said corporation shall judge best for the benefit, advantage and use of said poor.

May hold real estate not exceeding £500 by the year.

Shall have a common seal, and may make by-laws, &c. Ibid, § 4.

4. It was further enacted that the said corporation have a common seal and power, and said corporation was authorized to make by-laws and private statutes and ordinances not repugnant to the laws of the land, for the better government of the said corporation and its finances, to choose a treasurer, clerk, and other subordinate officers, as from time to time should be found necessary, and all or any of them again at pleasure to displace.

Instruments made, and acts done, shall be binding. Ibid, § 5.

5. It was further enacted that all instruments which said corporation should lawfully make by the name aforesaid and sealed with their common seal, and all acts done or matters passed upon by the consent of a major part of the said overseers for the time being, should bind said corporation and be valid in law.

BOYLSTON'S CHARITABLE DONATIONS.

Incorporation of the trustees of John Boylston's charitable donations. 1802, 44, § 1.

6. By an act, passed in 1803, Oliver Wendell, William Cooper, Ebenezer Storer, and William Smith, all of Boston, and John Pitts of Tyngsborough, in the county of Middlesex, Esquires, and the survivors and survivor of them, together with the overseers of the poor of the town of Boston for the time being, and their successors, and after the decease of the said Oliver Wendell, William Cooper, Ebenezer Storer, William Smith and John Pitts, the said overseers of the poor of the town of Boston for the time being and their successors forever, were incorporated into a body politic, by the name and title of The Trustees of John Boylston's charitable donations for the benefit and support of aged poor persons, and of orphans and deserted children,

and by that name and title endowed with perpetual succession.

7. All the bequests, devises and donations, made and granted by John Boylston, late of Bath, in the kingdom of Great Britain, deceased, for the purposes above mentioned, were vested in the said corporation, to be held and disposed of by them conformably to the directions of the said will. And the said corporation were required to insert among their records a copy of the said act, and also of all the clauses of the said last will and testament which have relation to the said two charitable donations for the benefit of aged poor persons, and for the support of orphans and deserted children; and in the management and disposal of the funds granted in said will, the said corporation were required to conform to and be governed by the directions therein contained.

Bequests, &c., made by John Boylston, vested in said corporation. Ibid, § 2.

8. It was further enacted, that the said corporation should have a perpetual succession by the name and title aforesaid, to sue or be impleaded; to purchase and hold lands, or other real estate, not exceeding the value of three thousand dollars, by the year; to hold personal estate not exceeding the value of sixty thousand dollars; and to manage, lease, bargain, and sell or otherwise dispose of, all or any part thereof, subject to the directions of the said will; and to do all acts as natural persons may do, as the said corporation from time to time should judge best to carry into effect the charitable intentions of the said will: and that the real or personal estate which the said corporation were thereby empowered to hold, should not be considered as part of that which the overseers of the poor of the town of Boston were already empowered by their former act of incorporation to hold; but as altogether distinct and separate from the same.

Said corporation to have perpetual succession; and to hold real and personal estate. Ibid, § 3.

9. It was further enacted, that the said corporation should have a common seal, with power to break and alter the same; and said corporation was authorized to make by-laws and private statutes and ordinances not repugnant to the laws of the land, for the better government of said corporation and its finances; to choose a treasurer, clerk,

Shall have a common seal, and may make by-laws, &c. Ibid, § 4.

and other subordinate officers, as from time to time should be found necessary, and all or any of them again at pleasure to displace.

Instruments and acts shall be binding. Ibid, § 5.

10. It was further enacted, that all instruments which said corporation should lawfully make by the name aforesaid, and sealed with their common seal, and all acts done or matters passed upon by the consent of a major part of the members of said corporation, should bind the said corporation and be valid in law.

Corporation authorized to bind out poor persons, orphans, &c. 1813, 171.

11. By an additional act, passed February 26, 1814, the last mentioned corporation were authorized and empowered to bind out in virtuous families, or to reputable trades, or useful arts or occupations, such poor persons, orphans, or deserted children, as then received, or might thereafter receive, the benefit of the said Boylston's charitable donations, until they should arrive at the age of twenty-one years, in such manner as to the said corporation might seem expedient; and for this purpose authority was given to the corporation to establish any rules and regulations, and enter into any indenture or covenant relative to such objects, not repugnant to the laws of the commonwealth, as the said corporation might deem necessary or expedient.

Power of surrendering indigent boys to the Boston asylum for indigent boys, shall be exercised by the overseers of the poor. 1823, 53. But see 1835, 28, § 4.

12. The power recognized in the act to incorporate the Boston asylum for indigent boys, (1813, ch. 153,) of the parent or guardian of any indigent boy or boys, to surrender in writing him or them to the managers of said asylum, for the purposes mentioned in said act, shall, in case said boy or boys have no parent or guardian within the city of Boston, nor legal settlement in any other town in this commonwealth, be possessed and exercised by the overseers of the poor of the city of Boston.[1]

---

[1] For enactments respecting the Boston Asylum and Farm School, see stat. 1813, c. 153; 1823, c. 53; 1833, c. 135; 1835, c. 28; and 1838, c. 16.

PAUPERS.

STATUTES.

1. Towns shall support their poor.
2. Powers and duties of overseers of the poor.
3. Further powers of overseers.
4. Towns may provide alms-houses.
5. Certain kindred of poor persons, if able, shall support them.
6. Court of common pleas may assess such kindred.
7. Court of common pleas may also assess for future expenses.
8. Costs in such proceedings, how taxed.
9. The court may order with whom of such kindred the pauper shall live.
10. Proceedings on complaints made to court of common pleas.
11. Other kindred than those named in the complaint may be summoned.
12. Court may make new orders from time to time.
13. Overseers, to provide for immediate relief of strangers, &c., and their remedy.
14. When a recovery shall establish the fact of settlement.
15. Towns removing a pauper within thirty days, to pay only one dollar a week.
16. Overseers shall support, and in case of decease, bury, indigent strangers. Remedy therefor.
17. Foreign paupers may be conveyed from the state to the place where they belong.
18. Towns liable to their own inhabitants, after notice, &c.
19. Paupers may be removed to places of settlement.
20. Process in cases of removals. If a removal is not made or objected to by the town notified, then, &c.
21. Effect of notifications, &c., to towns sent by mail.
22. What minor children may be bound out by overseers.
23. Penalty for leaving paupers in towns to which they do not belong, with intent, &c.
24. Penalty on shipmasters for landing convicts, &c., from other states.
25. Overseers, or persons by them authorized, may prosecute, &c.
26. Overseers of the poor empowered to take the effects of deceased paupers, and apply them to reimburse expenses.
27. Overseers of poor and directors of house of industry to make returns respecting paupers.
28. Penalty for not making return.
29. Overseers and directors to make returns of children under 14 supported at public charge.
30. Blank forms to be provided.
31. Who shall not be considered state paupers.
32. Rates of charge for state paupers.
33. Particulars of account for state paupers, and how certified.
34. Accounts to be rendered yearly, on or before the third Wednesday of November.
35. Certificate that whole amount has been expended.
36. Accounts for support of state paupers sick with infectious disease, to what time to be made up, and when rendered.

Towns shall support their poor. R. S. 46, § 1.

1. Every town[1] shall relieve and support all poor and indigent persons, lawfully settled therein,[2] whenever they shall stand in need thereof, and may raise moneys therefor, and for their employment, in the same way, that moneys for other town charges are raised.

Powers and duties of overseers of the poor. Ibid, § 2.

2. The overseers of the poor shall have the care and oversight of all such poor and indigent persons, so long as they remain at the charge of their respective towns, and shall see that they are suitably relieved, supported and employed, at the charge of such town, either in the workhouse, or almshouse, provided by the town, or in such other manner as the town shall direct, or otherwise, at the discretion of said overseers.

Further powers of overseers. Ibid, § 3.

3. The overseers of the poor shall have the same power and authority over persons who may be placed under their care, which directors or masters of workhouses have over persons committed thereto, by force of the provisions concerning workhouses, contained in the sixteenth chapter of the Revised Statutes.

Towns may provide almshouses. Ibid, § 4.

4. Any town may erect or provide an almshouse, for the reception and employment of their poor; or any two or more towns may, at their joint charge and for their common benefit, erect or provide such a house, in like manner as they are authorized to join in providing a workhouse, by the said sixteenth chapter of the Revised Statutes.

Certain kindred of poor persons, if able, shall support them. Ibid, § 5.

5. The kindred of any such poor person, if any he shall have, in the line or degree of father or grandfather, mother or grandmother, children or grand children, by consan-

---

[1] In the construction of statutes, the word "town" may be construed to include all cities, &c. Rev. Stat. c. 2, § 6, clause 17. See note, on p. 280.

[2] For the law in relation to what constitutes a settlement, see Rev. Stat. c. 45.

guinity, living within this state, and of sufficient ability, shall be bound to support such pauper, in proportion to their respective ability.

6. The court of common pleas in the county, where any one of such kindred to be charged shall reside, upon complaint made by any town, or by any kindred, who shall have been at any expense, for the relief and support of such pauper, may, on due hearing, either upon the appearance or default of the kindred supposed to be chargeable, assess and apportion, upon such of the kindred as they shall find to be of sufficient ability, and in proportion thereto, such sum as they shall judge reasonable, for or towards the support of the pauper, to the time of such assessment, and may enforce payment thereof, by an execution in common form; provided, that such assessment shall not extend to any expense for relief, afforded more than six months previous to the filing of the complaint.

Court of common pleas may assess such kindred. Ibid, § 6.

7. The said court may further assess and apportion, upon the said kindred, such weekly sum, as they shall judge sufficient for the future support of the pauper, to be paid quarter yearly, until the further order of court; and upon application, from time to time, of the town, or kindred to whom the same shall have been ordered to be paid, the clerk of said court shall issue and may renew an execution, for the arrears of any preceding quarter.

Court of common pleas may also assess for future expenses. Ibid, § 7.

8. When the court shall adjudge two or more of the kindred of any pauper to be of sufficient ability to contribute to his support, they shall tax no more costs against any one respondent, than shall have been occasioned by his default or separate defence.

Costs in such proceedings, how taxed. Ibid, § 8.

9. The said court may further order, with whom of such kindred, that may desire it, such pauper shall live and be relieved, and such time with one, and such time with another, as they shall judge proper, having regard to the comfort of the pauper, as well as the convenience of the kindred.

The court may order with whom of such kindred, the pauper shall live. Ibid, § 9.

10. The complaint to be made by any town, or kindred of a pauper, as provided in the forty-sixth chapter of the Revised Statutes, shall be filed in the clerk's office of the

Proceedings on complaints made to C. C. Pleas. Ibid, § 10.

court of common pleas, and a summons shall be thereupon issued, requiring the kindred therein named to appear and answer thereto; which summons shall be directed to any officer, who is qualified to serve civil process between the same parties, and shall be served like an original summons, fourteen days at least before the sitting of the court to which it is returnable.

Other kindred than those named in the complaint may be summoned. Ibid, § 11.

11. Upon a suggestion that there are other kindred of ability, not summoned in the original process, such other kindred may be summoned, and after due notice, whether they appear or are defaulted, the court may proceed against them, in the same manner as if they had been summoned upon the original complaint.

Court may make new orders from time to time. Ibid, § 12.

12. The said court may take further order, from time to time, in the premises, upon application of any party interested, and may alter such assessment and apportionment, according to the circumstances; and upon all such complaints, they may award costs to either party, as justice shall require.

Overseers, to provide for immediate relief of strangers, &c., and their remedy. Ibid, § 13. 2 Pick. 341.

13. The said overseers, in their respective towns, shall also provide for the immediate comfort and relief of all persons, residing or found therein, not belonging thereto, but having lawful settlements in other towns, when they fall into distress and stand in need of immediate relief, and until they shall be removed to the places of their lawful settlements; the expenses whereof, incurred within three months next before notice given to the town to be charged, as also of their removal or of their burial, in case of their decease, may be sued for and recovered, by the town incurring the same, against the town which is liable therefor, in an action at law; provided, that such action for damages be instituted within two years after the cause of action shall have arisen, but not otherwise.

When a recovery shall establish the fact of settlement. R. S. 46, § 14.

14. A recovery in such civil action shall bar the town, against which it shall be had, from disputing the settlement of such pauper with the town so recovering, in any future action brought for the support of such pauper.

Towns, removing a pauper within 30 days, to pay only $1

15. When any person shall be supported in any town, other than that in which he has his settlement, the town that

is liable for his support shall not, in any case, be required to pay therefor more than at the rate of one dollar a week; provided the town that is liable for the support of the pauper shall cause him to be removed, within thirty days from the time of receiving legal notice that such support has been furnished.

a week.
Ibid, § 15.
4 Pick. 45.
7 Pick. 155.

16. The overseers of the poor of each town shall also relieve, support, and employ all poor persons, residing or found in their towns, having no lawful settlements within this state, and in case of their decease, shall decently bury them; the expense whereof may be recovered of their kindred, if they have any chargeable by law for their support, in the manner herein before provided; otherwise, it shall be paid out of the treasury of the commonwealth, as hereinafter provided.

Overseers shall support, and, in case of decease, bury indigent strangers.
R. S. 46, § 16.

Remedy therefor.

17. Upon complaint of the said overseers of any town, any justice of the peace, may, by warrant directed to, and to be executed by, any constable, or any other person therein designated, cause such pauper to be sent and conveyed, at the expense of the state, by land or water, to any other state, or to any place beyond sea, where he belongs, if the justice thinks proper, and if he may be conveniently removed; but if he cannot be so removed, he may be sent to, and relieved and employed in, the house of correction or workhouse, at the public expense.

Foreign paupers may be conveyed from the state to the place where they belong.
Ibid, § 17.

18. Every town shall be held to pay any expense, which shall be necessarily incurred, for the relief of a pauper, by any person, who is not liable by law for his support, after notice and request made to the overseers of the said town, and until provision shall be made by them.

Towns liable to their own inhabitants after notice, &c.
Ibid, § 18.

19. The said overseers may, in all cases, send a written notification, stating the facts relating to any person actually become chargeable to their town, to one or more of the overseers of the place, where his settlement is supposed to be, and requesting them to remove him, which they may do by a written order, directed to any person therein designated, who is hereby authorized to execute the same.

Paupers may be removed to places of settlement.
Ibid, § 19.

20. If such removal is not effected by the last mentioned overseers, within two months after receiving such

Process in cases of removals.
If a removal is

not made nor objected to by the town notified, then, &c. Ibid, § 20.

notice, they shall, within said two months, send a written answer, stating therein their objections to the removal of the pauper, signed by one or more of them, to one or more of the overseers, requesting such removal; and if they shall fail so to do, the overseers, who requested the removal of the pauper, may cause him to be removed to the said place of his supposed settlement, by a written order directed to any person therein designated, who is hereby authorized to execute the same; and the overseers of the town, to which the pauper is so sent, shall be obliged to receive and provide for him, and their town shall be liable for the expenses of his support and removal, to be recovered by an action by the town incurring the same, and shall be barred from contesting the question of settlement with the plaintiffs in such action.

Effect of notifications, &c., to towns, sent by mail. Ibid, § 21.

21. The notification and answer, mentioned in the two preceding sections, may be sent by mail; and such notification or answer, directed to the overseers of the poor of the town, intended to be notified or answered, (the postage being paid and indorsed thereon,) shall be deemed a sufficient notice and answer, and shall be considered as delivered to the overseers, to whom it is directed, at the time when it is received in the post office of the town, to which it is directed, and in which the said overseers reside.

What minor children may be bound out by overseers. Ibid, § 22.

22. The said overseers may bind out the minor children of any poor person, who has become chargeable to their town, as having a lawful settlement therein, or who is supported there in whole or in part at the charge of the state, and also other minor children, who are poor and chargeable to the town, in the manner provided in the eightieth chapter of the Revised Statutes.[1]

Penalty for leaving paupers in towns, to which they do not belong, with intent, &c. Ibid, § 24. 2 Greenl. 5. 1 Pick. 465. 16 Mass. 393. 1849, 66.

23. If any person shall bring into and leave any poor and indigent person in any town of this state, wherein such pauper is not lawfully settled, knowing him to be poor and indigent, and with intent to charge such town with his support, he shall forfeit a sum not exceeding one hundred dollars for any such offence; which penalty shall be forfeited

---

[1] The 23d section of Rev. Stat. c. 46, was repealed by stat. 1837, c. 178, § 3.

to the use of, and may be sued for and recovered by, the town intended to be so charged.

24. If any master or other person, having charge of any vessel, shall therein bring into, and land, or suffer to be landed in, any place within this state, any person, before that time convicted, in any other state or in any foreign country, of any infamous crime, or any for which he hath been sentenced to transportation, knowing of such conviction, or having reason to suspect it, or any person of a notoriously dissolute, infamous and abandoned life and character, knowing him to be such, he shall, for every such offence, forfeit a sum not exceeding five hundred dollars.

Penalty on shipmasters for landing convicts, &c., from other states. R. S. 46, § 25.

25. In all actions and prosecutions, founded on the provisions of the forty-sixth chapter of the Revised Statutes, the overseers of the poor of any town, or any person by writing under their hands appointed, shall and may appear, prosecute or defend the same to final judgment and execution, in behalf of such town.

Overseers, or persons by them authorized, may prosecute, &c. R. S. 46, § 26.

26. Upon the death of any pauper, who, at the time of his decease, shall be actually chargeable to any town within this commonwealth, the overseers of the poor of such town may take into their possession all the personal property belonging to such pauper. And if no administration shall be taken upon the estate of such pauper within thirty days after his decease, the said overseers may sell so much of the said property as may be necessary to repay the expenses incurred for such pauper. And if any part of such property shall be withheld from the said overseers, they shall have the same remedy for the recovery of such property, or the value thereof, that an administrator of the estate of the said pauper might have in like case.

Overseers of the poor empowered to take the effects of deceased paupers, and apply them to reimburse expenses 1837, 54.

27. The overseers of the poor of the several towns in this commonwealth, and the directors of the house of industry in the city of Boston, shall on or before the third Wednesday of November in each year, make out and return to the secretary of this commonwealth, a statement of the paupers in said town,[1] as they are on the first day of said November; which return shall contain true and correct answers to the

Overseers of poor and directors of house of industry to make returns respecting paupers. 1837, 194, § 1. 1841, 116, § 1.

---

[1] See note to § 1, p. 286, *ante*.

following inquiries, viz: What number of persons have been relieved or supported as paupers during the year in your town? Of these, how many have a legal settlement in your town, or elsewhere in this commonwealth? How many state paupers does your town support? How many of those are foreigners? How many of the foreigners are from England and Ireland? Have you an alms-house? What number of acres of land is attached to your alms-house? What is the estimated value of your alms-house establishment? What number of persons have been relieved in your alms-house during the year? What is the average number supported in alms-house? What is the average weekly cost of supporting each pauper in alms-house? What number of persons in your alms-house who are unable to perform any kind or amount of labor? What is the estimated value of all the labor performed by paupers in your alms-house? How many persons do you aid and support out of alms-house? What is the average weekly cost of supporting paupers out of alms-house? How many does your town support or relieve who are insane? How
1844, 146. many do you relieve or support who are idiots? What number of persons relieved or supported as paupers during the year in your town, have become paupers by reason of
1837, 194, § 1. insanity or idiocy? What proportion of your paupers, in your opinion, have been made dependent by intemperance in themselves, or those who ought to have been their supporters? What number of your foreign paupers have come into this commonwealth within one year? What is the total net amount of expense of supporting or relieving paupers in your town for one year, including interest on your alms-house establishment? What amount does your town receive from the treasury of this commonwealth to-
1841, 116, § 1. wards the support of state paupers? And the secretary of this commonwealth shall, in the month of September annually, furnish the overseers of the poor of each town with a blank form of return which shall contain in substance the foregoing interrogatories.[1]

[1] Stat. 1837, c. 194, § 2, and 1841, 116, § 2, make it the duty of the secretary of state to make out abstracts of such returns, for the use of the legislature.

28. If the overseers of the poor of any town in this commonwealth, or the directors of the house of industry in the city of Boston, shall refuse or neglect to make the return as aforesaid, they shall forfeit a sum not exceeding one hundred dollars, to be recovered by indictment in any court of competent jurisdiction.

Penalty for not making return. 1837, 194, § 3.

29. The overseers of the poor of the several towns, and the directors of the alms-houses of the several cities, shall make, and transmit to the secretary of the commonwealth, on or before the third Monday in November, in each and every year, correct returns of all the children in their respective towns and cities, under fourteen years of age, who are supported at the public charge; and, in said returns, shall specify the name, age, and sex, of each child so supported.

Overseers and directors to make returns of children under 14, supported at public charge. 1848, 247, § 1.

30. Suitable blank forms for such returns shall be furnished to each town and city by the secretary of the commonwealth; and he shall prepare yearly abstracts thereof, and shall lay the same before the general court.

Blank forms to be provided, &c. Ibid, § 2.

STATE PAUPERS.

31. No male person over the age of twelve years, while of competent health to labor, shall be considered a state pauper, and entitled to support as such.

Who shall not be considered state paupers. R. S. 46, § 30.

32. All accounts against the commonwealth, presented for allowance by any city, town, or keeper of any house of correction, for the support of state paupers, shall be made out and charged at a fixed price by the day, and the allowance shall not exceed in any case seven cents a day, for the support of paupers over twelve years of age, and four cents a day, for the support of paupers under that age, and five dollars for the funeral expenses of each pauper over twelve years of age, and two dollars and fifty cents, for the funeral expenses of each pauper under that age.[1]

Rates of charge for state paupers. Ibid, § 32.

33. All accounts made out against the commonwealth, for the support of state paupers, shall show the name of each pauper, his age and place of nativity, and the time when he first came into this state, the time when he became

Particulars of account for state paupers, and how certified. Ibid, § 33.

---

[1] See section 24 p. 225, *ante*.

chargeable, and when he ceased to be so, or in case of his death, the time of his death, or if he still continues chargeable, the time to which such charge is made, and the number of days for which each of said paupers has been chargeable; and in all cases, where said charge is for the support of any pauper, not already mentioned on the list of state paupers, said account shall be accompanied by a certificate of the overseers of the poor of the towns, and in Boston, a certificate of the directors of the house of industry of that city, stating that neither of said paupers has a legal settlement in this state, and also that he has no kindred within this state obliged by law to support him; and in all such certificates, the said overseers, and the directors of the house of industry in the city of Boston, respectively, shall state that they made the same on the best evidence they could obtain, and that no part of the account is for the support of any person over the age of twelve years, while of competent health to labor.

Accounts to be rendered yearly on or before the 3d Wednesday of November. 1841, 116, § 3.

34. All accounts against the commonwealth for allowance to cities and towns for support of state paupers shall be rendered to the secretary of the commonwealth on or before the third Wednesday of November annually, and shall be so made as to include all claims for such charges up to the third day of the said month of November, and the secretary shall lay all accounts so received before the legislature at the opening of the session thereof.

Certificate that whole amount has been expended. R. S. 46, § 31.

35. The selectmen, or overseers of the poor, of any town, or the keeper of any house of correction, and the directors of the house of industry in the city of Boston, respectively, shall certify that the whole amount charged in their account has been expended, for the support of the persons named in the same, for the time therein specified.[1]

Accounts for support of state paupers sick with infectious disease, to what time to be made up, and when rendered. 1849, 151, § 1.

36. All accounts against the commonwealth for allowance to cities and towns for support of state paupers sick with an infectious disease, dangerous to the public health, shall be so made out as to include all claims for such sup-

---

1 The remainder of Rev. Stat. c. 46, § 31, appears to be repealed, in effect, by stat. 1841, 116, § 3; i. e. § 34 of the text.

port up to the first day of November, annually; and shall be rendered to the secretary of the commonwealth, on or before the third Wednesday of said November.

37. All accounts against the commonwealth, for allowance for the support of lunatic state paupers, shall be so made out as to include all claims for such support up to the first day of December, annually, and shall be rendered to the secretary of the commonwealth, on or before the third Wednesday of said December.

Accounts for support of lunatic paupers. Ibid, § 2.

38. No account for the support of any state pauper shall be allowed by the auditor of accounts, unless the same shall be rendered within the time specified by law.

Not to be allowed unless rendered as directed. Ibid § 3.

39. It shall be the duty of the secretary of the commonwealth to transmit all claims against the commonwealth, rendered to his office, to the auditor of accounts.

Secretary shall transmit claims to auditor of accounts. Ibid, § 4.

40. Whenever any county of this commonwealth shall present any claim or claims for the support of any state lunatic pauper, it shall be the duty of said county to present satisfactory evidence to the committee, to which such claim or account may be referred, that said insane person has been supported in a suitable and comfortable manner, and at an expense equal to the amount to be allowed by the commonwealth, and that no allowance or payment shall be made unless this act shall have been complied with.[1]

Accounts for support of state lunatic paupers to be accompanied by proof of suitable support. 1849, 207.

---

[1] For other general provisions respecting paupers, work-houses, settlement, &c., see Rev. Stat. c. 16, 45, 143; 1837, c. 178; 1839, c. 156; 1841, c. 77; 1846, c. 88; 1848, c. 291. See also Alien Passengers, House of Correction, House of Industry, Lunatics, and Overseers of the Poor.

PILOTS.[1]

Two commissioners of pilots to be appointed for Boston.
R. S. 32, § 15.

1. The governor, with the advice and consent of the council, is authorized to appoint and commission two persons, to execute the office of commissioners of pilots for the harbor of Boston, who shall hold their office during the term of three years, unless sooner removed by the governor and council; provided always, that the said persons shall first be recommended by the trustees of the Boston marine society, and that no such commissioner shall at the same time be one of said trustees.

---

[1] The pilotage district, which includes the harbor of Boston, extends from Nahant rock, on the North, to the highlands of Marshfield on the South; and the words "port of Boston," or "harbor of Boston," as used in reference to the regulations of pilotage, include all the ports which use the several channels leading to the city of Boston, and the mouths of the rivers which enter into that harbor. *Martin v. Hilton*, (9 Metc. 371.)

2. The said commissioners shall grant commissions for pilots, and warrants for apprentices, to such persons as may be approved by the trustees of the Boston marine society; and they may, upon satisfactory evidence of misconduct, carelessness or neglect of duty, suspend until the meeting of the trustees then next ensuing, any pilot or apprentice who now holds or shall hereafter hold a branch, commission or warrant; and if the said trustees, at their said next meeting, shall decide that such branch, commission or warrant ought to be revoked, the said commissioners of pilots may revoke the same, or may, at their discretion, continue the suspension of such pilot or apprentice, until the next stated meeting of said trustees, and no longer, for the same offence.

Commissioners may grant and revoke commissions and warrants, &c. Ibid, § 16.

3. No person shall receive a commission or exercise the office of a pilot, for the harbor of Boston, until he shall have deposited, with the treasurer of the commonwealth, a bond in the penal sum of two thousand dollars, payable to the said treasurer, and with sureties satisfactory to the said commissioners, for the faithful performance by himself and his apprentices of all the duties required by law of any pilot or apprentice.

Pilots to give bond to state treasurer. Ibid, § 17.

4. Any surety on such bond of a pilot may, at the end of any year after signing the same, terminate his liability as surety for the future acts of such pilot, by giving notice of his determination, in writing, at least thirty days before the expiration of any such year, to the treasurer of the commonwealth and to the commissioners of pilots; and thereupon the said commissioners shall give notice to the said pilot, that unless he shall procure some other surety, his commission will be annulled at the end of such year, and the same shall in such case be annulled by them and delivered up accordingly; and if any such pilot shall, after demand made, refuse to deliver up his commission, he shall forfeit the sum of fifty dollars for every month, during which he shall retain the same.

Sureties on pilots' bonds may be released therefrom. Ibid, § 18.

5. The commissioners of pilots shall keep an office, and shall be in attendance during a part of each day, to receive and consider complaints by and against pilots, and to exam-

Commissioners, to keep an office, hear complaints, &c. Ibid, § 19.

ine the evidence concerning the same; and in case any pilot, either by himself or his apprentice, shall be guilty of any act, whereby the condition of his bond shall be broken, the said commissioners shall make immediate complaint thereof to the treasurer of the commonwealth, who shall cause a suit to be forthwith commenced and security to be taken, for the benefit of all persons who may have suffered by the misconduct or negligence of such pilot or apprentice; and the like proceedings and judgment shall be had and rendered in such suit, as in the case of sheriffs' bonds.

Pilots to render quarterly accounts to commissioners. Ibid, § 20.

6. Once in every three months, each branch pilot for the harbor of Boston shall render, to the said commissioners of pilots, an account of all vessels piloted, and of all moneys received by him or by any person for him for pilotage; and he shall pay to the said commissioners five per cent. on the amount thereof, which shall be taken in full for their official services and for the expenses of the office; and the said pilots may add five per cent. to the rates established by law, at the time when they shall perform the service of piloting any vessel, and they may collect the same in the like manner, as they are now authorized to collect the pilotage fees; and if any pilot shall make a false return of moneys so received, he shall forfeit a sum not exceeding fifty dollars.

Additional fees.

Penalty for a false return.

Commissioners may make regulations for pilots, &c. Ibid, § 21. 12 Metc. 346.

7. The commissioners of pilots may, from time to time, alter or amend any of the existing regulations, for the pilotage of the harbor of Boston, and may make any new regulations therefor; and all such altered, amended and new regulations, after being approved by the trustees of the Boston marine society, and being published one week in two of the newspapers printed in Boston, shall be binding on all persons; and the said commissioners, at least twice a year, shall publish as aforesaid all the regulations, which shall at such times be in force, concerning the pilotage of the harbor of Boston, and also shall see that the said regulations and the laws concerning said pilotage are duly observed and executed.

Regulations to be published.

Commissioners to keep fair records of their

8. The commissioners of pilots shall keep fair records of all their doings, under the provisions of this chapter, and

shall exhibit the same to the trustees of the Boston marine society, as often as once in every six months, and whenever the said trustees shall require the same.

proceedings, &c. R. S. 32, § 22.

9. If any person, not having a branch, commission or warrant, as a pilot or pilot's apprentice, for the harbor of Boston, shall undertake to pilot into or out of the said harbor any vessels, excepting such as are excepted in the seventh section of the thirty-second chapter of the Revised Statutes,[1] he shall forfeit a sum not exceeding fifty dollars for each offence.[2]

No person except a pilot, &c., to pilot vessels, except, &c. Ibid, § 23. 5 Metc. 412.

10. In case no Boston branch pilot shall offer his services to the master of a vessel bound into the harbor of Boston, before such vessel shall have passed a line drawn from Harding's Rocks to the Outer Graves, and from thence to Nahant Head, such master shall be at liberty to pilot his own vessel, or to employ any other person to pilot his vessel into the said harbor, without incurring the penalty mentioned in the preceding section.[3]

When a ship master may pilot his own vessel. R. S. 32, § 24. 5 Metc. 412.

11. If at any time it shall appear to the commissioners of pilots that the bonds given by any pilot are insufficient, the said commissioners shall require him to give a new bond or bonds to their satisfaction, within such time as they shall order.

Commissioners may require new bonds. 1844, 168.

12. Every branch pilot appointed agreeably to the provisions of the thirty-second chapter of the Revised Statutes, is authorized and directed, by himself or his deputy, to take charge of any vessel bound into or going out of the port assigned to him, except fishing vessels, and all American vessels of less than two hundred tons, bound from any port within the United States to a port or place within this state, and excepting also, all other vessels bound from a

Pilots to take charge of all vessels bound into or going out of ports assigned to them, except, &c. 1841, 45, § 1.

---

1 The vessels excepted in the section referred to, are fishing vessels, and vessels bound to or coming from any port within the state, and all vessels of less than two hundred tons, sailing under a coasting license. The section referred to was repealed by stat. 1841, c. 45, § 2.

2 This ninth section was subsequently modified by stat. 1847, c. 279, § 1. See § 15, on the next page.

3 This section appears to be modified by stat. 1841, c. 45, § 1. See § 12, on this page.

port within this state, to another port within the state, unless such vessel shall then be in the completion of a voyage from a port or place without the state; the said pilot first showing his branch or warrant to the master of any such vessel, if required.

Pilots liable for negligence while in charge of vessels. R. S. 32, § 11. 8 Pick. 23.

13. If any vessel, while under the charge of a branch or warrant pilot or his deputy, shall be lost or run aground, or sustain any damage, through the negligence or unskilfulness of such pilot or deputy, such pilot shall be liable, both for himself and his deputy, to pay all damages sustained by any person interested in such vessel or her cargo; and may, moreover, be removed from his office.

When masters may pilot their own vessels. R. S. 32, § 12. 5 Metc. 412. 9 Metc. 371. 12 Metc. 346.

14. Any master of a vessel, other than such as are excepted in the seventh section of the thirty-second chapter of the Revised Statutes,[1] who may choose to pilot his own vessel into or out of any port, shall be permitted so to do; but he shall, notwithstanding, be liable to pay to such pilot of the port, as shall first come on board of his vessel, the full pilotage, according to the fees specified in his warrant; [except as provided in the following section.]

Masters, &c., of a vessel may pilot it into any port, other than that of the destination, &c. 1847, 279, § 1.

15. On and after the first day of May, 1847, the master or commander of any ship or vessel may pilot his own vessel into, or out of, any port in this commonwealth, other than the port of her destination; and no ship or vessel, so piloted, shall be subjected to pay pilotage on entering or leaving any port as aforesaid: *provided*, that, if the master or commander of any such ship or vessel shall require and receive the aid of a pilot to conduct his vessel as aforesaid, then such pilot shall render his services, and be entitled to receive the rates of pilotage established for said port.

Rates of pilotage to be in proportion to draft of water. Ibid, § 2.

16. The rates of pilotage established in the several ports of this commonwealth, shall be paid in proportion for the depth of water any vessel may draw.

Pilots to demand certificates of master, &c. Ibid, § 3.

17. It shall be the duty of every pilot who shall have conducted any ship or vessel into, or out of, any port in this commonwealth, to demand, from the captain or commander of such ship or vessel, a certificate, containing the name of the ship or vessel, the pilot's name, and the

---

[1] See note 1, to § 9, p. 299, *ante*.

draught of water in feet and inches; and such certificate shall be conclusive evidence, against the owner, of the draught of water of such ship or vessel.

18. Any ship or vessel, requiring the aid of a pilot to enter any port in this commonwealth, shall receive the first person offering his services, and holding a branch for the port into which the vessel is bound, whether he be within his district or not; and if such pilot, so offering his services, shall not be received, and the master or commander shall afterwards receive another pilot, the first pilot offering shall be entitled to receive full pilotage for the draught of water such vessel may draw.

First pilot offering himself, to be received. Ibid, § 4.

19. Pilots are exempted from military duty in this commonwealth.

Pilots exempted from military duty. R. S. 12, § 1.

POLICE OFFICERS.

STATUTE.

The mayor and aldermen may appoint police officers.

The mayor and aldermen of Boston may, from time to time, appoint such police officers for said city as they may judge necessary, with all or any of the powers of the constables of said city, except the power of serving and executing any civil process; and the said police officers shall hold their offices during the pleasure of the said mayor and aldermen.[1]

Mayor and aldermen may appoint police officers. 1838, 123.

---

[1] The law does not require that a police officer of the city of Boston, appointed pursuant to stat. 1835, c. 123, should be sworn to the faithful discharge of the duties of his office; and therefore a party indicted for assaulting such police officer, and obstructing him in the discharge of the duties of his office, cannot defend by showing that he had never been sworn. *Commonwealth v. Dugan*, (12 Metc. 233.)

L. was appointed by the mayor and aldermen of Boston, under stat. 1838, c. 123, " a police officer (at the National Theatre) with the power of

PORTERS.

STATUTE.

1. Selectmen, (mayor and aldermen,) to appoint porters. To regulate their wages. Porters to wear badges.
2. Penalty for persons unlicensed acting as porters.
3. Penalty for asking more than selectmen allow, for services. For appearing without badge.
4. Security to be given by porters. They may be removed for disorderly conduct.

Selectmen (mayor and aldermen) to appoint porters. 1741, § 1. 1796, 69. 3 Special laws, Appendix, 6 & 25.

1. By an act for the better regulating porters employed within the town of Boston,[1] passed in 1741, and originally to continue for seven years, and no longer, but made perpetual, March 7, 1797, it was provided, that the selectmen[2] of the town of Boston for the time being, should have full power and authority to order what number, and who should be employed, and take upon them the business of carrying goods, wares and merchandizes, for pay or wages, as common porters within the said town; and what rate or price such

To regulate their wages.

---

a constable, except the power of serving civil process." Held, that if L.'s power was limited to a part of the city, yet that it was not limited to the space within the walls of the theatre, but extended to the environs, so far as the special vigilance of an officer might be required to keep the peace and preserve order among persons frequenting the theatre, or carrying others to and from it, or supplying refreshments; and also to shops, stalls and stands, kept in the vicinity, for the purpose of supplying refreshments. *Commonwealth v. Hastings*, (9 Metc. 259.)

[1] The preamble of this act was as follows:—

"Whereas the trade and business managed in the town of Boston, between the inhabitants thereof and others trafficking there, occasions many persons to resort to and attend about the wharves, docks, and other parts of the town, to convey and carry goods, wares and merchandizes from place to place, some of whom are not so well known as such an employment requires, others of no good character, yet ofttimes have goods of a considerable value put into their custody for conveyance as aforesaid, and some taking upon them the business of porters, impose upon those making use of them, more especially strangers, by exacting exorbitant wages for their labor, or refusing business, though not before employed, if they cannot have their unreasonable demands: Therefore, to avoid such inconveniencies for the future, Be it enacted," &c.

[2] By the city charter, § 13, the powers previously vested in the selectmen, were vested in the mayor and aldermen. See p. 13, § xx, *ante*.

persons should ask, receive and take, for their labor, service and attendance, according to the distance of place or other circumstances, the selectmen should order and ascertain; all which persons, so admitted by the selectmen, should at all times when in the service or doing the business of porters, wear a badge or ticket, with the figure of a pine tree marked thereon, on some part of his upper garment or girdle; which badge or ticket should be numbered, and a fair entry of each porter's ticket made in the selectmen's book, as also the wages they were to ask and receive, within ten days after the approbation of the selectmen as aforesaid.

Porters to wear badges.

2. It was further provided, that whosoever should presume to take up the business and employ of a common porter, and convey or carry goods and merchandize from place to place, within the town of Boston, for hire or wages, without being admitted by the selectmen, as aforesaid, should forfeit and pay the sum of twenty shillings, for every time he should be convicted thereof, before any one of his majesty's justices of the peace, within the county of Suffolk, at Boston aforesaid; the one half of which fine or forfeiture, should be disposed of to and for the use of the poor of the town of Boston, the other half to him or them that should inform and sue for the same.

Penalty for persons unlicensed acting as porters. Ibid, § 2.

3. It was further enacted, that whosoever, being admitted as a porter as aforesaid, should ask, take, and receive any more than what the selectmen should allow, for any work or service, should for every such exaction, forfeit and pay the sum of twenty shillings, to be recovered and disposed of as hereinbefore directed; and if any person admitted and approved of as aforesaid, as a common porter, should officiate or concern himself in the business of transporting goods or merchandize, not having his badge or ticket, should, for every such breach of the said act, forfeit and pay the sum of twenty shillings, to be recovered and disposed of as aforesaid.

Penalty for asking more than selectmen allow, for services. Ibid, § 3.

Appearing without badge.

4. It was further enacted, that the selectmen should require and take bond of each one of the porters, admitted as aforesaid, with sufficient surety, in a sum not exceeding

Security to be given by porters. Ibid, § 4.

fifty pounds, for their orderly and faithful acting in the business; more especially their safe conveying and delivering such goods as should be committed to them; and that upon complaint made to the selectmen, that any whom they might have admitted as aforesaid, did not behave and conduct themselves orderly, peaceably and quietly, towards their employers, it being made to appear, the party accused being seasonably notified thereof, such person might be removed, and other meet and orderly person admitted in his room.

They may be removed for disorderly conduct. 1821, 110, § 13.

PRINTING.

ORDINANCE OF THE CITY.[1]

A joint standing committee on printing to be appointed.

A joint standing committee on printing to be appointed. Dec. 24, 1846.

There shall be appointed annually, in the month of January, a joint standing committee of the city council, to be called the committee on printing, consisting of one member of the board of mayor and aldermen, and two members of the common council, whose duty it shall be to contract for the city printing, to see that the work performed, and the materials provided, are in conformity with the terms of the contract; and to approve all bills for printing.

---

[1] An ordinance relating to printing, passed December 24, 1846.

PUBLIC BUILDINGS.

STATUTES.

1. In the county of Suffolk, the court houses, jails, house of correction, fire proof offices, and all other necessary public buildings, for the use of the county, shall be provided by the city of Boston, at its own expense.

In county of Suffolk, public buildings to be provided by Boston. R. S. 14, § 10.

2. The mayor and aldermen, among other powers and duties of county commissioners, have authority to provide for the erecting and repairing of court houses, jails, and other necessary public buildings, within and for the use of the county.

Mayor and aldermen to provide for erecting and repairing county buildings. Ibid, §§ 29, 31.

ORDINANCE OF THE CITY.[1]

Committee on public buildings to be appointed. July 1, 1850.

SECT. 1. In the month of January in each year there shall be appointed a joint committee of the city council, to be called the committee on public buildings, to consist of three members of the board of mayor and aldermen, and five members of the common council.

To have care and custody of school houses and other city buildings, except, &c. Ibid.

SECT. 2. The said committee shall have the care and custody of all the school houses and other buildings belonging to the city, and of the erection, alteration and repair thereof, except as otherwise provided in this, and other ordinances of the city, and subject to such rules, orders and regulations as the city council may from time to time adopt.

To lease buildings belonging to city, subject, &c. Ibid.

SECT. 3. The said committee are authorized to lease any building belonging to the city, which is not otherwise appropriated, for any period not exceeding three years, and upon such terms and conditions as they may deem expedient, subject, however, to the approval of the board of mayor and aldermen; and in such case the lease shall be signed and executed by the mayor.

Lease to be signed by mayor.

Committee to prepare plans and specifications of buildings to be erected, altered, or repaired. Ibid.

SECT. 4. Whenever any building for the use of the city shall be erected, altered or repaired, the expense of which may exceed the sum of five hundred dollars, it shall be the duty of the committee that may have charge of the same, to prepare, or cause to be prepared, the requisite plans and specifications of the work to be done.

To publish notice of time and place for exhibition of same. Ibid.

SECT. 5. The said committee shall give notice in the newspapers in which the ordinances of the city are published, of the time and place for the exhibition of such plans and specifications, as may be necessary to enable contractors to make their estimates of the proposed work.

Proposals for work to be sealed. Ibid. How opened.

SECT. 6. No proposal shall be received by the said committee, from any person offering to contract for such work, unless the same is sealed; and no proposal shall be opened except in committee actually assembled; and the

---

[1] An ordinance concerning the public buildings, passed July 1, 1850.

contents of no proposal shall be made known to any person not a member of the committee, until after a contract shall have been made; provided, always, that if any such proposals shall be offered by persons, who, in the judgment of the said committee, shall be incompetent to perform their contracts in a workmanlike manner, or irresponsible in respect to their means of faithfully executing the same, the said committee may, in their discretion, reject any such proposal, notwithstanding the same be at a lower rate than other proposals offered for the same work.

Not to be disclosed till contract is made. Proviso.

SECT. 7. In all cases where the amount of any contract shall exceed the sum of five hundred dollars, the contract shall be in writing, and signed by the mayor on the part of the city; and, after being signed by the parties, no such contract shall be altered in any particular, unless three-fourths of the said committee shall signify their assent thereto in writing under their respective signatures, indorsed on the said contract.

Contracts exceeding $500, to be in writing, and signed by the mayor. Ibid. Not to be altered, unless, &c.

SECT. 8. The amount of expenditures for the foregoing purposes in any one year, shall never exceed the appropriations made by the city council for the same; and no expenditure exceeding two hundred dollars shall ever be made, in the alteration or repair of any building, without an express vote of the city council authorizing the same.

Expenditures not to exceed appropriations. Ibid.

SECT. 9. Whenever the city council shall order the purchase of any land, for the purpose of erecting any building thereon, such purchase shall be made under the direction of the said committee on public buildings.

Purchases of land for erecting buildings, to be made under direction of committee. Ibid.

SECT. 10. The preceding sections shall not apply to the jail, the court house, the registry of deeds, the house of correction, or any other buildings of which the erection, care or maintenance is devolved by law on the mayor and aldermen.

Certain buildings excepted from preceding section. Ibid.

SECT. 11. There shall be chosen in the month of April or May, in each year, and whenever a vacancy occurs, by concurrent vote of the two branches of the city council, a superintendent of public buildings, who shall hold his office until a successor is appointed, or he is removed. He shall be removable at the pleasure of the city council, and

Superintendent of public buildings. Ibid.

shall receive such compensation as the said council may from time to time determine.

To give bond. Ibid.

SECT. 12. The said superintendent, before entering on the duties of his office, shall give bond, with one or more sureties, to the approbation of the mayor and aldermen, with condition that he will not, directly or indirectly, for himself or others, or by others in trust for him, or on his account, have any interest or concern in any contract or agreement for the erection, alteration or repair of any building belonging to the city, or in any purchase, sale or lease made by the city under and by virtue of this ordinance.

Condition of bond.

To have care and custody of school houses and other buildings. Ibid.

SECT. 13. The said superintendent, under the direction of the committee on public buildings, or of the mayor and aldermen as the case may be, shall have the care and custody of all the school houses and other buildings belonging to the city, except as otherwise provided, whether used for county purposes or otherwise; he shall keep himself acquainted with their condition; he shall employ suitable mechanics, and shall himself superintend all repairs that may be ordered on the same; and, in general, he shall render such services as may be required of him, in relation to such buildings, by the mayor and aldermen, by the committee on public buildings, or by any other committee or board appointed by the city council.

His duties.

To keep record. Ibid.

SECT. 14. The said superintendent shall keep an accurate record of all buildings belonging to the city, and lands appurtenant to such buildings; and in the month of January, in each year, he shall present to the city council a report in relation to the same, showing their condition, and the nature and amount of expenditures that shall have been made in relation thereto.

To report to city council.

No building or land appurtenant to be sold without an order from the city council. Ibid.

SECT. 15. No building, or land appurtenant thereto shall be sold by any committee of the city council, without an order from the city council authorizing such sale.

PUBLIC LANDS.

STATUTE.

The city of Boston authorized to make a branch railroad from the Old Colony railroad to the city flats, by a bridge over the South Bay. 1848, 37, § 1. (Accepted by city council, April 24, 1848. City Records, vol. 26, p. 156.)

1. By an act passed March 3, 1848, the city of Boston was authorized to locate and construct a branch railroad, from some convenient point on the Old Colony railroad, in Boston, on the southwesterly side of the turnpike, so called; thence running across the marshes and flats, and over South Bay, by a suitable bridge, to the flats belonging to the said city, and lying between the easterly line of Front street, and the sea wall lately erected by the said city, with power, from time to time, as convenience might require, to locate branch tracks thereupon, for the purpose of filling up or grading any streets, passage-ways, or lands, in that vicinity, situate easterly of Washington street; and for the purpose aforesaid, the said city of Boston was vested with all the powers and privileges, and made subject to all the duties, liabilities, and restrictions,

set forth in the forty-fourth chapter of the Revised Statutes, and in that part of the thirty-ninth chapter of said statutes relating to railroad corporations, and in all statutes which had been, or should be thereafter, passed relating to railroad corporations; excepting, however, that the said city was not required to make any annual report to the legislature, unless thereafter specially directed so to do.

To be connected with the Old Colony railroad. 1848, 37, § 2.

When to be removed.

2. The said branch railroad was permitted to be connected with the Old Colony railroad, upon such terms and conditions as might be agreed between the said city of Boston, and the Old Colony Railroad Company; and the said branch railroad, and also all branch tracks therefrom, that might be constructed under the first, second and third sections, were to be removed within five years from the first day of February, in the year one thousand eight hundred and forty-eight; and all piles not taken up, were to be cut off at least six feet below the surface of the mud.

Bridge over South Bay, how to be constructed. Ibid, § 3.

3. The city of Boston were required to cause the bridge above authorized, to be constructed with convenient draws over the channel of South Bay, to be at least thirty feet wide, and with suitable piers, at the expense of said city, and to maintain and tend the same, so as to afford all reasonable and proper accommodation for vessels having occasion to pass by day or night through the same; and to improve the channels on said South Bay, the said city were required to remove from each channel at least twelve thousand eight hundred cubic yards of mud or earth, at their own expense, within six months from the first day of April, 1848, under the direction of Allen Putnam, of Roxbury, and Charles Heath, of Boston, or, in case of their death or inability to act, then under the direction of the mayor of Roxbury for the time being. [1]

---

[1] The act of 1848, c. 37, § 4, provided that the said act should take effect from and after its passage; and that upon its acceptance by the city council, all the powers and privileges conferred upon the city of Boston, by the act of the legislature approved by the governor on the twenty-third day of April, in the year one thousand eight hundred and forty-seven, entitled "An act to authorize the city of Boston to construct a railroad from the Providence railroad to South Bay," should be deemed to be surrendered

ORDINANCE OF THE CITY.[1]

SECT. 1. In the month of January, in each year, there shall be appointed a joint committee of the city council, to be called the committee on public lands, to consist of two aldermen and five members of the common council, and of the mayor, who shall be chairman *ex officio*. Committee on public lands to be appointed. July 22, 1850.

SECT. 2. The said committee shall have the care and management of the public lands belonging to the city, so far as relates to the improvement, sale and disposal of the same, subject to the limitations, mentioned in this and other ordinances of the city, and to such rules, orders and regulations, as the city council may from time to time adopt. To have care and management of public lands. Ibid.

SECT. 3. The said committee are authorized to lay out and make such streets, passage-ways and squares on the public lands, to lay such sewers therein, and to make such alterations in the lots, as they may deem expedient, subject to the approval of the mayor and aldermen. May lay out streets, &c. Ibid. May lay sewers, &c.

SECT. 4. There shall be chosen annually in the month of April or May, and whenever a vacancy occurs, by concurrent vote of the two branches of the city council, a superintendent of public lands, who shall hold his office until a successor is appointed, or he is removed. He shall be removable at the pleasure of the city council, and shall receive such compensation as the said council may from time to time determine. Superintendent of public lands to be chosen. Ibid.

SECT. 5. The said superintendent, before entering on the duties of his office, shall give bond, with one or more sureties, to the approbation of the mayor and aldermen, with condition that he will not, directly or indirectly, for himself or others, or by others in trust for him, or on his account, have any interest or concern in any purchase, Shall give bond. Ibid. Condition of bond.

---

by the said city, and said last mentioned act become null and void, being in such case repealed. See 1847, c. 250.

For the powers of the city council in relation to the public lands, see city charter and amendments, § 25, pp. 16, 17, *ante*.

[1] An ordinance concerning the public lands, passed July 22, 1850.

lease, contract or agreement, to be made in pursuance of this ordinance.

Duties of superintendent. Ibid.

SECT. 6. The said superintendent shall devote himself to the care, improvement and sale of the public lands, and, under the direction of the said committee, shall cause them to be surveyed and laid out into convenient lots, and contract for the sale, and actually sell or lease the same, at public or private sale. But this and the third section shall not apply to the common, the land and flats west of Charles street, the city wharf, the lands connected with the public institutions at South Boston, or to any other lands purchased or held for specific purposes, unless by special vote of the city council.

May contract to defray expenses by transfer of lands. Ibid.

SECT. 7. The said superintendent may, under the direction of the said committee, contract and agree for defraying in part, or in whole, the cost or expense incident to, or arising out of the performance of any acts which he is by this ordinance authorized to do and perform, by transfer of lands to the contracting parties, in lieu of money, when the same can be done with advantage to the city.

His duties in relation to the laying out of streets, &c. Ibid.

SECT. 8. The said superintendent shall at all times perform such services as may be required of him by the mayor and aldermen, in the laying out, alteration or widening of streets, and in the trial or settlement of any and all claims for damages, in consequence of such laying out, alteration or widening, and in the care and improvement of the common and public squares.

All contracts, &c., to be signed by the mayor, and countersigned by superintendent. Ibid.

SECT. 9. All contracts, deeds, conveyances and leases, made by virtue of this ordinance, shall be signed and executed by the mayor, in the same manner as if the same were made by order of the city council, and shall be countersigned by the said superintendent.

Superintendent to make quarterly reports. Ibid.

SECT. 10. The said superintendent shall, at least once in three months, and as often as required, make a true and correct report of his proceedings under this ordinance, and exhibit proper schedules and accounts of all lands sold, moneys received and securities taken, to the mayor and aldermen, which shall be by them sent to the common council.

SECT. 11. The said superintendent shall keep an accurate record or account of all the vacant lands belonging to the city; and whenever any such land shall be purchased by the city, for any purpose, it shall be the duty of the person or persons so purchasing the same, to make report thereof forthwith to the said superintendent.

To keep record or account of all vacant lands. Ibid.

SECT. 12. All money agreed to be paid by any purchaser or lessee of the public lands, and all notes, bonds, mortgages and securities for moneys, arising or accruing from or in virtue of any contract made by said superintendent, shall be paid to and deposited with the treasurer.

Moneys, securities, &c., to be paid to and deposited with the treasurer. Ibid.

SECT. 13. No conveyance of any estate in fee or for life in any lands belonging to the city, shall be delivered, until the purchase money is paid, or secured by a mortgage of the same land or other land of equal value; and the mayor may from time to time release to any mortgagor or his assigns, any part of the mortgaged premises, on payment of an equivalent portion of the purchase money. And in all cases where lands other than those sold are proposed to be taken as collateral security, the consent and approbation of the mayor in writing shall he first obtained.

No conveyance to be delivered till purchase money is paid or secured. Ibid.

SECT. 14. There shall be no expenditure of money, or contract requiring the expenditure of money to be made, under or by virtue of this ordinance, without the sanction of the city council, by an appropriation first made to meet such expenditure.

No expenditure, &c., to be made without sanction of city council. Ibid.

RAILROADS.

STATUTES.

1. Damages for land, &c., taken for railroads, to be assessed by the mayor and aldermen.
2. Either party may apply to C. C. Pleas for a jury.
3. Railroads not to obstruct other roads in crossing.
4. Proceedings when railroad corporations wish to raise or lower turnpikes, &c.
5. If the parties do not agree as to

Damages for land, &c., taken for railroads, to be assessed by the mayor and aldermen. R. S. 39, § 63.

1. If any railroad corporation shall, by virtue of their charter, take any land or other property, within the city of Boston, without the consent of the owner of such land or other property, the mayor and aldermen of said city shall, except as provided in the following section, have all the power of commissioners in the like cases; and the like proceedings shall be had, before the said mayor and aldermen, for the purpose of ascertaining, securing and obtaining payment of damages, and subject to the same limitations, as in case of an application to the said commissioners.

2. Either party, if dissatisfied with the estimate of damages thus made by said mayor and aldermen, may apply for a jury to the court of common pleas, next to be held within the county of Suffolk, after the said estimate is made known to the parties; and thereupon the same proceedings shall be had, as in case of estimating and enforcing payment of damages for laying out ways within the said city. Either party may apply to C. C. Pleas for a jury. Ibid, § 64.

3. If any railroad shall be so laid out as to cross any turnpike road or other way, it shall be so made as not to obstruct such turnpike road or way. Railroads not to obstruct other roads in crossing. R. S. 39, § 66.

4. Every railroad corporation, which has been or may be established, may raise or lower any turnpike or way, for the purpose of having their railroad pass over or under the same; but before proceeding to make any alteration in such turnpike or way, said railroad corporation shall, in writing, notify the president or clerk of the corporation owning such turnpike, or the selectmen of the town in which such way is situated; and said turnpike corporation or said selectmen, respectively, within thirty days after receiving such notice, shall, in writing, notify said railroad corporation of the alterations, if any, which they may require to have made therein for the purpose aforesaid. Proceedings when railroad corporations wish to raise or lower turnpikes, &c. Ibid, § 67.

5. If the parties shall not agree what alterations are necessary, the said railroad corporation, as well as the said proprietors of the turnpike, and said selectmen, may apply to the commissioners in the county where the said portion of turnpike, or way is situated, at their next regular meeting after the expiration of said thirty days, to determine whether any and what alterations shall be made, and their decision shall be final; and in case said corporation shall unreasonably neglect to make such alteration as the said commissioners shall determine to be proper, the said proprietors or selectmen shall have the same remedies as are prescribed for the recovery of damages caused by making such railroad. If the parties do not agree as to alterations, either may appeal to commissioners. Ibid. § 68.

6. If, after the laying out and making of any railroad already granted, or which may be hereafter granted, any turnpike road or other way shall be so laid out as to cross said railroad, the said turnpike road or way may be so Railroads not to be obstructed by turnpikes, &c., subsequently laid out. Ibid, § 69.

made as to pass under or over said railroad, and said turnpike or way shall in all cases be so made as not to obstruct or injure such railroad.

Proceedings where it is necessary that a highway, &c., crossed by a railroad, should be raised, or lowered. 1842, 22. See R. S., 29, § 66-69.

7. If the selectmen of any town, or the mayor and aldermen of any city, wherein any turnpike, highway or town-way, crossed by any railroad, on a level therewith, is situated, shall be of opinion that it is necessary for the security of the public that said turnpike, highway or town-way should be raised or lowered, so as to pass over or under said railroad, said selectmen, or mayor and aldermen, may, in writing, request the corporation to which said railroad belongs to raise or lower said ways; and if said corporation shall neglect or refuse so to do, said selectmen, or mayor and aldermen, may apply to the county commissioners of the county within which said town is situated, to decide upon the reasonableness of such request; and if said commissioners, after due notice and hearing the parties, shall decide that the raising or lowering of said ways is necessary, for the security of the public, said corporation shall comply with said decision, and shall pay the costs of the application; and if the said commissioners shall be of opinion that such alteration of said ways is not necessary, the said selectmen, or mayor and aldermen shall be liable to pay the costs of their application; and if said corporation shall unreasonably neglect or refuse to carry into effect the decision of said commissioners, such selectmen, or mayor and aldermen, may proceed to do it, and may institute and prosecute to final judgment and execution, in any court proper to try the same, an action of the case against said corporation, and recover the amount of all charges, expenses, labor and services occasioned by making such alteration, with costs of suit.

Application to county commissioners, for their decision thereon.

Railroads to be constructed so as to cross over or under highway, &c. 1846, 271, § 1.

8. Every railroad corporation which may construct a railroad across any turnpike, highway, or town-way, shall construct it, so as to cross over or under the turnpike, highway or town-way, and if the railroad shall be constructed to cross over the turnpike, highway, or town-way, a sufficient space shall be left under the railroad conveniently to accommodate the travel upon the turnpike, highway or town-way. And such railroad corporation shall build, keep

Space to be left under railroad, sufficient for travel.

up and maintain in good repair, such bridges, with suitable and convenient approaches thereto, as may be required to accommodate the travel upon the turnpike, highway or town-way, over such crossing, except such as are provided for in the following section.

Bridges, &c., to be built and maintained in good repair to accommodate travel.

9. The county commissioners of the county in which such crossing is situated, upon the application of the railroad corporation, or of the proprietors of the turnpike, or of the selectmen of the town, or of the mayor and aldermen of the city in which the crossing is situated, after due notice to the railroad corporation, the proprietors of the turnpike and such selectmen, or mayor and aldermen, not being themselves the applicants, and to any other persons of parties, as they may direct, and after hearing the parties, may authorize and require the railroad corporation to construct their railroad at such crossing, upon a level with the turnpike, highway or town-way, in such manner as they may direct; and if they shall consider it necessary, may require the railroad corporation to erect and maintain a gate across the railroad at such crossing, and to provide an agent to open and close the same, as is provided in the eightieth section of the thirty-ninth chapter of the Revised Statutes. And the railroad corporation shall pay the cost of every such application, excepting in cases where the county commissioners shall deny the application of the proprietors of a turnpike or the selectmen of any town, or the mayor and aldermen of any city.

Railroad corporation may be authorized and required by county commissioners, upon application, to construct their railroad on a level with highway, &c., at crossings. Ibid, § 2.

May be required to erect and maintain a gate, and provide an agent at such crossings, as provided in R. S. 39, § 80.

Cost of application, by whom to be paid. See § 15, *post.*

10. Every railroad corporation shall erect and maintain suitable fences, with convenient bars, gates or openings therein, at such places as may reasonably be required, upon both sides of the entire length of any railroad which they may construct, except at the crossings of any turnpike, highway or other way, or in places where the convenient use of the railroad would be obstructed thereby. And shall also construct and maintain sufficient barriers, at such places as may be necessary, where it is practicable to do so, to prevent the entrance of cattle upon the railroad.

Fences, &c., to be erected and maintained at such places as may be reasonably required, upon both sides of the railroad, except, &c. Ibid, § 3.

Sufficient barriers to be maintained to keep cattle from the railroad.

11. Any railroad corporation which shall unreasonably neglect to comply with any of the provisions of the three

Penalty. Ibid, § 4.

preceding sections shall, for each and every such neglect, forfeit a sum not exceeding two hundred dollars, for every month during which such neglect shall have continued.

Railroad corporations may alter the course of highway, subject to the direction of the county commissioners. 1849, 159, § 1.

12. If any railroad corporation, which has been or may be established, shall think proper to alter the course of any highway or town-way, for the purpose of facilitating the crossing of the same by their railroad, or for the purpose of permitting their railroad to pass at the side of such way, without crossing the same, they may make such alteration in such manner as shall be directed by the commissioners of the county where such way is situated; *provided* the commissioners, after due notice to the selectmen of the town where such way is situated, shall be of opinion that such alteration will not essentially injure such way; *and provided further*, that any damage occasioned to private property thereby shall be paid by the corporation, as in case of land taken for the construction of the railroad.

Bell to be attached to locomotive engines, and to be rung, &c. R. S. 39, § 78.

13. Every railroad corporation shall cause a bell, of at least thirty-five pounds in weight, to be placed on each locomotive engine passing upon their road; and the said bell shall be rung, at the distance of at least eighty rods, from the place where said railroad crosses any turnpike, highway or town-way, upon the same level with the railroad, and shall be kept ringing until the engine has crossed such turnpike or way.

Sign boards to be erected at the crossings of roads. Ibid, § 79.

14. Every railroad corporation shall cause boards to be placed, well supported by posts or otherwise, and constantly maintained across each turnpike, highway or town-way, where it is crossed by the railroad, upon the same level therewith; the said posts and boards to be of such height, as shall be easily seen by travellers, without obstructing the travel; and on each side of said boards, the following inscription shall be printed, in capital letters of at least the size of nine inches each,—RAILROAD CROSSING—LOOK OUT FOR THE ENGINE WHILE THE BELL RINGS.

Gates, &c., shall also be erected if necessary. Ibid, § 80.

15. If the selectmen of any town, wherein any turnpike, highway or town-way, so crossed by any railroad, is situated, shall be of opinion, that the provisions contained

in the two preceding sections are not a sufficient security to the public, in any particular case, and that it is necessary for such security, that gates should be erected across the railroad, and that an agent should be stationed to open and close said gates, whenever any engine passes, the said selectmen may in writing request said railroad corporation to erect such gates and station an agent as aforesaid; and if said corporation shall neglect or refuse so to do, the said selectmen may apply to the commissioners, to decide upon the reasonableness of such request; and if said commissioners, after due notice, and hearing the parties, shall decide that the erection of such gates, and providing such agent, are necessary for the security of the public, said railroad corporation shall comply with said decision, and shall pay the costs of the application; and if the said commissioners shall be of opinion, that the establishment of said gates and agent is not required as aforesaid, the said selectmen shall be liable to pay all the costs of their application.

Penalty for neglecting to comply with the foregoing provisions, and liability for damages. Ibid, § 81.

16. If any railroad corporation shall unreasonably neglect or refuse to comply with the requisitions, contained in the three preceding sections, they shall forfeit, for every such neglect or refusal, a sum not exceeding one thousand dollars; and if any agent stationed as aforesaid shall neglect to open or close said gates, for the safe passing of the engine on the railroad, or the traveller on the turnpike, highway or town-way, he shall, for every such neglect, forfeit a sum not exceeding one hundred dollars; and the said railroad corporation shall also be liable for all damages, sustained by any person by reason of such neglect of any of their agents, to be recovered in an action on the case, by the person sustaining such damages.

Applications, as to railroads crossing other roads, in Boston, may be made to the mayor and aldermen. 1849, 222, § 1.

17. By an act passed May 2, 1849, it was provided that the application required by the eightieth section of the thirty-ninth chapter of the Revised Statutes[1] to be made by selectmen to county commissioners, in the matter of a crossing, by a railroad, of any turnpike, highway, or town-way, may, when said crossing is within the limits of the city of Boston, be made by any two inhabitants of said city,

---

[1] That is, § 15, *ante*.

to the mayor and aldermen thereof, and such inhabitants shall be liable for costs when the railroad corporation shall be the prevailing party, and before the hearing of the application, shall give bonds, with sufficient surety, for the payment of such costs, if the mayor and aldermen shall so adjudge.

The preceding section, and R. S. 39, §§ 79, 80 and 81, extended. Ibid, § 2.

18. The provisions of the preceding section, and of the seventy-ninth, eightieth, and eighty-first sections of the thirty-ninth chapter of the Revised Statutes,[1] are declared applicable to all crossings by railroads of any highway, turnpike, town-way, or travelled place, upon the same level therewith, which did, at the passage of said statute of 1849, or might thereafter exist; *provided*, that, whenever it shall be adjudged that a railroad corporation shall provide security against a travelled place, not laid out and adjudged to be a town-way or a highway, the said corporation shall provide a gate for the same, or bars, as the county commissioners shall order.

Corporation shall provide a gate, or bars, when adjudged necessary.

County commissioners may direct gates to be built acoss highway, &c. Ibid, § 3.

19. The county commissioners may direct gates to be built across the turnpike, highway or town-way, when the same crosses such railroad, instead of across said railroad.

Shall have original jurisdiction of questions as to obstructions by railroads. Ibid § 4.

20. The original jurisdiction of all questions touching obstructions to turnpikes, highways, or town-ways, caused by the construction or operation of railroads, shall be vested in the county commissioners of the respective counties wherein such obstructions shall occur.

S. J. Court, shall have equity jurisdiction to enforce decisions of county commissioners. Ibid § 5.

21. The supreme judicial court shall have jurisdiction in equity, and may compel railroad corporations to raise or lower any turnpike, highway or town-way, when the county commissioners have decided, or may decide, in due and legal form, that such raising or lowering of any such way is necessary for the security of the public, and to compel railroad corporations to comply with the orders, decrees, and judgments of county commissioners, in all cases touching obstructions, by railroads, in any of said ways.[2]

---

[1] That is, §§ 14, 15, and 16, *ante*.

[2] For other provisions respecting railroads, see R. S. c. 39, §§ 45–86, and c. 130, § 21; 1836, c. 278; 1837, c. 226; 1838, c. 99; 1839, c. 76; 1840, c. 83, 85; 1841, c. 34, 69, 125; 1843, c. 10, 68; 1845, c. 191; 1846, c. 97, 190; 1847, c. 181; 1848, c. 140, 327; 1849, c. 131, 153, 161, 172, 191; 1850, c. 44. For the act respecting a temporary branch railroad over South Bay, see Public Lands, p. 309, *ante*.

REGISTRY OF BIRTHS, MARRIAGES AND DEATHS.

STATUTES.

1. By the provisions of the Revised Statutes, the city clerk[1] was required to keep a record of the births and deaths of all persons within the city, and coming to his knowledge; and to specify in such record the day of each

City clerk to record all births and deaths in the city. R. S. 15, § 46. Ibid, 2, § 6, clause 17.

[1] See § 10, p. 324, *post*, providing for the choice of a city registrar, to perform the duties herein imposed upon the city clerk.

birth and death, and the names of the parents of such persons, if known.

Parents and others, to give notice to city clerk, of births and deaths. Ibid. R. S. 15, § 47.

2. Parents in the city shall give notice to the city clerk of all the births and deaths of their children; and every householder shall give the like notice of every birth and death happening in his house; and the eldest person next of kin shall give such notice of the death of his kindred; and the keeper of any alms-house, work-house, house of correction, prison or hospital, and the master or other commanding officer of any ship, shall give the like notice of every birth and death, happening among the persons under his charge; and every person, neglecting to give such notice, for the space of six months, after the birth or death shall have happened, shall forfeit to the use of the city a sum not exceeding five dollars.

Clerks to transmit to secretary of the commonwealth copies of record of births, marriages and deaths. 1844, 159, § 1. 1849, 202, § 5.

3. The clerks of the several cities and towns in this commonwealth shall, annually, on or before the first day of February, return to the secretary of the commonwealth copies of the records of the births, marriages, and deaths, which have occurred within their respective cities and towns during the next preceding year ending December thirty-first.

Births, how to be recorded, and with what particulars.

The births shall be numbered and recorded in the order in which they are received by the clerk. The record of births shall state in separate columns the date of the birth, the place of birth, the name of the child, (if it have any,) the sex of the child, name and surname of one or both of the parents, occupation of the father, residence of the parents, and the time when the record was made.

Marriages.

The marriages shall be numbered and recorded in the order in which they are received by the clerk. The record of marriages shall state in separate columns, the date of the marriage, the place of the marriage, the name, residence, and official station of the person by whom married, the names and surnames of the parties, the residence of each, the age of each, the condition of each, (whether single or widowed,) the occupation, names of the parents, and the time when the record was made.

The deaths shall be numbered and recorded in the order in which they are received by the clerk. The record of deaths shall state in separate columns the date of the death, the name and surname of the deceased, the sex, condition, (whether single or married,) age, occupation, place of death, place of birth, names of the parents, disease, or causes of death, and the time when the record was made. Deaths.

4. The school committee of each city or town shall, annually, in the month of May, ascertain from actual inquiry or otherwise, all the births which have happened within such city or town, during the year next preceding the first day of said May, together with the facts concerning births required by the preceding section, and shall make an accurate return thereof to the clerk of such city or town, on or before the last day of said May; and the said school committee, or other person authorized by them to make such returns, shall be entitled to receive from the treasury of such city or town, five cents for each and every birth so returned. School committees to make annual returns of births, to town and city clerks. 1844, 159, § 2.

5. Every justice, minister, and clerk, or keeper of the records of the meeting wherein any marriages among the Friends or Quakers shall be solemnized, shall make a record of each marriage solemnized before him, together with all the facts relating to marriages required by the third section; and each such justice, minister, clerk, or keeper, shall, between the first and tenth days of each month, return a copy of the record for the month next preceding, to the clerk of the city or town in which the marriage was solemnized; and every person as aforesaid, who shall neglect to make the returns required by this section, shall, upon conviction thereof, forfeit for each neglect a sum, not less than twenty, nor more than one hundred dollars; one moiety thereof to the use of the county in which he resides, and the other moiety to the use of the person who shall prosecute therefor. Persons solemnizing marriages, to keep a record thereof, and to make returns, monthly, to town and city clerks. Ibid, § 3. R. S. 75, § 18.

6. Each sexton, or other person, having the charge of any burial ground in this commonwealth, shall, on or before the tenth day of each month, make returns of all the facts required by the third section, connected with the death of Persons having charge of burial grounds to make returns of burials monthly, to town and city clerks. 1844, 159, § 4.

any person whose burial he may have superintended during the month next preceding, to the clerk of the city or town in which such deceased person resided at the time of his death. And such sexton, or other person, shall be entitled to receive from the treasury of the city or town in which the return is made, five cents for the return of each death made agreeably to the provisions of this act.[1]

Clerks to distribute blank forms of returns. Ibid, § 6.

7. It shall be the duty of the clerks of the several cities and towns, to make such distribution of blank forms of returns as shall be designated by the secretary of the commonwealth.

Secretary of the commonwealth to furnish clerks with books and blanks, and to prepare and report abstract of returns to the legislature annually. Ibid, § 7.

8. The secretary of the commonwealth shall prepare and furnish to the clerks of the several cities and towns in this commonwealth, blank books of suitable quality and size, to be used as books of record, according to the provisions of the five preceding sections, and also blank forms of returns as herein before specified, and shall accompany the same with such instructions and explanations as may be necessary and useful; and he shall receive said returns, and prepare therefrom such tabular results, as will render them of practical utility, and shall make report thereof annually to the legislature, and generally shall do whatever may be required to carry into effect the provisions of this and the five preceding sections.

Penalty for neglect by clerks. Ibid, § 8.

9. Any clerk, who shall neglect to comply with the requirements of the six preceding sections, shall be liable to a penalty of ten dollars, to be recovered for the use of any city or town where such neglect shall be proved to have existed.[2]

Clerks to obtain and record information. 1849, 202, § 1. Registrar may be chosen to perform this duty, in certain cases.

10. Town and city clerks are authorized and required to obtain, record, and index, the information concerning births, marriages, and deaths, now required by law. Towns and cities, containing more than ten thousand inhabitants, may choose a person, other than the town or city clerk, to

---

[1] The 5th section of stat. 1844, c. 159, providing for the fees of the clerk, appears to be superseded by subsequent provisions. See § 11, p. 325, *post*.

[2] Stat. 1844, c. 159, § 9, repealed Stat. 1842, c. 95.

be town or city registrar, to perform this duty, instead of the town or city clerk; and said registrar shall take an oath faithfully to perform the duties of the office. **Oath.**

11. The fees of the clerk and registrar, for obtaining, recording, and indexing, the information required by this act, shall be as follows:—For each birth, twenty cents; for each intention of marriage, including the certificate to the parties, fifty cents; for each marriage solemnized, ten cents; for each death, five cents; and the undertaker shall be allowed ten cents for information concerning each death which he returns to the clerk or registrar; said fees for births, deaths, and marriages solemnized, shall be paid by the town; and for intentions of marriage, by the parties having such intentions; *provided, however*, that the aggregate compensation, allowed to any clerk or registrar, may be limited by any town or city, containing over ten thousand inhabitants, but in no case so as to prevent the full execution of this and the tenth, twelfth, and thirteenth sections. **Fees. Ibid, § 2.** **Compensation may be limited**

12. Any undertaker, or other person having the superintendence of the burial of any deceased person, who shall neglect or refuse to obtain and return the information required by this act concerning each person deceased, whose burial shall come under his superintendence, shall be liable to a penalty not exceeding twenty dollars for each neglect, and, if an undertaker, to be deprived of his office. And every clerk or registrar, who wilfully neglects or refuses to perform the duties herein prescribed, shall be liable to a penalty of not less than twenty, nor more than one hundred dollars, for each neglect or refusal. All penalties and forfeitures, under this section, may be recovered by any person who shall sue for the same, one half thereof to the use of said complainant, and the other half to the use of the town or city in which the forfeiture shall have been incurred. **Penalties for neglect by undertakers, &c. Ibid, § 3.** **How recovered.**

13. The blank forms of such returns shall be printed on paper of uniform size; and those for each year, when filled out and returned to the office of the secretary of state, shall be bound together in one or more volumes, and **Blank forms of returns. Ibid, § 5.** **See § 3, p. 322, *ante*.**

shall be furnished with an index. Blank books for indexes to the town registrars, shall be prepared by the secretary of state, and furnished to the several towns and cities at the expense of the commonwealth.[1]

Intentions of marriage to be entered with clerk, registrar, &c. 1850, 121, § 1.

14. All persons intending to be joined in marriage shall cause notice of their intention to be entered before their marriage, in the office of the clerk, registrar, or other officer appointed for such purpose, of the city or town in which they may respectively dwell, (if within the state;) and if there be no such clerk in the place of their residence, the like entry shall be made with the clerk of an adjoining town.

Clerk shall deliver to the parties a certificate. Ibid, § 2.

15. The clerk shall deliver to the parties a certificate under his hand, specifying the time when notice of the intention of marriage was entered with him, which certificate shall be delivered to the minister or magistrate, in whose presence the marriage is to be contracted, before he shall proceed to solemnize the same.

Parties going out of the state to be married, shall file a certificate within seven days after their return. Ibid, § 3.

16. Whenever parties living in this commonwealth shall go out of it for the purpose of having a marriage solemnized between them in another state, and a marriage shall be so solemnized, and they shall return to dwell here, they are hereby required to file a certificate or declaration of their marriage, including the facts concerning marriages now required by law, with the clerk or registrar of the town or city where either of them lived at the time, within seven days after their return, under a penalty of ten dollars, to be recovered in the manner and to the uses specified in the third section of the "act relating to the registration of births, marriages, and deaths," passed on the second day of May, in the year eighteen hundred and forty-nine.[2]

Fee. Ibid, § 4.

17. The fee of the clerk or registrar, for making the record of such marriage, shall be fifty cents, to be paid by the said parties.

---

[1] Stat. 1849, c. 202, § 6, contained a general repeal of all inconsistent provisions.

[2] § 12, p. 325, *ante*.

18. So much of the seventy-fifth chapter of the Revised Statutes as is inconsistent with the four preceding sections, is hereby repealed: *provided, nevertheless*, that nothing herein contained shall be so construed as to modify or alter the provisions of the twenty-second section of the said seventy-fifth chapter, which relates to marriages among the people called Friends or Quakers, but the same shall remain in full force.

Repeal of so much of R. S. 75, as is inconsistent. Ibid, § 5. Proviso.

ORDINANCE OF THE CITY.[1]

SECT. 1. There shall be chosen in the month of February or March, in each year, and whenever a vacancy occurs, by concurrent vote of the two branches of the city council, a city registrar, who shall hold his office until a a successor is appointed, or he is removed, and who shall be removable at the pleasure of the city council.

City registrar to be chosen. Sept. 9, 1850.

SECT. 2. The said city registrar shall perform the duties required by law to be performed by town and city clerks, or town and city registrars, in relation to births, marriages and deaths; and he shall have the custody of all records, books and papers, belonging to the city, relating to these matters.

To perform duties of clerks and registrars in relation to births, marriages and deaths. Ibid.

SECT. 3. The said city registrar shall, in the month of January, annually, report to the city council a statement of the number of births, of intentions of marriage entered according to law, of marriages solemnized, and of deaths recorded during the previous year, with such other information, and suggestions in relation thereto, as he may deem useful; and he shall perform such other duties as may be required of him by the mayor and aldermen or the city council.

To report to city council. Ibid.

---

[1] An ordinance providing for the appointment of a city registrar, passed Sept. 9, 1850.

Assistant registrars. Ibid.

SECT. 4. The said city registrar is authorized to employ one or more assistants, to act under his authority and direction, in obtaining information concerning all matters which may legally come under his superintendence.

Compensation of registrar. Ibid.

SECT. 5. The said city registrar shall receive, in full compensation for all his services under the general laws and the ordinances of the city, such salary, and such additional allowance for necessary clerk hire and assistants, as the city council may from time to time determine.

Compensation of undertakers. Ibid. See § 51, p. 213, and § 6, p. 323, *ante*.

SECT. 6. The compensation required by law to be paid for obtaining and returning to the city registrar the information required concerning persons deceased, shall be understood as included in the fees, provided to be paid to undertakers, in the fifty-first section of an ordinance relating to the public health, passed on the twentieth day of August, in the year eighteen hundred and fifty; and this section shall be considered as a part of their agreement, in accepting office.

REWARDS.[1]

STATUTE.

Selectmen, or mayor and aldermen, may offer a reward not exceeding $200 for securing offenders. 1840. 75, § 1.

1. The Selectmen of any town or the mayor and aldermen of any city, are authorized, whenever, in their opinion, the public good may require it, to offer a suitable reward, to be paid by such town or city, not exceeding two hundred

---

[1] The mayor and aldermen of the city of Boston passed an order, "that a reward of $500 be offered to any person who shall give information, so that any person shall be convicted of setting fire to any building, for the purpose of burning the same:" an advertisement was inserted in the

dollars in any one case, to any person who shall in consequence of such offer, secure any person charged with any capital crime, or other high crime or misdemeanor, committed in such town or city, and such reward shall be paid by the treasurer of such town or city, upon the warrant of the selectmen or mayor and aldermen.

2. When more than one claimant shall appear and apply for the payment of such reward, the selectmen or mayor and aldermen shall determine to whom the same shall be paid, and if to more than one person, in what proportion to each, and their determination shall be final and conclusive in law upon all persons whatsoever.

Payment, when there is more than one claimant.
Ibid, § 2.

---

city newspapers which were published on the next morning after said order was passed, reciting that sundry houses and other buildings had been recently set on fire, and offering a reward of $500 to any person "who shall give information, so that any perpetrator of these outrages shall be convicted." This advertisement purported to be "by order of the mayor and aldermen," and was signed by the city clerk. *Held*, that the advertisement must be taken to be the official act of the mayor and aldermen. *Held*, also, that the order and the advertisement were to be construed together, as parts of the same transaction, and that by the true construction thereof, the reward was offered for information that would lead to the conviction of offences previously committed, and not offences thereafter committed. *Freeman v. City of Boston*, (5 Metc. 56.) The mayor of the city of Boston caused an advertisement to be published, for about a week, in the daily papers of the city, stating that there had been a frequent and successful repetition of incendiary attempts, and offering a reward, to be paid by the city, for the apprehension and conviction of any person engaged in those attempts. Held, that this was not to be regarded as an unlimited offer, continuing till it should be formally withdrawn, but as limited to a reasonable time; and that it ceased to be an offer, after the lapse of three years and eight months. *Loring v. City of Boston*, (7 Metc. 409.)

As to the right of city officers to claim rewards offered by the city authorities, see *Poole v. City of Boston*, decided in the S. J. Court, November Term, 1849. See also *Meads v. City of Boston*, decided at the same term.

RIOTS.

Unlawful assemblies, how suppressed. R. S. 129, § 1. 10 Mass. 518. 5 Metc. 536. Thacher's Crim. Cases, 118.

1. If any persons, to the number of twelve or more, being armed with clubs or other dangerous weapons, or if any persons, to the number of thirty or more, whether armed or not, shall be unlawfully, riotously, or tumultuously assembled in any city or town, it shall be the duty of the mayor and of each of the aldermen of such city, and of each of the selectmen of such town, and of every justice of the peace, living in any such city or town, and also of the sheriff of the county and his deputies, to go among the persons so assembled, or as near to them as may be with safety, and in the name of the commonwealth to command all the persons, so assembled, immediately and peaceably to disperse; and if the persons, so assembled, shall not thereupon immediately and peaceably disperse, it shall be the duty of each of the said magistrates and officers to command the assistance of all persons there present, in seizing, arresting and securing in custody, the persons so unlawfully assembled,

so that they may be proceeded with for their offence, according, to law.

2. If any person present, being commanded by any of the magistrates or officers, mentioned in the preceding section, to aid or assist, in seizing and securing such rioters or persons so unlawfully assembled, or in suppressing such riot or unlawful assembly, shall refuse or neglect to obey such command, or, when required by any such magistrate or officer to depart from the place of such riotous or unlawful assembly, shall refuse or neglect so to do, he shall be deemed to be one of the rioters, or persons unlawfully assembled, and shall be liable to be prosecuted and punished accordingly.

Punishment for refusing assistance, when required. Ibid, § 2.

Refusing to disperse, when commanded.

3. If any mayor, alderman, selectman, justice of the peace, sheriff or deputy sheriff, having notice of any such riotous or tumultuous and unlawful assembly, as is mentioned in the two preceding and four succeeding sections, in the city or town in which he lives, shall neglect or refuse immediately to proceed to the place of such assembly, or as near thereto as he can with safety, or shall omit or neglect to exercise the authority, with which he is invested by said sections, for suppressing such riotous or unlawful assembly, and for arresting and securing the offenders, he shall be deemed guilty of a misdemeanor, and punished by a fine not exceeding three hundred dollars.

Neglect of mayor or other officer to suppress, &c. Ibid § 3.

4. If any persons, who shall be so riotously or unlawfully assembled, and who have been commanded to disperse, as before provided, shall refuse or neglect to disperse, without unnecessary delay, any two of the magistrates or officers, before mentioned, may require the aid of a sufficient number of persons, in arms or otherwise, as may be necessary, and shall proceed, in such manner as in their judgment shall be expedient, forthwith to disperse and suppress such unlawful, riotous or tumultuous assembly, and seize and secure the persons composing the same, so that they may be proceeded with according to law.

Officers may quell unlawful assemblies, by force, &c. Ibid, § 4.

5. Whenever an armed force shall be called out, in the manner provided by the twelfth chapter of the Revised

Armed force, if called out, to obey orders of

governor, judge, &c. Ibid, § 5.

Statutes,[1] for the purpose of suppressing any tumult or riot, or to disperse any body of men, acting together by force, and with intent to commit any felony, or to offer violence to persons or property, or with intent, by force or violence, to resist or oppose the execution of the laws of this commonwealth, such armed force, when they shall arrive at the place of such unlawful, riotous or tumultuous assembly, shall obey such orders for suppressing the riot or tumult, and for dispersing and arresting all the persons, who are committing any of the said offences, as they may have received from the governor, or from any judge of a court of record, or the sheriff of the county, and also such further orders, as they shall there receive from any two of the magistrates or officers, mentioned in the first section.

Officers, &c., to be held guiltless, though death be inflicted. Ibid § 6.

6. If, by reason of any of the efforts made by any two or more of the said magistrates or officers, or by their direction, to disperse such unlawful, riotous or tumultuous assembly, or to seize and secure the persons composing the same, who have refused to disperse, though the number remaining may be less than twelve, any such person, or any other persons then present as spectators or otherwise, shall be killed or wounded, the said magistrates and officers, and all persons acting by their order, or under their direction, shall be held guiltless and fully justified in law; and if any of the said magistrates or officers, or any person acting by their order, or under their direction, shall be killed or wounded, all the persons so unlawfully, riotously or tumultuously assembled, and all other persons who, when commanded or required, shall have refused to aid and assist the said magistrates or officers, shall be held answerable therefor.

Rioters, &c., to be severally responsible.

Riotously destroying dwelling house, &c. Ibid, § 7.

7. If any of the persons, so unlawfully assembled, shall demolish, pull down or destroy, or shall begin to demolish, pull down or destroy any dwelling house, or any other building, or any ship or vessel, he shall be punished by imprisonment in the state prison, not more than five years, or

---

[1] The Rev. Stat. c. 12, §§ 134–136, here referred to, contain provisions for calling out the militia in case of tumults, riots, mobs, &c., similar to those contained in stat. 1840, c. 92, §§ 27–29, (§§ 13–15, p. 333, *post*); these sections of the latter statute being a re-enactment, with some variations, of the provisions of the Revised Statutes.

by fine not exceeding one thousand dollars, and imprisonment in the county jail, not more than two years, and shall also be answerable to any person injured, to the full amount of the damage, in an action of trespass.

8. The sixth section above shall be applicable to proceedings had, and cases arising under the provisions of the fourth and fifth sections above, or either of them. Provisions of former law extended. 1839, 54, § 1.

9. Whenever any property of the value of fifty dollars or more, shall be destroyed, or be injured to that amount by any persons to the number of twelve or more, riotously, routously, or tumultuously assembled, the city or town within which said property was situated, shall be liable to indemnify the owner thereof to the amount of three-fourths of the value of the property so destroyed, or the amount of such injury thereto, to be recovered in an action of the case in any court proper to try the same: *provided*, the owner of such property shall use all reasonable diligence to prevent its destruction, or injury, by such unlawful assembly, and to procure the conviction of the offenders. Cities and towns to pay three-fourths of the value of property destroyed or injured by rioters. Ibid, § 2. Proviso.

10. Any city or town which shall pay any sum under the provisions of the preceding section, may recover the same against any or all of the persons who shall have destroyed or injured such property. Town or city, after payment, may recover the amount against any or all of the offenders. Ibid, § 3.

11. The active militia of this commonwealth shall consist and be composed of volunteers, or companies raised at large, and in all cases shall first be ordered into service, in case of war, or invasion, or to prevent invasion, to suppress riots, or to aid civil officers in the execution of the laws of the commonwealth. Active militia to be ordered out first in case of war, riots, &c. 1840, 92, § 11.

12. For unnecessarily neglecting to appear when ordered, or disobeying order, in case of any tumult, riot, or other cause, as provided in the following section, or advising any other person to do the like, every non-commissioned officer, musician, or private, belonging to the active militia of the commonwealth, shall forfeit and pay fifty dollars. Fine for soldiers not obeying orders to appear in case of riot, &c. Ibid, § 26.

13. Whenever there shall be, in any county, any tumult, riot, mob, or any body of men acting together by force, with intent to commit any felony, or to offer violence to persons or property, or by force and violence to break Proceedings to be adopted for ordering out volunteer corps in case of riots, or the like. Ibid, § 27.

and resist the laws of this commonwealth, or any such tumult, riot or mob shall be threatened, and the fact be made to appear to the commander in chief, or the mayor of any city, or to any court of record sitting in said county, or if no such court be sitting therein, then to any justice of any such court, or if no such justice be within the county, then to the sheriff thereof, the commander in chief may issue his order, or such mayor, court, justice, or sheriff may issue his precept directed to any commanding officer of any division, brigade, regiment, battalion, or corps, to order his command, or any part thereof, describing the kind and number of troops, to appear at a time and place within specified, to aid the civil authority in suppressing such violence, and supporting the laws; which precept, if issued by a court, shall be in substance as follows:

Form of requisition on commanding officer.

————————, ss.

COMMONWEALTH OF MASSACHUSETTS.

{ L. S. } To { Insert the officer's title. } A. B. commanding. { Insert his command. }

Whereas it has been made to appear to our justices of our , now holden at , within and for the county of , that (here insert one or more of the causes above mentioned,) in our county of , and that military force is necessary to aid the civil authority in suppressing the same: Now, therefore, we command you, that you cause, (here state the number and kind of troops required,) armed, equipped, and with ammunition, as the law directs, and with proper officers, either attached to the troops or detailed by you, to parade at , on , then and there to obey such orders as may be given them, according to law. Hereof fail not, at your peril, and have you there this writ, with your doings returned thereon.

Witness, L. S., Esquire, at , on the day of , in the year

C. D., *Clerk.*

And if the same be issued by any mayor, justice, or sheriff, it should be under his hand and seal, and otherwise varied to suit the circumstances of the case.

14. The officer to whom the order to [of] the commander in chief, or such precept shall be directed, shall forthwith, order the troops therein mentioned, to parade at the time and place appointed; and if he shall refuse or neglect to obey such order or precept, or if any officer shall neglect or refuse to obey an order issued in pursuance thereof, he shall be cashiered, and be further punished by fine or imprisonment, not to exceed six months, as a court martial may sentence. And any non-commissioned officer or soldier who shall neglect or refuse to appear at the place of parade to obey any order in such case, or any person who shall advise or endeavor to persuade any officer or soldier to refuse or neglect to appear at such place, or to obey such order, shall suffer the penalty provided in such case in the twelfth section.

Penalty on officers and soldiers for disobeying orders. Ibid, § 28.

15. Such troops shall appear at the time and place appointed, armed and equipped, and with ammunition, as for inspection of arms, and shall obey and execute such orders as they may then and there receive, according to law.[1]

Troops to appear with ammunition, &c. Ibid, § 29.

SCHOOLS.

---

[1] See Rev. Stat. c. 12, §§ 134—136, c. 130, § 17; 1838, c. 143; 1847, c, 104; 1849, c. 59; and 1821, 110, § 4, (p. 4, § v, *ante.*)

1. In every town[1] in this commonwealth, there shall be kept, in each year, at the charge of the town, by a teacher or teachers of competent ability and good morals, one school for the instruction of children in orthography, reading, writing, English grammar, geography, arithmetic, and good behavior, for the term of six months, or two or more such schools for terms of time which shall together be equivalent to six months; and in every school in this commonwealth containing fifty scholars as the average number, the school district or town to which such school belongs shall be required to employ a female assistant or assistants, unless such school district or town shall, at a meeting regularly called for that purpose, vote to dispense with the same. *What schools shall be provided by every town. 1839, 56, § 1.*

2. In every town, containing one hundred families or householders, there shall be kept in each year one such school,[2] for the term of twelve months, or two or more such schools, for terms of time, that shall together be equivalent to twelve months. *What by towns of 100 families. R. S. 23, § 2.*

3. In every town, containing one hundred and fifty families or householders, there shall be kept in each year *What by towns of 150 families. Ibid, § 3.*

---

[1] The word "town" may be construed to include "cities," &c. Rev. Stat. c. 2. § 6, clause 17.

[2] The word "such" in this section refers to the first part of § 1, ending with the words "equivalent to six months," which follows the language of Rev. Stat. c. 23, § 1. The remainder of § 1, was first enacted in 1839.

two such schools, for nine months each, or three or more such schools, for terms of time, that shall together be equivalent to eighteen months.

What by towns of 500 families. Ibid, § 4.

4. In every town, containing five hundred families or householders, there shall be kept in each year two such schools for twelve months each, or three or more such schools, for terms of time, that shall together be equivalent to twenty-four months.

Additional school in towns of 500 families, except, &c. Ibid, § 5.

5. Every town, containing five hundred families or householders, shall, besides the schools prescribed in the preceding section, maintain a school, to be kept by a master of competent ability and good morals, who shall, in addition to the branches of learning before mentioned, give instruction in the history of the United States, book-keeping, surveying, geometry and algebra; and such last mentioned school shall be kept for the benefit of all the inhabitants of the town, ten months at least, exclusive of vacations, in each year, and at such convenient place, or alternately at such places in the town, as the said inhabitants at their annual meeting shall determine; and in every town containing four thousand inhabitants, the said master shall, in addition to all the branches of instruction, before required in this chapter, be competent to instruct in the Latin and Greek languages, and general history, rhetoric and logic.

In towns of 4000 inhabitants.

Towns within the 5th section, but containing less than 8000 inhabitants, exempted from its requirements, on certain conditions. 1850, 274.

6. Towns coming within the requirements of the preceding section, but of less than eight thousand inhabitants by the next preceding decennial census, may be exempt from said requirements: *provided*, that they maintain, in each year, two or more schools, in such districts as the school committee shall approve, for terms of time that shall, together, be equivalent to twelve months, and for the benefit of all the inhabitants, kept by masters who, in addition to the branches of instruction enumerated in the first section of said chapter, shall be competent to give instruction in the history of the United States, book-keeping, surveying, geometry, and algebra, and also, in towns containing four thousand inhabitants, in the Latin and Greek languages, general history, rhetoric and logic: *provided, also*, that no one of said schools shall be kept for a less term than three months.

7. Any town, containing less than five hundred families or householders, may establish and maintain such a school as is first mentioned in the fifth section, for such term of time, in any year, or in each year, as they shall deem expedient.

Towns of less than 500 families may maintain such school as mentioned in § 5. R. S. 23, § 6.

8. It shall be the duty of the president, professors, and tutors of the university at Cambridge, and of the several colleges, and of all preceptors and teachers of academies, and all other instructors of youth, to exert their best endeavors, to impress on the minds of children and youth, committed to their care and instruction, the principles of piety, justice, and a sacred regard to truth, love to their country, humanity and universal benevolence, sobriety, industry, and frugality, chastity, moderation, and temperance, and those other virtues, which are the ornament of human society, and the basis upon which a republican constitution is founded; and it shall be the duty of such instructors to endeavor to lead their pupils, as their ages and capacities will admit, into a clear understanding of the tendency of the above mentioned virtues to preserve and perfect a republican constitution, and secure the blessings of liberty, as well as to promote their future happiness, and also to point out to them the evil tendency of the opposite vices.

Duty of instructors. R. S. 23, § 7. See also Constitution, ch. 5, § 2.

9. It shall be the duty of the resident ministers of the gospel, the selectmen, and the school committees, in the several towns, to exert their influence, and use their best endeavors, that the youth of their towns shall regularly attend the schools established for their instruction.

Duty of ministers and town officers. R. S. 23, § 8.

10. The several towns are authorized and directed, at their annual meetings, or at any regular meeting called for the purpose, to raise such sums of money, for the support of the schools aforesaid, as they shall judge necessary; which sums shall be assessed and collected in like manner as other town taxes.[1]

Towns may raise money for schools. Ibid, § 9.

11. The school committee of the city of Boston shall consist of the mayor, of the president of the common coun-

School committee of Boston. 1835, 128, § 1.

---

[1] See also § 44, p. 348, *post*.

(Adopted by citizens in ward meetings, April 29, 1835. Records of returns of votes from the wards, April 29, 1835.) 1821, 110, § 19.

cil, and of twenty-four other persons, two of whom shall be chosen in each ward, and who shall be inhabitants of the wards in which they are chosen; said twenty-four members to be chosen by the inhabitants at their annual election of municipal officers; and said school committee shall have the care and superintendence of the public schools.[1]

School committee, to examine into the qualifications of instructors. R. S. 23, § 13.

12. The school committee shall require full and satisfactory evidence of the good moral character of all instructors, who may be employed in the public schools in their town, and shall ascertain, by personal examination, their literary qualifications and capacity for the government of schools.

Instructors not to be paid unless the committee certify, &c. Ibid, § 14. But see 1850, 115.

13. Every instructor of a town or district school shall obtain of the school committee of such town, a certificate in duplicate, of his qualifications, before he opens such school, one of which shall be filed with the town treasurer, before any payment is made to such instructor on account of his services.

Committee to decide on admission of scholars into school kept for the whole town. R. S. 23, § 15.

14. The school committee shall determine the number and qualifications of the scholars, to be admitted into the school, kept for the use of the whole town, as aforesaid, and visit such school, at least quarter yearly, for the purpose of making a careful examination thereof, and of ascertaining that the scholars are properly supplied with books; and they shall, at such examination, inquire into the regulation and discipline of the school, and the habits and proficiency of the scholars therein.

Committee to visit all the district schools. Ibid, § 16.

15. The school committee, or some one or more of them, shall, for the purposes aforesaid, visit each of the district schools in their town, on some day during the first or second week after the opening of such schools, respectively, and also on some day during the two weeks preceding the closing of the same; and shall also, for the same purposes, visit all the schools kept by the town, once a month, without giving previous notice thereof to the instructors.

---

[1] As to the right to establish in the city of Boston, separate schools for colored children, see the case of *Roberts v. City of Boston*, decided in the Supreme Judicial Court, March T. 1850.

16. The school committee of each town shall direct what books shall be used in the several schools kept by the town; and may direct what books shall be used in the respective classes.

Authority of committee as to school books. Ibid, § 17.

17. The scholars at the town schools shall be supplied by their parents, masters or guardians, with the books prescribed for their classes.*

Parents, &c., to supply the books prescribed. Ibid, § 18.

18. The school committee of each town may procure, at the expense of the town, or otherwise, a sufficient supply of such class books, for all the schools aforesaid, and shall give notice of the place, where such books may be obtained; and the books shall be supplied to the scholars, at such prices, as merely to reimburse the expense of the same.

Books may be provided by the school committee. R. S. 23, § 19. 13 Pick. 229.

19. In case any scholar shall not be furnished by his parent, master, or guardian, with the requisite books, he shall be supplied therewith by the school committee, at the expense of the town.

Books to be furnished at expense of the town, in case, &c. R. S. § 20.

20. The school committee shall give notice, in writing, to the assessors of the town, of the names of the scholars so supplied by them with books, and of the books so furnished, the prices thereof, and the names of the parents, masters or guardians, who ought to have supplied the same; and said assessors shall add the price of the books so supplied, to the next annual tax of such parents, masters or guardians; and the amount so added shall be levied, collected, and paid into the town treasury, in the same manner as the town taxes.

Expense of books so supplied, to be taxed to parents, &c. R. S. 23, § 20.

21. In case the assessors shall be of opinion, that any such parent, master or guardian is unable to pay the whole expense of the books so supplied on his account, they shall omit to add the price of such books, or shall add only a part thereof, to the annual tax of such parent, master or guardian, according to their opinion of his ability to pay.

If parents are unable to pay, such tax may be wholly or partially omitted. Ibid, § 22.

22. The school committee shall never direct to be purchased or used, in any of the town schools, any school books, which are calculated to favor the tenets of any particular sect of christians.

Books not to be bought which favor any particular sect of christians. Ibid, § 23.

Committee to select teachers. 1838, 105, § 2.

23. The school committees shall select and contract with the teachers for the town and district schools.[1]

Committee to keep records, &c. Ibid, § 3.

24. The school committee in each town shall be provided with a record book, in which all votes, orders and proceedings of the committee shall be duly recorded, and said record shall be delivered over by the committees, at the expiration of the year, to their successors in office.[2]

Committee empowered to dismiss teachers. 1844, c. 32.

25. The school committee of any town is authorized to dismiss from employment any teacher in such town, whenever the said committee may think proper, and from the time of such dismissal such teacher shall receive no further compensation for services rendered in that capacity.

Proceeds of Maine lands and militia claim, appropriated to school fund. R. S. 11, § 13.

26. All moneys and stocks in the treasury, on the first day of January, in the year one thousand eight hundred and thirty-five, which shall have been derived from sales of the commonwealth's lands in the state of Maine, and from the claim of the commonwealth on the government of the United States for military services, and which shall not be otherwise appropriated, together with one half of the moneys thereafter received from the sale of lands in Maine, shall constitute a permanent fund, to be called the Massachusetts school fund, for the encouragement of common schools, according to the provisions of the twenty-fourth chapter of the Revised Statutes;[3] provided, that said fund shall never exceed one million of dollars.

Investment of school fund. Ibid, § 14.

27. The investment of all moneys, appropriated to the said school fund, shall be made by the treasurer of the commonwealth, with the approbation of the governor and council.[4]

Committees to make returns to secretary. Ibid, § 62.

28. The school committees of the several towns and of the city of Boston shall, on or before the first day of No-

---

[1] In towns, the teachers may be selected and contracted with by the prudential committee, whenever the town shall so determine. See the whole section, 1838, c. 105, § 2.

[2] A provision is made by law for the compensation of school committees, except in the city of Boston. Stat. 1838, 105, § 4.

[3] There appears to be an error in the Revised Statutes in this reference; c. 23 should have been referred to.

[4] See also stat. 1838, c. 154; and 1846, 219, § 2.

vember, in each year, make official returns, to the secretary of the commonwealth, of all the public schools in such towns and city, respectively, whether such schools are kept for school districts, or for the common benefit of all the inhabitants.

29. The school committee of each city and town shall, as soon as may be after the first day of May, annually, ascertain by actual examination or otherwise, the number of persons between the ages of five and fifteen years belonging to such city or town, on the said first day of May, and shall make a certificate thereof, under oath, and also of the sum raised by such city or town for the support of schools, including only wages and board of teachers, and fuel for the schools, during the said year; and shall transmit the same to the secretary of the commonwealth, on or before the last day of the following April, which certificate shall be in the following form to wit:

School committee to ascertain and report, annually, the number of persons between 5 and 15 years of age in their city or town. 1846, 223, § 2. 1849, 117, § 1.

We, the school committee of ———, do certify, from the best information we have been able to obtain, that, on the first day of May, in the year ———, there were belonging to the said town the number of ——— persons, between the ages of five and fifteen years; and we further certify, that said town raised the sum of ——— dollars for the support of common schools for the said year, including only the wages and board of teachers, and fuel for the schools.

Form of certificate.

——— ———,
——— ———,
——— ———, } School Committee.

——— ss. On this ——— day of ——— personally appeared the abovenamed school committee of ———, and made oath that the above certificate by them subscribed is true.

Before me,

——— ———, Justice of the Peace.

30. The form of the blanks, and the inquiries provided for by the statute of the year one thousand eight hundred and

Board of education shall prescribe form of

blanks and inquiries, for school returns. 1846, 223, § 3.

thirty-seven, chapter two hundred and twenty-seven,[1] shall be prescribed by the board of education; and it shall be the duty of said board, in the month of January, annually, to transmit to the secretary of the commonwealth, copies of said blanks for the several cities and towns. It shall be the duty of said secretary to cause said blanks to be forwarded to the sheriffs of the several counties, who shall transmit them as soon as may be to the clerks of the several cities and towns within their counties respectively, and said clerks shall forthwith transmit the same to the school committees. The school committees of the several cities and towns shall return said blanks duly filled up, to the office of the secretary of the commonwealth, on or before the last day of April. If any school committee shall fail to receive such blank form of return on or before the last day of March, they shall forthwith give notice thereof, to the secretary of the commonwealth, who shall transmit such blank as soon as may be.

Secretary to forward the same.

School committee to return the same, duly filled up, to secretary of commonwealth.

School committee to make, annually, a detailed report of the condition of the public schools. Ibid, § 4.

31. The school committees shall annually make a detailed report of the condition of the several public schools in their respective cities and towns, which report shall contain such statements and suggestions in relation to such schools as the said committee shall deem necessary or proper to promote the interests thereof; and a certified copy of such report shall be transmitted by said committees to the office of the secretary of the commonwealth, on or before the last day of April. Said report shall also be deposited in the office of the clerk of the city or town;

To be deposited with clerk, and read in town meeting, &c.

---

[1] The Revised Statutes, c. 23, §§ 63, 64, prescribed a form of blanks and inquiries for school returns. The statute of 1837, c. 227, referred to in the text, prescribed a different form, and repealed those sections of the Revised Statutes, but provided that all reference to those sections, contained in other sections of c. 23, should be considered as applying to the act of 1837. By stat. 1838, c. 105, § 5, the form of the blanks and inquiries, and the time of returning them, was left to be prescribed by the board of education. By stat. 1841, c. 17, § 4, the provision giving the board authority to prescribe the time, was repealed. By stat. 1846, c. 223, § 3, the provision giving the board authority to prescribe the form of blanks and inquiries was re-enacted, as given in the text.

and shall either be read in open town meeting, in the month of February, March or April, or at the discretion of the school committee, shall be printed for the use of the inhabitants.[1]

The income of the school fund, except, &c., to be apportioned according to number of persons between 5 and 15. Ibid, § 5. 1849, 117, § 2.

32. The income of the Massachusetts school fund, to the first day of June in each year, except the sum of two hundred and forty dollars appropriated to the support of schools among the Indians, shall be apportioned by the secretary and treasurer of the commonwealth, and paid over by the said treasurer on the tenth day of July, to the treasurer of the several cities and towns, for the use of the common schools therein, according to the number of persons therein, between the ages of five and fifteen years, ascertained and certified as provided in the twenty-ninth section. Provided, however, that no such apportionment shall be made to any city or town which shall have failed to comply with any of the provisions of this act, or which shall not have raised by taxation, for the support of schools, including only wages, and board of teachers, and fuel for the schools, during the said year, a sum equal at least to one dollar and fifty cents for each person between the ages of five and fifteen years, belonging to said city or town, on the first day of May of said year.[2]

Ibid, § 1. Proviso. 1846, 223, § 5. 1849, 117, § 3.

Committees shall state, in their returns, the amount received from the school fund. 1850, c. 179.

33. In addition to the returns required of school committees, by the twenty-third chapter of the Revised Statutes,[3] such committees shall hereafter be required to state the sum or sums of money received from the school fund, by their several towns and cities respectively; and also to specify the purposes to which such sums may have been appropriated.

Secretary of board of education to transmit forms, &c. 1850, 41.

34. It shall be the duty of the secretary of the board of education to send the blank forms of inquiry, the school registers, the abstract of school returns, and the annual

---

[1] This section appears to supersede stat. 1838, 105, § 1.

[2] By 1849, c. 117, § 4, nothing in the said act is to be considered as prohibiting the attendance upon the schools, of scholars under five or over fifteen years of age.

[3] See § 28, p. 342, *ante*, and note to § 30, p. 344, *ante*.

report of the board of education, and that of its secretary, to the clerks of the several towns and cities of the commonwealth, as soon as may be after they are ready for distribution.

Clerks of cities and towns to distribute the same.
1849, 65, § 2.

35. It shall be the duty of the clerk of each of the several cities or towns to deliver the blank forms of inquiry, and the registers, when the same shall be received by him, to the school committee; it shall also be his duty to deliver one copy of the said abstract and reports to the secretary of the school committee of the city or town, to be by him carefully kept for the use of the said committee, and handed over to his successor in office; and also two additional copies of said reports, for the use of said committee; and further, it shall be the duty of the clerks of the several cities or towns to deliver one copy of the said reports to the clerk of each of the school districts in the respective cities or towns, to be by him deposited in the district school library, if there be one; and, if not, to be by him carefully kept for the use of the prudential committee, the teachers, and the inhabitants of the district, during his continuance in office, and then to be handed over to his successor; and, in case the city or town shall not be districted, the said reports shall be delivered to the school committee, and so placed by them that they shall be accessible to the several teachers, and to the citizens; and they shall be deemed to be the property of the town or city, and not of any officer, teacher or citizen thereof.

Abstracts of school returns to be made up by board of education.
1847, 183, § 1.

36. The abstracts of school returns, prescribed by the statute of eighteen hundred and thirty-seven, chapter two hundred and forty-one,[1] shall hereafter be made up by the secretary of the board of education.

City or town may withhold compensation of school committee, who fail to make returns.
Ibid, § 2.

37. Any city or town may withhold such compensation as the school committee of such city or town are now authorized, by law, to receive, if such town shall have for-

[1] Stat. 1837, c. 241, § 2, here referred to, provided, that the board of education should prepare and lay before the legislature, in a printed form, on or before the second Wednesday of January, annually, an abstract of the school returns received by the secretary of the commonwealth.

feited its due portion of the income of the school fund through the failure of such committee to comply with the provisions of the law in relation to school returns, or to comply with the provisions of the thirty-first section.[1] 1848, c. 173.

38. Whenever, in consequence of vacancies occurring in the school committee of any city or town in this commonwealth, after the date of the warrant for the annual town meeting for the election of their successors, or the inability, arising after said date, of any of the members of said committee to act, such committee shall be reduced to a minority of its original number, the remaining members of said committee shall be competent to make the returns required to be made and transmitted to the office of the secretary of the commonwealth; and such returns shall be accompanied by a certificate of the person or persons so making them, setting forth the existence of such vacancies or disabilities, and the time when the same arose.

Where school committees become reduced in number, the remaining members empowered to make returns. 1849, c. 144.

39. The board of education shall prescribe a blank form of a register, to be kept in all the town and district schools in the commonwealth; and the secretary of state shall forward a sufficient number of copies of the same to the school committees of the respective towns; and said committees shall cause registers to be faithfully kept in all said schools, according to the form prescribed.

Registers to be provided, and transmitted to school committees. 1838, 105, § 6.

To be faithfully kept, according to form prescribed.

40. Instead of the school registers, in book form, now transmitted to school committees, the secretary of the board of education is hereby required to transmit registers in such form as the said board shall prescribe; and no school teacher shall be entitled to receive payment for his or her services, until the register of his or her school, properly filled up and completed, shall be deposited with the school committee, or with such person as they may designate to receive it.

Board of education to prescribe form of school registers. 1849, 209, § 1.

No teacher entitled to pay, until the register of the school is completed, &c.

41. Nothing contained in the twenty-third chapter of the Revised Statutes shall affect the right of any corporation, which is or may be established in any town, to manage any estate or funds, given or obtained for the purpose of

Provisions of R. S. c. 23, not to affect funds, &c., of corporations for supporting schools. R. S. 23, § 59.

---

[1] See note (2) to § 24, p. 342, *ante*.

supporting schools therein, or, in any wise, to affect any such estate or funds; but such corporate powers and such estate and funds shall remain, as if the provisions in said chapter had not been enacted.

Forfeiture if towns neglect to raise money for schools; and how appropriated. Ibid, § 60.

42. If any towns shall refuse or neglect to raise money for the support of schools, as required by the twenty-third chapter of the Revised Statutes, such town shall forfeit a sum, equal to twice the highest sum, which had ever before been voted for the support of schools therein; and, if any town shall refuse or neglect to choose a school committee to superintend said schools, or to choose, for the purposes before mentioned in the said chapter, prudential committees in their several districts, when it is the duty of the town to choose such prudential committee, such town shall forfeit a sum not less than one hundred nor more than two hundred dollars, which shall be paid into the treasury of the county; and one-fourth thereof shall be for the use of the county, and three-fourths thereof shall be paid by the county treasurer to the school committee of such town, if any, and if not, to the selectmen of the town, for the support of schools therein.

School committee, &c., to receive and appropriate sums forfeited. Ibid, § 61.

43. Every such school committee, or board of selectmen, shall forthwith receive, from the treasurer of the county, any money so payable to them, and shall apportion and appropriate the same, to the support of the schools of such town, in the same manner it should have been appropriated, if it had been regularly raised by the town for that purpose.

Any city or town may appropriate further sums of money for instructing adults in reading, &c. 1847, 137, § 1.

44. In addition to the grants of money for common schools which cities and towns are now, by law, authorized to make, any city or town may appropriate such further sums of money as it may deem expedient, for the support of schools for the instruction of adults in reading, writing, English grammar, arithmetic, and geography.

Such moneys to be assessed, &c., in the same manner as taxes. Ibid, § 2.

45. Such moneys shall be assessed, levied, collected, and paid into the treasury, in the same manner that other town or city taxes are, and shall then be at the disposal of the school committee of the town or city, to be expended

by them, for the purpose aforesaid, in such manner as they may deem expedient.

46. The inhabitants of any school district, in any city or town, and of any city or town not divided into school districts, in this commonwealth, may, at any meeting called for that purpose, raise money for the purchase of libraries, and necessary school apparatus, in the same manner as school districts may now raise money for erecting and repairing school houses in their respective districts.

School districts, &c., may raise money for the purchase of libraries, &c.
1849, c. 81, § 1.

47. Physiology and hygiene shall hereafter be taught in all the public schools of this commonwealth, in all cases in which the school committee shall deem it expedient.

Physiology and hygiene to be taught in the schools.
1850, 229, § 1.

48. All school teachers shall hereafter be examined in their knowledge of the elementary principles of physiology and hygiene, and their ability to give instructions in the same.

Teachers to be examined in those branches.
Ibid, § 2.

49. The two preceding sections shall take effect on and after the first day of October, one thousand eight hundred and fifty-one.

When to take effect.
Ibid, § 3.

50. Every person who shall wilfully interrupt or disturb any school or other assembly of people, met for a lawful purpose, within the place of such meeting, or out of it, shall be punished by imprisonment in the county jail, not more than thirty days, or by fine not exceeding fifty dollars.

Punishment for disturbing school, &c.
1849, c. 59.

51. Any child, unlawfully excluded from public school instruction, in this commonwealth, shall recover damages therefor, in an action on the case, to be brought in the name of said child, by his guardian or next friend, in any court of competent jurisdiction to try the same, against the city or town by which such public school instruction is supported.[1]

Remedy for the unlawful exclusion of a child from public school instruction.
1845, c. 214.
Roberts v. Boston, S. J. C. March T. 1850.

---

[1] For other and general laws respecting schools, see R. S. c. 15, § 33; c. 23; c. 94, § 54; c. 97, § 22; 1836, c. 245; 1837, c. 147, 227, 241; 1838, c. 55, 105, 154, 159, 189; 1839, c. 56, 137; 1840, c. 7, 76; 1841, c. 17; 1842, c. 42, 60; 1843, c. 85; 1844, c. 6, 32; 1845, c. 100, 157, 214; 1846, c. 99, 219; 1848, c. 10, 237, 274, 279, 283; 1849, c. 62, 81, 206, 215, 220; 1850, c. 115, 213, 286, 294, 301; some of which are, in whole or in part, repealed. See also Truants.

ORDINANCE OF THE CITY.[1]

School committee to elect and remove instructors, and determine their salaries, &c. March 24, 1822.

SECT. 1. The school committee are authorized to elect all such instructors as they may think necessary, for the public schools, and to determine the amount of their respective salaries; also to remove any instructor from said schools, when in their discretion it may be proper; and generally to execute all the powers, which the selectmen of towns or school committees are authorized by the laws of this commonwealth to exercise.

To apportion salaries of instructors, so as not to exceed the appropriations made by city council. March 23, 1830.

SECT. 2. The school committee are authorized to distribute the annual sum which shall be appropriated by the city council for salaries of instructors in the public schools, so fixing the amount of the salary of each instructor, as that in no case shall the aggregate amount of all said salaries exceed the whole sum which shall have been so appropriated by said council.

SECOND HAND ARTICLES.

---

[1] An ordinance providing for the election, and providing for the compensation of instructors in the public schools, passed March 24, 1822. An ordinance in addition to an ordinance providing for the election and compensation of instructors in the public schools, passed March 23, 1830.

STATUTE.

1. The mayor and aldermen of any city, and the selectmen of any town, may license such persons as they deem suitable to be keepers of shops for the purchase, sale, or barter of junk, old metals, or of any second hand articles, and to be dealers therein.

Licenses may be granted to deal in old and second hand articles. 1839, 53, § 1.

2. The licenses to such persons shall designate the place where the business is to be carried on, and contain such conditions and restrictions as may be prescribed by the ordinances and by-laws of the city or town wherein the same are granted, and shall continue in force for one year unless sooner revoked.

Place of dealing to be designated. Conditions and terms of license. Ibid, § 2.

3. No person, unless licensed as aforesaid, shall keep any shop for the purchase, sale or barter of the articles aforesaid, or be a dealer therein; nor shall any person so licensed, keep such shop, or be a dealer in said articles in any other place or manner than as is designated in his license, or after notice to him that said license has been revoked, under the penalty of a sum not exceeding twenty dollars for every offence, to be recovered by complaint in any police court, or by indictment in any court of record in the county where such offence may be committed.

Penalty for dealing in such articles without license, or at places not designated, &c. Ibid, § 3.

4. The city council of any city may suspend or dispense with the provisions of this and the three preceding sections, so far as the same apply to each city, *provided*, that no offence committed and no penalty incurred before such suspension shall take effect, shall be affected thereby; and the provisions of the said sections shall not extend to any town unless the inhabitants thereof shall, at a legal meeting, adopt the same.

City council may suspend this act. Ibid, § 4.

Act not to take effect in towns, unless adopted in town meeting.

ORDINANCE OF THE CITY.[1]

Licenses to contain conditions. May 6, 1839.

SECT. 1. All licenses which shall be granted by the mayor and aldermen of the city, to any persons to be keepers of shops for the purchase, sale or barter of junk, old metals, or any second hand articles, and to be dealers therein, shall contain the following conditions and restrictions:—

Fee for license.

First—That every person, at the time of receiving said license, shall pay therefor the sum of one dollar.

Keeper of licensed shop shall keep a book, &c.

Second—That every keeper of such shop shall keep a book in which shall be written, at the time of every purchase, a description of the article or articles purchased, the name and residence of the person from whom, and the day and hour when, such purchase was made; and that such book shall at all times be open to the inspection of the said mayor and aldermen, or of any person by them authorized.

Shall put up sign, designating that he is licensed.

Third—That every keeper of such shop shall put in some suitable place a sign designating that he is licensed as such, and containing his name.

Shops to be kept open at certain hours only.

Fourth—That the said shops shall not be kept open, except at such hours as shall be specially allowed by the terms of the license; and that no purchases of any of the articles aforesaid, shall be made by the keepers thereof, or by any person for them, except during such hours as shall be designated in the license. And that the said shops shall at all times be open to the inspection of the said mayor and aldermen, or of any person by them authorized.

Keeper shall not deal with minor or apprentice.

Fifth—That no keeper of such shop shall, directly, or indirectly, either purchase, or receive by way of barter or exchange, any of the articles aforesaid of any minor or apprentice, knowing or having reason to believe him to be such.

Penalty. Ibid.

SECT. 2. Any person or persons having obtained a license under the provisions of this ordinance, who shall

---

[1] An ordinance concerning junk shops and dealers in second hand articles, passed May 6, 1839.

violate any of the conditions thereof, shall upon conviction thereof, pay a fine of not less than one, nor more than twenty dollars, to be recovered by complaint before the justices of the police court.

SEWERS.

Mayor and aldermen, &c., may lay, &c., main drains and common sewers. 1841, 115, § 1. (Accepted by city council, April 5, 1841. City Records, vol. 19, p. 76.)

1. The selectmen of the several towns, and the mayor and aldermen of the several cities, in the commonwealth, may lay, make, maintain and repair all main drains or common sewers in their respective towns and cities; and all the main drains or common sewers which have heretofore been, or which may hereafter be constructed by any town or city, shall be taken and deemed to be the property of such town or city.

Persons entering particular drains into common sewer, &c., shall pay a proportional part of the expense. Ibid, § 2. 1 Metc. 130.

2. Every person who may hereafter enter his particular drain into any main drain or common sewer so constructed as aforesaid, for the draining of his cellar or land, or in obedience to the by-laws or ordinances of the town or city, or who, by any more remote means, shall receive any benefit thereby, for draining his cellar or land, shall pay to the town or city a proportional part of the charge of making and repairing such main drain or common sewer, to be ascertained and assessed by the selectmen in case of towns, and by the mayor and aldermen in case of cities, and by them certified and notice thereof given to the party to be charged, or his tenant or lessee.

Assessments to be a lien, for one year, on real estate. Estate may be sold for payment. 1841, 115, § 3.

3. And all assessments, so made, shall constitute a lien on the real estates assessed for one year after they are laid, and may, together with all incidental costs and expenses be levied by sale thereof if the assessment is not paid within three months after a written demand of payment, made either upon the person assessed, or upon any person occupying the estate; such sale to be conducted in like manner as sales for the non-payment of taxes.

Any person aggrieved by assessment may appeal to C. C. Pleas, &c. Ibid, § 4.

4. Any person who may deem himself aggrieved by any such assessment, may, at any time within three months from receiving notice thereof, appeal to the county commissioners, or if the case arise in the city of Boston or in the town of Chelsea, to the court of common pleas, which court, in such case, shall appoint three disinterested persons, who may be inhabitants of Boston or other town, to settle and assess the share to be charged to such person; and the same county commissioners and referees may examine the parties, and any other persons, on oath, touching the matter submitted to them, and shall settle and determine the

proper amount of charge or assessment, and the said referees, in the case of the city of Boston or the town of Chelsea, shall make return of their doings to the said court of common pleas, and in all cases the decision of said county commissioners and of the said referees shall be final, and in case the assessment made by the selectmen or mayor and aldermen shall not be reduced on such appeal, the town or city shall recover costs, but otherwise shall pay costs: *provided, however*, that in all cases of an appeal as aforesaid, the appellant, before entering it, shall give one month's notice, in writing, to the selectmen or mayor and aldermen, of his intention to appeal, and shall therein particularly specify the points of his objection to the assessment made by them, to which specification he shall be confined upon the hearing of the appeal.

City, &c., may pay a part of expense. City of Boston shall pay one quarter. Ibid, § 5.

5. Nothing contained in this and the four preceding sections shall prevent any town or city from providing, by by-law, ordinance or otherwise, that a part of the expense of constructing, maintaining and repairing main drains or common sewers, shall be paid by such town or city; and in the city of Boston not less than one quarter part of such expense shall be paid by said city, and shall not be charged upon those using the said main drains or common sewers.[1]

Duty of South Cove Corporation as to certain drains. 1833, 17, § 11.

6. By the act to establish the South Cove Corporation, passed January 31, 1833, it is provided, that said corporation should be holden to extend and carry out all drains and common sewers which then had their termination in said cove, before they should so fill up said cove as to obstruct and affect their use; and that the same should be done in such manner as should be approved by the mayor and aldermen of the city of Boston. And if any other drains or common sewers should from time to time thereafter be made by said mayor and aldermen into said cove, as far as it should have been filled up at the time of making such other drains or common sewers, and the said corporation should

---

[1] For provisions applicable to common sewers and main drains, in other cases, see Rev. Stat. c. 27.

thereafter further proceed to fill up said cove beyond the termination of such other drains or common sewers, then the said corporation should be further holden to extend and carry out from time to time, such other drains and common sewers before the said cove should be farther filled up, so that the said filling up should not obstruct and affect the use of such other drains and common sewers.

City authorized to lay drains, &c., under land extended by B. and R. Mill Corporation. 1844, 58.

7. By an act authorizing the Boston and Roxbury Mill Corporation to extend their wharf, passed March 6, 1844, it was provided, that the authorities of the city of Boston should have the right to extend Byron street, so called, to the channel over the land to be made as authorized by the act, and to lay, continue, and maintain, all necessary drains under the same.

ORDINANCE OF THE CITY.[1]

Common sewers to be laid near centre of street. June 14, 1841. Manner of construction.

SECT. 1. All common sewers which shall be considered necessary by the mayor and aldermen, in any street or highway, shall be laid as nearly as possible in the centre of such street or highway, and shall be built of such materials, and of such dimensions, as the mayor and aldermen shall direct. And where it is practicable and advisable, they shall be of a sufficient size to be entered and cleaned without disturbing the pavement above.

Size.

Drains entering into same, to be built as mayor and aldermen shall direct. Ibid.

SECT. 2. All particular drains, which shall hereafter enter into such common sewer, shall be built of such materials as the mayor and aldermen shall direct; and shall be laid under the direction of the said mayor and aldermen; and they shall be laid in such direction, of such size, and with such descent, and (where required) with such strainers as they shall require; and shall, if practicable, be of a size,

Size.

---

[1] An ordinance in relation to common sewers and drains, passed June 14, 1841, and an ordinance in addition thereto, passed March 7, 1844.

sufficient to be cleared from the common sewer without disturbing the pavement above.

SECT. 3. The mayor and aldermen shall have power, in all cases where there is any common sewer in any street or highway, to cause every owner of land, adjoining such street or highway, his agent or tenant, to make a sufficient drain from his house, yard or lot, whenever in their opinion the same shall be necessary, and shall thereupon give such owner, agent or tenant, notice in writing, specifying the time within which such drain shall be completed; and in case the said owner, agent or tenant, shall neglect to complete the same within the time specified, the mayor and aldermen shall cause the same to be done; and shall recover the whole amount of the expense thereof, together with ten per cent. damages, by an action of the case, to be brought in the name of the city of Boston before any court proper to try the same; provided, however, that in no case shall ten per cent. claimed by way of damage, exceed the sum of twenty dollars.[1]

Mayor and aldermen shall have power to cause owners of land to make drains. Ibid.

Shall make same, at owner's expense, in case they neglect.

SECT. 4. It shall be lawful for all persons, having the care of any buildings, at their own expense, to carry the rain water from the roofs of said buildings, into any common sewers, free of any charge from the city; *provided*, that the same be done by tight water spouts and tubes under ground, and under the direction of the Mayor and aldermen.

Rain water from roofs may be carried into common sewers. Ibid.

SECT. 5. Every person entering his or her particular drain into any common sewer, without a permit in writing from the mayor and aldermen, or superintendent of common sewers hereinafter mentioned, shall forfeit and pay the sum of twenty dollars, and shall also be liable to pay all such damage by way of indemnification as the mayor and aldermen shall deem just and reasonable. And all persons to whom the said permits shall be granted, shall pay therefor a sum not less than ten dollars, as the mayor and aldermen may fix and determine.

Penalty for entering drain into common sewer, without permit. Ibid.

Fee for permit. See sec. 6, p. 203, *ante*.

---

[1] See also §§ 4 and 7, pp. 202, 203, *ante*.

Superintendent of common sewers to be chosen. Ibid.

SECT. 6. There shall be appointed annually, in the month of May or June, by concurrent vote of the city council, a superintendent of common sewers, who shall hold his office until removed, (or a successor be appointed,) who shall receive such compensation as the city council shall determine, and who shall be removable at the pleasure of the city council, and in case said office shall at any time become vacant, the same shall be filled in the manner before prescribed.

Shall have supervision of common sewers. Ibid.

SECT. 7. The said superintendent shall, under the direction of the mayor and aldermen, take the general supervision of all common sewers, which now are, or hereafter may be built and owned by the city, or which may be permitted to be built or opened by its authority, and he shall take charge of the building and repairs of the same, and make all contracts for the supply of labor and materials therefor.

Shall ascertain and insert in a book the dimensions, &c., of sewers to be built. Ibid.

SECT. 8. The said superintendent, whenever any common sewer is ordered to be built or repaired, shall ascertain its depth, breadth, mode of construction and general direction, and take the plan thereof, and insert the same, with all those particulars, in a book, to be kept for that purpose, and forthwith ascertain and insert on said plan all entries made into such sewer.

Shall keep account of expense of each, and report to mayor and aldermen, &c. Ibid.

SECT. 9. The said superintendent shall keep an accurate account of the expense of constructing and repairing each common sewer, and shall report the same to the mayor and aldermen, together with a list of the persons and estates deriving benefit therefrom, and an estimate of the value of the lands, upon which said expense ought to be assessed; the value of such lands to be estimated independently of any buildings or improvements thereon.

Mayor and aldermen, in making assessments, shall deduct not less than one quarter of the expense. March 7, 1844.

SECT. 10. It shall be the duty of the mayor and aldermen, in making assessments for defraying the expense of constructing or repairing common sewers, pursuant to the provisions of this ordinance, to deduct from the said expense such part, and not less than one quarter part, as they may deem expedient, to be charged to, and paid by the city;

Manner of assessment.

and to assess the remainder thereof upon the persons and estates deriving benefit from such common sewer, either by the entry of their particular drains therein, or by any more remote means; apportioning the assessment according to the value of the lands thus benefited, independently of any buildings or improvements thereon; and also to prescribe and establish the time when the proportion of the said assessments, which is charged upon persons benefited, shall be paid.

Manner of entering, demanding, and collecting assessments. June 14, 1841.

SECT. 11. The said superintendent shall enter in books, to be kept for that purpose, all such assessments made by the mayor and aldermen, and shall forthwith make out bills for the same, and deliver them to the city treasurer for collection; and the said treasurer shall forthwith demand payment in writing, of the said bills, in the manner prescribed by law; and in case any bills or dues under this ordinance shall remain unpaid at the expiration of three months after demand for payment as aforesaid, the said treasurer shall cause the same to be collected, by a resort to the proper legal process.

Same duties to be performed in relation to common sewers heretofore constructed. Ibid.

SECT. 12. It shall also be the duty of the mayor and aldermen, to make assessments for all common sewers heretofore constructed by the city, the expenses of which have not already been assessed and collected, in the same manner as it is made their duty by this ordinance to make assessments for those which may hereafter be constructed; and the said superintendent shall render all the services and perform all the duties, in regard to the common sewers heretofore constructed, the expenses of which have not already been assessed and collected, which he is herein required to render and perform in regard to those hereafter to be constructed.

SOLICITOR.

ORDINANCE OF THE CITY.[1]

City solicitor to be chosen. His qualifications. April 29, 1846.

SECT. 1. In the month of June, annually, and whenever a vacancy in the office shall occur, there shall be chosen, by concurrent vote of both branches of the city council, a solicitor for the city of Boston, who shall be a resident citizen thereof, and who shall have been admitted an attorney and counsellor of the courts of the commonwealth, and who shall not hold any other office under the city government, during the period for which he is elected; and he shall be removable at the pleasure of the city council.

His duties. Ibid.

SECT. 2. It shall be the duty of said city solicitor, by himself, or by some person by him duly authorized, for whose conduct, skill and faithfulness, he shall be accountable, to draft all bonds, deeds, obligations, contracts, leases, conveyances, agreements, and other legal instruments, of whatever nature, which may be required of him, by any ordinance or order of the mayor and aldermen, or of the city council, or which, by any ordinance or order heretofore passed, may be requisite to be done and made by the city of Boston, and any person or persons contracting with the city in its corporate capacity, and which, by law, usage and agreement, the city is to be at the expense of drawing.

To commence and prosecute suits for city. Ibid.

SECT. 3. It shall be the duty of said city solicitor to commence and prosecute all actions and suits to be commenced by the city before any tribunal in this common-

[1] An ordinance providing for the appointment of a city solicitor, and prescribing his duties, passed April 29, 1846.

wealth, whether in law or equity; and also to appear in, defend and advocate the rights and interests of the city, or any of the officers of the city, in any suit or prosecution for any act or omission in the discharge of their official duties, wherein any estate, right, privilege, ordinances or acts of the city government, or any breach of any ordinance, may be brought in question. And said solicitor shall also appear before the legislature of the commonwealth, or any committee thereof, whether of either or both branches of the same, and there, in behalf of the city, represent, answer for, defend, and advocate the interests and welfare of said city, whenever the same may be directly or incidentally affected, whether to prosecute or defend the same; and he shall in all matters do all and every professional act, incident to the office which may be required of him by the city government, or by any joint or special committee thereof, or by any ordinance or order heretofore passed; and he shall, when required, furnish the mayor and aldermen, the common council, or any joint or special committee of either branch thereof, and to any officer of the city government, who may require it in the official discharge of his duties, with his legal opinion on any subject touching the duties of their respective offices.

To defend suits against city.

To appear before the legislature, and committees thereof.

To furnish legal opinions.

SECT. 4. In full compensation for all the services of said solicitor, he shall receive such salary as the city council may from time to time fix and determine. In all cases, however, when his attendance may be required out of the city, his reasonable travelling expenses shall be allowed him; and in suits and prosecutions, he shall be entitled to receive and retain for his own use the legal taxable costs which may be recovered of the adverse party, where the city shall recover the same, according to the usage and practice of the courts.

Salary. Expenses, &c. Ibid.

STEAM ENGINES AND FURNACES.

No furnace for melting iron, or steam engine for planing, &c., or in which any other fuel than coal is used, to be erected, &c., without license. 1845, 197, § 1. Accepted by city council, April 21, 1849. (City Records, vol. 23, p. 122.)

1. No furnace for melting of iron, or stationary steam engine, designed for use in any mill for the planing or sawing of boards, or turning of wood in any form, or when any other fuel than coal is used to create steam, shall hereafter be erected, or put up to be used, in any city or town in this commonwealth, unless the mayor and aldermen of such city, or selectmen of such town, shall have previously granted license therefor, designating the place where the building or buildings shall be erected, in which such steam engine or furnace shall be used, the materials and construction thereof, and such other provisions and limitations, as to the height of flues, and protection against fire, as they shall judge necessary for the safety of the neighborhood; such license to be granted on written application, and to be recorded in the records of such city or town. [1]

Mayor and aldermen, &c., to prescribe rules, &c., as to fur-

2. Whenever the mayor and aldermen of any city, or the selectmen of any town, after due notice in writing to the owner of any such steam engine or furnace erected, or

[1] For provisions respecting furnaces for glass, see p. 143, *ante*.

in use, previous to the passage of the act of 1845, and a hearing of the matter, shall adjudge the same to be dangerous, or a nuisance to the neighborhood, they may make and record an order, prescribing such rules, restrictions and alterations, as to the building in which such steam engine or furnace is constructed or used, the construction and height of its smoke flues, or other provisions, as they shall deem the safety of the neighborhood to require; and it shall be the duty of the city or town clerk to deliver a copy of such order to a constable, who shall serve such owner with an attested copy thereof, and make return of his doings thereon to said clerk, within three days from the delivery thereof to him.

naces and engines previously erected or in use, in certain cases. Ibid, § 2.

3. Any such engine or furnace hereafter erected, without license made and recorded as aforesaid in section first, shall be deemed and taken to be a common nuisance, without any other proof thereof than proof of its use; and any steam engine or furnace used contrary to the provisions of section second, shall be taken and deemed to be a common nuisance.

Engine or furnace hereafter erected without license, to be deemed a common nuisance. Ibid, § 3.

4. The mayor and aldermen of any city, or selectmen of any town, shall have the same power and authority to abate and remove any such steam engine or furnace erected or used contrary to the preceding provisions, as are given to the board of health, in the tenth and eleventh sections of the twenty-first chapter of the Revised Statutes.

May be abated and removed by mayor and aldermen, &c. Ibid, § 4.

See note 1, on p. 190, *ante*.

5. Whenever application shall be made for license as aforesaid, the mayor and aldermen of any city, or selectmen of any town, shall assign a time and place for the consideration of the same, and shall cause public notice thereof to be given at least fourteen days beforehand, in such manner as said mayor and aldermen or selectmen may direct, and at the expense of the applicant, in order that all persons interested may be heard before the granting of a license.

Proceedings on an application for a license. Ibid, § 5.

6. Any owner of a steam engine or furnace, aggrieved by any such order, as provided in section second, may apply to the court of common pleas, if sitting in the county, in which such engine or furnace is situated, or to any justice thereof in vacation, for a jury, and such court or justice

Persons aggrieved by any order under § 2, may apply to C. C. P. for a jury. Ibid, § 6.

shall issue a warrant for a jury to be impanelled by the sheriff, in the same manner as is provided in the twenty-fourth chapter of the Revised Statutes, in regard to the laying out of highways; such application shall be made within three days after such order is served upon the said owner; and the said jury shall be impanelled within fourteen days from the issuing of said warrant.

An injunction to restrain the use of such engine, &c., may be issued, on such application. Ibid, § 7.

7. Upon any application to said court of common pleas, or to any justice thereof, for a jury, said court or justice, on granting the same, may, in its or his discretion, issue an injunction restraining the further use of said engine or furnace, until the final determination of such application by the jury and court to which such verdict may be returned.

Verdict of the jury, how found, returned and accepted, and effect thereof. Ibid, § 8.

8. The jury shall find a verdict either affirming or annulling the said order in full, or making alterations therein, as they may see fit: which verdict shall be returned to the next term of the said court by the sheriff for acceptance, in like manner as in the case of highways, and which verdict being accepted, shall be binding to the same effect as the original order would have been without such appeal.

Damages and costs, when and in what manner to be awarded. Ibid, § 9.

9. If the verdict shall affirm such order, costs shall be recovered by the city or town against such applicant; if the verdict shall annul such order in whole, damages and costs shall be recovered by the complainant against such city or town; and in case the verdict shall alter such order in part, the court may render such judgment as to costs, as to justice shall appertain.[1]

No steam boiler to be used, unless provided with fusible safety plug, &c. 1850, 277, § 1.

10. No person or corporation shall use, or cause to be used, any steam-boiler in this commonwealth, unless the same be provided with a fusible safety plug, to be made of lead, or some other equally fusible material, and to be of a diameter of not less than one-half an inch, which plug shall be placed in the roof of the fire-box, when a fire-box is

[1] The statute of 1845, c. 197, § 10, provided that the preceding sections should not be in force in any town or city, unless the inhabitants of the town or the city council of the city, should adopt the same, at a legal meeting of said inhabitants or city council, called for that purpose. The city council of Boston accepted the same April 21, 1849. (City Records, vol. 23, p. 122.)

used, and, in all cases, shall be placed in a part of the boiler fully exposed to the action of the fire, and as near the top of the water line as any part of the fire-surface of the boiler; and, for this purpose, it shall be lawful to use Ashcroft's "protected safety fusible plug."

Penalty for removing such plug. Ibid, § 2.

11. If any person shall, without just and proper cause, remove from the boiler the safety plug thereof, or shall substitute therefor any material more capable of resisting the action of the fire than the said safety plug so removed, he shall be punished by a fine not exceeding one thousand dollars.

Penalty for using steam boiler without such safety plug. Ibid, § 3.

12. If any person or corporation shall use, or cause to be used, in this commonwealth, for the space of six consecutive days, a steam-boiler unprovided with a safety fusible plug, as named in the tenth section, such person or corporation so offending, shall be punished by a fine not exceeding one thousand dollars.[1]

STREETS.

---

[1] Stat. 1849, c. 139, upon the same subject, was repealed by stat. 1850, c. 277, § 4.

therefor. Individuals may object to paving, &c.
12. Canopy, balcony, platforms and cellar doors. Penalty.
13. Posts. Trees. Porticoes, porches and bow-windows. Projecting signs. Penalty.
14. Placing goods in the street. Boxes, barrels, &c. Penalty.
15. How fines shall be distributed.
16. Articles shall not be raised, for the purpose of storage, from any street, &c., into second story, &c., except, &c.
17. City council may elect mayor and aldermen surveyors of highways.
18. Streets may be macadamized, and same provisions shall apply.
19. Streets, laid out over private land, by the owners, how to be graded.
20. No street to be opened less than 30 feet wide, except, &c.
21. Ways dedicated and opened shall not become chargeable upon city, unless, &c.
22. Entrances to such ways to be closed up, &c.
23. City liable, unless notice is given.
24. Abutters on such ways shall construct sidewalk. Otherwise, the mayor and aldermen may construct the same at expense of abutters. Such expense shall be a lien. Proviso. Additional proviso.
25. Right of gas company to sink pipes, &c., under the control of the mayor and aldermen.
26. Mayor and aldermen authorized to lay out streets in continuation of Broad and Commercial streets.
27. In continuation of Front street.
28. Compensation for land, &c.

ORDINANCE.

1. Streets to retain their names till altered.
2. Superintendent of streets.
3. He may appoint assistants.
4. Superintendent to attend at his office. To keep record, and books, &c. To make reports.
5. To superintend streets, &c. City not responsible for his acts, unless, &c.
6. Superintendent to have care of city stables. Of cleaning streets, manure, house offal, &c.
7. Penalty for digging up streets, &c.
8. Person so digging, to repair the same, &c.
9. When drain or aqueduct is repaired, a fence and lights to be put up.
10. Notice to be given of intention to build. Regulations in such case.
11. Placing coal or firewood in streets, regulated.
12. Playing at foot-ball, throwing stones and snow-balls.
13. Shooting with bow and arrow forbidden.
14. Exposing gaming tables.
15. Coursing or coasting upon sleds.
16. Bathing in waters surrounding the city.
17. Taking street dirt without license.
18. Obstructing street by moving buildings.
19. Suspending goods so as to project into street.
20. Awnings and shades.
21. Projecting signs, lanterns, &c.
22. Same subject.
23. Ringing bells or blowing horns.
24. Standing to grind cutlery.
25. Projecting porches, doors, windows, steps, &c.
26. Cellar doors and cellar doorways.
27. Steps descending from street to be enclosed and lighted.
28. Apertures under street, coalholes, &c.
29. Gratings in streets.

30. Coal-holes and gratings may be authorized, &c.
31. Feeding animals in streets forbidden.
32. Riding or driving faster than 6 miles an hour, forbidden.
33. Horses, kine, swine, &c., not to go at large.
34. Surveyors of highways to regulate the width and height of sidewalks. May accept the same.
35. After acceptance, &c., sidewalks to be maintained by the city, provided, &c.
36. City clerk to keep record of names of streets, and acceptance of sidewalks.
37. Carriages forbidden on sidewalks, except, &c.
38. Sawing firewood on sidewalks.
39. Standing in a group so as to obstruct the passage.
40. Placing lumber, bales, &c., on sidewalks.
41. Snow to be removed from sidewalks by abutters.
42. To extend to snow falling from any building.
43. Sidewalks encumbered with ice to be made safe, &c.
44. Ice or snow thrown into street to be broken up, &c.
45. Meaning of the word "street" defined.
46. Who shall be liable to penalties.
47. Acts forbidden to be done without license, may be licensed
48. Rights and duties of surveyors of highways, not limited by this ordinance.
49. When to take effect.

STATUTES.

1. Under a provision in the act of 1799, chapter 31, the selectmen, (whose powers were afterwards transferred to the mayor and aldermen by the city charter,) were empowered, whenever in their opinion the safety and convenience of the inhabitants of Boston should require it, to lay out or widen any street, lane or alley of Boston; and for that purpose to remove any building or buildings of what nature soever. *Laying out and widening streets. 1799, 31, § 3. 1821, 110, § 13.* And it was further provided, that the owner or owners of such building should be entitled to receive compensation for the damages which he or they might sustain by such removal, which damages should be ascertained, determined, and recovered in the way and manner pointed out in the act entitled "An Act directing the method of laying out highways." *Compensation for buildings removed.* *1786, 67, repealed by Rev. Stat.* That act provided for an estimation of such damages by a committee of freeholders, appointed by the court of general sessions of the peace; with a privilege to any party aggrieved of applying to the court for a hearing before a jury, or a new committee. By an additional act, passed March 4, 1805, the selectmen were in like manner *1804, 73.*

empowered to lay out any new street, or to widen any street, lane or alley, and for that purpose to take any land that might be required for the same, and to remove any building or buildings of what nature soever; and that the same street, lane and alley, being recorded in the town's books, should be thereby established as such; and that the owner or owners of the land or buildings that should be so taken or removed, should receive such recompense for the damages sustained, as the party interested and the selectmen should agree upon, to be paid by the town, or the individual person or persons for whose use such street, lane or alley should be laid out or widened, or as should be ordered by the justices of the court of general sessions of the peace, upon an inquiry into the same by a jury to be summoned for that purpose, who should be drawn out of the jury box of the supreme judicial court of the town of Boston by the selectmen of said town, upon the application of the sheriff of the county of Suffolk, and if, by accident or challenge, there should happen not to be a full jury, said officer was to fill the panel *de talibus circumstantibus;* or by a special committee, if the parties should agree thereto.[1]

Compensation for land taken, &c.

11 Mass. 447.

Discontinuance of streets, &c. 1816, 90, § 1. 1821, 110, § 13.

2. By an act passed December 13, 1816, the selectmen were, and in consequence, by the city charter, the mayor and aldermen are also empowered whenever in their opinion the safety or convenience of the inhabitants of the said city shall require it, to discontinue any street, lane or alley of the said city or to make any alteration in the same, in part or in whole; reserving however, in all cases, to individuals who may sustain damage thereby, recompense for the same, to be ascertained and allowed in the same manner as is provided in the preceding act.

1804, 73.

Previous orders, &c., of selectmen confirmed. 1816, 90, § 2.

3. All orders, votes and determinations of the said selectmen of the town of Boston, had and passed, previous to

1 The court of general sessions of the peace has since been abolished, and its functions in this and other matters transferred to the court of common pleas. (See Stat. 1782, 14; 1803, 154; 1807, 11, 57; 1809, c. 18; 1811, c. 81, 93; 1813, 197; 1818, 120; 1819, 139; 1820, 79; 1821, 51, 109; R. S. c. 82.) The provisions for the recovery of damages have been modified by subsequent statutes, as stated in the succeeding sections. See §§ 5, 6, 7 and 8, pp. 369–372, *post*.

the act of 1816, for the discontinuance of any street, lane or alley of said town, or respecting any alteration in the same, in whole or in part, shall be held and considered as good and valid to all intents and purposes, as if the said act of 1799, c. 31, had explicitly vested said authority in the said selectmen; reserving always to individuals recompense for damages sustained thereby, as is provided in the said act.

Record of streets. Ibid, § 3. 1821, 110, § 13.

4. The selectmen were, and the mayor and aldermen are required to keep a record of all the streets, lanes and alleys, and of all votes and proceedings relative to the same; and copies thereof, certified by the clerk, shall be valid to all intents and purposes.

County commissioners authorized to lay out, &c., highways. Rev. Stat. 24.

5. By the twenty-fourth chapter of the Revised Statutes, the authority to lay out, alter, and discontinue highways, and to assess damages therefor, is given to the county commissioners; with a right to any party aggrieved to apply for a jury; and the method of proceeding is prescribed in detail. By the fifty-fourth section, it is provided that in the county of Suffolk, the mayor and aldermen of the city of Boston shall, within the said city, have the like powers and perform the like duties, as are exercised and performed by the commissioners of other counties, in respect to the laying out, altering and discontinuing of ways, and assessing damages therefor, except as is provided in the following section.[1]

Mayor and aldermen have the same authority in Boston. Ibid, § 54. Ibid, 84, § 9.

---

[1] Whether the authority of the mayor and aldermen to lay out and widen streets depends upon the Revised Statutes, c. 24, § 54, or upon stat. 1799, c. 31, § 3, stat. 1804, c. 73, and stat. 1821, c. 110, § 13, (City Charter) appears to be an open question. The practice has been to proceed upon the latter statutes. Upon this point see *Stone v. City of Boston*, (2 Metc. 220), *Parks v. City of Boston*, (8 Pick. 218), *Commonwealth v. City of Boston*, (16 Pick. 442), *Goddard's case*, (16 Pick. 504.)

The mayor and aldermen cannot legally lay out a street, without first giving to all persons interested notice of their intention so to do. *Stone v. City of Boston*, (2 Metc. 220.)

Where the mayor and aldermen laid out a street over land belonging to minors without giving any previous notice, and without making any estimate of the amount of damage thereby sustained by the owners, and more than a year elapsed before either of the owners came of age; a writ of *certiorari* was ordered, on a petition filed by one of the owners, at the first term after he came of age, although notice had been given to the tenant

Any party aggrieved may petition C. C. Pleas, for a jury. Ibid, 24, § 55.

6. When any party shall be aggrieved by the doings of the said mayor and aldermen, in the cases mentioned in the preceding section, he may apply for a jury, by petition to the court of common pleas, within and for the county of Suffolk, at any term of said court that shall be there held, within one year after the laying out, altering or discontinuing of any way in said city, and not afterwards;[1] and thereupon the said court shall, after due notice to the said city, order a trial by jury to be had in the case, at the bar of said court, in the same manner, in which other civil causes are there tried by the jurors there returned and empanelled; and if either party request it, the jury, to whom the cause may be committed, shall view the place in question.[2]

Trial.

View.

---

in possession to remove the buildings from the land, and he had communicated that notice to the guardian of said minors, within a year after the street was thus laid out. *Ibid.* See also *Parks v. Mayor and Aldermen of the City of Boston*, (8 Pick. 218.)

Where the mayor and aldermen shall adjudge that the laying out or altering of a street is required by public safety and convenience, their having taken a bond from an individual to contribute towards the expense will not vitiate their proceedings, provided the bond was not made the basis of their proceedings, and the adjudication was not colorably for the use of the city, and really for the benefit of the individual. *Ibid.* See also *Crockett v. City of Boston*, S. J. C. Nov. T. 1850.

Where parties, interested in the alteration of a street or highway, had actual notice of the proceedings, and attended, and were heard concerning them, and have acquiesced therein for many years, a writ of *certiorari* to remove those proceedings will not be granted, merely because it does not appear that they had the official notice prescribed by law, nor because one of them was *non compos mentis*, and had no guardian. *Hancock v. City of Boston*, (1 Metc. 122).

[1] But see the succeeding section.

[2] Where part of a lot of land under lease is taken by the mayor and aldermen for the purpose of widening a street, the lease is not thereby extinguished: nor is the lessee discharged from his liability to pay the reserved rent during the residue of the term. But the lessor and lessee are each entitled to recover compensation for the damage so sustained by them respectively. *Parks v. City of Boston*, (15 Pick. 198).

Where land is taken by the mayor and aldermen for the purpose of widening a street, it is to be estimated at its value at the time of the taking, in the assessment of damages. *Ibid.*

Where a jury empanelled in the C. C. P. to assess the damages sus-

7. By a subsequent statute, it is enacted, that in all cases, where any suit shall hereafter be brought, wherein the validity or legal effect of the proceedings of the mayor and aldermen, in respect to the laying out, altering or discontinuing of any way, which laying out, altering or discontinuing, shall take place after the passage of said statute shall be drawn in question, the time limited for applications for a jury to assess the damages shall be so far extended, that such application may be made at any time within one year after the final determination of any such suit; *pro-*

Time for petition extended, in certain cases. 1849, 200.

---

tained by the owner of such land, under Stat. 1821, c. 109, § 8, by which the jurisdiction of the court of sessions in the county of Suffolk, in such case, is transferred to that court, have viewed the land, the jurors may exercise their own judgment and knowledge of like subjects, in estimating the damages: but *it seems*, that if a juror has knowledge of any fact, bearing upon the case, he must disclose and testify to it, in court. *Ibid.*

Under Stat. 1820, c. 79, § 5, a bill of exceptions lies to the instructions and rulings of the C. C. P. upon such trial. *Ibid.*

Where the lessee of a store in Boston was prohibited, under certain penalties, by the terms of the lease, from making any alterations in the store without the consent of the the lessor, and subsequently to the execution of the lease, the street was widened by the city authorities, it was *held*, that the city was not responsible to the lessee, for any damage occasioned by a delay on the part of the lessor to give his consent to the alterations rendered necessary by the widening of the street. *Brooks v. City of Boston*, (19 Pick. 174.)

In an action for damages brought, in such case, by the lessee against the city, evidence that his sales were less during the time when the street, as widened, was being fitted for use, than in the corresponding season of the next year, after the alteration had been completed, is not admissible, unless it is connected with other evidence tending to show that the diminution of business was in fact occasioned by operation of widening the street. *Ibid.*

A city or town is not responsible in damages for the inconvenience and loss of business occasioned to the abutters on a street, by incumbrances and obstructions placed in the street for the purpose of repairing it, or by opening a common sewer in the street. *Ibid.*

The complainant took a lease of a store in the city of Boston, for three years, covenanting to pay the rent and to leave the premises in good repair at the end of the term, and the lessor reserving a right to enter and make improvements. The front part of the land was taken, and the front wall of the building was cut off by the city, for the purpose of widening the street. It was *held*, that this act of the city did not put an end to the term, nor release the lessee from his covenants to pay rent and make repairs. *Patterson v. City of Boston*, (20 Pick. 159.)

vided, that such suits shall have been brought within one year from the time of such laying out, altering or discontinuance.

Several parties to go to the same jury, in certain cases. Rev. Stat. 24, § 56.

8. In the said county of Suffolk, whenever there shall be several parties, having several estates or interests, at the same time, in any land or any buildings thereon, within the city of Boston, and the said land or buildings shall be taken or otherwise damaged, in whole or in part, by the laying out, altering or discontinuing of any highway or town way, and any one of such parties shall make application, by petition

---

Whether the erection of a new wall on the new line fixed for the street, was in the nature of a reparation which the lessee's covenant bound him to make, or whether it was not rather an addition or improvement, *quære. Ibid.*

But the lessee, in the first instance, and if he decline, the lessor, had a right to build such wall, and the expense of it is a proper item of claim for damages against the city. *Ibid.*

Whether the lessee has built such wall himself, or paid the lessor for building it, does not affect his claim for damages against the city, unless the lessor built it on his own account, and received remuneration from the city; in which case he was not entitled to recover the amount from the lessee, and the city is not to be charged a second time for the same damage. *Ibid.*

The damage sustained by the lessee in being deprived of the use of his store, and for which he is entitled to recover of the city, is to be computed for such time as would be reasonably necessary to remove his goods and make the repairs and remove back again: and the loss or the value of the store to him for that period, and not the rent and taxes specifically, is the measure of his indemnity. *Ibid.*

The lessee is also to be remunerated for the diminished value of the premises caused by the taking of part, for the residue of the term he continuing to pay at the same rate the rent and taxes. *Ibid.*

It seems he is not entitled to damages for loss of custom, occasioned by his being obliged to occupy a less advantageous place of business while the repairs are making. *Ibid,*

In estimating the damages sustained by an individual by reason of his land being taken for public use, the jury may rightfully be influenced by their general knowledge and experience of like subjects, as well as by the testimony and opinion of the witnesses. *Ibid.*

Soon after the commencement of a lease for three years, of a warehouse or store in Boston, in which lease the lessee covenanted to pay the rent during the term, and to leave the premises in good repair, the city took the front part of the land on which the building stood, and cut down the front wall, for the purpose of widening the street. The building remained in this condition about two years, when the lessor took it down, and erected a new store on the same site, but diminished by the strip of land taken by

to the court of common pleas, for a jury to ascertain his damages, as provided in the like cases in the 24th chapter of the Revised Statutes, the said court shall order the petitioner to give the like notice, as is required in the like cases before the commissioners of other counties, to all the other parties interested, to appear at the next term of the said court, and become parties to the proceedings under the said petition; and at the said next term, or at any succeeding term, as the court may direct, the said parties shall all be heard by the same jury, at the bar of the court, in such manner as the court shall direct; and thereupon the like proceedings shall be had, in the estimation of damages, the returning of the verdict, and the adjudication of the court thereon, as are in said chapter required to be had on verdicts in the like cases, returned to the court of common pleas in other counties.

Paving of streets and sidewalks. 1799, 31, § 1.

9. By the act of 1799, chapter 31, § 1, it was provided that all streets in Boston should be paved agreeably to the following regulations, viz: The foot path or walk on each side of every street, shall be of the breadth of one

---

the city. Before the wall was taken down, the lessee removed into another store, and remained there until the new one was erected, when he removed back to the new one. In a complaint by the lessee against the city for damages, it was *held*, that the plaintiff was entitled to recover the expenses of removing his goods from and back to his original place of business, and for the loss of earnings for the few days occupied in such removals, and a reasonable sum for the rent of another store for so long a time as would reasonably have been required for putting up a new front wall: (or, if he had suspended his business, that he might have recovered for the loss of earnings during a reasonable time for rebuilding the wall:) that he had a right forthwith to rebuild the wall, carrying it up to the roof, and if he had done so, inasmuch as he could not have compelled a contribution from the lessor, he would have been entitled to recover the whole cost from the city; but that, as in fact he did not put up the wall, but left the lessor to make his full claim of damages on the city, he could recover only such proportion of the estimated expense, as his interest, (regard being had to the portion of the store occupied by him and the time which his lease had to run,) bore to the value of the whole estate. *Patterson v. City of Boston.* (23 Pick. 425.)

For provisions respecting the recovery of damages for the raising or lowering of highways, see Rev. Stat. c. 25, § 6. See also *Brown v. Lowell*, (8 Metc. 172.)

sixth part of the width of the whole street, and shall be laid or paved with bricks or flat stones, and secured with a beam or cut stone along the out side thereof: and the middle or remaining four-sixths of every street, shall remain as a passage-way for carriages of burden or pleasure; and shall

Gutters.

have a gutter on each side thereof, or otherwise, as the surveyors of highways in the said town shall determine; and shall be paved with good and sufficient paving stones: *provided, always*, that if in any street so to be paved, the sides shall not exactly range, the gutter or outside of the foot walk shall be laid out as nearly in a straight line, as the street

Squares, &c.

will admit of; and in all squares, and other large open spaces, and in all streets the breadth of which shall not conform to this law, the breadth of the foot walk, and the ascent and descent, and the crowning of the pavement in every street, shall be regulated by the surveyors of highways.

Regulation of width and height of sidewalks, and acceptance thereof. 1833, 128.

10. The provisions of the preceding section were essentially modified by the act of 1833, c. 128, which provided, that the city council of the city of Boston, may from time to time, by any ordinance or ordinances, empower the surveyors of highways of said city so to regulate the width and height of the sidewalks of any public squares, places, streets, lanes or alleys, in said city, as shall, in the judgment of said surveyors, be most conducive to the convenience and interest of said city, any law of the commonwealth to the contrary notwithstanding; and may also empower said surveyors to accept such sidewalks, after the same shall be put in good and perfect repair by the abutters on said squares, places, streets, lanes and alleys, and after the same shall have been relinquished in writing to the said city by such abutters; and may also order, that, after such relinquishment, such sidewalks may be maintained at the expense of said city.[1]

Owner to pave the sidewalks at his own expense. 1799, 31, § 2.

11. Where the cartway in any public street shall be ordered to be paved, every owner of the lot or lots of ground upon such street shall, without delay, at his own cost, cause

---

[1] See the ordinance of the city in relation to streets, § 34, *p.* 391, *post*.

the footway in front of his ground to be paved with bricks or flat stones, and kept in repair; and in paving or repairing the pavement of any street, no person shall place timber or wood in front of his or her house or lot, to support the foot walk, but the same shall be supported with hammered or cut stone; the same to be done under the direction of, and to the approbation of the surveyors of highways; and if the owner or owners of such lots shall neglect to pave with bricks or flat stones and to support the footway, for the space of twenty days after he, or the tenant of such lot, or the attorney of the said owner or owners, shall have been thereto required by any of the surveyors of highways, then it shall be lawful for the said surveyors of highways, and they are enjoined and required, to pave the said footways with brick or flat stones, and to support and to defend the same, and to repair the same; and shall recover the whole amount thereof by action of the case to be brought by the surveyors of highways, before any court proper to try the same: *provided, nevertheless*, that in all cases where applications may be made for new paving of streets, any individuals who may be affected thereby, may make their objections to the mayor or aldermen, or surveyors of highways, who are directed to take them into consideration while deliberating on the expediency of said application, and to pave the same at the expense of said town, whenever they shall think it expedient.[1]

Materials therefor. 1809, 28, § 1.

1799, 31, § 2.

Individuals may object to paving, &c.

12. No canopy, balcony, platform or cellar door, or step, in any street, lane, or alley in the city of Boston, shall project into such street, more than one-tenth part of the width of the street, and in no case more than three feet; and all cellar doors hereafter to be made or repaired, shall be built with upright cheeks, and shall not project from the line of the house, more than six inches; and if any propri-

Canopy, balcony, platforms and cellar doors. Ibid, § 4.

[1] This section originally contained a provision, "that where there are any vacant lots of land in any such streets, the surveyors of highways may, at their discretion, allow the owner or owners thereof to cover the foot-path with planks, which shall be removed, and the brick, or flat stone pavement shall be completed, whenever it may become necessary in the judgment of said surveyors;" but this provision would appear to be repealed by stat. 1809, c. 28, § 1, as incorporated in the section in the text.

Penalty. etor or owner of any such canopy, balcony, platform, or cellar door, or steps, shall refuse or neglect to remove or take down the same, within five days after notice and direction given him or them by the surveyors of highways, or any person empowered by them to that purpose, such owner or proprietor, shall forfeit and pay the sum of two dollars, for each and every day the same shall remain after the expiration of the said five days.

Posts. Ibid, § 5. 13. No post shall be erected or set in any of the streets of the said city of Boston, except at the corners or intersection of two streets, and in such other places as the surveyors of highways may authorize and direct, and the said surveyors may remove the same; and no person shall plant any tree in any street of the said city of Boston, without leave first obtained from the surveyors of highways, who shall have power to remove the same:[1] and no person shall in future make, erect, or have any portico or porch, any bow window, or other window, which shall project into the streets of the said city of Boston, more than one foot beyond the front of his or her house; or hang any sign, or any goods, wares, or merchandize, which shall project into the street more than one foot beyond the front of his or her house or lot; and if any person shall hereafter offend against this provision, every person so offending, shall forfeit and pay the sum of one dollar for each and every day, such portico or porch, bow window, or other window shall be continued, after notice given to him by the surveyors of highways, or by any person by them authorized to that purpose.

Trees. Porticoes, porches and bow windows. Projecting signs. Penalty.

Placing goods in the street. Ibid, § 6. 14. If any person or persons shall continue to place in the street, contrary to the meaning of this act, any goods, wares, or merchandizes, it shall be lawful for the surveyors of highways of the said city of Boston, or any person empowered by them, to remove such goods, wares, and merchandizes, and to keep them in safe custody; and the proprietor or owner of such goods, wares, and merchandize,

[1] A portion of this section, in relation to carriages and wheelbarrows, was repealed by stat. 1847, c. 224, § 3.

shall not have the same goods restored, until he or they shall have paid to the person or persons so removing them, all expenses of removing and storing them, and a reasonable compensation for the time so employed in their removal, as well as the fine aforesaid: and if any person shall place or pile any empty boxes, barrels, hogsheads, or other conveniency capable of containing goods or merchandize, or that may have contained goods or merchandize, in any part of the streets of the said city of Boston, more than five minutes after notice given to remove the same, such person shall forfeit and pay the sum of two dollars, for each and every such offence, to be recovered by action of debt, by the surveyors of highways, before any justice of the peace in the said county.[1]

Boxes, barrels, &c.

Penalty.

15. All the forfeitures and fines which may be recovered in pursuance of the five preceding sections, shall go and be distributed, one moiety thereof to the poor of the city of Boston, and the other moiety to the surveyors of highways.[2]

How fines shall be distributed. Ibid § 8.

16. No person shall raise up from any street, wharf, or place of public resort, within the city of Boston, for the purpose of storing the same, any cask, bale of goods, or other articles of merchandize, into the second or any higher story of any house, store, or other building, upon or adjoining the same, and on the outside of such buildings; and no person shall deliver, from the second or any higher story of any house, store, or other building, on the outside of the same, which shall adjoin upon any street, wharf or place of public resort, within the said city of Boston, any cask, bale of goods, or other article of merchandize, except at such times and places, and under such restrictions and limitations, as the mayor and aldermen for the time being shall, by writing, authorize and direct. And every person who

Articles shall not be raised, for the purpose of storage, from any street, &c., into second story, &c., except, &c. 1816, 90, § 4. 1821, 110, §§ 1, 13.

---

[1] By Rev. Stat. c. 87, § 11, it is provided, that the justices court for the county of Suffolk shall have and exercise, exclusively, the same jurisdiction in all civil actions in the county of Suffolk, that is exercised by justices of the peace in other counties.

[2] The 7th section of stat. 1799, c. 31, was repealed by stat. 1847, c. 224, § 3.

shall offend in manner aforesaid, shall forfeit and pay to the commonwealth, for each and every such offence, a sum not exceeding one hundred dollars, nor less than ten dollars, to be recovered by indictment in the municipal court for the city of Boston, with costs of prosecution: *provided*, that this shall not be construed to extend to the raising any materials or other articles which may be necessary in erecting, repairing or taking down any building within the said city of Boston, or for the convenience thereof, or for removing any merchandize or other article in case of danger by fire, or other inevitable casualty.

City council may elect mayor and aldermen surveyors of highways. 1823, 2.

17. The city council of the city of Boston, shall have the power and authority of electing, if they see fit, the mayor and aldermen of said city, surveyors of highways for said city, any thing in the act establishing the city of Boston to the contrary notwithstanding.[1]

Streets may be macadamized, and same provisions shall apply. 1831, 17.

18. The surveyors of highways of the city of Boston, whenever they shall judge it expedient, may order any street of said city to be macadamized; and the several provisions of an act entitled, "An act to regulate the paving of streets in the town of Boston, and for removing obstructions in the same," passed on the twenty-second day of June, in the year of our Lord one thousand seven hundred and ninety-nine, and of the several acts in addition thereto, shall be deemed and taken to apply to streets ordered to be macadamized, as well as to streets ordered to be paved in said city, and the macadamizing of any of said streets shall, to all intents and purposes of said several acts, be deemed equivalent to the paving of the same, and shall create the same liabilities in all respects, under the said several acts, as would be created under them by the paving of such streets.

Streets, laid out over private land, by the owners, how to be graded. 1845, 236, § 1.

19. When any street or way, which now is, or hereafter shall be opened in the city of Boston, over any private land, by the owners thereof, and dedicated to, or permitted to be used by the public, before such street shall have been ac-

---

[1] For general provisions respecting surveyors of highways, see Rev. Stat. 15, § 81—84; c. 24, 25; and 1839, c. 144.

cepted and laid out according to law, it shall be the duty of the owners of the lots abutting thereon, to grade such street or way at their own expense, in such manner as the safety and convenience of the public shall, in the opinion of the mayor and aldermen of said city, require; and if the owners of such abutting lots shall, after reasonable notice given by the said mayor and aldermen, neglect or refuse to grade such street or way in manner aforesaid, it shall be lawful for the said mayor and aldermen to cause the same to be graded as aforesaid, and the expense thereof shall, after due notice to the parties interested, be equitably assessed upon the owners of such abutting lots, by the said mayor and aldermen, in such proportions as they shall judge reasonable; and all assessments so made shall be a lien upon such abutting lands, in like manner as taxes are now a lien upon real estate: *provided, always*, that nothing contained in this act shall be construed to affect any agreements heretofore made respecting any such streets or ways as aforesaid, between such owners and said city: *provided, also*, that any such grading of any street or way by the mayor and aldermen as aforesaid, shall not be construed to be an acceptance of such street or way by the city of Boston.

No street to be opened less than 30 feet wide, except, &c. Ibid, § 2.

20. No street or way shall hereafter be opened as aforesaid in said city, of a less width than thirty feet, except with the consent of said mayor and aldermen, in writing, first had and obtained for that purpose.[1]

Ways opened and dedicated shall not become chargeable upon city, unless, &c. 1846, 203, § 1.

21. No way heretofore opened and dedicated to the public use, and not already become a public way, and no way hereafter opened and dedicated to the public use, shall become chargeable upon any city or town, unless such ways shall be laid out and established by such city or town, in the manner prescribed by the statutes of this commonwealth.

---

[1] This act, which was passed March 26, 1845, was to take effect in thirty days from the passing thereof, unless the city council of said city should within that time, vote not to accept the same. No such vote appears to have been passed.

Entrances to such ways to be closed up, &c. Ibid, § 2.

22. It shall be the duty of the mayor and aldermen of each city, and of the selectmen of each town in this commonwealth, and they are hereby authorized and required, whenever, and so long as the public safety may demand it, to direct and cause the entrances of all the ways aforesaid, entering on and uniting with any existing public way, to be closed up, or, by other sufficient means, to caution the public against entering upon such ways.

City liable, unless notice is given. Ibid, § 3.

23. In case any city or town shall not close up the entrances to the ways aforesaid, or give other sufficient notice that the same are dangerous, such city or town so neglecting, shall be liable for any damages arising from any defects therein, in the same manner as if such ways were duly laid out and established.

Abutters on such ways shall construct sidewalk. 1849, 133.

24. When any street or way, which now is,[1] or hereafter shall be opened, in the city of Boston, over any private land, by the owners thereof, and dedicated to, or permitted to be used by, the public, before such street shall have been accepted, and laid out, according to law, it shall be the duty of the owners of lots abutting thereon, to construct convenient sidewalks on each side of such street or way, at their own expense, in such manner as the safety and convenience of the public shall, in the opinion of the mayor and aldermen of said city, require; and if the owners of such abutting lots shall, after reasonable notice given by the said mayor and aldermen, neglect or refuse to construct said sidewalks in such street or way, in manner aforesaid, it shall be lawful for the said mayor and aldermen to cause the same to be constructed as aforesaid; and the expense thereof shall, after due notice to the parties interested, be equitably assessed upon the owners of such abutting lots, by the said mayor and aldermen, in such proportions as they shall judge reasonable; and all assessments so made shall be a lien upon such abutting lands, in like manner as taxes are now a lien upon real estate; *provided, always*, that nothing contained in this section, shall be con-

Otherwise, the mayor and aldermen may construct the same at expense of abutters.

Such expense shall be a lien.

Proviso.

---

[1] The grammatical construction of this part of the statute does not appear very clear.

strued to affect any agreement heretofore made respecting any such street or way, as aforesaid, between such owners and said city; *provided*, *also*, that any such constructing of sidewalks in any street or way, by the mayor and aldermen, as aforesaid, shall not be construed to be an acceptance of such street or way by the city of Boston.[1]

Additional proviso.

25. The Boston Gas Light Company, with the consent of the mayor and aldermen, shall have power and authority to open the ground in any part of the streets, lanes and highways, in the city, for the purpose of sinking and repairing such pipes and conductors as [it] may be necessary to sink for the purpose expressed in the act incorporating said company. And the said corporation, after opening the ground in the said streets, lanes or highways, shall be held to put the same again in repair, under the penalty of being prosecuted for a nuisance; provided, that the said mayor and aldermen for the time being shall at all times have the power to regulate, restrict and control the acts and doings of said corporation, which may, in any manner, affect the health, safety or convenience of the inhabitants of said city.[2]

Right of gas company to sink pipes, &c., under the control of the mayor and aldermen. 1822, 41, § 3.

26. By an act passed March 26, 1833, the mayor and aldermen of the city of Boston were authorized to lay out a new street, in continuation of Broad street, beginning at or near the then easterly end of said Broad street, and thence running partly over the margin of Fort Hill, and over other land near the harbor of Boston, to a point, at or near the place

Mayor and aldermen authorized to lay out streets, in continuation of Broad and Commercial streets. 1833, 185, § 1.

---

[1] This act, passed April 23, 1849, was not to take effect, if, within thirty days from the passage thereof, the city council of said city should vote not to accept the same. For further general provisions respecting streets and highways, see Rev. Stat. c. 24, 25, 27, § 1; stat. 1836, c. 278; 1837, c. 164; 1838, c. 30; 1839, c. 76, 90, 144; 1841, c. 105; 1842, c. 46, 86; 1843, c. 70; 1846, c. 222; 1847, c. 254; 1848, c. 98, 123, 192; 1850, c. 5.

By Rev. Stat. c. 2, § 6, clause sixth, in the construction of all statutes, the word "highway" may be construed to include county bridges; and it shall be equivalent to the words "county way," "county road," and "common road."

[2] A similar provision is inserted in subsequent acts of incorporation of gas companies. See 1846, c. 36; 1847, c. 21; 1850, c. 202.

where Summer street meets Sea street; and also to lay out a new street extending from the then termination of Commercial street, near Lewis's wharf, so called, to the marine railway on Ann street. And the said streets were directed to be laid out respectively, of such widths, in such directions, and through and over such docks, then used for the purposes of navigation, as the public safety or convenience of the inhabitants of said city should, in the opinion of said mayor and aldermen, require.

In continuation of Front street. 1834, 65, § 1.

27. By an act passed March 11, 1834, the mayor and aldermen of the city of Boston were authorized to lay out a new street, in continuation of Front street, beginning at or near the southerly end of said Front street, and thence running in a south-westerly direction over the tide waters to Northampton street. And said street was required to be laid out in such direction, and through and over such docks and flats, as the public safety or the convenience of the inhabitants of said city should, in the opinion of said mayor and aldermen, require.[1]

Compensation for land, &c. Ibid, § 2. 1833, 185, § 2.

28. It was provided by the said acts, that the owner or owners of any building, wharf or other erection which might be removed, and of any land or flats which might be taken for said streets, should be entitled to receive compensation for the damages occasioned thereby.

ORDINANCE OF THE CITY.[2]

Streets to retain their names till altered. Sept. 30, 1850.

SECT. 1. The several streets in the city shall continue to be called and known by the names given to them respectively, by the selectmen of the town of Boston, the

---

[1] See "An act to incorporate certain Persons for the Purpose of making a Street from Rainsford's Lane, in the Town of Boston, to the Bridge proposed to be built from, at or near the Town's Landing to Dorchester Neck," 1803, c. 114, 3 Special Laws, p. 375; and two acts in addition thereto, viz. 1804, c. 3, ibid, p. 442, and 1805, c. 92, 4 Special Laws, p. 28.

[2] An ordinance in relation to streets, passed September 30, 1850.

mayor and aldermen of the city, or the city council, until the same shall be altered by the mayor and aldermen.

Superintendent of streets. Ibid.

SECT. 2. There shall be chosen, annually, in the month of January or February, and whenever a vacancy occurs, by concurrent vote of the two branches of the city council, a superintendent of streets, who shall hold his office until a successor is appointed, or he is removed. He shall be removable at the pleasure of the city council, and shall receive such compensation as the said council may from time to time determine.

He may appoint an assistant. Ibid.

SECT. 3. The said superintendent is authorized to appoint an assistant, to act under his control and direction, who shall be approved by the mayor and aldermen, and who shall receive such compensation as the city council may from time to time determine. The said assistant may be removed at any time by the said superintendent, or the mayor and aldermen.

Superintendent to attend at his office. To keep record, and books, &c. Ibid.

SECT. 4. The said superintendent shall attend at his office a portion of each day. He shall keep a record of all his proceedings, and a set of books, in which shall be entered, under appropriate heads, the receipts and expenditures in his department, with the names of all persons who have furnished materials, and of all workmen, and the amount paid to each individual; and he shall make a quarterly report thereof to the city council. On or before the tenth day of January, annually, he shall make a report to the city council, containing a general statement of the expenses of his department during the preceding year, the amount expended on the various streets, and such other information as he may consider desirable, together with an estimate in detail of the property under his charge belonging to the city.

To make reports.

To superintend streets, &c. Ibid.

SECT. 5. It shall be the duty of the said superintendent, under the direction and control of the mayor and aldermen, or the surveyors of highways for the time being, to superintend the general state of the streets; to attend to the laying out, widening, elevation and repairs of the same, and to make all contracts for the supply of labor and materials therefor; to give notice to the mayor or the city marshal, of any nuisance, obstruction or encroachment thereon. And the city shall not be responsible for any of his doings that have not been ordered by the city council, the mayor and aldermen, or the surveyors of highways, or sanctioned by express vote.

City not responsible for his acts, unless, &c.

Superintendent to have care of city stables. Ibid.

Of cleaning streets, manure, house offal, &c.

SECT. 6. The said superintendent, under the direction and control of the mayor and aldermen, shall have the care and superintendence of the city carts and stables, and shall make all necessary arrangements for cleaning the streets, disposing of manure, and removing house dirt and house offal.

Penalty for digging up streets, &c. Ibid.

SECT. 7. No person or persons shall break or dig up, or assist in breaking or digging up, any part of any street, or remove any gravel or other similar thing therefrom, without having first obtained the license of the mayor and aldermen, in writing, or of some person by them authorized for that purpose, under a penalty of not less than five nor more than twenty dollars; and a like sum for every day that he shall neglect or refuse to repair the same to the satisfaction of the mayor and aldermen.[1]

Persons so digging, to repair the same, &c. Ibid.

SECT. 8. Whosoever shall, by virtue of such license, break or dig up, or cause to be dug or broken up, any part of any street, shall, within such time as the mayor and aldermen, or some person by them authorized, may order, cause the same to be repaired and amended, to the satisfaction of the mayor and aldermen, under a penalty of not less than five dollars, nor more than twenty dollars, for each and every day he or they shall neglect or refuse so to do, after such order.

When drain or aqueduct is repaired, a fence and lights to be put up. Ibid.

SECT. 9. When any drain or aqueduct shall be opened or laid, or any aperture shall be made, in any street, the person or persons, or either of them, by or for whom the said drain or aqueduct shall be opened or laid, or such

---

[1] By Rev. Stat. c. 27, § 1, it is provided that if any person shall dig or break up the ground in any highway, street or lane, in any town, for the laying, altering or repairing of any drain, or common sewer, without the consent of the selectmen, in writing, he shall forfeit the sum of five dollars for each offence, to the use of the town, to be recovered by the treasurer thereof.

aperture made, shall cause a rail or other sufficient fence to be placed and fixed, so as to enclose such drain, aqueduct, or other aperture, and the dirt, gravel, or other material, thrown into the street, as aforesaid; and such fence shall be continued during the whole time such drain, aqueduct or aperture shall be open. And a lighted lantern, or some other proper and sufficient light, shall be fixed to some part of such fence, or in some other proper manner, over or near such open drain, aqueduct or aperture, and the dirt, gravel or other material taken from the same, and so kept from the beginning of the twilight of the evening through the whole of the night, and shall be continued every evening and night, during all the time such drain, aqueduct or aperture shall be open, or in a state of repair; and whosoever shall be guilty of a breach of any part of this section, shall be liable to a penalty for each offence, of not less than five nor more than twenty dollars.

Notice to be given of intention to build, &c. Ibid.

SECT. 10. Every person intending to erect or to repair any building upon land abutting on any of the streets, shall make the same known to the mayor and aldermen, who shall have power and authority to allot such portion of the street, thereto adjoining, as they or some person duly authorized shall deem expedient and necessary. And the part or portion so allotted, if any, and no other part of said street, shall be used for laying all the materials for any such building or repairing, and for receiving the rubbish arising therefrom. And all the rubbish arising therefrom or thereby, shall be carried away by the person or persons so building or repairing, at such convenient time as the mayor and aldermen, or other person by them authorized as aforesaid, may direct; and in case of neglect or refusal so to do, it shall be removed by the superintendent of streets, or other person authorized as aforesaid, at the expense of such person or persons. And, in all cases, the portion so allotted shall be enclosed and lighted as prescribed in the preceding section. Every person offending against any of the provisions of this section, shall be liable to a penalty for each offence, of not less than five nor more

Regulations in such case.

than twenty dollars, and a like sum for every day such offence shall be repeated or continued. And such portion of the street allotted as aforesaid shall not be used more than thirty days, on one application.

Placing coal or firewood in streets, regulated. Ibid.

SECT. 11. Neither the purchaser nor seller of any coal or firewood shall place or permit any such coal or firewood to remain in any street, more than thirty minutes after sunset in the evening; nor shall any greater quantity than two loads of such wood or coal, in any case, be permitted, either by the purchaser or seller, or other person having the charge thereof, to lie or continue in any street. Nor shall any purchaser, or seller or other person as aforesaid, permit any such wood or coal, at any time, by day or night, to remain in any street, so as unnecessarily to obstruct the passage in the same, nor more than two hours in any case. Whosoever shall be guilty of a breach of any of the provisions of this section, shall be liable to a penalty for each offence of not less than three dollars, nor more than twenty dollars.

Playing at football, throwing stones and snowballs. Ibid.

SECT. 12. No person shall play at football, or throw stones or snowballs, within any of the streets, or throw stones on the common, or in any of the public squares, under a penalty for each offence of not less than one dollar nor more than twenty dollars.

Shooting with bow and arrow forbidden. Ibid.

SECT. 13. No person shall shoot with, or use a bow and arrow, in any street, or on the common, or in any of the public squares, under a penalty of not less than one nor more than twenty dollars.

Exposing gaming tables. Ibid.

SECT. 14. No person shall expose, in any street, or on the common, or in any public square, any table or device of any kind whatsoever, upon, or by which, any game of hazard or chance can be played; and no person shall play at any such table or device, or at any unlawful game, in any street, or on the common, or in any public square, under a penalty of not less than ten dollars nor more than twenty dollars for either of the said offences.

Coursing or coasting upon sleds. Ibid.

SECT. 15. Whosoever shall course or coast upon a sled in any street, shall forfeit and pay for each offence a sum not less than one dollar, nor more than twenty dollars, to be paid by each offender respectively.

SECT. 16. No person shall swim or bathe in the waters surrounding the city which are adjacent to any of the wharves, bridges, avenues or railroads leading into the same, so as to be exposed to the view of the spectators, under a penalty of not less than four nor more than twenty dollars for each offence.

Bathing in waters, surrounding the city. Ibid.

SECT. 17. No person shall take any quantity of street dirt or manure, collected from any street, without the license of the mayor and aldermen first obtained, under a penalty for every offence of not less than three nor more than twenty dollars.

Taking street dirt without license. Ibid.

SECT. 18. No person shall obstruct any street, or any part thereof, by placing therein any house, barn, shop, or other building; and no person shall remove or draw, through or upon any street, any house, barn, shop or other building, without the permission of the mayor and aldermen. Any person offending against either of the provisions of this section, and any person who shall aid and assist in so offending, shall be liable to a penalty of not less than ten nor more than twenty dollars, and of a like sum for every twelve hours that the said obstruction shall continue, or that the said house, barn, shop or other building, shall remain in or upon any street.[1]

Obstructing street by moving buildings. Ibid.

SECT. 19. No person shall place, or cause to be placed, or shall suspend or cause to be suspended, from any house, shop, store, lot or place, over any street, any goods, wares or merchandize whatsoever, or any other thing, so that the same shall extend or project from the wall or front of said house, store, shop, lot, or place, more than one foot towards, or into the street, under a penalty of not less than three nor more than twenty dollars for every offence.

Suspending goods, so as to project into street. Ibid.

SECT. 20. It shall be lawful to place, or continue to maintain, awnings and shades before any house, shop or store in any street, upon the terms and under the regulations mentioned in this section, and not otherwise; *provided*,

Awnings and shades. Ibid.

---

[1] See the case of *Pike v. Brimmer*, (9 Law Reporter, 221.)

that the mayor and aldermen, as to particular buildings or streets, may order that no awnings or shades shall be erected. Such awnings and shades shall be safely fixed and supported, in such manner as not to interfere with passengers, and so that the lowest part thereof shall never be less than nine feet in height, above the sidewalk or street, and in no case to extend beyond the line of the sidewalk; and the person so placing or continuing to maintain the same, shall in all respects conform to any directions in relation to the materials, the construction and maintenance thereof, which shall be given by the mayor and aldermen. Any person violating any of the provisions of this section, or any such direction of the mayor and aldermen, shall be liable to a penalty of not less than three nor more than twenty dollars, and to a like penalty for every day that any such awning or shade shall be continued in violation of such provision or direction.

Projecting signs, lanterns, &c. Ibid.

SECT. 21. No person shall hang, affix, erect or fasten any sign, show bill, lantern or show board, of any description whatsoever, which shall project into any street more than one foot, under a penalty of not less than four nor more than twenty dollars for each offence, and the like penalty for every day such sign, show bill, lantern, or other board shall be continued, after an order to remove the same, given by the mayor and aldermen, or any person authorized by them.

Same subject. Ibid.

SECT. 22. No sign, show bill, lantern, show board or other thing, which at its lowest part is less than nine feet in height above the sidewalk or street, shall project into any street more than six inches, under a penalty of not less than four nor more than twenty dollars for each offence, and the like penalty for every day such sign, show bill, lantern, show board, or other thing shall be continued after an order to remove the same, given by the mayor and aldermen, or any person authorized by them.

Ringing bells or blowing horns. Ibid.

SECT. 23. No person, unless duly licensed by the mayor and aldermen, shall ring, or cause to be rung, any bell, or use or cause to be used any horn or other instrument, in any street, to give notice of the exercise of any business or calling, or for the sale of any article, under a penalty of not less than three nor more than twenty dollars for each offence.

Standing to grind cutlery, &c. Ibid.

SECT. 24. No person shall stand in any street, for the purpose of grinding cutlery, or for the sale of any article, or for the exercise of any other business or calling, unless duly licensed by the mayor and aldermen, under a penalty of not less than three nor more than twenty dollars for each offence.

Projecting porches, doors, windows, steps, &c. Ibid.

SECT. 25. No person shall construct or place, or cause to be constructed or placed, any portico, porch, door, window, or step, which shall project into any street, under a penalty of not less than four nor more than twenty dollars for each offence, and a like penalty for every day that the said portico, porch, door, window or step, shall be continued as aforesaid, after notice to remove the same, from the mayor and aldermen, or some person by them authorized.

Cellar doors and cellar door ways. Ibid.

SECT. 26. It shall not be lawful to construct or to continue to maintain, any cellar door or cellar door way in any sidewalk, or projecting into any street, for the purpose of being kept open as a common entrance, except as herein provided. No occupant or other person having the care of any building, shall suffer any cellar door, or cellar door way, connected with such building, which projects into any street, to remain open, or the platform thereof to be removed, more than fifteen minutes, during any part of the night time, or for more than two hours in the whole during the day time, unless duly licensed so to do by the mayor aldermen, under a penalty of not less than ten nor more than twenty dollars for every offence ; and this section shall apply to any cellar door or cellar door way, which is now or shall hereafter be made.

Steps descending from street to be enclosed and lighted. Ibid.

SECT. 27. Every entrance or flight of steps, descending immediately from any street, into any cellar or basement story of any building, where such entrance or flight of steps shall not be safely and securely covered, shall be enclosed with a railing on each side, permanently put up, at least three feet high from the top of the sidewalk or pavement, together with either a gate to open inwardly, or two iron chains across the front of the entrance way, one near the top and the other half way from the ground to the top of the railing; and such gate or chains shall, unless there be a burning light over the steps to prevent accidents, be closed during the night. And any person, who shall be guilty of a violation of any of the provisions of this section, shall be liable to a penalty of not less than ten nor more than twenty dollars, and a like penalty for each and every day during which or any part of which such violation continues; which penalty may be recovered of the owner, occupant or other person having charge of such building.

Apertures under street, coal holes, &c. Ibid.

SECT. 28. No person shall make, or cause to be made, any aperture in or under any street, for the purpose of constructing coal holes, or receptacles for any other article, or for light and air, or for an entrance, or for any other purpose, without the license of the mayor and aldermen, under a penalty of not less than ten nor more than twenty dollars for each offence, and a like penalty for every day the same shall remain. And no person shall leave such coal hole or other aperture open or unfastened after sunset, nor in the day time, unless while actually in use with a person or persons by the same, under a penalty of not less than two nor more than twenty dollars for each offence.

Gratings in streets. Ibid.

SECT. 29. No person shall affix or place, or cause to be affixed or placed, or continue, in any street, any grating, without the license of the mayor and aldermen, under a penalty of not less than ten nor more than twenty dollars for each offence, and a like penalty for every week the same shall remain.

Coal holes and gratings may be authorized, &c. Ibid.

SECT. 30. The mayor and aldermen, upon the application of any person, may authorize the construction of coal holes or other apertures, and of gratings, as hereinbefore mentioned, in such manner, and under the direction of such person, as they may deem suitable, at the expense of the applicant; and they may also authorize the continuance of any grating already constructed; *provided*, that in no case shall any grating be authorized to extend more than eighteen inches into the street.

SECT. 31. No owner, or person having for the time being, the charge or use of any horse, oxen, or other grazing animal, shall bait or feed the same in any street, under a penalty of not less than two dollars nor more than twenty dollars for each offence.[1]

Feeding animals in streets forbidden. Ibid.

SECT. 32. No owner, or person having for the time being the care or use of any horse, or other beast of burden, carriage or draught, shall ride, drive, or permit the same to go at a faster rate than six miles an hour, in any street, under a penalty of not less than five nor more than twenty dollars for each offence.[1]

Riding or driving faster than 6 miles an hour forbidden. Ibid. 3 Pick. 462.

SECT. 33. No owner, or person having the charge of any horse, kine, swine, sheep, goat, or other grazing animal, shall turn or permit the same to go at large or loose into or in any street, under a penalty of not less than five nor more than twenty dollars for each offence.

Horses, kine, swine, &c., not to go at large. Ibid.

SIDEWALKS.

SECT. 34. The surveyors of highways are hereby empowered so to regulate the width and height of the sidewalks of any streets, as shall in their judgment be most conducive to the convenience and interest of the city, and they may accept such sidewalks, after the same shall be put in good and perfect repair by the abutters on such streets, and after the same shall be relinquished in writing to the said city by such abutters.[2]

Surveyors of highways to regulate the width and height of sidewalks. Ibid. May accept the same.

SECT. 35. After such relinquishment and acceptance, such sidewalks shall be maintained at the expense of the city: *provided*, that when any sidewalk shall require repairs, in consequence of any defect in the cellar door, curb, step, or steps, cellar window, coal hole, cellar wall, or from any other cause within the control of the owner or occupant of the estate to which such sidewalk adjoins, then and in that case such repairs shall be made at the expense of such owner or occupant.

After acceptance, &c., sidewalks to be maintained by the city, provided, &c. Ibid.

---

[1] The orders of the mayor and aldermen, §§ 53, 57, *ante*, pp. 74, 76, apply to horses, &c, *harnessed to carriages*.

[2] See stat. 1833, c. 128, § 10, p. 374, *ante*.

City clerk to keep record of names of streets, and acceptances of sidewalks. Ibid.

SECT. 36. The city clerk shall keep a book in which the names of the streets shall be alphabetically arranged, and in which all the sidewalks which now are or may hereafter be accepted as aforesaid, shall be entered, with the date of such acceptance, the length and width of such sidewalk, and the names of the owners of the estate to which it belongs, and of the owner or owners of the adjoining estates.

Carriages forbidden on sidewalks, except, &c. Ibid.

SECT. 37. No person shall drive, wheel or draw any coach, cart, hand-cart, hand-barrow, or other carriage of burthen or pleasure, whether of the same description or not, except children's hand-carriages, containing children only, and drawn by hand, or drive or permit any horse under his care to go or stand upon any foot-path or sidewalk in the city, under a penalty of not less than five nor more than twenty dollars.

Sawing firewood on sidewalks. Ibid.

SECT. 38. No person shall saw any fire-wood, or place the same, upon the foot or sidewalk of any street, and no person shall stand on any such foot or sidewalk, with his woodsaw or horse, so as to obstruct a free passage for foot passengers, under a penalty of not less than one dollar nor more than twenty dollars.

Standing in a group, so as to obstruct the passage. Ibid.

SECT. 39. Three or more persons shall not stand in a group, or near to each other, on any sidewalk, in such a manner as to obstruct a free passage for foot passengers, for a longer time than twenty minutes, under a penalty of not less than three nor more than twenty dollars; nor more than five minutes after a request to move on, made by the mayor, any police officer, or watchman, under a like penalty.

Placing lumber, bales, &c., on sidewalks. Ibid.

SECT. 40. No person shall place, or cause to be placed, upon any foot path or sidewalk in the city, any lumber, iron, coal, trunk, bale, box, crate, cask, package, or article or thing whatsoever, whether of the same description or not, so as to obstruct a free passage for foot passengers for more than five minutes, under a penalty of not less than three nor more than twenty dollars: and if such person shall suffer such obstruction to foot passengers to remain more than one hour after it is first placed there, or more than ten minutes after notice to remove the same, given by the mayor, or some other person by him authorized, the person or persons so offending shall be liable to a penalty of not less than five dollars nor more than ten dollars for every such offence; and for each and every hour thereafter, that the same shall be suffered to remain, the person or persons so offending shall be liable to a penalty of not less than five nor more than ten dollars. *Provided*, that nothing contained in this section shall be deemed to extend to such goods, wares or merchandize as shall, in conformity with such rules, regulations and orders as shall be made by the mayor and aldermen upon the subject, be placed in any street, lane, court, alley, square or place, for the purpose of being sold at public auction.

Snow to be removed from sidewalks by abutters. Ibid.

SECT. 41. The tenant, occupant, and, in case there shall be no tenant, the owner, or any person having the care of any building or lot of land bordering on any street, lane, court, square or public place within the city, where there is any footway, or sidewalk, shall, after the ceasing to fall of any snow, if in the day time, within one hour, and if in the night time, before nine of the clock in the forenoon succeeding, cause the same to be removed therefrom, and in default thereof, shall forfeit and pay a sum not less than two dollars, nor more than ten dollars; and for each and every hour thereafter that the same shall remain on such footway or sidewalk, such tenant, occupant, owner or other person shall forfeit and pay a sum not less than one dollar nor more than ten dollars.[1]

---

[1] A by-law of a city, requiring the owners or occupants of houses bordering on streets to clear the snow from the sidewalks adjoining their respective houses and lands, is not, strictly speaking, a by-law levying a tax; and inasmuch as the burden created by it is imposed on a numerous class, and upon all persons equally who come within the description of such class, and as they commonly derive a peculiar benefit from the duty required, and are peculiarly able to perform it, with the promptness, which the good of the community demands, the by-law is not partial and unequal, within the sense of the provision of the constitution, that assessments, rates and taxes, imposed and levied on the inhabitants of the commonwealth, shall be proportional and reasonable; but such by-law is reasonable and valid. *Goddard, Petitioner*, (16 Pick. 504.)

Such a by-law is not invalid on account of a part of the city peculiarly situated being expressly exempted from its operation. *Ibid.*

To extend to snow falling from any building. Ibid.

SECT. 42. The provisions of the preceding section shall also apply to the falling of snow from any building.

Sidewalks encumbered with ice to be made safe, &c. Ibid.

SECT. 43. Whenever the sidewalk, or any part thereof, adjoining any building or lot of land, on any street, shall be encumbered with ice, it shall be the duty of the occupant, and in case there is no occupant, of the owner, or any person having the care of such building or lot, to cause such sidewalk to be made safe and convenient, by removing the ice therefrom, or by covering the same with sand or some other suitable substance; and in case such owner, or occupant, or other person shall neglect so to do for the space of six hours during the day time, he shall forfeit and pay a sum not less than two nor more than five dollars, and a like sum for every day that the same shall continue so encumbered.

Ice or snow thrown into street, to be broken up, &c. Ibid.

SECT. 44. Every person who shall lay, throw or place, or cause to be laid, thrown or placed, any ice or snow into any street, within the city, shall cause the same to be broken into small pieces, and spread evenly on the surface of such street; and, in default thereof, shall be liable to a penalty of not less than two dollars, nor more than five dollars for every offence.

Meaning of the word "street" defined. Ibid.

SECT. 45. Whenever the word "street" or "streets" is mentioned in this ordinance, it shall be understood as including alleys, lanes, courts, public squares and public places; and it shall also be understood as including the sidewalks, unless the contrary is expressed, or such construction would be inconsistent with the manifest intent of the city council.

Who shall be liable to penalties. Ibid.

SECT. 46. Whenever any thing is prohibited in this or any other ordinance, as well the person actually doing such prohibited thing, as his agent or employer, shall be liable to the penalty prescribed.

Acts forbidden to be done without license, may be licensed. Ibid.

SECT. 47. Whenever, in this or any other ordinance, anything is prohibited to be done without the permission or license of any officers or board, such officers or board shall have the power to permit or license such thing to be done.

Rights and duties of surveyors of highways not limited by this ordinance. Ibid.

SECT. 48. The foregoing provisions shall not be taken or construed as limiting in any manner the legal rights and duties of the surveyors of highways to make any alterations and repairs in the streets, which they may deem the safety and convenience of the inhabitants to require.

SECT. 49. This ordinance shall take effect and go into operation on and after the first day of October, in the year eighteen hundred and fifty. When to take effect. Ibid.

TAXES.

STATUTES.

1. The city council shall have power, from time to time, to lay and assess taxes for all purposes, for which towns Powers of the city council in relation to the assessment of

city and county taxes. 1821, 110, § 15. 1822, 85.

are by law required or authorized to assess and grant money, and also for all purposes, for which county taxes may be levied and assessed, so long as the town of Chelsea shall continue not to be liable to taxation therefor; *provided, however*, that in the assessment and apportionment of all such taxes upon the polls and estates of all persons liable to contribute thereto, the same rules and regulations shall be observed, as are now established by the laws of this commonwealth, or may be hereafter enacted, relative to the assessment and apportionment of town taxes. The said city council shall also have power to provide for the assessment and collection of such taxes, and to make appropriations of all public moneys, and provide for the disbursement thereof, and take suitable measures to ensure a just and prompt account thereof; and for these purposes, may either elect such assessors, and assistant assessors, as may be needful, or provide for the appointment or election of the same, or any of them, by the mayor and aldermen, or by the citizens, as in their judgment may be most conducive to the public good, and may also require of all persons entrusted with the collection, custody or disbursement of public moneys, such bonds, with such conditions and such sureties, as the case may in their judgments require.

Same rules to be observed, as in relation to town taxes. 1821, 110, § 15.

City council may provide for assessment and collection of taxes.

May elect assessors, &c., or provide for same.

May require bonds.

County and city taxes, how assessed. R. S. 7, § 26.

2. In the city of Boston, all taxes, assessed for city or county purposes, may be assessed separately, as county taxes, and as city taxes, or under the denomination of city taxes only, as the city council shall from time to time direct.

City treasurer shall be collector of taxes. 1802, 7, § 3. 1821, 110, §§ 1, 13. (See *ante*, pp. 2, 13, §§ I, XX.)

3. By virtue of the act of 1802, chapter 7, section three, as modified by the first and thirteenth sections of the city charter, the treasurer of the city of Boston shall be the collector of taxes in the said city, and is empowered to substitute and appoint under him such and so many deputies or assistants as the service may be found to require, who shall give bonds for the faithful discharge of their duty, in such sums, and with such sureties, as the mayor and aldermen shall think proper; and the said collector, and his deputy or deputies, shall have the same powers as are in-

vested by law in collectors of taxes chosen by other towns in this commonwealth.

Treasurer, &c., may collect taxes outstanding when he was chosen. 1803, 15, § 1. 1821, 110, §§ 1, 13. (See *ante*, pp. 2, 13, §§ I, XX.)

4. By virtue of the act of 1803, chapter 15, as modified by the city charter, the treasurer, his deputy or deputies, is empowered to collect all such taxes as may be outstanding and uncollected, at the time of his being chosen to the office of treasurer; such treasurer and his deputies first giving bonds for the faithful discharge of their duty, in such sums and with such sureties as the mayor and aldermen shall think proper.

Treasurer may issue his warrant for part of the rates, to his deputies. 1803, 15, § 2. 1821, 110, § 1.

5. The said treasurer may issue his warrant to his deputy or deputies, for the collecting and gathering in such part of the rates or assessments as, in his discretion, he shall think proper to commit to such deputy or deputies; which warrant shall be in the same tenor with the warrant prescribed to be issued by the selectmen or assessors, for the collecting and gathering in of the state rates or assessments, *mutatis mutandis*.

Power of distraining for taxes, how to be exercised. 1807, 134, § 1. 1821, 110, § 1.

6. By virtue of the act of 1807, chapter 134, as modified by the city charter, the treasurer and collector is authorized to issue his warrant to the sheriff of the county of Suffolk, his deputy, or to any constable of the city of Boston, directing them to distrain the persons or property of any person or persons, who may be delinquent in the payment of taxes, after the time has expired, that is or may be fixed for payment, by any vote of said town.[1] Which warrants shall be of the same tenor with the warrant prescribed to be issued by selectmen or assessors for the collecting or gathering in of the state rates or assessments, *mutatis mutandis*. And the said officers shall make a return of their warrants, with their doings thereon, to the said treasurer and collector, within thirty days from the date thereof: *provided, however*, That nothing in the said act shall prevent the said treasurer and collector, whenever there may be a probability of losing a tax, from distraining the person

---

[1] By the act of 1821, c. 110, § 15, (City Charter) all the powers by law then vested in the town of Boston, or in the inhabitants thereof, as a municipal corporation, were vested in the mayor and aldermen and common council. See p. 14, § XXIV, *ante*.

or property of any individual, before the expiration of the time fixed by the votes of said town.[1]

Same subject. 1807, 134, § 2.

7. By the same act it was made the duty of the said officers, to execute all warrants they may receive from said treasurer and collector, pursue the same process in distraining the persons or property of delinquents, as collectors of taxes were then authorized by law to do and perform; and for collecting the sum of money due on said warrant, receive the fees that were then allowed by law for levying executions in personal actions: *provided, however*, before the said officers shall serve any warrant, they shall deliver to the delinquent, or leave at his or her usual place of abode, a summons from said treasurer and collector, stating the amount due; and that unless the same is paid within ten days from the time of leaving said summons into the city treasury, with twenty cents for said summons, his or her property will be distrained according to law.[2]

ORDINANCE OF THE CITY.[3]

Assessors to be chosen. Oct. 24, 1850.

SECT. 1. There shall be chosen annually, in the month of March, by concurrent vote of the two branches of the city council, seven assessors of the public taxes; four of whom shall be voted for upon one ballot, and shall devote

---

[1] See note (1) on the preceding page.

[2] An act passed Feb. 4, 1764, (3 Special Laws, Appendix, p. 19,) and made perpetual March 7, 1797, (1796, c. 69,) seems to be no longer applicable, its provisions being superseded by the Revised Statutes, c. 8, §§ 14, 15. For general laws respecting taxes, see R. S. c. 7, 8, 9, 15; act of amendment, § 1; stat. 1837, c. 86, 176; 1839, c. 111, 139; 1841, c. 127; 1842, c. 34; 1843, c. 21, 85, 87, 98; 1844, c. 36, 90, 145, 147, 165; 1845, c. 190; 1846, c. 195; 1847, c. 226; 1848, c. 166, 235; 1849, c. 149, 213; 1850, c. 57, 79, 98, 218, 267, 276, 308.

[3] An ordinance concerning the assessment and collection of taxes, passed October 24, 1850.

their whole time to the service of the city, and shall receive such compensation as the city council may determine; and the remaining three shall be voted for on one ballot, and shall receive for their services four dollars per day each, while going through the wards, taking a list of the ratable polls, and estimating the value of real and personal estates; and three dollars per day in full for their services while engaged in other duties of their office. All the said assessors shall serve during the year, and until others are chosen and qualified in their stead.

Their duties, and compensation.

SECT. 2. In the month of February annually, a committee of the common council, consisting of one member from each ward, shall be appointed, whose duty it shall be to nominate assistant assessors, from the several wards, selecting, as nearly as may be, a just representation from the various callings of the persons to be taxed.

Committee to nominate assessors. Ibid.

SECT. 3. In the month of March annually, there shall be chosen, by concurrent vote of the two branches of the city council, twenty-four assistant assessors, two from each ward, who shall serve during the year, and until others are chosen and qualified in their stead; and they shall receive such compensation, in full for all their services, as the city council may determine.

Assistant assessors to be chosen. Ibid.

Compensation.

SECT. 4. Each of the officers mentioned in the preceding sections shall be removable at any time by the city council; and in case of any vacancy, by death, resignation, removal, or otherwise, it shall be filled in the manner before provided.

Assessors, &c., may be removed. Ibid.

Vacancies to be filled.

SECT. 5. The assessors shall meet as soon as practicable after their election, and organize themselves into a board, by the choice of a chairman and secretary, which secretary shall also be the secretary of the board provided for in the next section.

Organization of assessors. Ibid.

SECT. 6. The assessors and assistant assessors shall meet, as soon as practicable after their election, and organize themselves into a board, by the choice of a chairman; and a majority of the board shall constitute a quorum for the transaction of business. But nothing in this, or the preceding section, shall be construed to restrain the city

Organization of assessors and assistant assessors. Ibid.

council from electing one of the assessors to be chairman of both boards, whenever it may see fit so to do.

Secretary to keep records of both boards. Ibid.

SECT. 7. It shall be the duty of the said secretary of the two boards, thus organized, to keep the records of the doings of both boards in the same book, in the order in which the meetings occur, always designating the board whose doings are recorded.

Committee on the assessors department. Ibid.

SECT. 8. A joint committee on the assessors department, consisting of two of the board of mayor and aldermen, and three of the common council, shall be annually appointed, whose duty it shall be to confer with the assessors, and make such provision for their assistance, as the exigency of that department may from time to time require.

Duties of assistant assessors. Ibid.

SECT. 9. It shall be the duty of one or more of the said assistant assessors to visit, in company with one or more of the assessors, the different estates in their respective wards, and to assist the assessors in taking a list of the polls, in estimating the value of their personal property, and in appraising the value of the real estate.

Chairman of assessors, or other assessor, to remain at assessors' room. Ibid.

SECT. 10. During the season when the assessors are called upon to perform street duty, it shall be the duty of the chairman, or such other assessor as he may designate, to remain at the assessors' room, during office hours, to attend to such business as may be required to be transacted there.

Abatements to be recorded, &c. Ibid.

SECT. 11. Abatements of taxes, which shall be at any time allowed, shall be recorded by the assessors, and the record thereof shall contain the names of all persons whose taxes shall be abated in whole or in part, with the amount originally assessed, and the amount of abatements; and the reasons for abatement shall be stated on the said record, against the name of each person whose tax shall be abated; and this record shall be laid before the city council, annually, on or before the fourth day of March. And that this record may be perfect, the city clerk is instructed to inform the assessors of all abatements made by the mayor and aldermen, at the time they are made, in all which last mentioned cases the reasons of abatement may be omitted.

SECT. 12. It shall be the duty of the assessors to make out and deliver, to the treasurer and collector, tax bills for all taxes assessed on all persons and estates, on or before the first day of October, in each year.

Assessors to deliver tax bills to the treasurer, on or before Oct. 1. Ibid.

SECT. 13. The city treasurer and collector shall immediately issue the tax bills, and if the same are not paid within thirty days thereafter, he shall issue a summons to each delinquent person assessed; and if such person shall not pay his taxes within ten days after the receipt of such summons, or after the service thereof upon him in the usual form, the said treasurer shall issue his warrant for the collection of said taxes according to law.

How taxes shall be collected. Ibid.

SECT. 14. The said assessors may, at their discretion, transfer the amount of taxes, assessed on real estate not owned at the time of assessment by the persons charged with such taxes, to the persons by whom the said real estates were owned at the time.

Assessors may transfer taxes on real estate to the owner. Ibid.

SECT. 15. The said assessors shall assess, upon the owners of real estate, lying within the city, the amount of taxes for which such real estate may be taxable: provided, that, in any case where the assessors may deem it to be more for the public interest to assess the tenant or occupant, instead of the owner, they may so assess such tenant or occupant: and provided, also, that nothing herein shall affect the rights which owners and tenants may have, respectively, by reason of any agreement made between themselves concerning such taxes.

Real estate to be assessed to the owner. Ibid.

Proviso.

Further proviso.

TRUANTS.

STATUTE.

1. Cities and towns empowered to make provisions, &c., concerning truants.
2. They may appoint three or more persons to make complaint to judicial officer, &c.
3. Truants may be placed in an institution of instruction, or house of reformation.

STATUTE.

Cities and towns empowered to make provisions, &c., concerning truants. 1850, 294, § 1.

1. Each of the several cities and towns, in this commonwealth, is authorized and empowered to make all needful provisions and arrangements concerning habitual truants, and children not attending school, without any regular and lawful occupation, growing up in ignorance, between the ages of six and fifteen years; and, also, all such ordinances and by-laws, respecting such children, as shall be deemed most conducive to their welfare, and the good order of such city or town; and there shall be annexed to such ordinances, suitable penalties, not exceeding, for any one breach, a fine of twenty dollars: *provided*, that said ordinances and by-laws shall be approved by the court of common pleas for the county, and shall not be repugnant to laws of the commonwealth.

They may appoint three or more persons to make complaint to judicial officer, &c. Ibid, § 2.

2. The several cities and towns, availing themselves of the provisions of this act, shall appoint, at the annual meetings of said towns, or annually by the mayor and aldermen of said cities, three or more persons, who alone shall be authorized to make the complaints, in every case of violation of said ordinances or by-laws, to the justice of the peace, or other judicial officer, who, by said ordinances, shall have jurisdiction in the matter, which persons, thus appointed, shall alone have authority to carry into execution the judgments of said justices of the peace, or other judicial officer.

Truants may be placed in an institution of instruction, or house of reformation. Ibid, § 3.

3. The said justices of the peace, or other judicial officers, shall, in all cases, at their discretion, in place of the fine aforesaid, be authorized to order children, proved before them to be growing up in truancy, and without the benefit of the education provided for them by law, to be placed, for such periods of time as they may judge expedient, in such institution of instruction, or house of reformation, or other suitable situation, as may be assigned or pro-

vided for the purpose, under the authority conveyed by the first section, in each city or town availing itself of the powers herein granted.

ORDINANCE OF THE CITY.[1]

SECT. 1. The city of Boston hereby adopts the two hundred and ninety-fourth chapter of the laws of the commonwealth for the year one thousand eight hundred and fifty, entitled "an act concerning truant children and absentees from school," and avails itself of the provisions of the same.

Act of 1850, c. 294, respecting truant children, &c., adopted. Oct. 21, 1850.

SECT. 2. Any of the persons described in the first section of said act, upon conviction of any offence therein described, shall be punished by fine not exceeding twenty dollars; and the senior justice by appointment, of the police court, shall have jurisdiction of the offences set forth in said act.

Punishment for truancy, &c. Ibid.

Senior justice of police court to have jurisdiction.

SECT. 3. The house for the employment and reformation of juvenile offenders is hereby assigned and provided as the institution of instruction, house of reformation, or suitable situation, mentioned in the third section of said act.

House of reformation, &c., to be the institution, &c., mentioned in said act. Ibid.

---

[1] An ordinance concerning truant children and absentees from school, passed October 21, 1850. This ordinance was presented to the court of common pleas for the county of Suffolk, at the October term, 1850, and was approved by the court.

WARDS.

ORDINANCE OF THE CITY.[1]

New division of the wards. June 24, 1850.

SECT. 1. The present division of the wards of the city is hereby altered,[2] and a new division thereof is hereby made, and the same shall hereafter be known and constituted as follows, viz:—

Boundaries of the wards. Ward No. 1.

Ward No. 1. Beginning at the water, on the southerly side of the Eastern Packet Pier; thence across Commercial street to Richmond street; thence by the centre of Richmond street, across Hanover street, to Salem street; thence by the centre of Salem street to Cooper street; thence by the centre of Cooper street, crossing Charlestown street, to Beverly street; thence by the centre of Beverly street to Causeway street; thence across Causeway street, and in the same direction with Beverly street, to the water; thence by the water to the point begun at.

Ward No. 2.

Ward No. 2. All that part of the city called East Boston, and all the islands in the harbor.

Ward No. 3.

Ward No. 3. Beginning at the water, on the north side of the Fitchburg Railroad Depot, on a line which would strike the central line of Beverly street if extended to the water; thence by such line and the centre of Beverly street to Charlestown street; thence across Charlestown street, and by the centre of Cooper street, to Salem street; thence by the centre of Salem street to Richmond street; thence by the centre of Richmond street to Hanover street;

---

[1] An ordinance providing for a new division of the city into wards, passed June 24, 1850.

[2] See p. 3, § III, *ante*, as to the power of the city council to alter the divisions of wards.

thence by the centre of Hanover street to Court street; thence by the centre of Court street to Green street; thence by the centre of Green street to Leverett street; thence by the centre of Leverett street to Causeway street; thence by the centre of Causeway street to Lowell street; thence by the centre of Lowell street, and by a line in the same direction with Lowell street, to the water; thence by the water to the point begun at.

Ward No. 4. Beginning at the water, on the southerly side of the Eastern Packet Pier; thence across Commercial street to Richmond street; thence by the centre of Richmond street to Hanover street; thence by the centre of Hanover street to Court street; thence by the centre of Court street to Green street; thence by the centre of Green street to Staniford street; thence by the centre of Staniford street to Cambridge street; thence by the centre of Cambridge street to Temple street; thence by the centre of Temple street, and Mount Vernon street, to Park street; thence by the centre of Park street to Tremont street; thence by the centre of Tremont street to Winter street; thence by the centre of Winter street to Washington street; thence by the centre of Washington street to Milk street; thence by the centre of Milk street to India street; thence crossing India street by a straight line, to the water on the south side of Central wharf; thence by the water to the point begun at. **Ward No. 4.**

Ward No. 5. Beginning at the water at the easterly end of Cambridge Bridge; thence by the centre of Cambridge street to Staniford street; thence by the centre of Staniford street to Green street; thence by the centre of Green street to the junction of Lynde and Leverett streets; thence by the centre of Leverett street to Causeway street; thence by the centre of Causeway street to Lowell street; thence by the centre of Lowell street, and by a line in the same direction with Lowell street, to the water; thence by the water to the point begun at. **Ward No. 5.**

Ward No. 6. Beginning at the water, at the easterly end of Cambridge Bridge; thence by the centre of Cambridge street to Temple street; thence by the centre of **Ward No. 6.**

Temple street, and Mount Vernon street, to Beacon street; thence by the centre of Beacon street, and the Western avenue, to the boundary line between Boston and Roxbury, on the Western avenue; thence northerly by said boundary line, to the water; thence by the water to the point begun at.

Ward No. 7. Ward No. 7. Beginning at the water, on the south side of Central wharf; thence across India street, by a straight line, to Milk street; thence by the centre of Milk street to Washington street; thence by the centre of Washington street to Winter street; thence by the centre of Winter street to Tremont street; thence by the centre of Tremont street to West street; thence by the centre of West street, and Bedford street, to Kingston street; thence by the centre of Kingston street to Essex street; thence by the centre of Essex street to South street; thence by the centre of South street to Summer street; thence by the centre of Summer street, and by a straight line in continuation thereof, to the water, on the northerly side of Summer street wharf; thence by the water to the point begun at.

Ward No. 8. Ward No. 8. Beginning at the water on the northerly side of Summer street wharf; thence by a straight line in continuation of the centre of Summer street, and by the centre of Summer street to South street; thence by the centre of South street to Essex street; thence by the centre of Essex street to Kingston street; thence by the centre of Kingston street to Bedford street; thence by the centre of Bedford street and West street to Tremont street; thence by the centre of Tremont street to Eliot street; thence by the centre of Eliot street to Washington street; thence across Washington street to Kneeland street; thence by the centre of Kneeland street to Sea street; thence crossing Sea street by a straight line, to the water on the southerly side of Howe's wharf; thence by the water to the point first begun at.

Ward No. 9. Ward No. 9. Beginning at the boundary line between Boston and Roxbury, on the Western avenue; thence by the centre of the Western avenue and Beacon street to Park street; thence by the centre of Park street to Tremont street; thence by the centre of Tremont street to Warren street; thence by the centre of Warren street to Washington street; thence by the centre of Washington street to West Castle street; thence by the centre of West Castle street to Tremont street; thence by the centre of Tremont street to the Railroad bridge; thence by the centre of the Boston and Worcester railroad to the boundary line between Boston and Roxbury; thence by said boundary line to the point begun at.

Ward No. 10. Beginning at the water on the southerly side of Howe's wharf; thence by a straight line across Sea street to Kneeland street; thence by the centre of Kneeland street to Washington street; thence across Washington street to Eliot street; thence by the centre of Eliot street to Tremont street; thence by the centre of Tremont street to Warren street; thence by the centre of Warren street to Washington street; thence by the centre of Washington street to Dover street; thence by the centre of Dover street to the water at the northwesterly end of the Boston South Bridge; thence by the water to the point begun at. Ward No. 10.

Ward No. 11. Beginning at the boundary line between Boston and Roxbury, on the Boston and Worcester railroad; thence by the centre of the Boston and Worcester Railroad to the Railroad bridge; thence by the centre of Tremont street to West Castle street; thence by the centre of West Castle street to Washington street; thence by the centre of Washington street to Dover street; thence by the centre of Dover street to the water at the northwesterly end of the Boston South Bridge; thence by the water to the boundary line between Boston and Roxbury; thence by said boundary line to the point begun at. Ward No. 11.

Ward No. 12. All that part of the city called South Boston, and the Boston South Bridge and Boston Free Bridge. Ward No. 12.

Sect. 2. This ordinance shall take effect on and after the second Monday of December, in the year one thousand eight hundred and fifty. When this ordinance shall take effect. Ibid.

WATCH.

STATUTES.

1. Mayor and aldermen may appoint watchmen. Constables of divisions to report every morning.
2. Powers and duties of watchmen.
3. Powers and duties of watchmen. To prevent and suppress disturbances and disorders, &c. To walk the rounds. Constable to carry his badge of office. Officer of watch to carry quarter-pike. Watchmen to carry staff.
4. Expenses of watch, how raised.
5. Mayor and aldermen may set the watch at such hour after sunset as they shall judge expedient.
6. Watch may disperse any assembly of three or more persons, such as mentioned in R. S. 17, § 4, &c.

Mayor and aldermen may appoint watchmen. 1801, 26, § 1. 1821, 110, §§ 1, 13. (See *ante*, pp. 2, 13, §§ I, XX.)

1. The act of 1801, chapter 26, authorized the selectmen of the town of Boston, (whose powers, by the thirteenth section of the city charter, are transferred to the mayor and aldermen,) from time to time, to appoint such a number of the inhabitants, to be watchmen by night, in the town of Boston, as they should judge expedient; to be paid at the charge of that town; and the said selectmen were also further authorized, and empowered, from time to time, to appoint a head constable to superintend said watch, as also a constable for each division thereof; and the several constables of divisions were required to report every morning an account of their doings, and of the state of the town during the night, to the said head constable, in order that the same might be communicated to the chairman of the selectmen daily.

Constables of divisions to report every morning.

Powers and duties of watchmen. 1801, 26, § 2. 1796, 82, § 2.

2. The head constable, the several constables of divisions, and the watchmen appointed by virtue of the said act, shall have the same powers, and shall be held and obliged to perform the same duties, as are required of watchmen, by a law of this commonwealth, passed March the 10th, 1797, entitled "An act for keeping watches and wards in towns, and for preventing disorders in streets and public places."

3. The act of 1796, chapter 82, referred to in the preceding section,[1] gave the power to direct and order a suitable watch or watches to be kept nightly, from and after Powers and duties of watchmen. 1796, 82, § 2.

[1] Whether the provisions of the act of 1796, c. 82, in relation to the powers and duties of watchmen, are still in force in Boston, by virtue of the act of 1801, c. 26, § 2, or whether the provisions of the Revised Statutes, c. 17, are applicable to Boston, superseding the former enactments, —— *quære.* The act of 1796, c. 82, is among the general laws that were repealed by the Revised Statutes. The following are the provisions of the Revised Statutes, c. 17, upon this subject.

SECT. 3. When a military watch shall not be appointed to be kept, the selectmen of each town shall have power, from time to time, to order a suitable watch to be kept nightly, within their town, from such hour in the evening as they shall appoint, until sun rising in the morning; and also a guard to be kept in the day time and evening, when they shall think such watch or guard necessary; and they may direct the number of persons, of which the watch or guard shall consist, the places and the hours for keeping the same; and they may give orders in writing, accordingly, directed to any constable of the town, requiring him from time to time to warn such watch or guard, and to see that all persons so warned do attend, and perform their duty in such manner as shall be required; and in the warning thereof, care shall be taken, by the said selectmen, that some able householders, or other sufficient persons, be joined in each watch or guard.

SECT. 4. The constable or selectmen shall charge the watch to see that all disturbances and disorders in the night be prevented and suppressed; and, for that purpose, the watch shall have authority to examine all persons, whom they shall see walking abroad in the night after ten o'clock, and whom they shall have reason to suspect of any unlawful design, and to demand of them their business abroad at such time, and whither they are going; to enter any houses of ill fame, for the purpose of suppressing any riot or disturbance therein, and to arrest any persons there found, making or aiding and abetting in such riot or disturbance; and all persons, so walking abroad and suspected of any unlawful design, as aforesaid, who shall not give a satisfactory account of their so being abroad, and of their business, and all persons, so arrested in such houses of ill fame, shall be secured by imprisonment or otherwise, to be safely kept until the next morning, and shall then be taken before one of the nearest justices of the peace, to be examined and proceeded against, according to the nature of their offences.

SECT. 5. The watchmen shall walk the rounds, in and about the streets, wharves, lanes and principal inhabited parts, within each town, to prevent any danger by fire, and to see that good order is kept; taking particular observation and inspection of all houses and families of evil fame; and they shall in all things strictly observe the charge given them as aforesaid.

SECT. 6. Each constable when attending watch or guard, shall carry with him the usual badge of his office.

nine o'clock in the evening until sunrising in the morning; and also in the day time and evenings, when it should be thought necessary. And the watch were to be charged "to see that all disturbances and disorders in the night be prevented and suppressed; and to examine all persons whom they shall see walking abroad in the night after ten o'clock, and whom they shall have reason to suspect of any unlawful intention or design, of their business abroad at such season, and whither they are going; and in case they give not reasonable satisfaction therein, then to secure, by imprisonment or otherwise, all such disorderly and suspicious persons, to be safely kept until morning; then to carry them before one of the next justices of the peace to be examined, and proceeded against, according to the nature of their offences, as is by law directed. And such watchmen shall walk the rounds in and about the streets, wharves, lanes, and principal inhabited parts within such town or district, to prevent any danger by fire, and to see that good order is kept, taking particular observation and inspection of all houses and families of evil fame, and shall strictly observe the charge to be given them as aforesaid. And each constable, when attending watch or ward, shall carry with him the usual badge of his office." The same act also prescribed, that whenever a watch should be appointed and agreed upon different from a constable's watch, the person appointed officer of the watch to take the charge and command of such watch, as the badge of his office, should carry a quarter-pike, with a spire on the top thereof; and that every watchman, as well in this as in the constable's watch, should carry a staff with a bill fastened thereon, as was usual.

To prevent and suppress disturbances and disorders, &c.

To walk the rounds.

Constable to carry his badge of office.

Officer of watch to carry quarter pike.
Ibid, § 4.

Watchmen to carry staff.

4. The expenses that may be incurred, by reason of the establishment of the watch aforesaid, shall be raised, levied and collected, as the other expenses of said city are or may be raised, levied or collected; any law to the contrary notwithstanding.

Expenses of watch, how raised.
1801, 26, § 3.
1821, 110, § 1.

5. Whenever the mayor and aldermen of the city of Boston shall establish a watch within said city, in pursuance of the preceding provisions, the said mayor and aldermen

Mayor and aldermen may set the watch at such hour after sunset as may, and they are hereby authorized to set such watch, at such hour after sunset, as they shall judge expedient; and from and after such hour, the said watch shall and may exercise all the powers given in and by the several acts aforesaid, any thing in the said acts to the contrary notwithstanding. they shall judge expedient. 1833, 62.

6. The watch in any city or town in this commonwealth shall have authority to disperse any assembly of three or more persons, such as are mentioned in chapter seventeenth, section four, of the Revised Statutes,[1] at any time after the setting of such watch for the night and before the discontinuance of the same the next morning, and any such person as is in said section mentioned, to examine, arrest and secure during said time, and him to keep and proceed against, as therein mentioned. Watch may disperse any assembly of three or more persons, such as mentioned in R. S. 17, § 4, &c. 1850, 186.

WATER.

STATUTES.

1. City may obtain water from Long Pond, &c., in Natick, &c. May take and hold land. Shall file, in registry of deeds, a description of lands, ponds, &c., taken.
2. May construct aqueducts, dams, reservoirs, &c. May distribute water throughout the city, lay pipes, &c. May dig up highways, &c., when necessary.
3. Commissioners to be appointed. Their duties.
4. Compensation.
5. Their powers to be exercised by the city, after their office shall cease.
6. City of Boston shall be liable to pay all damages, sustained by taking land, &c. Application to C. C. P. in case of disagreement. Court may appoint three freeholders to assess damages.
7. Parties may claim a trial by jury, if dissatisfied with award.
8. No application to be made for damages for taking water, until actually diverted, &c.

---

[1] See note to § 3, p. 409, *ante*.

9. Where persons sustaining damages neglect to institute proceedings therefor, the city may commence such proceedings. How such persons shall be barred.
10. City may tender to petitioner, for damages, or bring into court, such sum as it shall think proper. Effect of such tender or payment.
11. City council may issue water scrip, to defray expenses.
12. City council may make temporary loans, to be redeemed within five years by water scrip.
13. Additional scrip may be issued by city council.
14. They may also issue scrip for payment of interest. But not after expiration of two years from completion of aqueducts, &c. Form of scrip. Record to be kept of same.
15. City council to regulate the price of water. Net surplus income to be applied to payment of principal and interest of scrip.
16. If surplus income is insufficient to pay the interest, the supreme judicial court may, on petition, &c., appoint commissioners, who may raise the price of water.
17. If such income is more than sufficient, &c., the court may appoint commissioners, on petition, &c., who may reduce the price of water. Reduction shall not be so great, that such income will be insufficient, &c. Costs, on such petitions.
18. Occupant of tenement, and owner, both liable for price of water. Action for use of water without consent of city. Inhabitants of Natick, &c., may use a portion of same.
19. Penalty for diverting or corrupting water.
20. City may purchase property, &c., of the Aqueduct Corporation.
21. Water may be conveyed to East Boston, through Charlestown and Chelsea. Over or under tide waters, with approval of a commissioner to be appointed, and with consent of city council.
22. City may lay the water pipes under the bridges of the Eastern Railroad Co.

ORDINANCE.

1. Cochituate water board, how chosen, &c.
2. Their organization.
3. Their general powers. To appoint subordinate officers, &c.
4. To make annual reports. Reports of city engineer and water registrar.
5. Schedule of water rates.
6. Cochituate water board may sell or lease property, &c.
7. Bills for expenditures, how drawn, examined, &c.
8. Duties of president of the board.
9. City engineer, how chosen, &c.
10. To have charge of lake, aqueducts, lands, reservoirs, &c.
11. To have charge of plans of streets. To make all surveys, &c.
12. May appoint an assistant.
13. To make an annual report.
14. Water registrar, how chosen, &c.
15. To assess water rates. To visit premises of takers, make out bills, &c.
16. To make annual report.
17. Water rent payable in advance, January 1.
18. Supply to be cut off in case of non payment
19. Abatements may be made.
20. Water registrar to keep books, &c.
21. No member of the board, or officer, to be interested in any

STATUTES.[1]

1. The city of Boston is hereby authorized, by and through the agency of three commissioners, to be appointed in the manner hereinafter provided, to take, hold, and convey to, into, and through the said city, the water of Long Pond, so called, in the towns of Natick, Wayland, and Framingham, and the waters, which may flow into and from the same, and any other ponds and streams within the distance of four miles from said Long Pond, and any water rights connected therewith; and may also take and hold, by purchase or otherwise, any lands or real estate necessary for laying and maintaining aqueducts for conducting, discharging, disposing of, and distributing water, and for

City may obtain water from Long Pond, &c., in Natick, &c. 1846, 167, § 1.

May take and hold land.

[1] An act for supplying the city of Boston with pure water, was passed March 25, 1845, (Stat. 1845, c. 220,) containing a provision that the act should be void, unless accepted by a majority of the legal voters of the city, in their respective wards, within sixty days from its passage. The act was rejected, by a vote of 3,670 yeas to 3,999 nays. (*Records of returns of votes from the several wards, May* 19, 1845.) The act of 1846, c. 167, given in the text, was passed March 30, 1846, and contained the following provisions, viz: *Sect.* 17. The mayor and aldermen of the city of Boston shall notify and warn the legal voters of the said city, to meet in their respective wards, on such day as the said mayor and aldermen shall direct, not exceeding thirty days from and after the passing of this act, for the purpose of giving their written votes upon the question, whether they will accept the same; and if a majority of the votes so given upon the question aforesaid, shall be in the negative, this act shall be null and void. *Sect.* 18. This act shall take effect from and after its passage. The act was accepted, April 13, 1846, by a vote of 4,637 yeas to 348 nays. (*Records of returns of votes from the several wards, April* 13, 1846)

forming reservoirs; and may also take and hold any land on and around the margin of said Long Pond, not exceeding five rods in width, measuring from the verge of said Pond, when the same shall be raised to the level of eight feet above the floor of the flume at the outlet thereof, and on and around the said other ponds and streams, so far as may be necessary for the preservation and purity of the same, for the purpôse of furnishing a supply of pure water for the said city of Boston. The city of Boston shall, within sixty days from the time they shall take any lands or ponds or streams of water for the purposes of this act, file in the office of the registry of deeds, for the county where they are situate, a description of the lands, ponds or streams of water so taken, as certain as is required in a common conveyance of lands, and a statement of the purpose for which taken, which said description and statement shall be signed by the said mayor.

Shall file, in registry of deeds, a description of lands, ponds, &c., taken.

May construct aqueducts, dams, reservoirs, &c. Ibid, § 2.

2. The said city may, by and through the same agency, make and build one or more permanent aqueducts, from any of the aforesaid water sources, to, into and through the said city, and secure and maintain the same by any works suitable therefor; may connect the said water sources with each other; may erect and maintain dams to raise and retain the waters therein; may make and maintain reservoirs within and without the said city; may make and establish such public hydrants, in such places as may, from time to time, be deemed proper, and prescribe the purposes for which they may be used, and may change or discontinue the same; may distribute the water throughout the city, and for this purpose may lay down pipes to any house or building in said city, the owner or owners thereof having notice and not objecting thereto; may regulate the use of the said water within and without the said city, and establish the prices or rents to be paid therefor. And the said city may, for the purposes aforesaid, carry and conduct any aqueducts, or other works, by them to be made and constructed, over or under any water course, or any street, turnpike-road, railroad, highway, or other way, in such manner as not to obstruct or impede travel thereon;

May distribute water throughout the city, lay pipes, &c.

May dig up highways, &c., when necessary.

and may enter upon and dig up any such road, street or way, for the purpose of laying down pipes beneath the surface thereof, and for maintaining and repairing the same; and, in general, may do any other acts and things necessary, or convenient and proper, for the purposes of this act.

3. Three commissioners shall be appointed by the city council, who shall, during their continuance in office, execute and perform, and superintend and direct, the execution and performance of, all the works, matters and things mentioned in the preceding sections which are not otherwise specially provided for in this act; they shall be subject to such ordinances, rules and regulations, in the execution of their said trust, as the city council may, from time to time, ordain and establish, not inconsistent with the provisions of this act and the laws of this commonwealth; they shall respectively hold their said offices for the term of three years next after their said appointment, unless the aqueducts and works aforesaid shall be sooner completed: but they, or either of them, after having had an opportunity to be heard in his or their defence, may be removed at any time by a concurrent vote of two thirds of each branch of the city council; and in case of a vacancy in the board of commissioners, by death, resignation, or removal, such vacancy shall be filled by the appointment of another commissioner, in manner aforesaid, who shall hold his said office for the residue of the said term of three years, with all the powers and subject to all the restrictions aforesaid. A major part of said commissioners shall be a quorum for the exercise of the powers and the performance of the duties of the said office: they shall, once in every six months, and whenever required by the city council, make and present in writing, a particular report and statement of all their acts and proceedings, and of the condition and progress of the works aforesaid.

Commissioners to be appointed. Their duties. Ibid, § 3.

4. Before the appointment of the commissioners aforesaid, the city council shall establish and fix the salaries, or compensation, to be paid to the commissioners for their services; and the said salaries of the said commissioners,

Compensation of commissioners. Ibid, § 4.

so established and fixed as aforesaid, shall not be reduced during their continuance, respectively in said office.

Their powers to be exercised by the city, after their office shall cease. Ibid, § 5.

5. Whenever the said office of commissioners shall cease, either by the expiration of the said term of three years from the original appointment, or by the completion of the aqueducts and works mentioned in the preceding sections of this act, all the rights, powers and authority, given to the city of Boston by this act, shall be exercised by the said city, subject to all the duties, liabilities and restrictions herein contained, in such manner, and by such agents, officers and servants, as the city council shall, from time to time, ordain, appoint, and direct.

City of Boston shall be liable to pay all damages, sustained by taking land, &c. Ibid, § 6.

Application to C. C. P. in case of disagreement.

6. The said city of Boston shall be liable to pay all damages that shall be sustained by any persons, in their property, by the taking of any land, water, or water rights, or by the constructing of any aqueducts, reservoirs, or other works for the purposes of this act. And if the owner of any land, water, or water rights, which shall be taken as aforesaid, or other person who shall sustain damage as aforesaid, shall not agree upon the damages to be paid therefor, he may apply, by petition, for the assessment of his damages, at any time within three years from the taking of the said land, water, or water rights as aforesaid, and not afterwards, to the court of common pleas, in the county in which the same are situate; such petition may be filed in the clerk's office of said court, in vacation or in term time, and the clerk shall thereupon issue a summons to the city of Boston, returnable, if issued in vacation, to the then next term of the said court, and if in term time, returnable on such day as the said court shall order, to appear and answer to the said petition; the said summons shall be served fourteen days, at least, before the return day thereof, by leaving a copy thereof, and of the said petition, certified by the officer who shall serve the same, with the mayor or clerk of the said city; and the said court may, upon default or hearing of the said city, appoint three judicious and disinterested freeholders of this commonwealth, who shall, after reasonable notice to the parties, assess the damages, if any, which such petitioner

Court may appoint three freeholders to assess damages.

may have sustained as aforesaid, and the award of the said freeholders, or of the major part of them, being returned into and accepted by the said court, shall be final, and judgment shall be rendered and execution issued thereon for the prevailing party, with costs, unless one of the said parties shall claim a trial by jury, as hereinafter provided.

7. If either of the parties mentioned in the preceding section, shall be dissatisfied with the amount of damages awarded as therein expressed, such party may, at the term at which such award was accepted, or the next term thereafter, claim, in writing, a trial in said court, and have a jury to hear and determine, at the bar of said court, all questions of fact relating to such damages, and to assess the amount thereof; and the verdict of such jury, being accepted and recorded by the said court, shall be final and conclusive, and judgment shall be rendered and execution issued thereon; and cost shall be recovered by the said parties, respectively, in the same manner as is provided by law, in regard to proceedings relating to the laying out of highways.

Parties may claim a trial by jury, if dissatisfied with award. Ibid § 7.

8. No application shall be made to the court, for the assessment of damages for the taking of any water rights, until the water shall be actually withdrawn or diverted by the said city under the authority of this act; and any person or corporation, whose water rights may be thus taken and affected, may make his application aforesaid, at any time within three years from the time when the waters shall be first actually withdrawn or diverted as aforesaid.

No application to be made for damages for taking water, until actually diverted, &c. Ibid, § 8.

9. Whenever any damages shall have been sustained by any persons in their property, by the taking of any land, water, or water rights, or by the constructing of any aqueducts, reservoirs, or other works, for the purposes of this act, and of the act entitled "An act for supplying the city of Boston with pure water," chapter one hundred and sixty-seven, of the Acts and Resolves of the year eighteen hundred and forty-six, and such persons shall neglect to institute proceedings against the city of Boston, according to the provisions of the said act, for the space of five months, it shall be lawful for the city of Boston to commence such

Where persons sustaining damages neglect to institute proceedings therefor, the city may commence such proceedings. 1849, 187, § 2. (Accepted by city council, May 28, 1849. City Records, vol. 27, p. 239.)

proceedings, which shall go on, and be determined, in the same manner as if commenced by the persons who shall have sustained such damage. And, if such persons, on receiving due notice, shall not come in and prosecute the proceedings so instituted, judgment shall be entered against them, and they shall be forever barred from recovering any damages under said act.

How such persons shall be barred.

City may tender to petitioner, for damages, or bring into court, such sum as it shall think proper. 1850, 316.

10. In every case of a petition to the court of common pleas, by any person, for the assessment of damages, as provided in the sixth, seventh and eighth sections above, the city of Boston, by any of its officers, may tender to the complainant, or his attorney, any sum that it shall think proper, or may bring the same into court, to be paid to the complainant for the damages claimed in his petition; and if the complainant shall not accept the same, with his costs up to that time, but shall proceed in the suit, he shall be entitled to his costs up to the time of the tender, or such payment into court, and not afterwards, and the said city shall be entitled to recover its costs afterwards, unless the complainant shall recover greater damages than were so offered.

Effect of such tender or payment.

City council may issue water scrip, to defray expenses. 1846, 167, § 9.

11. For the purpose of defraying all the costs and expenses of such lands, estates, waters and water rights, as shall be taken, purchased or held for the purposes mentioned in this act, and of constructing all aqueducts and works necessary and proper, for the accomplishment of the said purposes, and all expenses incident thereto, the city council shall have authority to issue, from time to time, notes, scrip, or certificates of debt, to be denominated, on the face thereof, "Boston Water Scrip," to an amount not exceeding in the whole, the sum of three millions of dollars, bearing interest at a rate not exceeding the legal rate of interest in this commonwealth; and said interest shall be payable semi-annually, and the principal shall be payable at periods not more than forty years from the issuing of the said scrip, notes, or certificates respectively. And the said city council may sell the same, or any part thereof, from time to time, at public or private sale, or pledge the same for money borrowed for the purposes aforesaid, on

such terms and conditions as the said city council shall judge proper.

12. Nothing in the preceding section shall be construed to prohibit the city council of the city of Boston, from making temporary loans, for the purposes therein set forth, to be redeemed within five years by the "Boston Water Scrip:" *provided*, that the amount of said scrip shall in no case, exceed the amount named in the said section.

City council may make temporary loans, to be redeemed within five years by water scrip. 1848, 33.

13. In addition to the notes, scrip, or certificates of debt, authorized to be issued by the eleventh section, the city council of the city of Boston are authorized to issue, from time to time, notes, scrip, or certificates of debt, to be denominated on the face thereof, "Boston Water Scrip," to an amount not exceeding, in the whole, the further sum of one million five hundred thousand dollars, for the same purposes, and in the same manner, and upon the terms and conditions specified in said section.

Additional scrip may be issued by city council. 1849, 187, § 1. (Accepted by city council, May 28, 1849. City Records, vol. 27, p. 239.)

14. In addition to the sum of three millions of dollars mentioned in the eleventh section, the said city council may, whenever and so far as deemed necessary, issue and dispose of notes, scrip, or certificates of debt, in the manner prescribed in the said eleventh section, to meet all payments of interest which may accrue upon any scrip by them issued; *provided*, *however*, that no scrip shall be issued for the payment of interest as aforesaid, after the expiration of two years from the completion of said aqueducts and other works; but payment of all interest that shall accrue after that time, shall be made from the net income, rents, and receipts for the use of the water, if they shall be sufficient for that purpose; and if not, then the payment of the deficiency shall be otherwise provided for by the city council. All notes, scrip, and certificates of debt, to be issued as aforesaid, shall be signed by the treasurer and auditor, and countersigned by the mayor of the said city, and a record of all such notes, scrip, and certificates shall be made and kept by the said treasurer and auditor respectively.

They may also issue scrip for payment of interest. 1846, 167, § 10.

But not after expiration of two years from completion of aqueducts, &c.

Form of scrip.

Record to be kept of same.

15. The city council shall, from time to time, regulate the price or rents for use of the water, with a view to the

City council to regulate the price of water. Ibid, § 11.

payment, from the net income, rents, and receipts therefor, not only of the semi-annual interest, but ultimately of the principal also of the "Boston Water Scrip," so far as the same may be practicable and reasonable. And the said net surplus income, rents and receipts, after deducting all expenses and charges of distribution, shall be set apart as a sinking fund, and shall be appropriated for and towards the payment of the principal and interest of the said scrip; and shall, under the management, control, and direction of the mayor, treasurer, and auditor of the city, or the major part of them for the time being, who shall be trustees of the said fund, be applied solely to the use and purpose aforesaid, until the said scrip shall be fully paid and discharged. And the said trustees shall, whenever thereto required by the city council, render a just, true, and full account to the said city council, of all their receipts, payments, and doings under the provisions of this section.

Net surplus income to be applied to payment of principal and interest of scrip.

(See City Doc. for 1848, No. 45.)

16. At any time after the expiration of two years, from the completion of the works mentioned in the second section, and before the reimbursement of the principal of the "Boston Water Scrip" herein before mentioned, if the surplus income and receipts for the use of the water distributed under the provisions of this act, at the price established by the city council, after deducting all expenses and charges of distribution, shall, for any two successive years, be insufficient to pay the accruing interest on the said scrip, then the supreme judicial court, on the petition of one hundred or more of the legal voters of the said city, praying that the said price may be raised and increased so far as may be necessary for the purpose of paying, from the said surplus income and receipts, the said accruing interest, and upon due notice of the pendency of such petition given to the said city in such manner as the said court shall order, may appoint three commissioners, who, upon due notice to the parties interested, may raise and increase the said price, if they shall judge proper, so far as may be necessary, in their judgment, for the purpose aforesaid, and no farther. And the award of said commissioners, or the major part of them, being returned to the

If surplus income is insufficient to pay the interest, the supreme judicial court may, on petition, &c., appoint commissioners, who may raise the price of water. 1846, 167, § 12.

said court, at the then next term thereof for the county of Suffolk, and accepted by the said court, shall be binding and conclusive, for the term of three years next after the said acceptance, and until the price so fixed by the commissioners shall, after the expiration of said term, be changed or altered by the city council.

17. If the surplus income and receipts for the use of the water, distributed under the provisions of this act, at the price established by the city council, after deducting all expenses and charges of distribution, shall, for any two successive years, be more than sufficient to pay the accruing interest on the "Boston Water Scrip," herein before mentioned, then the supreme judicial court, on the petition of one hundred or more of the legal voters of the said city, who may deem the said price unreasonably high, and pray for the reduction thereof; and upon due notice of the pendency of said petition given to the said city in such manner as the said court shall order, may appoint three commissioners, who, upon due notice to the parties interested, may, if they shall judge proper, reduce the price established by the city council; *provided*, that such reduction shall not be so great that the surplus income and receipts aforesaid, will, in the judgment of the said commissioners, be thereafter insufficient for the payment of the said accruing interest. And the award of the said commissioners, or the major part of them, being returned and accepted as mentioned in the preceding section, shall be binding and conclusive in the same manner, and to the same extent, as therein provided in regard to awards made pursuant to the provisions of that section.

If such income is more than sufficient, &c., the court may appoint commissioners, on petition, &c., who may reduce the price of water. Ibid, § 13.

Reduction shall not be so great, that such income will be insufficient, &c.

And the said court may, at their discretion, order the costs on such petitions as are mentioned in this and the preceding section, and of the proceedings thereon, or any part thereof, to be paid by either of the said parties, and may enter judgment and issue execution therefor accordingly.

Costs, on such petitions.

18. The occupant of any tenement shall be liable for the payment of the price or rent for the use of the water in such tenement; and the owner thereof shall be also

Occupant of tenement, and owner, both liable for price of water. Ibid, § 14.

liable, if, on being notified of such use, he does not object thereto; and if any person or persons shall use any of the said water, either within or without the city, without the consent of the city, an action of trespass on the case may be maintained against him or them, by the said city, for the recovery of damages therefor; *provided*, *however*, that this act shall not be so construed as to prevent the inhabitants of Natick, Framingham, Sherburne, and Wayland, from using so much of the water hereby granted as shall be necessary for extinguishing fires, and for all ordinary household purposes, under such regulations of the said city council as may be essential for the preservation of the purity of the same.

Action for use of water without consent of city.

Inhabitants of Natick, &c., may use a portion of same.

Penalty for diverting or corrupting water. Ibid, § 15.

19. If any person or persons shall wantonly or maliciously divert the water, or any part thereof, of any of the ponds, streams, or water sources, which shall be taken by the city pursuant to the provisions of this act, or shall corrupt the same, or render it impure, or destroy or injure any dam, aqueduct, pipe, conduit, hydrant, machinery or other property, held, owned or used by the said city, by the authority and for the purposes of this act; every such person or persons shall forfeit and pay to the said city, three times the amount of the damages that shall be assessed therefor, to be recovered by any proper action. And every such person or persons may, moreover, on indictment and conviction of either of the wanton and malicious acts aforesaid, be punished by fine, not exceeding one thousand dollars, and imprisonment not exceeding one year.

City may purchase property, &c., of the Aqueduct Corporation. Ibid, § 16.

20. The said city of Boston is hereby authorized to purchase and hold all the property, estates, rights and privileges of the Aqueduct Corporation, incorporated by an act passed February 27th, in the year one thousand seven hundred and ninety-five, and by any convenient mode may connect the same with their other works.[1]

---

[1] For acts respecting the Aqueduct Corporation, see stat. 1794, c. 55; 1796, c. 1; 1803, c. 35.

21. The city of Boston is authorized to convey the water of Long Pond to, into, and through, that part of Boston called East Boston, by laying their aqueduct, or water pipes, through the city of Charlestown and town of Chelsea; and, for that purpose, may have all the rights and privileges, and shall be subject to all the liabilities, mentioned in the act entitled "An act for supplying the city of Boston with pure water." And the said city of Boston may make any suitable structures for the purpose of conveying the said water over or under the tide waters within the jurisdiction of this commonwealth, provided that such structures shall be approved of by a commissioner, to be appointed for that purpose by the governor and council, and to be compensated by the city of Boston: *provided, further*, that the authority granted by this section shall not be exercised without the consent of the city council of said city first had and obtained.[1]

Water may be conveyed to East Boston, through Charlestown and Chelsea. 1849, 187, § 3. (Accepted by city council, May 28, 1849. City Records, vol. 27, p. 239.)

Over or under tide waters, with approval of a commissioner to be appointed, and with consent of city council.

22. By the act passed in 1849, authorizing the Eastern Railroad Company to extend their road, it is declared lawful for the city of Boston, under the direction of a commissioner to be appointed by the governor and council, and paid by the Eastern Railroad Company, to lay and construct their water pipes under, or by the side of the bridges, to be constructed by said railroad corporation, for the purpose of conveying water into and through East Boston, without compensation to the said railroad corporation; *provided, however*, that said pipes shall be so laid, maintained and repaired, as not to retard, or in any manner obstruct, the regular and convenient use of said bridges, for all the uses of said railroad company.

City may lay the water pipes under the bridges of the Eastern Railroad Co. 1849, 201, § 7.

---

[1] By an order of the city council, passed June 11, 1849, it was ordered, that the water commissioners be authorized and empowered, by virtue of the 3d section of the act of 1849, c. 187, to convey the waters of Long Pond to East Boston; provided, that the cost of the same shall not exceed the sum of four hundred thousand dollars; and that, in the execution of said authority, they shall have all the powers, so far as the same are proper and necessary, and be subject to all the duties and restrictions contained in the several ordinances of the city regulating the proceedings of the commissioners. (*City Records, vol.* 27, *p.* 272.)

ORDINANCE OF THE CITY.[1]

Cochituate water board, how chosen, &c. Oct. 31, 1850.

SECT. 1. There shall be chosen annually, in the month of March or April, by concurrent vote of the two branches of the city council, one alderman, one member of the common council, and five citizens at large, to constitute the Cochituate water board, who shall hold their offices until they are removed or others are chosen in their places; and they and each of them shall be removable at the pleasure of the city council, and no person shall be chosen as aforesaid for more than five consecutive years.

Their organization. Ibid.

SECT. 2. The persons so chosen shall meet, and organize themselves into a board, by the choice of a president from their own number, and of a clerk, and they may make such rules and regulations for their own government, and in relation to all subordinate officers by them appointed, as they may deem expedient.

Their general powers. Ibid.

SECT. 3. The Cochituate water board shall have and exercise all the powers, vested in the city council by an act of the legislature of Massachusetts, passed on the thirtieth day of March, in the year eighteen hundred and forty-six, entitled an Act for supplying the city of Boston with pure water, and by any acts in addition thereto, so far as the same can be legally delegated; and they shall, more especially, have the power to appoint all necessary subordinate officers, agents and assistants, and may fix their compensation, and of the clerk before mentioned, provided that the same shall not exceed in the whole the sum appropriated therefor by the city council; but all the powers mentioned in this section shall be subject to any limitations and restrictions, contained in the ordinances, regulations and orders of the city council.

To appoint subordinate officers, &c.

To make annual reports. Ibid.

SECT. 4. The Cochituate water board, on or before the fifteenth day of January, annually, shall present to the city council a report, containing a statement of the condi-

---

[1] An ordinance providing for the care and management of the Boston water works, passed October 31, 1850.

tion of all the water works, and of the lands and other property connected therewith, with an account of all receipts and expenditures, together with any information or suggestions which they may deem important; and they shall, at the same time transmit to the city council the report of the city engineer, and the water registrar, mentioned in the thirteenth and sixteenth sections. Reports of city engineer and water registrar.

SECT. 5. The Cochituate water board, whenever requested by the city council, shall prepare and send to the city council a schedule of water rates. Schedule of water rates. Ibid.

SECT. 6. The Cochituate water board are authorized to sell or lease such of the property connected with the water works as they may deem expedient, subject to the approval of the mayor and aldermen; and all necessary deeds and leases shall be executed by the mayor and countersigned by the president of the board. Cochituate water board may sell or lease property, &c. Ibid.

SECT. 7. All bills for expenditures by the Cochituate water board shall be drawn for by the president, examined by the auditor, and approved by the committee of accounts, before they are paid by the treasurer. Bills for expenditures, how drawn, examined, &c. Ibid.

SECT. 8. The president of the Cochituate water board shall exercise a general supervision over all the water works, and the materials and property connected therewith, and over all subordinate officers and agents. In case of his absence, or inability, his duties may be performed by a president pro tempore, to be chosen by the said board. Duties of president of the board. Ibid.

SECT. 9. There shall be chosen annually, in the month of September or October, and whenever a vacancy occurs, by concurrent vote of the two branches of the city council, a city engineer, who shall be a citizen of Boston, and who shall hold his office until a successor is appointed, or he is removed. He shall be removable at the pleasure of the city council, and shall receive such compensation as the said council may from time to time determine. City engineer, how chosen, &c. Ibid.

SECT. 10. The city engineer shall take such charge of Lake Cochituate, the aqueducts, lands, reservoirs, and other works and property connected with the water works, To have charge of lake, aqueducts, lands, reservoirs, &c. Ibid.

as the Cochituate water board may from time to time direct; and he shall perform all such services in relation thereto as may be required of him by the Cochituate water board, or the city council.

To have charge of plans of streets. Ibid.

To make all surveys, &c.

SECT. 11. The said city engineer, under the direction and control of the mayor and aldermen, shall have charge of all the plans of streets belonging to the city. He shall, by himself or his assistant, for whom he shall be responsible, make all such surveys, admeasurements, and levels, and perform such other services, as may be required of him by the mayor and aldermen, or any committee of the city council.

May appoint an assistant. Ibid.

SECT. 12. The said city engineer may appoint an assistant, subject to the approval of the mayor and aldermen, who shall receive such compensation as the city council may determine.

To make an annual report. Ibid.

SECT. 13. The city engineer, on or before the fifth day of January, annually, shall present to the Cochituate water board a report of the general condition of the water works, with a detailed statement of all expenditures in his department relating to the same, and such other matters as he or the said board may deem expedient.

Water registrar, how chosen, &c. Ibid.

SECT. 14. There shall be chosen, annually, in the month of September or October, and whenever a vacancy occurs, by concurrent vote of the two branches of the city council, a water registrar, who shall be a citizen of Boston, and who shall hold his office until a successor is appointed, or he is removed. He shall be removable at the pleasure of the city council, and shall receive such compensation as the said council may from time to time determine.

To assess water rates. Ibid.

To visit premises of takers, make out bills, &c.

SECT. 15. The water registrar, under the direction and control of the Cochituate water board, shall assess the water rates, according to the tariff established by the city council. He shall, once in each year, personally visit the premises of every person who takes the water, and shall make out and distribute all bills for the same, and he shall exercise a constant supervision over the use of the water, and attend to the enforcement of all regulations relative thereto.

SECT. 16. The water registrar, on or before the fifth day of January, annually, shall present to the Cochituate water board a report, containing a statement of the number of water takers, the number of cases where the water has been cut off, the number and amount of abatements, the expenditures in his department, and such other matters as he or the said board may deem expedient. To make annual report. Ibid.

SECT. 17. The annual rent for the use of the water shall be payable to the city treasurer in advance, on the first day of January in each year. All charges for specific supplies, or for fractional parts of the year, shall be payable in advance, and before the water is let on. Water rent payable in advance, January 1. Ibid.

SECT. 18. In all cases of non-payment of the water rent for sixty days after the same is due, the water registrar shall cut off the supply; and the water shall not again be let on, either for the present or any subsequent occupant, except upon the payment of the amount due, together with the sum of two dollars; provided, that, in cases of specific supplies, or for fractional parts of the year, where the water has been let on, it may be cut off immediately, after notice given at the place that the rent is not paid, and may be let on again upon the condition before mentioned. And the foregoing provisions shall apply, when two or more parties take the water through the same service pipes, although one or more may have paid the proportion due from him or them. Supply to be cut off in case of non-payment. Ibid.

SECT. 19. The water registrar, under the control of the Cochituate water board, may make abatements in the water rents, in all proper cases. Abatements may be made. Ibid.

SECT. 20. The water registrar shall keep suitable books, in which shall be entered the names of all persons who take the water, the kind of building, the name and number of the street, the nature of the use, the number of taps, and the amount charged, which shall be always open to the inspection of the Cochituate water board and any committee of the city council. He shall perform such other services as may be required of him by the city council, or the Cochituate water board. Water registrar to keep books, &c. Ibid.

No member of the board, or officer, to be interested in any contract, &c., in relation to the water works. Ibid.

SECT. 21. No member of the Cochituate water board, and no person appointed to any office, or employed, by virtue of this ordinance, or of the acts of the legislature mentioned in the third section, shall be interested, directly or indirectly, in any contract, bargain, sale, or agreement, in relation to the water works, or any matter or thing connected therewith, wherein the city is interested, without an express vote of the city council; and any and all contracts, bargains, sales or agreements, made in violation of this section, shall be utterly void as to the city.

Penalty for opening hydrant, &c. Ibid.

SECT. 22. If any person shall open any hydrant within the city of Boston, or lift or remove the cover of the same, without the license of the Cochituate water board, or of the city engineer or the water registrar, except in case of fire, he shall be liable to a penalty of not less than three nor more than twenty dollars.

For opening any pipe, or reservoir, &c. Ibid.

SECT. 23. If any person shall make any opening or connection with any pipe or reservoir, without the license mentioned in the preceding section, he shall be liable to a penalty of not less than three nor more than twenty dollars.

For turning on or turning off the water, &c. Ibid.

SECT. 24. If any person shall turn on or turn off the water in any of the water pipes or reservoirs, without the license mentioned in the twenty-second section, he shall be liable to a penalty of not less than three nor more than twenty dollars.

For injuring any other reservoir, &c. Ibid.

SECT. 25. Any person who shall injure any public reservoir, not connected with the Cochituate water works, or who shall break and enter the same, and draw off, or cause to be removed, any of the water therefrom, except in case of fire, or unless duly authorized by the mayor and aldermen, or chief engineer of the fire department, shall forfeit and pay a sum not less than one dollar nor more than twenty dollars.

Water not to be sold to parties out of the city, unless, &c. Ibid.

SECT. 26. The water shall not be sold or delivered to any parties out of the limits of the city, unless by special vote of the city council, except in cases where contracts have already been entered into and arrangements made for that purpose.

SECT. 27. The following regulations shall be considered a part of the contract with every person who takes the water; and every such person, by taking the water, shall be considered to express his assent to be bound thereby. They shall be printed upon every bill for water rent, and whenever any one of them is violated, the water shall be cut off from the building or place of such violation, although two or more parties may receive the water through the same pipe, and shall not be let on again, except by the order of the Cochituate water board, and on the payment of two dollars; and in case of any such violation, the said board shall have the right to declare any payment made for the water, by the person committing such violation, to be forfeited, and the same shall thereupon be forfeited. Regulations under which the water shall be taken. Ibid.

The said regulations are as follows, namely:—

1. All persons taking the water shall keep the service pipes within their premises, including any area beneath the sidewalk, in good repair, and protected from frost, at their own expense; and they will be held liable for all damage which may result from their failure to do so. Takers to keep service pipes in good repair.

2. They shall prevent all unnecessary waste of water, and there shall be no concealment of the purposes for which it is used. To prevent waste, and use no concealment.

3. No alteration shall be made in any of the pipes or fixtures inserted by the city, except by its agents, who are to be allowed to enter the premises supplied, to examine the apparatus, and to ascertain whether there is any unnecessary waste. No alteration to be made, except, &c.

4. No water is allowed to be supplied to parties not entitled to the use of it under the city ordinances, unless by special permission. Water not to be supplied to other parties, unless, &c.

5. The use of the hand hose is restricted to one hour before eight of the clock in the forenoon, and one hour after sunset. Use of hand hose restricted.

6. The water registrar may enter the premises of any water taker, to examine the quantity used, and the manner of use. Water registrar may enter premises to examine.

SECT. 28. This ordinance shall take effect on and after the first day of January in the year eighteen hundred and When this ordinance shall take effect. Ibid.

fifty-one: provided, however, that the officers provided therein to be chosen by the city council, may be chosen during the present municipal year.

WEIGHTS AND MEASURES.

STATUTES.

1. Appointment of sealers of weights and measures.
2. Same subject.
3. How removable.
4. Each town sealer to have complete sets of standards.
5. County and town treasurers to keep seals.
6. Sealer of weights and measures shall keep a house or office, where weights, measures, &c., shall be sent to be sealed.
7. Sealer shall go to houses, stores, and shops, of such as neglect to bring in weights, measures, &c., and shall seal the same. Double fees and expenses. Penalty for refusing to have weights, &c., sealed. Penalty for using same without sealing. Penalty for altering same.
8. Standard weights, measures and balances. To be in care and custody of treasurer of commonwealth.
9. Description of same.
10. Of seals to be used.
11. Treasurer to appoint deputy, and to make duplicates of standards for his use.
12. Fee for sealing.
13. Sealers to give notice annually, and to seal all weights, &c. Penalty for selling by weights, measures, &c., not sealed.
14. Trying and sealing hay-scales, &c. Fees. Penalty for using hay-scales, &c., not sealed.
15. County standards shall be tried once in ten years, &c. Penalty.
16. County and town treasurers shall keep sets of weights, measures and balances. How the same shall be made.
17. Standards shall be furnished by commonwealth.
18. County, city and town treasurers shall provide places for keeping the same.
19. Shall have care of same, keep them in repair, and replace them when lost, &c.
20. Penalty for neglect.
21. Town and city standards shall be sealed once in ten years. Penalty.
22. Sealers accountable to towns for preservation of standards.
23. Penalty for neglect of sealers.
24. Vibrating steel-yards allowed to be used, if sealed.
25. Provisions respecting measures for salt and grain.
26. "Hundred weight" to be construed the net hundred.
27. Public weighers to weigh according to the preceding section.
28. Who shall be deemed a public weigher. His duty in weighing. Penalty for breach thereof.

ORDINANCE.

Two sealers of weights and measures to be appointed.

STATUTES.

1. The Revised Statutes, chapter 15, section 38, provide that the selectmen of each town shall, in the month of March or April annually, appoint, unless the inhabitants themselves, at their annual meeting, shall choose the same, one sealer of weights and measures; and any other number which the inhabitants shall at their annual meeting, vote to have appointed.

Appointment of sealers of weights and measures. R. S. 15, § 38.

2. The Revised Statutes, chapter 30, section 12, provide, that one or more suitable persons shall be annually appointed in each town, in the manner provided in the fifteenth chapter, to be sealers of weights and measures for such town.

Same subject. R. S. 30, § 12.

3. The thirteenth section of the same chapter provides, that the selectmen may remove from office any sealer of weights and measures in their town, and may fill all vacancies occasioned by such removal or otherwise.[1]

How removable. Ibid, § 13.

4. The fourteenth section of the same chapter provided, that, when any town shall vote to have more than one sealer of weights and measures, the treasurer of the town shall, at the expense thereof, procure and preserve the necessary additional seals, weights and measures specified in said chapter; so that each sealer in such town may have complete sets of the same.

Each town sealer to have complete sets of standards. Ibid, § 14.

5. The fifth section provided, that the county treasurers shall keep a seal for sealing town standards, and preserve the same: and the eighth section provided, that every town treasurer shall keep a seal, for sealing the weights and measures of the inhabitants of the town.

County and town treasurers to keep seals. Ibid, §§ 5, 8.

6. By the statute of 1817, c. 50, it was provided, that it shall be the duty of the sealer of weights and measures,

Sealer of weights and measures shall

[1] Similar provisions to those stated in sections 1–4 in the text, were contained in stat. 1799, c. 60, which although afterwards repealed by the Revised Statutes, was in force at the time of the passage of the statute of 1821, c. 110, (City Charter.) By § 13 of the last mentioned statute, all the powers theretofore vested in the selectmen of the town of Boston, were vested in the mayor and aldermen. See § xx, p. 13, *ante*.

keep a house or office, where weights, measures, &c., shall be sent to be sealed. 1817, 50, § 1. 1821, 110, § 1.

within and for the town[1] of Boston, to be provided with a house, or office, and to which all persons using scale beams, steelyards, weights or measures within the town[1] of Boston, in trade, for the purpose of buying or selling any article, shall be required, after notice thereof shall have been given in two or more of the newspapers published within the said town[1] to send annually their scale beams, steelyards, weights and measures, for the purpose of having the same tried, proved and sealed.[2]

Sealer shall go to houses, stores, and shops, of such as neglect to bring in weights, measures, &c., and shall seal the same. 1817, 50, § 2. 1821, 110, § 1.

7. It was also provided by the same act, that the said sealer is authorized and required, to go to the houses, stores and shops of all such merchants, innholders, traders, retailers, and of all other persons living or residing within the said town of Boston, using beams, steelyards, weights or measures, for the purpose of buying and selling, as shall neglect to bring or send the same to the house or office of the sealer aforesaid: and there, at the said houses, stores and shops, on having entered the same with the assent of the occupant thereof, to try, prove and seal the same, or to send the same to his said house or office, to be tried, proved and sealed, and shall be entitled to demand and receive therefor, double the fees he would be entitled to demand and receive for the same, if such beams, steelyards, weights and measures, had been sent to his said house or office; with all expenses attending the removal and transportation of the same; and if any such person or persons shall refuse to have his, her or their beams, steelyards, weights or measures, so tried, proved and sealed, the same not having been tried, proved and sealed, within one year preceding such refusal, he, she or they shall forfeit and pay ten dollars for each offence; the one moiety to the use of the said town of Boston, the other moiety of the same to the sealer.

Double fees, and expenses.

Penalty for refusal to have weights, measures, &c., sealed.

---

[1] See § I, p. 2, *ante*.

[2] This section referred, for the manner of sealing, and fees to be demanded, to stat. 1799, c. 60, which was repealed by the Revised Statutes. Its provisions, with several modifications, were incorporated in R. S. c. 30, and several additional statutes upon the subject have been passed. See the subsequent sections. Whether §§ 6 and 7 in the text were not in effect repealed by the Revised Statutes, c. 30,—*quære*.

And if any such person or persons shall use any beam, steelyard, weight or measure, which shall not conform to the public standard, the same not having been tried, proved and sealed, within one year preceding such use of the same, he, she or they shall forfeit and pay ten dollars for each offence; the one moiety to the use of said town of Boston, and the other moiety of the same to the informer. And if any such person or persons shall alter any beam, steelyard, weight or measure, after the same shall have been tried, proved and sealed, so as that the same shall, by such alteration be made not to conform to the public standard, and shall fraudulently make use of the same, he, she or they shall forfeit and pay fifty dollars for each offence, the one moiety to the use of the said town of Boston, and the other moiety of the same to the informer.

Penalty for using same without sealing.

Penalty for altering same.

8. The several avoirdupois and troy weights and balances, procured from the government of the United States for this commonwealth, by the commissioners appointed for that purpose in the year one thousand eight hundred and thirty-five, and also all weights, measures, and balances, that have since been received from the said government, for the purpose of being used as standards, shall hereafter be used as the sole authorized public standard of weights and measures of this commonwealth, and shall be in the care and custody of the treasurer of the commonwealth.

Standard weights, measures, and balances. 1847, 242, § 1.

To be in care and custody of treasurer of commonwealth.

9. The said balances, weights, and measures shall be preserved by the treasurer and used as public standards, and are as follows, namely: one half bushel, one wine gallon, one wine quart, one wine pint, one wine half-pint, one yard measure; also, a set of avoirdupois weights consisting of fifty, twenty-five, twenty, ten, five, four, three, two, one pounds, and from eight ounces down to one dram; also, one set of troy weights, from five thousand pennyweights down to half a grain, and from one pound down to the ten-thousandth part of an ounce; and three sets of balances.

Description of same. Ibid, § 2.

10. The seals, used by the various sealers of weights and measures, shall hereafter be as follows, to wit: by the treasurer of the commonwealth and his deputy, the letters C. M.; by the county treasurers, the initial and final let-

Of seals to be used. Ibid, § 3.

ters of their respective counties, followed by the letters Co.; by town and city sealers, the name of their respective towns and cities, or such intelligible abbreviation thereof as the selectmen of the towns, or the mayor and aldermen of cities, may prescribe.

Treasurer to appoint deputy, and to make duplicates of standards for his use. R. S. 30, § 4.

11. The treasurer of the commonwealth shall keep the authorized public standard weights and measures in the state treasury; and he shall cause duplicates thereof to be made, which shall be kept by a deputy to be appointed by him; the said deputy shall be under oath, and shall give bonds for the faithful discharge of the duties of his office: and the said duplicates may be used by the said deputy for sealing weights and measures, in like manner, as the standards kept in the state treasury may be used by the treasurer, for the like purpose.

Fee for sealing. 1847, 242, § 4.

12. Each sealer of weights and measures, including the state deputy and county treasurer, shall receive a fee of three cents for every weight, measure, scale, beam or balance, by him sealed, except platform-balances; and a reasonable compensation for all repairs, alterations, and adjustments thereof, which may be necessary for him to make.

Sealers, to give notice, annually, and to seal all weights, &c. Ibid, § 5. R. S. 30, § 16.

13. Every sealer of weights and measures shall, in the month of May, annually, give public notice, by advertising in some newspaper, or posting up notifications in different parts of the town, stating the time and place when and where he will attend such of the inhabitants, as live within the limits described in the respective notifications, for every inhabitant of his town or city who uses weights and measures for the purpose of buying or selling, and for public weighers who have the same, to bring in their measures, weights, balances, scales, and beams, to be examined, adjusted, and sealed; and he shall forthwith adjust and seal all weights and measures brought to him for that purpose. And he shall deface and destroy all such as cannot be brought to the just standard. And every person who shall presume to sell by any other weights, measures, scales, beams, or balances, than those which have been sealed as before provided, or as provided in the following section, shall forfeit and pay a sum not exceeding twenty dollars

Penalty for selling by weights, measures, &c., not sealed.

for every such offence; one half to enure to the use of the town or city, the other half to the complainant.[1]

Trying and sealing hay scales, &c. 1847, 242, § 6.

14. The sealers of every town and city shall go, once in every year, to every hay scale and platform-balance, which cannot be readily removed, and try, adjust, and seal the same, for which he shall be entitled to a fee of one dollar and fifty cents for every such scale or platform-balance, weighing five thousand pounds and upwards; and for every scale or platform-balance, weighing less than five thousand pounds, he shall be entitled to a fee of fifty cents; and all repairs and alterations, which it shall be necessary for him to make, shall be the subject of an additional charge. Any person using such scale or platform-balance, in buying or selling, that has not been so tried, adjusted, and sealed, at least once in every year, shall be subject to the same forfeiture as provided in the preceding section, to be appropriated in the manner therein provided. And no sealer of weights and measures, except for the purposes of this section, shall carry his standard of weights, measures, and scales, from one place to another, for the purpose of adjusting others within the town or city.

Fees.

Penalty for using hay scales, &c., not sealed.

County standards shall be tried once in ten years, &c. Ibid, § 7.

15. Every county treasurer shall, once at least in every ten years, at the expense of the county, have the county standards tried, adjusted, and sealed, by the treasurer of the commonwealth, or his deputy; and every town and city sealer shall, once at least in five years, at the expense of the town or city, have the town or city standards tried,

---

[1] By Rev. Stat. c. 36, §§ 47, 48, a special provision is made for weights used in banks, as follows:—

SECT. 47. The directors of the several banks, once in five years, shall have all the weights used in their respective banks compared, proved and sealed by the treasurer of the commonwealth, or by some person specially authorized by him for that purpose; which shall supersede, so far as respects such banks, the sealing of their weights by the town sealer.

SECT. 48. No tender of gold, by any bank, weighed with weights other than those compared, proved and sealed, as required in the preceding section, shall be legal; and the payer or receiver may also require that the gold shall be weighed in each scale, and the mean weight resulting therefrom shall be considered as the true weight.

How far this provision is affected by stat. 1847, c. 242, § 5, as given in the text,—*quære*.

adjusted, and sealed, by the treasurer of the county in which the sealer resides, or by the treasurer of the commonwealth, or his deputy.[1] And every treasurer or sealer who shall refuse or neglect to have their standards sealed, as herein provided, shall forfeit to the use of the commonwealth a sum not exceeding fifty dollars.

Penalty.

County and town treasurer shall keep sets of weights, measures and balances. How the same shall be made. Ibid, § 8. 1848, 332, § 6.

16. The treasurer of each county, and the treasurer of each town, shall keep a complete set of the said weights, measures, and balances, except the troy weight. Said weights and measures shall be made of copper, cast brass, or cast iron; the weights of four pounds, and all under that weight, to be made of brass; the larger weights may be made of iron, and all to be turned and finished. The liquid and dry measures shall be made of durable thickness, and, if made of brass or iron, shall be turned inside and on the top edge or rim. The balances shall be made of brass, steel, or iron, and, in all cases, the edges and bearings shall be of hardened steel, or agate. The dry measures to be made, in form and dimensions, to conform to the aforesaid standard; all to be proved, sealed, and marked by said standard as aforesaid.

Standards shall be furnished by commonwealth. 1848, 332, § 1.

17. There shall be furnished, to the treasurer of each county, and the treasurer of each city and town, in this commonwealth, at the expense of the commonwealth, a complete set of the standard weights, measures, and balances, such as the treasurer of each county and the treasurer of each town is required to keep, by the provisions of the preceding section.

County, city, and town treasurers shall provide places for keeping the same. Ibid, § 2.

18. The treasurer of each county, and the treasurer of each city and town, shall provide, at the expense of such county, city, and town, respectively, some suitable place, in their said counties, cities, or towns, for the safe and suitable keeping and preservation of said weights, measures, and balances; and all expenses attending the boxing, putting up, transporting, and depositing, in their destined

[1] So much of this section as relates to town and city standards appears to be repealed by stat. 1848, c. 332, § 5. See § 21, p. 437, *post*.

locations, said weights, measures, and balances, shall be defrayed by the counties, cities, and towns, respectively.

19. The treasurer of each county, and the treasurer of each city and town, shall have the care and oversight of said weights, measures, and balances, and shall see that the same are kept in good order and repair; and, in case they are lost, destroyed, or irreparably damaged, shall replace the same by similar weights, measures, and balances; and all expenses incurred under the provisions of this section, shall be defrayed by the counties, cities, and towns, respectively.

Shall have care of same, keep them in repair, and replace them when lost, &c. Ibid, § 3.

20. If the treasurer of any county, city, or town, shall neglect to provide a suitable place, to keep the said weights, measures, and balances, or shall neglect to keep them in good order and repair, or shall suffer them to be lost, damaged, or destroyed, through his neglect, contrary to the true meaning and intent of this act, he shall forfeit the sum of two hundred dollars, to be recovered, by indictment, to the use of the commonwealth.

Penalty for neglect. Ibid, § 4.

21. Every town and city treasurer shall, once at least in ten years, at the expense of the town or city, have the town or city standards of weights, measures, and balances, tried, adjusted and sealed, by the treasurer of the county in which the city or town is situated, or by the treasurer of the commonwealth, or his deputy; and every town or city treasurer, who shall neglect to have the standards under his charge sealed, as herein provided, shall forfeit, to the use of the commonwealth, a sum not exceeding fifty dollars.

Town and city standards shall be sealed once in ten years. Ibid, § 5.

Penalty.

22. Every sealer of weights and measures shall receive of the town treasurer the town standards and seal, and shall give him a receipt therefor, expressing the condition in which the same may be; and he shall be accountable to the town for the due preservation of the same in the like condition, until he shall redeliver them to the treasurer.

Sealers accountable to towns for preservation of standards. R. S. 30, § 15.

23. If any sealer of weights and measures shall neglect to perform his duty, as prescribed in the thirtieth chapter of the Revised Statutes, he shall for each neglect forfeit to the use of the town a sum not exceeding twenty dollars.

Penalty for neglect of sealers. R. S. 30, § 21.

Vibrating steelyards allowed to be used, if sealed. Ibid, § 22.

24. The vibrating steelyards, which have been heretofore allowed and used in this state, may continue to be used; provided, that each beam, and the poizes thereof, shall be annually tried, proved and sealed, by a sealer of weights and measures, like other beams and weights.

Provisions respecting measures for salt and grain. Ibid, § 23.

25. Every measure, by which salt or grain shall be sold, in addition to being comformable in capacity and diameter to the public standards, shall have a bar of iron across the middle thereof at the top, to be approved by a sealer of weights and measures, and a bar or standard of iron from the centre of the first mentioned bar to the centre of the bottom of the measure, to be approved in like manner; and every such measure shall be filled by shovelling such salt or grain into the same; and the striking thereof shall always be lengthwise of the said first described bar; and if any person shall sell or expose to sale any salt or grain, in any other measure, or shall fill or strike such measure, in any other manner than is provided in this section, he shall forfeit, to the use of the town where the offence is committed, the sum of fifty cents, for every bushel of salt or grain measured, filled or stricken contrary to the provisions of this section; provided, that salt may be measured from vessels in such measures as are used by the government of the United States, and that nothing contained in this section shall prevent the measuring of salt in tubs, or any proportional parts of hogsheads without bars, as may be determined by any town; and that the regulations of this section shall not take effect in any town, except where they shall be adopted by a vote, at a legal meeting of the inhabitants, and such vote shall have been published for the space of one month, in some newspaper printed in such town, or in its vicinity, if none is printed in the town.

"Hundred weight" to be construed the net hundred. Ibid, § 25.

26. When any commodities shall be sold by the hundred weight, it shall be understood to mean the net weight of one hundred pounds avoirdupois; and all contracts concerning goods sold by weight shall be understood and construed accordingly.

Public weighers to weigh accord-

27. Every public weigher of goods or commodities shall

weigh the same, according to the provisions of the preceding section, and make his certificate accordingly. *ing to the preceding section. Ibid, § 26.*

28. Every public weigher, who shall offend against the provisions of the preceding section, shall for every such offence forfeit to the use of the town a sum not exceeding ten dollars; and every weigher of goods or commodities, appointed by any town, and every weigher of goods or commodities, for hire or reward, shall be deemed and taken to be a public weigher, so far as relates to the provisions of this and the preceding section.[1] *Who shall be deemed a public weigher; his duty in weighing, and penalty for breach thereof. Ibid, § 27.*

ORDINANCE OF THE CITY.[2]

Two sealers of weights and measures shall be appointed, within the city of Boston. *Two sealers of weights and measures to be appointed. July 22, 1822.*

WELLS AND PUMPS.

ORDINANCE OF THE CITY.[3]

1. Public wells to be provided with pumps. Expense to be assessed on persons using the same.
2. Owner of estate assessed to pay within ten days.
3. Owner of estate to be released in certain cases. Proviso.
4. Penalty for injuring, &c., public pumps.

---

[1] See 1837, c. 166. See also Wood, Bark and Charcoal.

[2] An order providing for the appointment of two sealers of weights and measures, passed July 22, 1822.

[3] An ordinance for the repair and keeping in order the public wells and pumps, passed December 30, 1833.

Public wells to be provided with pumps. Dec. 30, 1833.

SECT. 1. It shall be the duty of the mayor and aldermen, to keep supplied with suitable pumps, all wells belonging to the city, and to keep the same in good order and repair; and to cause the expense of providing such pumps, as well as keeping them in repair, and also a reasonable charge for the use of the same, to be annually assessed upon the owners of real estate in the vicinity of such well, and whose tenants make use of the same; and where such owners are absent or out of this commonwealth, or unknown, then they shall assess his or their proportion of the same, upon the tenants of such real estate, said assessment to be charged on said estate.

Expense to be assessed on persons using the same.

Owner of estate assessed to pay within ten days. Ibid.

SECT. 2. The owner or tenant of such real estate, as the case may be, being assessed as aforesaid, shall pay the amount thereof into the city treasury within ten days from the time of the delivery of such notice; and in case of neglect thereof for the space of ten days, it shall be the duty of the city treasurer to prosecute for the same.

Owner of estate to be released in certain cases. Ibid.

SECT. 3. If the said owner or tenant, being assessed as aforesaid, shall make it appear to the satisfaction of the mayor and aldermen, that he has, upon his own estate, a good and sufficient well of water, and that neither he, nor any tenant or occupant of his estate, has made any use of, or has any necessity to resort to such public pump or well, in such case it shall be in the power of the mayor and aldermen to release such owner or tenant from the payment of such assessment: provided, always, that in such case if it shall be made satisfactorily afterwards to appear, that any tenant or occupant of such estate, hath made use of said public well or pump, such owner or tenant shall be liable to pay double the amount of that, and of all other assessments, which may have been made upon such estate, if from the circumstances of the case, the mayor and aldermen shall see fit to demand the same.

Proviso.

Penalty for injuring, &c., public pumps. Ibid.

SECT. 4. Whoever shall break or otherwise injure any of the public pumps, or commit any trespass on the same, shall forfeit and pay a sum not less than one dollar nor more than twenty dollars, to be recovered by complaint before the justices of the police court.

WOOD, BARK AND CHARCOAL.

STATUTE.

1. All cord wood exposed to sale shall be either four feet, three feet, or two feet long, including half the carf; and the wood, being well and close laid together, shall measure in quantity equal to a cord of eight feet in length, four feet in width, and four feet in height. Dimensions of cord wood. R. S. 28, § 200.

2. If any fire wood or bark, exposed to sale in any market, or upon any cart or other vehicle, shall be offered for sale before the same shall have been measured by a public measurer of wood and bark, and a ticket thereof signed by him delivered to the driver, certifying the quantity of wood which the load contains, the name of the driver, and the town in which he resides, the driver and owner of such wood or bark shall, for each load thereof, severally forfeit the sum of five dollars, to the use of the town where such wood or bark shall be so offered for sale. Penalty for selling wood, &c., not measured. Ibid, § 201.

3. The measurers of wood and bark[1] in any town shall be entitled to such fees for their services, as the selectmen of such town shall establish; and the said fees shall, in Fees. Ibid, § 202.

[1] See Rev. Stat. c. 15, § 33, requiring measurers of wood and bark to be sworn to the faithful discharge of the duties of their office.

each case, be paid to the measurer, by the driver, and shall be repaid by the purchaser.

Wood, brought in by water, how measured. Ibid, § 203.

4. All cord wood, brought by water into any town for sale and landed, shall be measured by a measurer, sworn as aforesaid; and for that purpose, the wood shall be corded and piled by itself in ranges, making up in height what shall be wanting in length, and being so measured, a ticket shall be given to the purchaser. who shall pay the stated fees for such service; provided, that in the city of Boston, the city government may establish ordinances and regulations, with suitable penalties, for the inspection, survey, admeasurement and sale of wood, coal and bark for fuel, brought by water into said city for sale, and that the said city may also provide for the appointment of such surveyors, inspectors and other officers, and establish their fees of office.

Special provisions for Boston.

Carters to have tickets. Ibid, § 204.

5. Each wharfinger, carter or driver, who shall convey any firewood or bark from any wharf or landing place in any town, shall be furnished by the owner or seller of such wood or bark, with a ticket certifying the quantity which the load contains, and the name of the driver; and if any firewood or bark shall be conveyed as aforesaid, without such ticket accompanying the same, or if any driver shall refuse to produce and show such ticket on demand, to any measurer duly sworn as aforesaid, or to give his consent to have the same measured, or if such tickets shall certify a greater quantity of wood or bark than the load contains, in the opinion of the measurer aforesaid, after measuring the same, the driver and owner of such wood or bark shall, for each load thereof, forfeit the sum of five dollars, to the use of the town where the offence shall be committed; provided, nevertheless, that nothing contained in this chapter shall be construed to extend to any person who shall transport or cart, or cause to be transported or carted, from any wharf or landing place to his own dwelling house or store, any cord wood or bark which he shall have purchased on such wharf or landing place, or shall have landed thereon upon his own account.

6. All baskets, used in measuring charcoal for sale, shall contain two bushels, and shall be of the following dimensions, to wit; nineteen inches in diameter in every part thereof, and seventeen inches and a half deep, measuring from the top of the basket to the highest part of the bottom; and the basket shall be well heaped, and also be sealed by the sealer of the town, where the person so using the same shall usually reside; and every person, who shall measure any charcoal, offered for sale in any basket of less dimensions, or not sealed as aforesaid, shall forfeit for each offence fifty cents, to the use mentioned in the preceding section, and such basket shall also be destroyed.

Dimensions, &c., of charcoal baskets. Ibid, § 205.

7. The selectmen of any town may appoint some suitable person, to seize and secure all baskets, used for measuring coal, that shall not be of the dimensions prescribed in the preceding section, and sealed as therein required, and may also prosecute all persons, who shall offend against the said provisions.

Illegal baskets to be seized. Ibid, § 206.

8. In the sale of charcoal, it shall further be lawful to measure the same in boxes of the following capacities, namely; of two bushels, five bushels, ten bushels, and twenty bushels, said boxes being first duly sealed; and five thousand one hundred and twenty-eight cubic inches shall be deemed equal to two bushels, or the heaped basket above described.

Dimensions of charcoal boxes. Ibid, § 207.

9. Every person, who shall measure charcoal offered for sale in any box of other capacity, or not sealed as aforesaid, shall forfeit for each offence one dollar.

Penalty for using other measures. Ibid, § 208.

10. All the forfeitures, mentioned in the four preceding sections, may be recovered by indictment.[1]

Forfeitures, how recovered. Ibid, § 209.

---

[1] An act was passed in 1849, c. 143, respecting the sale of anthracite coal; but it was repealed by stat. 1850, c. 25.

ORDINANCE OF THE CITY.[1]

Places to be assigned for measuring wood and bark, and for the sale thereof. Oct. 31, 1850.

SECT. 1. The mayor and aldermen may assign as many places for the measuring of wood and bark, brought into the city by land for sale, as they may deem expedient; and they may assign places for the sale of such wood and bark.

Penalty for standing in place not assigned, &c. Ibid.

SECT. 2. Any person bringing wood or bark as aforesaid, into the city for sale, who shall, before or after the same has been duly measured, stand for the sale thereof in any other street or place than those appointed by the mayor and aldermen, shall forfeit and pay the sum of not less than two nor more than twenty dollars for each offence.

Measurers of wood and bark to be appointed. Ibid.

SECT. 3. The mayor and aldermen may annually appoint as many measurers of such wood and bark as they may deem expedient, who shall serve during the year, and until others are chosen and qualified in their stead, and who shall have all the powers, and perform all the duties of measurers of such wood and bark, mentioned in the laws of the commonwealth.

Fees. Ibid.

SECT. 4. Measurers of wood and bark shall be entitled to such fees for their services as the mayor and aldermen shall establish, to be paid according to law.

Measurers of wood and bark brought by water, &c. Ibid.

SECT. 5. The mayor and aldermen may annually appoint four or more measurers of wood and bark brought by water into the city for sale and landed, who shall serve during the year, and until others are appointed and qualified in their stead, and who shall be entitled to such fees as the mayor and aldermen shall establish, to be paid by the purchaser; and such measurers shall have all the powers and perform all the duties of measurers of wood and bark brought into the city by water for sale, mentioned in the laws of the commonwealth.

---

[1] An ordinance relating to the measuring of wood and bark, passed October 31, 1850.

REVISED ORDINANCES.

ORDINANCE OF THE CITY.[1]

1. The ordinances in this book declared to be the ordinances of the city.
2. Repeal of inconsistent ordinances, and of certain specified ordinances.
3. Saving of rights accrued, suits pending, &c.
4. How copies of the revised ordinances shall be kept, &c.
5. Copies for city council.

SECT. 1. All the ordinances printed and contained in the preceding pages, that is to say, in a certain book, prepared by the city solicitor, and printed under the direction of Henry B. Rogers, Moses Grant, William G. Brooks, Albert T. Minot, and Daniel N. Haskell, a committee duly appointed, and authorized for that purpose, by a vote of the city council of the city of Boston, passed on the eighteenth day of February, in the year eighteen hundred and fifty, shall be deemed and are hereby declared to be, ordinances of the said city, and shall have the force thereof.

The ordinances in this book declared to be the ordinances of the city. Nov. 7, 1850.

SECT. 2. All orders, ordinances and parts of orders and ordinances, inconsistent with any of the preceding ordinances, are hereby repealed, more particularly the orders, ordinances and parts of orders and ordinances, hereinafter specified in this section, that is to say:

Repeal of inconsistent ordinances, and of certain specified ordinances. Ibid.

An order to continue in force the by-laws and orders of the town of Boston, passed May 2, 1822.

An order for the election of certain city officers, passed May 9, 1822.

An ordinance authorizing the election and prescribing the duties, of the city marshal, passed June 18, 1823.

An ordinance for regulating the office hours of the public officers of the city, passed January 10, 1825.

An ordinance relative to the acts of the city council, and the enacting style, passed December 12, 1825.

---

[1] An ordinance in relation to the revised ordinances, passed November 7, 1850.

An ordinance directing the manner in which fines and penalties shall be recovered, passed December 22, 1825.

An ordinance directing the manner in which the ordinances of the city council, and the orders of the mayor and aldermen shall be promulgated, passed December 19, 1825.

An ordinance restraining the going at large of dogs within the city of Boston, passed December 26, 1825.

An ordinance for the regulation of public porters and handcartmen, passed September 18, 1826.

An ordinance to regulate common criers, passed October 9, 1826.

An ordinance forbidding the firing of guns, prohibiting fire works in certain cases, and to prevent damage by fire, passed December 18, 1826.

An ordinance to regulate theatrical exhibitions, passed December 18, 1826.

An ordinance regulating the admeasurement of wood and bark, passed December 27, 1826.

An ordinance providing for the appointment, and prescribing the duties, of an attorney and solicitor for the city of Boston, passed June 18, 1827.

An ordinance establishing the office of superintendent of the Boston Free Bridge, and prescribing the duties of the same, passed October 21, 1828.

An ordinance in addition to an ordinance, authorizing the election and prescribing the duties of the city marshal, passed May 25, 1829.

An ordinance concerning the names of the streets in the city, passed January 18, 1833.

An ordinance for the preventing and extinguishing fires, and establishing a fire department, passed July 15, 1833.

An ordinance for regulating the weighing of hay and other articles, passed July 15, 1833.

An ordinance establishing and regulating the quarantine of vessels, passed August 10, 1833.

An ordinance establishing the office of superintendent of streets, and prescribing the duties thereof; to prevent unlawful and injurious practices in the streets of the city, and in relation to sidewalks, passed August 22, 1833.

An ordinance for the regulation of horses and carriages within the city of Boston, passed September 9, 1833.

An ordinance for the regulation of Faneuil Hall Market, passed September 23, 1833.

An ordinance to regulate the interment of the dead, passed September 26, 1833.

An ordinance regulating the survey, and admeasurement of lumber brought into the city of Boston by water for sale, passed September 26, 1833.

An ordinance prescribing rules and regulations relative to nuisances, sources of filth, and causes of sickness, within the city of Boston, passed October 7, 1833.

An ordinance concerning the assessment and collection of taxes, passed October 21, 1833.

An ordinance in relation to the common, and common lands of the city, and regulating the going at large of cattle, passed November 4, 1833.

The sixth section of an ordinance concerning buildings and reservoirs in the city, and for preventing trespasses on the same, passed November 14, 1833.

An ordinance relative to sewers and drains, passed February 13, 1834.

An ordinance in addition to an ordinance to regulate the interment of the dead, passed April 11, 1834.

An ordinance to provide for the care and management of the public lands, passed April 10, 1834.

An ordinance concerning the assessment and collection of taxes, passed May 16, 1836.

An ordinance in addition to an ordinance to regulate the interment of the dead, passed April 20, 1837.

An ordinance establishing the office of superintendent of the Boston South Bridge, passed May 25, 1837.

An ordinance for preventing and extinguishing fires, and establishing a fire department, passed July 29, 1837.

An ordinance in addition to an ordinance establishing the office of superintendent of streets, and prescribing the duties thereof; to prevent unlawful and injurious practices in the streets of the city; and in relation to sidewalks, passed January 5, 1839.

An ordinance establishing the office of city attorney, passed April 16, 1839.

An ordinance concerning the erection, alteration and repair of public buildings, passed April 23, 1840.

An ordinance in addition to an ordinance to provide for the care and management of the public lands, passed September 17, 1840.

An ordinance in addition to an ordinance concerning the erection, alteration and repair of public buildings, passed October 23, 1840.

An ordinance in addition to an ordinance entitled "an ordinance establishing the office of superintendent of streets, and prescribing the duties thereof; to prevent unlawful and injurious practices in the streets of the city, and in relation to sidewalks," passed December 7, 1840.

An ordinance in addition to an ordinance entitled "an ordinance prescribing rules and regulations relative to nuisances, sources of filth and causes of sickness within the city of Boston," passed February 11, 1841.

The sixth and eleventh sections of an ordinance in relation to common sewers and drains, passed June 14, 1841.

An ordinance to establish the office of port physician, passed June 21, 1841.

An ordinance in addition to an ordinance to establish the office of port physician, passed December 20, 1841.

So much of the second section of an ordinance regulating the survey and admeasurement of lumber brought into the city of Boston by water for sale, passed July 25, 1842, as is inconsistent with an ordinance in addition thereto, passed December 31, 1847.

The first section of an ordinance relating to the Boston Lunatic Hospital, passed October 3, 1842, and so much of the fourth section of the same ordinance as is inconsistent with an ordinance in addition thereto, passed June 4, 1846.

An ordinance in addition to an ordinance, entitled "an ordinance for preventing and extinguishing fires and establishing a fire department," passed December 12, 1842.

An ordinance in relation to sidewalks, passed February 9, 1843.

An ordinance for the regulation of Faneuil Hall Market, passed March 2, 1843.

An ordinance concerning the removal of buildings through the streets of the city, passed May 18, 1843.

An ordinance concerning the sale of the public buildings, passed October 2, 1843.

An ordinance relating to obstructions in the streets, passed May 30, 1844.

An ordinance providing for the discharge of the duties of mayor in certain cases, passed February 7, 1845.

The first section of an ordinance in addition to an ordinance for the care and management of the public lands, passed February 9, 1846.

The fourth and seventh sections of an ordinance for the regulation of Faneuil Hall Market, passed October 26, 1846.

An ordinance in addition to an ordinance to provide for the care and management of the public lands, passed December 24, 1846.

An ordinance concerning the assessment, abatement and collection of taxes, passed March 30, 1848.

An order in relation to the election of assessors, passed by the city council, March 5, 1849.

An ordinance to prevent unlawful and injurious practices in the streets of the city, and in relation to sidewalks, passed May 11, 1848.

An ordinance in addition to an ordinance to provide for the care and management of the public lands, passed January 11, 1849.

An ordinance concerning the office and duties of city physician, and to establish health commissioners, passed May 10, 1849.

An ordinance concerning the duties of the harbor master, passed May 10, 1849.

An ordinance concerning the office and duties of port physician, passed May 17, 1849.

An ordinance in addition to an ordinance to regulate the interment of the dead, passed May 21, 1849.

An ordinance constituting the board of health for the city, passed June 18, 1849.

An ordinance providing for the appointment of a city registrar, and prescribing his duties, passed June 25, 1849.

An order concerning public lands, passed February 7, 1850.

The twentieth section of an ordinance in relation to streets, passed September 30, 1850.[1]

Saving of rights accrued, suits pending, &c. Ibid.

SECT. 3. The repeal in the preceding section shall not affect any act done or any right accruing or accrued, or established, or any suit or proceeding, had or commenced in any civil case, before the time when such repeal shall take effect, nor any offence committed, nor any penalty or forfeiture incurred, nor any suit or prosecution pending at the time of such repeal, for any offence committed, or for the recovery of any penalty or forfeiture incurred, under any of the provisions so repealed: and in all cases where any provisions of the preceding ordinances are made to go into operation at any time hereafter, the corresponding provisions, if any, of the said repealed ordinances or orders shall continue in force, until the said new provisions shall go into operation, subject, however, to any express regulations relating thereto which may be contained in the preceding ordinances: and all persons who, at the time when the said repeal shall take effect, shall hold any office under any of the ordinances or orders so repealed, shall continue to hold the same according to the tenure thereof, except those offices which may have been abolished, and those as to which a different provision shall have been made by the preceding ordinances: and no ordinance or order or part of an ordinance or order which has been heretofore repealed, shall be revived by the repeal, in the preceding section, of any of the ordinances or orders, or parts of ordinances or orders therein mentioned.

---

[1] The section repealed is omitted in this volume, and the succeeding sections are re-numbered.

SECT. 4. All copies of the revised ordinances, not otherwise disposed of, shall be deposited with the auditor, subject to the direction and control of the standing committee on ordinances, and shall be on sale at such price as shall be determined from time to time by the said committee.

How copies of the revised ordinances shall be kept, &c. Ibid.

SECT. 5. Every member of the city council shall be entitled to one copy of the revised ordinances.

Copies for city council. Ibid.

APPENDIX.

CITY CHARTER AND AMENDMENTS.

(1) AN ACT ESTABLISHING THE CITY OF BOSTON.

[Statute of 1821, Chap. 110.]

SECT. 1. *Be it enacted by the Senate and House of Representatives, in General Court assembled, and by the authority of the same,* That the inhabitants of the town of Boston, for all purposes, for which towns are by law incorporated, in this commonwealth, shall continue to be one body politic, in fact and in name, under the style and denomination of the city of Boston, and as such, shall have, exercise, and enjoy, all the rights, immunities, powers, and privileges, and shall be subject to all the duties and obligations, now incumbent upon, and appertaining to said town, as a municipal corporation. And the administration of all the fiscal, prudential, and municipal concerns of said city, with the conduct and government thereof, shall be vested in one principal officer, to be styled the mayor; one select council, consisting of eight persons, to be denominated the board of aldermen; and one more numerous council, to consist of forty-eight persons, to be denominated the common council; which boards, in their joint capacity, shall be denominated the city council, together with such other board of officers, as are herein after specified.

City, and its rights, powers, &c.

City officers.

SECT. 2. *Be it further enacted,* That it shall be the duty of the selectmen of Boston, as soon as may be, after the passing of this Act, to cause a new division of the said

To be divided into 12 wards.

town to be made into twelve wards, in such manner as to include an equal number of inhabitants in each ward, as nearly as conveniently may be, consistently with well defined limits to each ward; including, in such computation of numbers of inhabitants, persons of all descriptions, and taking the last census, made under the authority of the United States, as a basis for such computation. And it shall be in the power of the city council, herein after mentioned, from time to time, not oftener than once in ten years, to alter such divisions of wards, in such a manner as to preserve, as nearly as may be, an equal number of inhabitants in each ward.

Election of city officers.

SECT. 3. *Be it further enacted*, That on the second Monday of April, annually, the citizens of said city, qualified to vote in city affairs, shall meet together, within their respective wards, at such time and place, as the mayor and aldermen may, by their warrant, direct and appoint; and the said citizens shall then choose by ballot one warden and one clerk, who shall be resident in said ward, who shall hold their offices for one year, and until others shall be appointed in their stead. And it shall be the duty of such warden to preside at all meetings of the citizens of such ward, to preserve order therein; and it shall be the duty of such clerk, to make a fair and true record, and keep an exact journal of all the acts and votes of the citizens, at such ward meetings; to deliver over such records and journals, together with all other documents and papers held by him, in his said capacity, to his successor in such office. And if, at the opening of any annual meeting, the warden of such ward should not be present, the clerk of such ward shall call the citizens to order, and preside at such meeting until a warden shall be chosen by ballot. And if, at any other meeting, the warden shall be absent, the clerk, in such case, shall so preside, until a moderator or warden, *pro tempore*, shall be chosen; which may be done by nomination and hand vote, if the clerk so direct. At such meeting also, five inspectors of elections shall be chosen for such ward, being residents therein, by ballot, to hold their offices for one year. And it shall be the duty of the war-

Duty of warden and clerk.

Inspectors of elections.

den and inspectors, in each ward, to receive, sort, count and declare all votes, at all elections within such ward. And the warden, clerk, and inspectors, so chosen, shall respectively be under oath, faithfully and impartially to discharge their several duties, relative to all elections; which oath may be administered, by the clerk of such ward, to the warden, and by the latter, to the clerk and inspectors, or by any justice of the peace of the county of Suffolk; and a certificate of such oaths having been administered shall be entered in the record or journal, to be kept by the clerk of such ward.

Duties of inspectors.

SECT. 4. *Be it further enacted,* That the warden or other presiding officer of such ward meeting, shall have full power and authority to preserve order and decorum therein, and to repress all riotous, tumultuous, and disorderly conduct therein, and for that purpose, to call to his aid, any constable, or other peace officer, and also to command the aid and assistance of any citizen or citizens, who may be present; and any peace officer, or other citizen, neglecting or refusing to afford such aid, shall be taken and deemed to be guilty of a misdemeanor. And such warden shall also have power and authority, by warrant, under his hand, to cause any person or persons, who shall be guilty of any riotous, tumultuous, or disorderly conduct at such meeting, to be taken into custody, and restrained: *provided however,* That such restraint shall not continue after the adjournment or dissolution of such meeting: *and provided further,* that the person, so guilty of such disorderly conduct, shall be liable, notwithstanding such restraint, to be prosecuted and punished, in the same manner, as if such arrest had not been made.

Powers of warden.

Provisoes.

SECT. 5. *Be it further enacted,* That the citizens of said city, qualified to vote in city affairs, at their respective ward meetings, to be held on the second Monday in April, annually, shall be called upon to give in their votes for one able and discreet person, being an inhabitant of the city, to be mayor of said city, for the term of one year. And all the votes so given in, in each ward, being sorted, counted, and declared by the warden and inspectors of elections,

Choice of mayor.

shall be recorded at large, by the clerk, in open ward meeting; and in making such declaration and record, the whole

Returns of votes.

number of votes or ballots, given in, shall be distinctly stated, together with the name of every person voted for, and the number of votes given for each person respectively; such numbers to be expressed in words at length; and a transcript of such record, certified and authenticated by the warden, clerk, and a majority of the inspectors of elections for each ward, shall forthwith be transmitted or delivered by such ward clerk, to the clerk of the city. And it shall be the duty of the city clerk, forthwith to enter such returns, or a plain and intelligible abstract of them, as they are successively received, upon the journal of the proceedings of the mayor and aldermen, or some other book to be kept for that purpose.

Examination of votes.

And it shall be the duty of the mayor and aldermen to meet together, within two days after such election, and to examine and compare all the said returns, and to ascertain whether any person has a majority of all the votes given for mayor: and in case a majority is so given, it shall be their duty to give notice thereof, in writing, to the person thus elected, and also to make the same known to the inhabitants of said city.

Provision for new meeting in case no election is made at the first.

But if, on such an examination, no person appears to have a majority of all the votes given for mayor, the mayor and aldermen, for the time being, shall issue their warrants for meetings of the respective wards, for the choice of a mayor, at such time and place, as they shall judge most convenient: And the same proceeding shall be had in all respects, as are herein before directed, until a mayor shall be chosen by a majority of all the voters, voting at such election.

Provision in case of the death, absence, &c., of the mayor.

And in case of the decease, inability, or absence of the mayor, and the same being declared, and a vote passed by the aldermen and common council, respectively, declaring such cause, and the expediency of electing a mayor, for the time being, to supply the vacancy thus occasioned, it shall be lawful for the aldermen and common council to meet in convention, and elect a mayor to hold the said office until such occasion shall be removed, or until a new election.

SECT. 6. *Be it further enacted*, That the citizens in their respective ward meetings, to be held on the second Monday of April, annually, shall be called upon to give in their votes for eight persons, being inhabitants of said city, to constitute the board of aldermen, for the ensuing year; and all the votes so given, being sorted, counted, and declared by the warden and inspectors, shall be recorded at large, by the clerk, in open ward meeting; and in making such declaration and record, the whole number of votes or ballots given in shall be particularly stated, together with the name of every person voted for, and the number of votes given for each person; and a transcript of such record, certified by the warden and clerk, and a majority of the inspectors of each ward, shall, by the said clerk, within two days, be transmitted to the city clerk; whereupon the same proceeding shall be had, to ascertain and determine the persons chosen as aldermen, as are herein before directed in regard to the choice of mayor, and for a new election, in case of the whole number required not being chosen at the first election. And each alderman, so chosen, shall be duly notified in writing, of his election, by the mayor and aldermen for the time being.

Board of aldermen to be chosen annually.

SECT. 7. *Be it further enacted*, That the citizens of each ward, qualified to vote as aforesaid, at their respective ward meetings, to be held on the second Monday of April, annually, shall be called upon to give in their votes for four able and discreet men, being inhabitants of said ward, to be members of the common council: and all the votes given in as aforesaid, in each ward, and being sorted, counted, and declared by the warden and inspectors, if it appear that four persons have a majority of all the votes given at such election, a public declaration thereof, with the names of the persons so chosen, shall be made in open ward meeting, and the same shall be entered at large, by the clerk of such ward, in his journal, stating particularly the whole number of votes given in, the number necessary to make a choice, and the number actually given for each of the persons, so declared to be chosen. But in case four persons are not chosen at the first ballot, a new ballot

Common council to be elected annually

shall be opened for a number of common councilmen, sufficient to complete the number of four; and the same proceedings shall be had, as before directed, until the number of four shall be duly chosen: *Provided however*, That if the said elections cannot conveniently be completed on such day, the same may be adjourned to another day, for that purpose, not longer distant than three days. And each of the persons so chosen as a member of the common council, in each ward, shall, within two days of his election, be furnished with a certificate thereof, signed by the warden, clerk, and a majority of the inspectors of such ward; which certificate shall be presumptive evidence of the title of such person to a seat in the common council; but such council, however, shall have authority to decide ultimately upon all questions relative to the qualifications, elections and returns of its members.

Proviso for adjournment of meeting.

Qualification of electors.

SECT. 8. *Be it further enacted*, That every male citizen of twenty-one years of age and upwards, excepting paupers, and persons under guardianship, who shall have resided within the commonwealth one year, and within the city six months next preceding any meeting of citizens, either in wards, or in general meeting, for municipal purposes, and who shall have paid by himself or his parent, master or guardian, any state or county tax, which, within two years next preceding such meeting, shall have been assessed upon him, in any town or district in this commonwealth, and also every citizen who shall be, by law, exempted from taxation, and who shall be in all other respects qualified as above mentioned, shall have a right to vote at such meeting, and no other person shall be entitled to vote at such meeting.

Officers to enter on their duties on 1st of May.

SECT. 9. *Be it further enacted*, That the mayor, aldermen and common councilmen, chosen as aforesaid, shall enter on the duties of their respective offices on the first day of May, in each year, unless the same happen on a Sunday; and in that event, on the day following; and before entering on the duties of their offices, shall respectively be sworn, by taking the oath of allegiance and oath of office, prescribed in the constitution of this commonwealth, and an oath to support the constitution of the United States. And

Oath of office.

such oaths may be administered to the mayor elect, by any one of the justices of the supreme judicial court, or any judge of any court of record, commissioned to hold any such court, within the said city, or by any justice of the peace for the county of Suffolk. And such oaths shall and may be administered to the aldermen and members of the common council, by the mayor, being himself first sworn as aforesaid; and a certificate of such oaths having been taken, shall be entered in the journal of the mayor and aldermen, and of the common council, respectively, by their respective clerks.

SECT. 10. *Be it further enacted*, That the mayor and aldermen, thus chosen and qualified, shall compose one board, and shall sit and act together as one body, at all meetings, of which the mayor, if present, shall preside; but in his absence, the board may elect a chairman, for the time being. The said board, together with the common council, in convention, shall have power to choose a clerk, who shall be sworn to the faithful discharge of the duties of his office, who shall be chosen for the term of one year, and until another person is duly chosen to succeed him; removable, however, at the pleasure of the mayor and aldermen; who shall be denominated the clerk of the city, and whose duty it shall be to keep a journal of the acts and proceedings of the said board, composed of the mayor and aldermen; to sign all warrants issued by them, and to do such other acts in his said capacity, as may, lawfully and reasonably, be required of him; and to deliver over all journals, books, papers and documents, entrusted to him as such clerk, to his successor in office, immediately upon such successor being chosen and qualified as aforesaid, or whenever he may be thereto required by the said mayor and aldermen. And the city clerk thus chosen and qualified, shall have all the powers, and perform all the duties, now by law, belonging to the town clerk of the town of Boston, as if the same were particularly and fully enumerated, except in cases where it is otherwise expressly provided.

Mayor and aldermen to act as one body.

General powers.

May be chosen surveyors of highways.

1823, ch. 2.

Duties of clerk.

SECT. 11. *Be it further enacted*, That the persons, so chosen and qualified, as members of the common council of the said city, shall sit and act together as a separate body,

Common council to act as a separate body.

distinct from that of the mayor and aldermen, except in those cases in which the two bodies are to meet in convention; and the said council shall have power, from time to time, to choose one of their own members to preside over their deliberations, and to preserve order therein, and also to choose a clerk, who shall be under oath faithfully to discharge the duties of his office, who shall hold such office, during the pleasure of said council, and whose duty it shall be to attend said council, when the same is in session, to keep a journal of its acts, votes and proceedings, and to perform such other services in said capacity, as said council may require. All sittings of the common council shall be public; also all sittings of the mayor and aldermen, when they are not engaged in executive business. Twenty-five members of the common council shall constitute a quorum for the transaction of business.

General powers.

Clerk to be chosen

His duty.

SECT. 12. *Be it further enacted*, That the mayor of the said city, thus chosen and qualified, shall be taken and deemed to be the chief executive officer of said corporation: and he shall be compensated for his services by a salary, to be fixed by the board of aldermen and common council, in city council convened, payable at stated periods; which salary shall not exceed the sum of five thousand dollars annually, and he shall receive no other compensation or emoluments whatever; and no regulations enlarging or diminishing such compensation shall be made, to take effect until the expiration of the year, for which the mayor then in office shall have been elected. And it shall be the duty of the mayor to be vigilant and active at all times, in causing the laws for the government of said city to be duly executed and put in force; to inspect the conduct of all subordinate officers in the government thereof, and, as far as in his power, to cause all negligence, carelessness, and positive violation of duty, to be duly prosecuted and punished. He shall have power, whenever, in his judgment, the good of said city may require it, to summon meetings of the board of aldermen and common council, or either of them, although the meeting of said boards, or either of them, may stand adjourned to a more distant day. And it

Compensation of the mayor.

His duty—

—may call meetings of the city officers.

shall be the duty of the mayor, from time to time, to communicate to both branches of the city council all such information, and recommend all such measures as may tend to the improvement of the finances, the police, health, security, cleanliness, comfort, and ornament of the said city.

Powers of mayor and aldermen.

SECT. 13. *Be it further enacted*, That the administration of police, together with the executive powers of the said corporation generally, together also with all the powers heretofore vested in the selectmen of the town of Boston, either by the general laws of this commonwealth, by particular laws relative to the powers and duties of said selectmen, or by the usages, votes, or by-laws of said town, shall be, and hereby are vested in the mayor and aldermen, as hereby constituted, as fully and amply as if the same were herein specially enumerated. And further, the said mayor and aldermen shall have full and exclusive power to grant licenses to innholders, victuallers, retailers and confectioners, within the said city, in all cases wherein the court of sessions for the county of Suffolk, on the recommendation of the selectmen of Boston, have heretofore been authorized to grant such licenses; and in granting such licenses, it shall be lawful for the said mayor and aldermen to annex thereto such reasonable conditions in regard to time, places, and other circumstances, under which such license shall be acted upon, as, in their judgment, the peace, quiet and good order of the city may require. Also to take bonds of all persons so licensed, in reasonable sums, and with sufficient sureties, conditioned for a faithful compliance with the terms of their said licenses, and of all laws and regulations respecting such licensed houses: And said mayor and aldermen, after the granting of any such license, shall have power to revoke or suspend the same, if in their judgment the order and welfare of said city shall require it. And any person or persons who shall presume to exercise either of the said employments, within said city, without having first obtained a license therefor, or in any manner, contrary to the terms of said license, or after the same shall have been revoked or suspended, such person or persons shall be liable to the same penalties and

To grant licenses,

—and take bonds from persons licensed.

Forfeiture for acting as a taverner, &c., without license.

forfeitures, and to be prosecuted for, in the same manner as now by law provided, in case of exercising either of said employment without license from the court of sessions, for the county of Suffolk; and shall also be taken and deemed to have forfeited their bonds, respectively given aforesaid, upon which suits may be instituted against such licensed persons or their sureties, at the discretion of the said mayor and aldermen, and in such manner as they may direct, for the purpose of enforcing such forfeiture: *Provided, however*, That all innholders, retailers, confectioners, and victuallers, shall, on being licensed as aforesaid, pay the same sum now required by law; which sum shall be accounted for in the same way and manner as is now by law required.

Mayor and aldermen may license theatrical exhibitions, &c., and regulate them.

SECT. 14. *Be it further enacted*, That the mayor and aldermen shall have power to license all theatrical exhibitions and all public shows, and all exhibitions of whatever name or nature, to which admission is obtained on payment of money, on such terms and conditions as to them may seem just and reasonable; and to regulate the same, from time to time, in such manner as to them may appear necessary to preserve order and decorum, and to prevent the interruption of peace and quiet. And any person or persons who shall set forth, establish or promote any such exhibition or show, or publish, or advertise the same, or otherwise aid or assist therein, without a license so obtained as aforesaid, or contrary to the terms or conditions of such license, or whilst the same is suspended, or after the same is revoked by said mayor and aldermen, shall be liable to such forfeiture, as the city council may, by any by-law made for that purpose, prescribe.

SECT. 15. *Be it further enacted*, That all other powers now by law vested in the town of Boston, or in the inhabitants thereof, as a municipal corporation, shall be, and hereby are vested in the mayor and aldermen, and common council of the said city, to be exercised by concurrent vote, each board as hereby constituted, having a negative upon the other. More especially, they shall have power to

By-laws.

make all such needful and salutary by-laws, as towns by the laws of this commonwealth have power to make and establish, and to annex penalties, not exceeding twenty dollars, for the breach thereof, which by-laws shall take effect and be in force from and after the times therein respectively limited, without the sanction or confirmation of any court, or other authority whatsoever: *Provided*, That such by-laws shall not be repugnant to the constitution and laws of this commonwealth: *And provided also*, That the same shall be liable to be annulled by the legislature thereof. The said city council shall also have power, from time to time, to lay and assess taxes for all purposes, for which towns are by law required or authorized to assess and grant money, and also for all purposes, for which county taxes may be levied and assessed, whenever the city shall alone compose one county: *Provided, however*, That in the assessment and apportionment of all such taxes upon the polls and estates of all persons liable to contribute thereto, the same rules and regulations shall be observed, as are now established by the laws of this commonwealth, or may be hereafter enacted, relative to the assessment and apportionment of town taxes. The said city council shall also have power to provide for the assessment and collection of such taxes, and to make appropriations of all public moneys, and provide for the disbursement thereof, and take suitable measures to ensure a just and prompt account thereof; and for these purposes, may either elect such assessors, and assistant assessors, as may be needful, or provide for the appointment or election of the same, or any of them, by the mayor and aldermen, or by the citizens, as in their judgment may be most conducive to the public good, and may also require of all persons entrusted with the collection, custody, or disbursement of public moneys, such bonds with such conditions and such sureties, as the case may in their judgments require.

Provisoes.

Assessment of taxes.

Proviso.

Collection of taxes.

Assessors to be chosen.

SECT. 16. *Be it further enacted*, That the said city council shall have power, and they are hereby authorized to provide for the appointment or election of all necessary officers, for the good government of said city, not otherwise provided for; to prescribe their duties, and fix their compensation, and to choose a register of deeds, whenever the

City council may appoint all necessary city officers.

Choose directors of house of industry. 1822, ch. 56.

—and superintend public buildings.

city shall compose one county. The city council also shall have the care and superintendence of the public buildings, and the care, custody, and management of all the property of the city, with power to lease or sell the same, (except the Common, and Faneuil Hall,) with power also to purchase property, real or personal, in the name, and for the use of the city, whenever its interest or convenience may, in their judgment, require it.

Powers of board of health transferred to city council.

SECT. 17. *Be it further enacted*, That all the power and authority now by law, vested in the board of health for the town of Boston, relative to the quarantine of vessels, and relative to every other subject whatsoever, shall be, and the same is hereby transferred to, and vested in the said city council, to be carried into execution by the appointment of health commissioners, or in such other manner as the health, cleanliness, comfort and order of the said city may in their judgment require, subject to such alterations as the legislature may from time to time adopt.

City treasurer to be chosen.

SECT. 18. *Be it further enacted*, That the mayor and aldermen of said city, and the said common council shall, as soon as conveniently may be, after their annual organization, meet together in convention, and elect some suitable and trustworthy person to be the treasurer of said city.

Firewards.

SECT. 19. *Be it further enacted*, That the citizens, at their respective ward meetings, to be held on the second Monday of April, annually, shall elect, by ballot, a number of persons, to be determined by the city council, but not less than three in each ward, to be firewards of said city, who together shall constitute the board of firewards for said city, and shall have all the powers, and be subject to all the duties, now by law appertaining to the firewards of the town of Boston, until the same shall be altered or qualified by the legislature.

Overseers of the poor.

And the said citizens shall, at the same time, and in like manner, elect one person in each ward, to be an overseer of the poor; and the persons thus chosen shall together constitute the board of overseers for said city, and shall have all the powers, and be subject to all the duties, now by law appertaining to the overseers of the poor for the town of Boston, until the same shall be altered or qualified by the legislature. And the said citizens shall, at the same time, and in like manner, elect one person in each ward, to be a member of the school committee, for the said city; and the persons so chosen shall, jointly with the mayor and aldermen, constitute the school committee for the said city, and have the care and superintendence of the public schools. **School committee.**

SECT. 20. *Be it further enacted*, That all boards and officers, acting under the authority of the said corporation, and entrusted with the expenditure of public money, shall be accountable therefor to the city council, in such manner as they may direct. And it shall be the duty of the city council to publish and distribute, annually, for the information of the citizens, a particular statement of the receipts and expenditures of all public moneys, and a particular statement of all city property. **Expenditures of public money to be accounted for to city council.**

SECT. 21. *Be it further enacted*, That in all cases in which appointments to office are directed to be made by the mayor and aldermen, the mayor shall have the exclusive power of nomination; such nomination, however, being subject to be confirmed or rejected by the board of aldermen: *Provided however*, that no person shall be eligible to any office, the salary of which is payable out of the city treasury, who at the time of his appointment, shall be a member either of the board of aldermen or common council. **Mayor to nominate officers.** **Proviso.**

SECT. 22. *Be it further enacted*, That it shall be the duty of the two branches of the city council, in the month of May, in each year, after their annual organization, to meet in convention, and determine the number of representatives, which it may be expedient for the corporation to send to the general court in such year, within its constitutional limits, and to publish such determination, which shall be conclusive; and the number thus determined shall be specified in the warrant calling a meeting for the election of representatives; and neither the mayor, nor any alderman, or members of the common council, shall, at the same time, hold any other office under the city government. **City council to fix the number of representatives to general court.**

SECT. 23. *Be it further enacted*, That all elections for governor, lieutenant governor, senators, representatives,

representatives to congress, and all other officers, who are to be chosen and voted for by the people, shall be held at meetings of the citizens, qualified to vote in such elections, in their respective wards, at the time fixed by law for those elections respectively. And at such meetings, all the votes given in, being collected, sorted, counted and declared, by the inspectors of elections, in each ward, it shall be the duty of the clerk of such ward to make a true record of the same, specifying therein the whole number of ballots given in, the name of each person voted for, and the number of votes for each, expressed in words at length. And a transcript of such record, certified by the warden, clerk, and a majority of the inspectors of elections in such ward, shall forthwith be transmitted or delivered by each ward clerk to the clerk of the city. And it shall be the duty of the city clerk forthwith to enter such returns, or a plain and intelligible abstract of them, as they are successively received, in the journals of the proceedings of the mayor and aldermen, or in some other book kept for that purpose. And it shall be the duty of the mayor and aldermen to meet together within two days after every such election, and examine and compare all the said returns, and thereupon to make out a certificate of the result of such election, to be signed by the mayor and a majority of the aldermen, and also by the city clerk, which shall be transmitted, delivered, or returned, in the same manner as similar returns are by law directed to be made by the selectmen of towns; and such certificates and returns shall have the same force and effect in all respects, as like returns of similar elections, made by the selectmen of towns. And in all elections for representatives to general court, in case the whole number proposed to be elected, shall not be chosen by a majority of the votes legally returned, the mayor and aldermen shall forthwith issue their warrant for a new election, and the same proceedings shall be had in all respects as are herein before directed, until the whole number shall be elected: *Provided however*, That it shall be the duty of the selectmen of the said town of Boston, within twelve days from the passing of this Act, to call a meeting of the qualified voters

Ward meetings, for the choice of national and state officers.

Examination and return of votes.

Proviso.

of the said town to give in their ballots on the following question: Shall the elections for state and United States officers be holden in general meeting? And it shall be the duty of the selectmen to preside at the said meeting, to receive, sort, count and declare the votes given in, and to forward a certificate of the result to the secretary of the commonwealth, and publish the same in two or more of the newspapers printed in Boston; and if a majority of the votes so given in shall be in the negative, then the provisions of the preceding part of this section shall regulate the said elections in wards; but if a majority of the votes given in as aforesaid shall be in the affirmative, then the said elections for state and United States officers shall be holden in the manner prescribed by the constitution and laws of the commonwealth, with the exception that the mayor and aldermen and city clerk shall perform the duties now required by law to be performed by the selectmen and town clerk.

Ward lists of voters to be made—

SECT. 24. *Be it further enacted*, That prior to every election of city officers, or of any officer or officers under the government of the United States or of this Commonwealth, it shall be the duty of said mayor and aldermen to make out lists of all the citizens of each ward, qualified to vote in such election, in the manner in which selectmen and assessors of towns are required to make out similar lists of voters, and for that purpose they shall have free access to the assessors' books and lists, and be entitled to the aid and assistance of all assessors, assistant assessors, and other officers of said city. And it shall be the duty of said mayor and aldermen to deliver such list of the voters in each ward, so prepared and corrected, to the clerk of said ward, to be used by the warden and inspectors thereof at such election; and no person shall be entitled to vote at such election, whose name is not borne on such list. And to prevent all frauds and mistakes in such elections, it shall be the duty of the inspectors, in each ward, to take care that no person shall vote at such election, whose name is not so borne on the list of voters, and to cause a mark to be placed against the name of each voter, on such list, at the time of giving in his vote.

—and delivered to ward clerks for wardens' and inspectors' use at elections.

None to vote whose name is not on the list.

General meetings.

SECT. 25. *Be it further enacted*, That general meetings of the citizens, qualified to vote in city affairs, may from time to time be held, to consult upon the common good, to give instructions to their representatives, and to take all lawful measures to obtain a redress of any grievances, according to the right secured to the people by the constitution of this commonwealth. And such meetings shall and may be duly warned by the mayor and aldermen, upon the requisition of fifty qualified voters of said city.

Warrants for meetings to be issued by mayor and aldermen.

SECT. 26. *Be it further enacted*, That all warrants for the meetings of the citizens, for municipal purposes, to be had either in general meetings or in wards, shall be issued by the mayor and aldermen, and shall be in such form, and shall be served, executed, and returned at such time, and in such manner, as the city council may, by any by-law, direct and appoint.

Form of organizing the city.

SECT. 27. *Be it further enacted*, That for the purpose of organizing the system of government hereby established, and putting the same into operation in the first instance, the selectmen of the town of Boston, for the time being, shall seasonably, before the second Monday of April next, issue their warrants for calling meetings of the said citizens, in their respective wards, qualified to vote as aforesaid, at such place and hour as they shall think expedient, for the purpose of choosing a warden, clerk, and five inspectors of elections, and also to give in their votes for a mayor and eight aldermen, for said city, and four common councilmen, three firewards, one overseer of the poor, and one member of the school committee, for each ward; and the transcripts of the records of each ward, specifying the votes given for mayor and aldermen, firewards, overseers, and members of the school committee, certified by the warden, clerk, and a majority of the inspectors of such ward, shall, at said first election, be returned to the said selectmen of the town of Boston, whose duty it shall be to examine and compare the same. And in case said elections shall not be complete at the first election, then to issue a new warrant, until such election shall be completed, and to give notice thereof, in the manner herein before directed, to the several persons

Return of votes.

elected. And at said first meeting, the clerk of each ward, under the present organization, shall call the citizens to order, and preside until a warden shall be chosen; and at said first meeting, a list of voters in each ward, prepared and corrected by the selectmen of the town of Boston, for the time being, shall be delivered to the clerk of each ward, to be used as herein before directed.

SECT. 28. *Be it further enacted*, That so much of the act heretofore passed, relative to the establishment of a board of health for the town of Boston, as provides for the choice of members of the said board, and so much of the several acts relative to the assessment and collection of taxes within the town of Boston, as provides for the election of assistant assessors, also all such acts, and parts of acts, as come within the purview of this act, and which are inconsistent with, or repugnant to the provisions of this act, shall be, and the same are hereby repealed. **Repeal of acts.**

SECT. 29. And whereas by the laws of this commonwealth, towns are authorized and required to hold their annual meetings, some time in the months of March or April, in each year, for the choice of town officers; and whereas, such meeting, in the month of March, in the present year, for the town of Boston, would be useless and unnecessarily burthensome; Therefore,

Be it further enacted, That the annual town meetings, in the months of March or April, be suspended, and all town officers now in office shall hold their places until this act shall go into operation. **March meetings suspended.**

SECT. 30. *Be it further enacted*, That nothing in this act contained shall be so construed as to restrain or prevent the legislature from amending or altering the same, whenever they shall deem it expedient. **Legislative control.**

SECT. 31. *Be it further enacted*, That this act shall be void, unless the inhabitants of the town of Boston, at a legal town meeting, called for that purpose, shall, by a written vote, determine to adopt the same within twelve days.[1] [*Approved*, *Feb.* 23, 1822.] **Conditional clause.**

---

[1] This act was adopted by the citizens, March 4, 1822. (Boston Records, vol. 10, p. 457.)

(2) AN ACT PROVIDING FOR THE ASSESSMENT OF TAXES IN THE COUNTY OF SUFFOLK.

[Statute of 1822, Chap. 85.]

Be it enacted by the Senate and House of Representatives, in General Court assembled, and by the authority of the same, That the city council of the city of Boston shall have power, from time to time, to lay and assess taxes in the county of Suffolk, for all purposes for which county taxes may be levied and assessed, so long as the town of Chelsea shall continue not to be liable to taxation for any county purposes. [*Approved, Feb.* 10, 1823.]

City council may lay taxes.

---

(3) AN ACT CONCERNING SURVEYORS OF HIGHWAYS IN BOSTON.

[Statute of 1823, Chap. 2.]

Be it enacted by the Senate and House of Representatives, in General Court assembled, and by the authority of the same, That the city council of the city of Boston shall have the power and authority of electing, if they see fit, the mayor and aldermen of said city, surveyors of highways for said city, any thing in the act establishing the city of Boston to the contrary notwithstanding. [*Approved, June* 10, 1823.]

---

(4) AN ACT CONCERNING THE REGULATION OF THE HOUSE OF CORRECTION IN THE CITY OF BOSTON, AND CONCERNING THE FORM OF ACTIONS COMMENCED UNDER THE BY-LAWS OF SAID CITY, AND PROVIDING FOR FILLING VACANCIES IN THE BOARD OF ALDERMEN.

[Part of Statute of 1824, Chap. 28.]

Vacancies in the board of aldermen, how filled.

SECT. 6. *Be it further enacted,* That in case of the death or resignation of any member of the board of aldermen, the citizens of Boston shall have power to fill such vacancy at any regular meeting that may thereafter be convened for that purpose. [*Approved, June* 12, 1824.]

---

(5) AN ACT IN FURTHER ADDITION TO AN ACT, ENTITLED "AN ACT ESTABLISHING THE CITY OF BOSTON."

[Statute of 1824, Chap. 49.]

SECT. 1. *Be it enacted by the Senate and House of Representatives, in General Court assembled, and by the authority of the same*, That the election of the mayor, aldermen and common councilmen, and such other officers of the city of Boston, as are now by law to be chosen on the second Monday in April, annually, shall in future be made on the second Monday in December, annually, and the said officers so chosen shall hold their respective offices for the same term of time, and the same proceedings shall be had in relation to such elections, as is provided in and by the act, entitled "an act establishing the city of Boston," to which this is in addition: *provided, nevertheless*, that the next choice of the said city officers shall be made at such time, and in such manner, as are prescribed in and by the act aforesaid, and the officers so elected shall severally hold their offices until the first Monday of January next, any thing in this act to the contrary notwithstanding.

Time of election

Proviso.

SECT. 2. *Be it further enacted*, That the officers chosen under and by virtue of this act, shall enter on the duties of their respective offices on the first Monday of January in each year, and shall be liable to all the duties and restrictions, and shall exercise all the powers to which the said officers are respectively subject or entitled, under and by virtue of the act to which this is in addition, and of all other acts having relation to this subject matter.

Entrance upon office.

SECT. 3. *Be it further enacted*, That this act shall be void, unless the inhabitants of the city of Boston, at any general meeting duly warned by public notice, of at least fourteen days, by the mayor and aldermen, shall, within

This act, how void.

sixty days from the passing hereof, by written vote, adopt the same.[1]

Repeal.

SECT. 4. *Be it further enacted*, That all the provisions of the act to which this is in addition, or of any other act inconsistent with the provisions of this act, shall be, and hereby are repealed. [*Approved, Jan.* 27, 1825.]

---

(6) AN ACT PROVIDING IN CERTAIN CASES FOR THE ELECTION OF MAYOR OF THE CITY OF BOSTON.

[Statute of 1830, Chap. 7.]

Mayor, how elected in certain cases.

SECT. 1. *Be it enacted by the Senate and House of Representatives, in General Court assembled, and by the authority of the same*, That whenever, on examination by the mayor and aldermen of the city of Boston, of the returns of votes given for mayor, at the meetings of the wards holden for the purpose of electing that officer, last preceding the first Monday of January, in each year, no person shall appear to have a majority of all the votes given for mayor, the mayor and aldermen, by whom such examination is made, shall make a record of that fact, an attested copy of which it shall be the duty of the city clerk to produce and read, on the first Monday of January, in the presence of the members returned to serve as aldermen and common councilmen; and thereupon the oaths prescribed by law may be administered to the members elect, by any one of the justices of the supreme judicial court, or any judge of any court of record, holden in said city, or by any justice of the peace for the county of Suffolk: and thereupon the members of the board of aldermen shall proceed to elect a chairman, and the common council a president, in their respective chambers, and being respectively organized, shall proceed to business, in the same manner as provided in the

---

[1] This act was adopted by the inhabitants, Feb. 25, 1825. (City Records, vol. 28, p. 160.)

tenth section of the city charter, in case of the absence of the mayor: and the board of aldermen shall forthwith issue their warrants for meetings of the citizens of the respective wards, for the choice of a mayor, at such time and place as they shall judge most convenient; and the same proceedings shall be had, in all respects, as are directed in and by the provisions of the fifth section of the City Charter, and repeated, from time to time, until a mayor shall be chosen, by a majority of all the voters voting at such elections.

Refusal of office

SECT. 2. *Be it further enacted*, That, in case any person elected mayor of said city shall refuse to accept the office, the same proceedings shall be had in all respects, as are herein before directed, in cases wherein there has been no choice of mayor, until a mayor be chosen by a majority of votes. And in case of the unavoidable absence, by sickness or otherwise, of the mayor elect, on the first Monday in January, the city government shall organize itself in the mode herein before provided, and may proceed to business in the same manner as if the mayor were present.

Act to be void unless adopted by the city of Boston.

SECT. 3. *Be it further enacted*, That this act shall be void, unless the inhabitants of said city of Boston, at a legal city meeting, called for that purpose, shall, by a written vote, determine to adopt the same, within twelve days from the time of the passing of this act.[1] [*June* 5, 1830.]

---

(7) AN ACT IN FURTHER ADDITION TO AN ACT ENTITLED "AN ACT ESTABLISHING THE CITY OF BOSTON."

[Statute of 1831, Chap. 38.]

Time for city council to meet in convention.

Be it enacted by the Senate and House of Representatives, in General Court assembled, and by the authority of the same, That the time for the city council of the city of Boston to meet in convention, in order to determine the

[1] This act was adopted by the citizens, June 16, 1830. (Boston Records, vol. 10, p. 516.)

60

number of representatives which it may be expedient for said city to send to the general court, shall be in the month of October, instead of May, in each year, any thing in the act to which this is in addition to the contrary notwithstanding. [*June* 17, 1831.]

---

(8) AN ACT IN FURTHER ADDITION TO AN ACT ESTABLISHING THE CITY OF BOSTON.

[Statute of 1835, Chap. 128.]

Number of school committee.

SECT. 1. *Be it enacted by the Senate and House of Representatives, in General Court assembled, and by the authority of the same,* That the school committee of the city of Boston shall consist of the mayor of said city, of the president of the common council of said city, and of twenty-four other persons, two of whom shall be chosen in each ward of said city, and who shall be inhabitants of the wards in which they are chosen; said twenty-four members to be chosen by the inhabitants, at their annual election of municipal officers.

When to be chosen.

Repeal.

SECT. 2. *Be it further enacted,* That so much of the act to which this is in addition, as is inconsistent with the provisions of this act, is hereby repealed: *provided, however,* that the present school committee of said city shall continue in office, until a new committee shall be chosen under the provisions of this act.

Proviso.

Condition of this act.

SECT. 3. *Be it further enacted,* That this act shall be void, unless it shall be adopted by ballot by the inhabitants of said city of Boston, qualified to vote in city affairs, at a legal meeting of said inhabitants called for that purpose, and held in their respective wards, within thirty days from the passing hereof.[1] [*April* 7, 1835.]

---

[1] This act was adopted by the citizens, in ward meetings, April 29, 1835. (Records of returns of votes from the wards, April 29, 1835.)

(9) EXTRACTS FROM THE REVISED STATUTES.

[Chapter 3.]

SECTION 1. Every male citizen of twenty-one years of age and upwards, (excepting paupers and persons under guardianship,) who shall have resided within the state one year, and within the town, in which he may claim a right to vote, six months next preceding any election of town, county or state officers, or of representative to congress, and who shall have paid, by himself, or his parent, master or guardian, any state or county tax, which shall, within two years next preceding such election, have been assessed upon him, in any town of this state; and also every citizen, who shall be by law exempted from taxation, and who shall in all other respects be qualified as above mentioned, shall have a right to vote in all such elections; and no other person shall be entitled to vote in such elections.

Qualifications of voters at town, county, and other elections.

11 Pick. 538.

SECT. 2. The collector of state and county taxes, in each town, shall keep an accurate account of the names of all persons, from whom they shall have received payment of any state or county tax, and of the time of such payment; and, upon request, shall deliver, to the person making the payment, a receipt specifying his name and the time of such payment; and such receipt shall be admitted as presumptive evidence thereof.

Collectors of taxes, to keep a list of persons who have paid their taxes, and upon request to give receipt.

SECT. 3. The said collectors, whether the time, for which they were respectively chosen, shall have expired or not, shall, twice in each year, namely, once in the month of February, not more than twenty days nor less than fifteen days before the first Monday in March, and once in the month of October, not more than twenty days nor less than fifteen days before the second Monday in November, return to the selectmen of their respective towns, an accurate list of all persons, from whom they shall have received payment of any state or county tax, subsequently to the time, appointed for making their last preceding return.

Collectors, to return lists to selectmen twice a year.

4 Pick. 118.
7 ib. 286.

SECT. 4. Any collector, who shall neglect to make such a return, as is required in the preceding section, shall forfeit the sum of one hundred dollars, for every such neglect;

Penalty for neglect and for a false return.

and any collector, who shall make a false return, in respect to any part of such list, shall forfeit the sum of twenty dollars for every name, in respect to which he shall have made a false return.

Selectmen to make out and post up lists of voters.

SECT. 5. The selectmen shall, at least ten days before the first Monday of March, and at least ten days before the second Monday of November annually, make out correct alphabetical lists of all the persons, qualified to vote for the several officers, to be elected at those periods, respectively, and shall, at least ten days before the said elections, cause such lists, respectively, to be posted up in two or more public places, in their respective towns.

Selectmen to be in session, for receiving evidence of qualifications, and to give notice thereof.

SECT. 6. The selectmen shall be in session, at some convenient place, for a reasonable time, within forty-eight hours next preceding all meetings for the elections of any of the officers aforesaid, for the purpose of receiving evidence of the qualifications of persons, claiming a right to vote in such elections, and of correcting the lists of voters; and such session shall be holden for one hour at least, on the day of such election, and before the opening of the meeting; and notice of the time and place of holding the said sessions shall be given by the selectmen, upon the lists posted up as aforesaid.

Selectmen's sessions, where voters exceed one thousand. See also 1839, c. 42, § 4.

SECT. 7. In any town, where the number of qualified voters shall exceed one thousand, such session of the selectmen shall be holden on the day immediately preceding the meeting, and for as much longer time, previous to said day, as the selectmen shall judge necessary, for the purpose aforesaid; and when the day, immediately preceding such meeting, shall be Sunday, then such session shall be holden on the Saturday next preceding.

Penalty for giving false answers to selectmen at such sessions.

SECT. 8. If any person shall give a false name or any false answer to the selectmen, when in session as provided in the two preceding sections, he shall forfeit the sum of thirty dollars for each offence.

Selectmen, when not answerable for refusing to receive votes,

SECT. 9. The selectmen, in case they shall have duly entered on said list of voters the names of all persons, who shall have been returned to them by the collectors aforesaid, shall not be held answerable for any omissions in said list, nor for refusing the vote of any person, whose name is not borne thereon, unless the person, whose name may have been so omitted, shall, before offering his vote, furnish them with sufficient evidence of his having the legal qualifications of a voter at such meeting, and shall have requested them to insert his name on said list.

SECT. 10. The moderator of any town meeting shall receive the votes of all persons, whose names are borne on the list of voters, as certified by the selectmen; and he shall in no manner be held answerable, for refusing the vote of any person, whose name is not on the said list. Moderator shall receive votes of all persons on the lists. May refuse all others.

[Chapter 5.]

SECT. 1. At the election of governor, lieutenant governor, and senators, it shall be the duty of the selectmen and clerks of towns, and of the mayor and aldermen of the city of Boston, to make and seal up separate lists of persons voted for as governor, lieutenant governor, and senators of the commonwealth, with the number of votes for each person, written in words at length against his name, and to transmit said lists to the secretary of the commonwealth, or to the sheriffs of their respective counties; and when the said lists shall be received at the office of the secretary, the seals thereof shall not be broken, but the same shall be kept as they are received, until delivered by him to the two branches of the general court, or to the executive authority, according to the constitution and laws. Separate lists of votes for governor, &c., to be transmitted to the secretary or to sheriffs.

SECT. 11. In the city of Boston, the several elections, provided for in this chapter, shall be conducted according to the provisions of the act establishing the city of Boston, and of the several acts in addition thereto. Elections in Boston, how conducted.

[Chapter 6.]

SECT. 9. In the congressional district of the city of Boston, the said election[1] shall be held, and all the proceedings thereon had, and the returns thereof made, in Special provisions for such elections in Boston.

---

[1] This section relates to the election of representatives in congress.

conformity with the act establishing the city of Boston, and the several acts in addition thereto; and in case of no choice being made at such election, or in case of any vacancy happening in said district, the governor shall cause precepts for new elections, to be directed to the mayor and aldermen of said city, as often as occasion shall require; and such new elections shall be held, and all proceedings thereon had, and returns made, in conformity with the said acts.

Special provision for the city of Boston.

SECT. 18. In the city of Boston, the said elections[1] shall be holden, and the returns thereof made, in conformity with the act establishing the city of Boston, and the several acts in addition thereto; but the same shall be holden and made at and within the times directed in the five preceding sections.

[Chapter 14.]

In Suffolk, the mayor and aldermen of Boston to have the powers of commissioners, except, &c.

SECT. 29. In the county of Suffolk, the mayor and aldermen of the city of Boston shall have the like powers, and perform the like duties, within the city, as are exercised and performed by the county commissioners of other counties, except such as relate to trials by jury, and the recovery of damages on such trials, in case of the laying out, altering or discontinuing highways or townways in said counties.

[Chapter 15.]

Special provision respecting the municipal powers and duties of the city of Boston.

SECT. 86. The city of Boston shall continue to have and exercise all the powers and privileges, and be subject to all the duties and liabilities, mentioned in the act establishing the city of Boston, and in the several acts specially relating to said city.

[Chapter 24.]

Mayor and aldermen of Boston, to have powers, &c., of commissioners.

SECT. 54. In the county of Suffolk, the mayor and aldermen of the city of Boston shall, within the said city,

---

[1] This section relates to the election of electors of president and vice president of the United States.

have the like powers and perform the like duties, as are exercised and performed by the commissioners of other counties, in respect to the laying out, altering and discontinuing of ways, and assessing damages therefor, except as is provided in the following section.

C. C. Pleas may order a trial by jury to any party aggrieved by doings of the mayor, &c.

SECT. 55. When any party shall be aggrieved by the doings of the said mayor and aldermen, in the cases mentioned in the preceding section, he may apply for a jury, by petition to the court of common pleas, within and for the county of Suffolk, at any term of said court that shall be there held, within one year after the laying out, altering, or discontinuing of any way in said city, and not afterwards; and thereupon the said court shall, after due notice to the said city, order a trial by jury to be had in the case, at the bar of said court, in the same manner, in which other civil causes are there tried by the jurors there returned and empanelled; and if either party request it, the jury, to whom the cause may be committed, shall view the place in question.

Several parties to go to the same jury in certain cases.

SECT. 56. In the said county of Suffolk, whenever there shall be several parties, having several estates or interests, at the same time, in any land or any buildings thereon, within the city of Boston, and the said land or buildings shall be taken or otherwise damaged, in whole or in part, by the laying out, altering, or discontinuing of any highway or town way, and any one of such parties shall make application, by petition to the court of common pleas, for a jury to ascertain his damages, as provided in the like cases in this chapter, the said court shall order the petitioner to give the like notice, as is required in the like cases before the commissioners of other counties, to all the other parties interested, to appear at the next term of the said court, and become parties to the proceedings under the said petition; and at the said next term, or at any succeeding term, as the court may direct, the said parties shall all be heard by the same jury, at the bar of the court, in such manner as the court shall direct; and thereupon the like proceedings shall be had in the estimation of damages, the returning of the verdict, and the adjudication of the court thereon, as are in this chapter required to be had on verdicts in the like cases, returned to the court of common pleas in other counties.

---

(10) AN ACT PRESCRIBING THE TIME FOR MAKING RETURNS OF VOTES FOR ELECTORS OF PRESIDENT AND VICE PRESIDENT OF THE UNITED STATES.

[Statute of 1844, Chap. 167.]

Be it enacted by the Senate and House of Representatives, in General Court assembled, and by the authority of the same, as follows:

Votes for electors of president, &c., how and when to be transmitted by town and city officers to the secretary.

SECT. 1. The mayor and aldermen of the several cities, and selectmen of the several towns in the commonwealth, shall within three days next after the day of any election of electors of president and vice president of the United States, held by virtue of the laws of this commonwealth, or of the United States, deliver, or cause to be delivered the lists of votes therefor, sealed up, to the sheriff of the county in which said election is held, and the sheriff shall within four days after receiving said lists, transmit the same to the office of the secretary of the commonwealth, or the said mayor and aldermen, or the selectmen may, and when the office of sheriff is vacant, he or they shall themselves transmit the said lists to the said office within seven days after the election, and all votes not so transmitted shall be rejected.

Notice of this law to be given by the secretary to cities and towns.

SECT. 2. The secretary of the commonwealth shall, on or before the first day of October next, transmit to the mayor and aldermen of each city, and to the selectmen of each town in the commonwealth, a copy of this act. [*Approved by the Governor, March* 16, 1844.]

(11) AN ACT PROVIDING, IN CERTAIN CASES, FOR THE ELECTION OF CITY OFFICERS.

[Statute of 1845, Chap. 217.]

Be it enacted by the Senate and House of Representatives, in General Court assembled, and by the authority of the same, as follows:

In case of failure of election of mayor, or of a full board of aldermen, in cities whose city council shall adopt this act, the aldermen chosen shall issue their warrant for an election, &c.

SECT. 1. Whenever it shall appear, by the regular returns of the elections of the city officers, in any city in this commonwealth, which, by a vote of its city councils, shall adopt this act,[1] that a mayor has not been chosen, or that a full board of aldermen has not been elected, such of the board of aldermen, whether they constitute a quorum or not, as may have been chosen, shall issue their warrant, in usual form, for the election of a mayor, or such members of the board of aldermen as may be necessary, and the same proceedings shall be had and repeated, until the election of a mayor and aldermen shall be completed, and all vacancies be filled in the said board; and in case neither a mayor nor any aldermen shall be elected at the usual time for electing the same, and after the powers of the former mayor, and mayor and aldermen, shall have ceased, it shall be the duty of the president of the common council, to issue his warrant, in the same manner as the board of aldermen would have done, if elected, and the same proceedings shall be had and repeated, until a mayor, or one or more aldermen, shall be elected.

In case of failure to elect a mayor or any aldermen within the usual time, &c., the president of the common council shall issue his warrant, &c.

In case of a vacancy in the board of aldermen or in the common council, the mayor and aldermen shall issue their warrant, &c.

SECT. 2. Whenever it shall appear to the mayor and aldermen, that there is a vacancy in either the board of aldermen, or in the common council, or in any of the city or ward offices, it shall be the duty of the mayor and aldermen to issue their warrant for elections, in due form, to fill all such vacancies in each and all of the said boards and offices, at such time and place as in their judgment may be deemed advisable.

[1] This act was adopted by the city council, Oct. 6, 1845. See City Records, vol. 23, p. 406.

Ward officers shall perform their duties, &c., and in case of their absence their offices may be filled *pro tempore*, &c.

SECT. 3. It shall be the duty of all ward officers, authorized to preside and act at such elections, to attend and perform their respective duties, at the times and places appointed for elections of any officers, whether of the United States, state, city, or wards, and to make and sign the regular returns of the same ; and in case of the absence of any or either of the ward officers, at any meeting for elections, or other purposes, such office may be filled, pro tempore, by the legal voters present, which may be done by nomination and hand votes, if the voters present so determine.

In case of failure to elect a mayor, the chairman of the board of aldermen shall be mayor *pro tempore*, &c.

SECT. 4. In case of the non-election of a mayor, the chairman of the board of aldermen shall discharge all the duties incumbent on the mayor of the city, prescribed by the city charter, or any other law, or any ordinance of any city adopting this act, which now or hereafter may be required of him, until a mayor shall be chosen and duly sworn to the discharge of his duties ; and such chairman, with the board of aldermen, shall discharge all the duties incumbent on the mayor and aldermen.

City officers shall continue to act, notwithstanding removal from their ward.

SECT. 5. All city officers, after their election, shall be held to discharge the duties to which they have been elected, being residents of the ward at the time of their election, notwithstanding their removal afterwards out of their ward into any other ward of the city. [*Approved by the Governor, March* 25, 1845.]

---

(12) AN ACT TO AMEND AN ACT ESTABLISHING THE CITY OF BOSTON.

[Statute of 1850, Chap. 167.]

Be it enacted by the Senate and House of Representatives, in General Court assembled, and by the authority of the same, as follows :

Wards.

SECT. 1. The second section of an act entitled " an act to establish the city of Boston," passed February 23, 1822, is hereby amended so that the wards therein mentioned shall be altered in such manner as to preserve as nearly as may be, consistently with well-defined limits, an equal number of legal voters in each ward, instead of an equal number of inhabitants, as is now provided in said section: *provided*, that this act shall be void, unless accepted and adopted by the city council of said city, by a vote taken by yeas and nays, within thirty days from from its passage.[1]

Equal number of voters in each ward.

Proviso, as to acceptance of this act.

SECT. 2. This act shall take effect from and after its passage. [*Approved by the Governor, April* 6, 1850.]

HEALTH LAW OF 1816.

AN ACT TO EMPOWER THE TOWN OF BOSTON TO CHOOSE A BOARD OF HEALTH, AND TO PRESCRIBE THEIR POWER AND DUTY.

[Statute of 1816, Chap. 44.]

SECT. 1. *Be it enacted by the Senate and House of Representatives in General Court assembled, and by the authority of the same,* That the inhabitants of the town of Boston, qualified to vote for town officers, shall, on the first Wednesday of April, annually, meet in their respective wards, at such time and place as may be appointed by the present and succeeding boards of health of said town, and published in two of the newspapers printed in said town, seven days previous to the time of meeting, and choose one able and discreet person, being a freeholder and resident within the ward for which he shall be chosen, to be a member of a board of health, which board shall consist of one person from each ward, chosen by a majority of the voters present, and by ballot: And the members of the board of health, for the time being, shall preside each in his respective ward, at such meetings, and on the neglect of either of them, a committee chosen by the ward shall preside until a clerk for such ward is chosen by a majority of the voters present; whose duty it shall be to preside at future meetings of said ward, for the ensuing year, to call for the votes, receive, count and declare the same in open meeting; and in case it shall appear that no choice has been made, the ballot shall be repeated until a person shall be elected, at whose dwelling-house, the clerk shall, on the same day, leave a written notification of his being chosen as aforesaid; and upon his

Time of choosing members.

Repealed by 1821, ch. 110, § 28.

Powers of clerk.

---

[1] This act was adopted by the city council, April 29, 1850. See City Records, vol. 28, p. 160.

refusal or non-acceptance within four days, after notice as aforesaid, the clerk shall summon a new meeting of the inhabitants of his ward at a time and place to be specified in two of the newspapers as aforesaid, three days at least previous to the intended meeting; *provided, however*, in case of refusal to serve of any person, at the time of his election in any ward, the said ward shall proceed to a new choice, and in case of the acceptance of any person chosen as aforesaid, the clerk of the ward, where such person is chosen, shall notify the president of the board of health for the time being, or in case of his death or absence from Boston, the oldest member of said board, of such choice, within twenty-four hours after such choice is made; and in all cases the said board of health for the time being shall continue in power and office until a new board is chosen and organized agreeable to the provisions of this act.

Powers of president.

And the president of the board of health, for the time being, or in case of his death or absence from the town of Boston, or incapacity to attend, the oldest member of said board present, shall within five days after the return made to him, by two thirds of the clerks of the wards aforesaid, where and when two thirds of said members of said board of health are chosen as aforesaid, notify the new members chosen and returned as aforesaid, to meet at the usual place of the meeting of said board, and shall at such meeting preside until a president and secretary shall be elected by the members of said new board, for said board; and he hereby is authorized to administer to such secretary an oath faithfully to record all the votes, orders, proceedings and regulations of said board, and faithfully to perform all the duties of his said office, during his continuance therein, which oath shall be entered and subscribed by such secretary on the records of said board, and attested by the person administering the same, after which such secretary shall have the custody of the records, books and papers of said board; and a certified copy of the votes, orders, proceedings and regulations of said board, or a certified copy from the records of said board, by such secretary thereof, shall be received and admitted as evidence in all cases relating to the proceedings or concerns of said board.

Regulations.

Powers. 1821, ch. 110, § 17.

SECT. 2. *Be it further enacted*, That said board of health shall have power, and it is hereby made their duty, to examine into all causes of sickness, nuisances, and sources of filth that may be injurious to the health of the inhabitants of the town of Boston, which do, or may exist within the limits of the town of Boston, or on any island, or in any vessel within the harbor of Boston, or within the limits thereof, and the same to destroy, remove or prevent, as the case may require; and whenever said board shall think it necessary for the preservation of the lives or health of the inhabitants of Boston to enter forcibly any building, or vessel, having been refused such entry by the owner or occupier thereof, within the limits of the said town of Boston or the harbor thereof, for the purpose of examining into, destroying, removing or preventing any nuisance, source of filth, or cause of sickness aforesaid, which said board have reason to believe is contained in such building or vessel—any member of said board, by order of said board, may apply to any justice of the peace, within and for the county of Suffolk, and on oath complain and state, on behalf of said board, the facts as far as said board have reason to believe the same relative to such nuisance, source of filth or cause of sickness aforesaid; and such justice shall thereupon issue his warrant, directed to the sheriff of the county of Suffolk, or either of his deputies, or any constable of the town of Boston, therein requiring them or either of them, taking with them sufficient aid and assistance, and also in company with said board of health, or some two members of the same, between the hours of sunrise and sunset, to repair to the place where such nuisance, source of filth or cause of sickness complained of as existing as aforesaid; and there, if found, the same to destroy, remove or prevent, under the directions and agreeable to the order of said board of health, or such members of the same, as may attend and accompany such officer for such purpose; *provided however*, that no sheriff or deputy sheriff shall execute any civil process, either by arresting the body or attaching the goods and chattels of any person or persons under color of any entry made for the purposes aforesaid, unless such service could by law have been made without such entry; and all services so made, under color of such entry, shall be utterly void, and the officer making such service shall be considered as a trespasser to all intents *ab initio*. And in all cases where such nuisance, source of filth, or cause of

Proviso.

sickness shall be removed, destroyed or prevented in manner aforesaid, the cost of so removing, destroying or preventing the same, together with all costs attending the proceedings relative thereto, shall be paid by the person or persons, who caused or permitted the same nuisance, source of filth, or cause of sickness to exist, or in whose possession the same may be found. And in all cases where any contagious and malignant disorder exists, within the limits of the town of Boston, or on board of any vessel, or on any island within the harbor of Boston, and it appearing to said board of health, after the same has been examined into by the physician of said board, or some other respectable physician of the town of Boston, that the public safety requires that any person or persons affected with any contagious, malignant disorder, should be removed to the hospital on Rainsford Island, or to any other place within the limits of said town of Boston, on any island in the harbor of Boston, or should be confined or remain in the place where such person or persons thus affected then are; in every such case the said board of health shall pass an order relative to the same, which order, all persons, dwelling in or occupying such place, building or vessel, notified thereof by said board, or called on by said board, shall be obliged to obey; and any person refusing to obey such order or resisting any officer or person acting under the authority of said board or any member of said board in any of the duties or requirements in this section of this act, shall severally forfeit and pay for such offence, a sum not less than five, and not exceeding five hundred dollars, according to the nature and aggravation of the offence.

Rules and orders.

SECT. 3. *Be it further enacted*, That the said board of health shall have power to make such rules, orders, and regulations, from time to time, for the preventing, removing or destroying of all nuisances, sources of filth and causes of sickness within the limits of the town of Boston, or on board any vessel, or on any island in the harbor of Boston which they may think necessary; which rules, orders and regulations, from and after the same have been published in two newspapers, printed in the said town of Boston, shall continue in force and be obeyed by all persons until changed, altered or repealed by the same board who made them, or by some succeeding board of health. And any person or persons who disobey or violate any such rules, orders or regulations, so as aforesaid made by such board, shall severally forfeit and pay for such offence, a sum not less than one and not more than fifty dollars, according to the nature and aggravation of such offence.

May seize and destroy provisions.

SECT. 4. *Be it further enacted*, That the said board of health shall have power to seize, take and destroy, or to remove to any safe place without the limits of the town of Boston, or cause the same to be done, any unwholesome and putrid or tainted meat, fish, bread, vegetable or other articles of the provision kind, or liquor, which in their opinion, first consulting the physician of said board, or some other reputable physician of the town of Boston, shall not be fit for food and nourishment, and injurious to the health of those who might use the same: And the cost of such seizing, taking, destroying or removing shall be paid for by the person, or persons in whose possession the same unwholesome, putrid, or tainted article shall or may be found.

SECT. 5. *Be it further enacted*, That the said board of health shall have power, from time to time, to make and establish all such rules, orders and regulations relating to clothing or any article capable of containing or conveying any infectious disease, or creating any sickness, which may be brought into, or conveyed from the town of Boston, or into or from any vessel, or on or from any island in the harbor of Boston, as they shall think proper for public safety, or to prevent the spreading of any dangerous or contagious disease. And all such rules, orders and regulations, so as aforesaid by said board made and established, shall be obeyed by all persons from and after the same have been published in two of the newspapers, printed in the town of Boston, and shall continue to be in full force until altered or repealed by the board who made and established the same, or some other succeeding board; and every person who shall disobey or violate any of such rules, orders and regulations, shall forfeit and pay a sum not less than one

Fines.

dollar, and not more than one hundred dollars, according to the nature and aggravation of such offence.

Quarantine.

SECT. 6. *Be it further enacted*, That the said board of health shall have power to establish and regulate the quarantine to be performed by all vessels arriving within the harbor of the town of Boston, and for that purpose shall have power, from time to time, to establish, make and ordain all such orders, rules and regulations relating to said quarantine as said board shall think necessary for the safety of the public and the security of the health of the inhabitants of the said town of Boston; which said rules, orders and regulations, so as aforesaid established, made and ordained, shall be obeyed by all persons, and shall continue to be in force from and after the same shall have been published in two newspapers, printed in the town of Boston, until the same are altered or repealed by the said board establishing, making and ordaining the same, or by some succeeding board of health. And said rules, orders, and regulations may extend as well to all persons arriving in such vessels, and to their property and effects aboard such vessels, and to all such persons as may visit, or go on board such vessels, after their arrival in said harbor of Boston, and to the cargo of all such vessels, as to the vessels themselves—as also to every matter and thing relating to, or connected with such vessel, or the cargo of the same, or to any person or persons going on board or returning from the same; and every person who shall knowingly or wilfully violate or disobey any of such rules, orders and regulations, so as aforesaid made, established or ordained by said board of health, shall severally forfeit and pay a sum not less than five dollars, and not exceeding five hundred dollars, according to the nature and aggravation of such offence. And the board of health shall have power at all times, to cause any vessel arriving in the harbor of Boston, which is foul and infected, or whose cargo is foul and affected with any malignant and contagious disease, to be removed and placed on quarantine ground, and the same to be thoroughly cleansed and purified at the expense and charge of the owners, consignees or possessors of the same; and also all per-

Fines.

sons arriving in or going on board such infected vessel, or handling such infected cargo, to be removed to hospital or Rainsford Island, under the care of said board, and to the hospital on the same, there to remain under the orders and regulations of said board. All expenses incurred on account of any person under the quarantine rules, orders and regulations of said board of health, shall be paid by such persons.

SECT. 7. *Be it further enacted*, That said board of health shall have power, and it shall be their duty to elect and appoint a principal physician to said board, who shall reside in Boston, and an assistant physician, who shall, during the time of quarantine, reside on Hospital Island, also an island-keeper, to reside on said Hospital Island, boatmen and such other officers and servants as will be necessary to carry into effect the rules, orders and regulations of said board of health, as it respects the quarantine ; and shall prescribe to them their duty, and establish their salary and fees, and displace or remove them at pleasure, and elect and appoint others in their places; also said board shall, from time to time, establish and regulate the fees or expenses attending the said quarantine regulations, shall have the care of said Rainsford or Hospital Island, and of the hospital on the same, and of all property on said island and belonging to or connected with the hospital on the same; and shall annually in the month of January in each year, file in the secretary's office of this commonwealth, an exact and true account of the state of the property in and connected with the hospital establishment on said island, and of the property belonging to the commonwealth on said island, and of all money expended thereon.

Officers appointed for Hospital Island.

SECT. 8. *Be it further enacted*, That said board of health shall have power to elect and appoint scavengers, superintendents of burying grounds, funeral porters or undertakers, and such other officers and servants, as shall be necessary to carry into effect all the powers and duties in this act given to, or required of the said board of health, and to fix and establish their fees of office or compensation; and all officers elected or appointed by said board, shall be

Scavengers and funeral porters.

removable from their said offices, at the pleasure of said board, and others substituted, elected or appointed in their place. And a majority of said board shall be competent to transact any business which the whole board, were they all present, might or could transact.

1797, ch. 16. 1799, ch. 10. SECT. 9. *Be it further enacted*, That all the powers and duties which are given to, or required of the selectmen of the town of Boston, by a law of this commonwealth, passed the twenty-second day of June, in the year of our Lord one thousand seven hundred and ninety-seven, entitled "an act to prevent the spreading of contagious sickness," and by the several acts in addition thereto, shall be, and they hereby are transferred to and made the duty of the board of health of the town of Boston, any thing in said laws to the contrary notwithstanding. And for all expenses which may arise in the execution of their duty, the said board of health shall be authorized to draw upon the town treasurer of the

Expenses. town of Boston; and the accounts of said board including all receipts and expenditures of money shall be examined by the committee of accounts annually chosen by said town of Boston for that purpose, who shall report a state of them to the said town accordingly, and the same shall be paid by the treasurer of said town of Boston. And on the death or resignation of any member of said board of health, the said board may cause such vacancy to be filled by a new election from the ward from which said member was elected by directing the clerk of such ward to call a meeting of the inhabitants of such ward, qualified to elect a member of the board of health, to meet at such time and place, as shall be notified to him by said board; at which meeting such va-

Vacancies filled up. 1821, ch. 110, § 28. cancy shall be filled, and such proceedings be had as are directed in the first section of this act, as to the choice and return and notification of the person elected as a member of said board as aforesaid.

SECT. 10. *Be it further enacted*, That whenever any prisoner confined in the gaol in Boston, or within the limits of said prison, shall be attacked with any contagious, malignant disorder, which in the opinion of said board of health, first having consulted with the physician of said board, or some other respectable physician, of the town of Boston, endangers the safety and health of the other prisoners in said gaol, or the inhabitants of said town, and that the suffering such prisoners, so attacked as aforesaid, longer to remain in said gaol, or within the limits of said prison, is not consistent with the public safety, or the health of the inhabitants of said town, or the prisoners in said gaol; in every such case the said board of health shall make application in writing to any two justices of the peace, *quorum unus*, therein stating the facts relative to such case; and the said justices to whom such application shall be made, shall examine into such case, and if satisfied that the facts stated are true, shall issue their warrant to said board of health, authorizing and directing them to remove said prisoner so attacked with such contagious and malignant disorder, to the hospital on Rainsford Island, or to some other place of safety, there to remain under the directions of said board, until such prisoner either recovers or dies; and in case of recovery, then to be returned by said board to the place from which he was taken; and such warrant so executed by said board, or any member thereof, shall be by them returned, with their doings thereon, into the clerk's office of the court, from which the process for committing such prisoner to gaol, shall have issued; and the place to which such prisoner shall be removed by virtue of such order, shall be considered as the gaol of the county of Suffolk; and every prisoner removed as aforesaid, for the causes aforesaid, shall not thereby be considered as having committed any escape, so as to prejudice either himself, his bondsmen, or the persons who had the custody of him in his confinement aforesaid.

May remove sick prisoners.

SECT. 11. *Be it further enacted*, That the said board of health of the town of Boston are hereby authorized and empowered, from time to time, to make and establish rules, orders and regulations for the interment of the dead in said town, to establish the police of the burying grounds, appoint and locate the places where the dead may be buried in said town, and cause the places for the deposit of the dead in said town, and the burying grounds, to be repaired and

Burying grounds.

Funerals.

properly enclosed. Also to make regulations for funerals and funeral processions, and appoint all necessary officers and persons to carry the same into effect, and to appoint to them their duties and fees; and shall also have the power to establish such penalties for the violation of any such rules, orders and regulations, as they may think proper: *Provided*, no one penalty for any one violation, shall exceed the sum of fifty dollars. And all such rules, orders or regulations, so as aforesaid made and established by said board, shall be obeyed by every person, from and after the same have been published in two of the newspapers printed in Boston, and shall continue in full force, until the same are altered or repealed by the said board, who made and established them, or by some succeeding board.

Proviso for penalties.

SECT. 12. *Be it further enacted*, That the said board of health shall have power to grant permits for the removal of any nuisance, infected article, or sick person, within the town of Boston, when they think it safe and proper so to do; and said board, whenever they think justice requires it, may stop, discontinue, discharge or compromise any suit, complaint or information, originating under this act. And all fines, forfeitures, penalties, sums to paid or recovered, arising under any of the provisions of this act, shall be prosecuted for, by and in the name of "the board of health of the town of Boston," by complaint or information by said board, to be made in writing to some justice of the peace within and for the county of Suffolk; which said justice, upon said complaint or information being made to him as aforesaid, shall receive the same, and thereupon issue his warrant, therein reciting the said complaint or information, directed to the sheriff of the county of Suffolk, or either of his deputies, or any constable of the town of Boston, commanding them or either of them, to summon the party informed against or complained of, to appear before him at a time and place to be named in said warrant, to shew cause, if any they have, why they should not pay the sum demanded of them in such complaint or information: which said warrant, shall by the officer who receives the same, be served on the party informed or complained against as aforesaid,

Permits.

May prosecute.

at least seven days before the day in said warrant stated, as the said day of trial, by giving such party in hand, a copy of such warrant, reading the same to him, or leaving a copy thereof at the last and usual place of the abode of such party; and if such party shall not appear at the time and place appointed, or appearing shall not show sufficient cause as aforesaid, the said justice shall proceed to render judgment in every such case, that the said board of health shall recover such sum in damages or as fine, as the case may be, as according to the provisions of this act, they ought by law to recover, with costs, and shall proceed to issue his execution therefor, in the same manner as executions issue from justices of the peace in civil cases triable before them; and such executions shall be served and made returnable in the same manner as executions in civil actions are by law served, and made returnable, which issue on judgments rendered in the supreme judicial court of this Commonwealth: *Provided however*, that in all such prosecutions as aforesaid, if the said board of health shall discontinue such prosecution or become nonsuit, or the same on the merits should be decided by such justice trying such prosecution against them, in every such case, the said party informed against and complained of, shall recover his legal costs against said board, which costs shall be paid by the treasurer of the town of Boston. And in every prosecution under this act, before any justice of the peace as aforesaid, the party complained against in such prosecution, being dissatisfied with the judgment in the same, given by such justice, may appeal therefrom to the Boston court of common pleas, next to be holden at Boston, within and for the county of Suffolk, after such judgment is so as aforesaid given, or rendered by said justice; *provided* such appeal be entered within twenty-four hours after such judgment is given as aforesaid; and the same proceedings in all respects relating to such appeal, shall be had as are by law required on appeals from judgments rendered in civil causes by justices of the peace in this commonwealth; and on the entry of such appeal in said court, the said court shall have cognizance and jurisdiction of the same, and shall proceed to hear and de-

Forms of process.

Proviso.

Appeals.

termine the same in the same manner, and award execution in the same way and manner as they have cognizance and jurisdiction, proceed to hear and determine and award execution in civil causes, on appeals to them from judgments given by justices of the peace in this commonwealth. And in all cases of such appeals on prosecutions under this act, the party prevailing in the said court shall recover his costs, to be paid in the manner prescribed in this section of this act: *Provided however*, that no appeal shall be allowed or granted to said court in any prosecution under the provisions of this act, where the amount of the judgment rendered and had before, and by any justice of the peace, shall not amount to more than five dollars exclusive of costs. And all fines and forfeitures recovered by said board of health, under the provisions of this act, shall inure to the use of the inhabitants of the town of Boston, and be accounted for by said board of health, to and with the town treasurer of said town of Boston. *And provided also*, that in consequence of said appropriation of said fines and forfeitures, or the appropriation of any other moneys by virtue of this act, no inhabitant of the said town of Boston shall be disqualified as a justice of the peace, a witness or juror in any prosecution under this act, nor shall the said board of health, or any member of the same, or any officer of the same, be rendered thereby incompetent witnesses in any prosecution under this act; and the members of said board of health, while they continue in such office, shall be exempted from all militia duty and every other duty and service, which by law the selectmen of towns in this commonwealth are exempted from: and all laws heretofore made relating to a board of health in the town of Boston, so far as they are inconsistent with or contrary to the provisions of this act, shall be, and the same are hereby repealed. *Provided however*, that the election of the present board of health for the said town of Boston, and all their doings under the said laws are hereby confirmed, and they shall have and exercise all the powers and duties required or permitted by this present act; *and provided also*, that all prosecutions now pending, shall be proceeded in, in the same way and manner, as

Costs.

Proviso.

Exemptions.

Acts repealed.

though this act had never been passed. And in all prosecutions under this act, the persons prosecuted, may plead the general issue, and give any special matter in evidence under the same; and the complaint, information, pleadings or proceedings in any prosecutions under this act, may, by leave of court, before whom the same is, or may be pending, be amended in any state of such prosecution, without the payment of costs by either party. [*Approved, June* 20, 1816.]

May plead the general issue.

RULES AND REGULATIONS OF THE HOUSE OF CORRECTION.

DUTIES OF THE MASTER.

The master, under the direction of the overseers, shall have the control and management of all who are employed in the house of correction, as watchmen, superintendents, or in any the like capacity, and such officers shall be required to follow his directions, at all times, unless otherwise directed by the overseers. He shall also have the entire management and control of the convicts, subject to the rules and regulations legally established, and such directions as he may from time to time receive from the overseers. It shall be the duty of the master to report to the overseers, at the stated weekly meetings, at least one week before the same shall be needed, all such articles as may be wanted for the uses of the institution.

He shall also, in case any prisoner shall be about to leave, who may require a supply of clothing on going out, make a report thereof, at least one week beforehand, to the overseers, so that they may be suitably provided with the same, and also in cases where some pecuniary aid may be thought proper, which shall not exceed in amount five dollars in any case. The master shall regularly make a weekly report to the board of the number of committals and discharges of the past week, of the mode of employment of the inmates, stating the numbers of both sexes so employed, of goods received during the week for manufacture or use, of those who may be sick, with such remarks as may be suitable, and of the punishments that may have been inflicted during that time, or other occurrences of moment to the institution. And he shall, at all times, make such further communications or returns, as the overseers may desire. The master shall cause to be kept regular books, showing the quantity and amount of articles received at the institution for the supply of the wants of the same; all materials to be wrought by the inmates, and the amount, kind, and value of the work done by them, and also any moneys received for sales of produce or otherwise, and he shall keep such an account with each inmate as shall show, as near as may be, the actual amount of his or her earnings; these books to be at all times open to the examination of the overseers. He shall have charge of all materials of labor, and shall give out the same in suitable quantities for supplying the convicts with work, and he shall appoint the kind and quantity of work required of each, subject to the direction of the overseers. He shall countersign every bill for articles delivered at the house, for the purpose of showing that the same have been received. The watchmen, under the direction of the master, shall keep watch during the night time, in such manner and for such periods as he shall determine; and shall, during the day time, perform such other duties as he shall require.

The master shall have a system of rules for conducting the prison, to be approved by the overseers, and to be read in the chapel, at least once a month, to all the inmates.

DUTIES OF CHAPLAIN.

It shall be the duty of the chaplain to perform divine service on each Lord's day, and to visit the sick, and instruct the convicts in their moral and religious duties, and to report to the board any special cases which may fall under his cognizance for consideration, and he shall do such other things, in his said capacity, as the overseers may require of him.

DUTIES OF THE CLERK OF THE OVERSEERS.

He shall be present at all business hours at the office of the overseers, to attend to the business of the office, and at all meetings of the board, and keep exact and fair records of all their doings. He shall keep regular books of account, with an entry of all purchases and moneys paid out, and of all moneys received and paid over to the city treasurer. Shall make record of such returns as he may be directed by the overseers, and keep regular files of such papers as may be placed in his custody. He shall examine all bills and collect all moneys due to the institution, and pay over the same, when collected, immediately to the city treasurer, as provided for in the ordinance of the city made for that purpose, and he shall, under the direction of the overseers, make such purchases for the institution, and do all such other acts as the overseers may from time to time require of him.

DUTIES OF THE PHYSICIAN.

It shall be the duty of the physician to visit the house every day, and as much oftener as may be necessary, and to examine carefully into every case of sickness and inability to labor, and to prescribe such medicines and such course of diet as he may deem proper. It shall be his duty to furnish the overseers from time to time a list of such medicines as may be wanted for the house, and to report to the overseers any neglect or improper conduct on the part of the nurses, or those in attendance, that may come to his knowledge. No critical surgical operation or amputation of a limb shall be performed, excepting in case of urgent necessity requiring immediate action, without the sanction of the overseers. He shall keep a journal of patients in the hospital, designating the time of entry of each, with the nature of the complaint and treatment, and the time of discharge or death.

This journal shall at all times be open to the inspection of the overseers. The sustenance and diet of those in the hospital shall be regulated by the physician, whose requisitions shall be in writing, and shall in no case be given for a longer term than one week. He shall make a return once in every quarter to the overseers of all cases which have come under his care.

GENERAL REGULATIONS.

All bills, before payment, shall be approved by the chairman, at a regular meeting of the board, excepting in cases where purchases are made of persons residing out of the city, and immediate payment is necessary, when the bills may be approved by the chairman and one other member of the board.

The overseers shall, as a board, visit and examine the institution in all its parts, at least once in a month and a record shall be made of the doings of such visit and the result of the examination.

The overseers shall appoint such subordinate officers, assistants and clerks as they may find necessary, and shall fix their compensation, unless otherwise provided for by the ordinances of the city.

No persons, excepting the city council and the board of accounts, shall have a right to enter the premises of the institution without a permit from a member of the board of overseers.

The convicts, during the whole time when they are not taken out for work, or other purposes by order of the master, shall be kept locked in their respective cells, in no case more than one being allowed to each cell, and while so shut up, shall preserve perfect silence, speaking to no one, except in cases of illness, in which case they shall be allowed to speak to the officer then in charge of the cells. They shall be taken out for work, on all days but Sundays or other holidays specially excepted, at sunrise, and shall labor at the work assigned them until sunset, allowing a half hour's respite for each meal, when they shall be reconducted to their cells, receiving their food at some convenient place as they go. When they are taken out or returned to their cells, the males and females shall move at different times, allowing a sufficient interval for those of one sex to be entirely removed from observation, before those of the other are allowed to move; and they shall enter and go out at doors on different parts of the building, so as effectually to prevent their meeting. On Sundays, at the times of public worship, the females shall be conducted into the chapel, and seated beyond the screen, and afterwards the males shall be conducted in. During the times when they are moving to and from the chapel, or at and from their workshops, entire silence and the most perfect order and decorum shall be maintained, and the master shall introduce such regulations as to the precise manner in which they shall proceed, on these occasions, as he shall find to be suited to preserve order and regularity. Their food, which must always be eaten in their cells, shall be as follows—The daily sustenance of the convicts, not in the hospital, shall consist of the following rations: 16 ounces No. 1 beef, or 12 ounces No. 1 pork, 10 ounces fine flour, 5 ounces Indian meal, 1 gill molasses, for each prisoner; and for every 100 rations 2½ bushels potatoes, 2 quarts vinegar, 4 quarts salt, 2 ounces black pepper.

All the convicts shall have on clean shirts and stockings, and such other clothes as the master shall determine, every Sunday morning, and as much oftener as he shall direct; and the males shall also be required to be fresh shaved at the same time. No spirituous liquors shall be allowed to be drank, nor shall any prisoner be allowed to have tobacco in any shape.

No officer shall receive any perquisite, in any shape, in addition to the compensation fixed by the overseers, and no trafficking shall be allowed between the officers and the convicts. There shall be allowed no trafficking among the convicts, and they shall not be allowed to receive any thing from without the house, or hold any intercourse with persons outside the house, without express permission from the master or overseers. When there shall be visitors present, no convict shall be allowed to address them without permission, except in answer to such questions as may be asked by the judges of the board of accounts, or members of the city government, authorized to examine into the state of the establishment, and any one intruding upon visitors shall be liable to punishment.

For every failure, or refusal to comply with the foregoing requirements, for any insolent or insubordinate behavior while at work, or at other times, for any neglect or refusal to obey the orders of the master, or those having charge of the convicts by his direction, for gross or profane language towards the officers or each other, for defacing the cells or any of their furniture, or any part of the premises, and for any want of decent and proper deportment in the chapel, or in the presence of the chaplain, the convicts shall be punished by being kept upon bread and water, in solitary confinement for a time not exceeding ten days. And no convict shall be confined for a longer time than twenty-four hours, without authority from the overseers in writing; and no corporeal punishment, of any kind or degree, shall be allowed in any case, except that in flagrant and obstinate cases of insubordination, the use of the shower bath may be permitted, under the direction and limitation of the overseers, and in presence of one of their number. And it shall be the duty of the master to have any convict in solitary confinement visited by the physician once a day during that confinement.

In Common Council, October 19, 1843.

Passed.

EDWARD BLAKE, *President.*

In the Board of Aldermen, October 23, 1843.

Passed.

M. BRIMMER, *Mayor.*

ORIGIN OF THE HOUSE OF INDUSTRY.

At a meeting of the freeholders and other inhabitants of the town of Boston, holden at Faneuil Hall, on Monday, March 12, 1821, and adjourned to March 13, certain petitions on the subject of erecting a workhouse were read. Whereupon it was voted, that the subject be referred to a committee of thirteen, to be nominated from the chair; the said committee to consider the subject at large and report, and that the report be printed and distributed among the inhabitants; and the selectmen were requested to call a meeting to act on said report. The following gentlemen were nominated and appointed on the committee, viz: Hon. Josiah Quincy, Joseph Lovering, James Savage, Henry J. Oliver, Francis Welsh, Joseph May, Thomas Howe, William Thurston, Abraham Babcock, Samuel A. Wells, James T. Austin, Benjamin Rich and Joseph Woodward, Esqrs.

Origin of the house of industry.

Boston Records vol. 10, pp. 290, 296.

At a subsequent meeting, on Monday, May 7, 1821, the committee appointed on the 12th day of March, "on the subject of pauperism at large, and on the expediency of erecting a work house," within the said town, made a long report, in which they express themselves as unanimously of opinion, that the accommodations, provided for the poor at the almshouse in Boston, are not such as comport with the honor and interests of the town; and that, in aid of the present establishment, a workhouse, to be denominated a House of Industry, should be erected, with a sufficient quantity of land attached to it, &c.; and submitted the following votes, which were passed.

Ibid, pp. 305, 307

Voted, That it is expedient to establish, forthwith, within this town, a House of Industry.

Ibid, p. 326.

Voted, That a committee be appointed consisting of persons, with full authority to select a suitable place for the erection of a House of Industry, with an extent of land, attached to it, not less than fifty acres; and that the said committee be authorized to take any of the unappropriated lands, belonging to the town, for that purpose; or, in case they deem any other spot, or like extent of land, within the town, a better location for such an establishment than any the town now possesses, that they be authorized to purchase the same; and that the said committee be instructed to proceed forthwith to erect suitable buildings, and to form a system for the conduct of such institution; and to report their proceedings, in the premises, from time to time, to the town, as they may deem expedient.

Voted, That the committee appointed by the preceding vote, be authorized to draw on the town treasurer for such sum, or sums of money, as may from time to time be found necessary, for the carrying into effect the purposes therein expressed; provided always that the amount of said drafts shall never exceed twenty thousand dollars.

Voted, That the report this day made to the town on the subject of pauperism and a house of industry, be referred to the committee appointed by the preceding votes, and that they be instructed to take into consideration the various subjects suggested in it, and particularly to inquire into the general state of the poor, within the town, and concerning the operations, effects, modes, and principles of extending relief to the poor, adopted by the various charitable institutions existing in it; and from time to time to report such measures in relation to the whole, or any, of the subjects aforesaid, as they may deem it expedient for the town to adopt.

Ibid, p. 334. Hon. Josiah Quincy, Joseph Lovering, James Savage, Henry J. Oliver, Francis Welsh, Ebenezer Francis, Thomas Howe, William Thurston, Abram Babcock, Samuel A. Wells, James T. Austin, Benjamin Rich, and Joseph Woodward, Esquires, were nominated from the chair and appointed a committee, in conformity to the second vote.

Ibid, pp. 388, 410. At a meeting of the freeholders, &c., held by adjournment from September 25, 1821, on October 22, 1821, the chairman of the committee made a long report, stating that the committee had procured a tract of land at South Boston, containing fifty-three acres, owned by Samuel Brown, Esq., and were proceeding with the work of erection; and that the establishment was then advancing to the third story. The thanks of the town were voted to the chairman and members of the committee, and the sum of $6,000 in addition to that previously voted, was placed at their disposal. Ibid, p. 430.

The committee made a further report March 28, 1822; and it was voted that the sum of $15,000 be put at their disposition. They were also instructed to prepare a system for the general conduct and management and discipline of said house, and of the land connected with it, and lay the same before the city authorities as soon as practicable after their organization. Ibid, pp. 462, 473.

May 3, 1822, the committee represented, that they apprehend, that the power of devising rules for the management and discipline of the institution is vested in the board of overseers of the poor, under the act of 8 and 9 George II., (1735); and the committee therefore postponed any action in relation to this duty, until the action of the city council; and they suggest either an application to the legislature, or a reference of the subject matter to the board of overseers. This report was read and committed to a joint committee. City Records, vol. 1, p. 7.

May 7, 1822, the joint committee on the subject recommended a reference of the matter to the board of overseers of the poor and the committee for building the house of industry conjointly; which report was read and accepted. Ibid, p. 12.

May 24, 1822, the board and committee made a report recommending an application to the legislature for an act, authorizing the establishment of a new board; which report was read and committed. Ibid, p. 30.

June 4, 1822, the committee reported a bill to be presented to the general court. Ibid, p. 36.

Sept. 16, 1822, the committee for building the house of industry reported the house as substantially completed; and stated that a balance of expense of $5,406.71 remained, for which provision was yet to be made. The report was read and committed. Ibid, p. 79.

May 21, 1823, $8,000 was appropriated for completing the house of industry, outbuildings, fences, and for the purpose of stock, furniture, &c., and for carrying the said Ibid, p. 221.

house of industry into effective operation, and the directors of the said house of industry were authorized to draw their warrants on the city treasurer therefor from time to time as occasion might require.

After the erection of the house of industry, there appears to have been considerable difficulty between the directors of the institution, the city council and the overseers of the poor, respecting the rights and duties of the latter in relation to the poor. The following report and resolutions, drawn up by Mr. Quincy, the mayor, were accepted and adopted by the city council May 12, 1825.

Mr Quincy's report. (Accepted by the city council May 12, 1825.)

"The committee of both branches of the city council, to whom was referred the application of the overseers of the poor, for the providing of a suitable house for the accommodation of the poor and distressed, and expressing their readiness to take the oversight, care and government of such house, respectfully report:

"That such a house is already provided in this city, established by law, and placed under the oversight and care of the directors of the house of industry, who are invested in this respect by the statutes of this commonwealth, with all the powers and authorities "had and exercised by overseers of the poor," that the state of this house under the wise and active management of those directors is, in every respect satisfactory; the poor of every class content; and the moral and physical condition of the inmates placed upon a new system, calculated to ameliorate both in as high a degree as, in the nature of things is possible under the wise arrangements of these directors, annually chosen by and responsible to the city council.

"While your committee are happy in being thus able to state the results and prospects of this institution, they are not less gratified, that the city council are able, consistent with the legally invested rights of the directors of that house, to avail themselves in relation to it of the general aid of the overseers of the poor, and at the same time to grant them all the practical and useful facilities, relative to providing for the poor, which from the tenor of their application they desire; and thus the general arrangements of the poor of the city enjoy the advantage of the intelligence and experience of the members of both the overseers of the poor and of the directors of the house of industry.

"Their general views will be developed in the subjoined resolutions, which they respectfully report to the city council for its consideration and adoption.

"*Resolved*, (1) That the overseers of the poor be and they are hereby authorized and requested to grant permits for the admission of any person, in their judgment entitled to receive the support of the city in the tenement of the city denominated the House of Industry at South Boston, in like manner as the directors of said house are authorized by law; and that the superintendent of said house be and he hereby is authorized and directed to receive and take charge of persons to whom such permits have been granted; and to provide for their relief, support, and employment in said house, according to the regulations, and under the superintendence of the directors of the House of Industry.

"*Resolved*, (2) That the overseers of the poor be and they hereby are authorized and requested, at their discretion, with, or without notice, to visit the establishment called the House of Industry at South Boston, to inquire into the condition, treatment and employment of the poor who may be inmates therein, and to make such representations and suggestions, from time to time, to the city council, in relation to their said condition, treatment and employment, as their wisdom and experience may suggest.

"*Resolved*, (3) That the mayor and aldermen be and they hereby are authorized to provide a suitable vehicle for the conveyance to the House of Industry, of sick, decrepid persons, or those otherwise incapacitated from going of themselves to such house, and that the same be, at all times, subject to the order of the overseers of the poor, and of the directors of the House of Industry, for the purpose above specified."

Subsequently to the adoption of these resolutions, a committee of the city council, to whom was referred a communication from the overseers of the poor, reported that they had laid the whole subject before counsel learned in the law, Hon. William Prescott, Charles Jackson and Daniel Webster, Esquires; and the committee reported the following resolves which were passed.

"*Resolved*, That the overseers of the poor be and they hereby are directed to cause all persons who, from the nature of the illness under which they labor, or of the accident which has befallen them, are incapable, without endangering life, to be removed from the place where they are, to be relieved and supported in such place, until they are capable so to be removed, and as soon as they are capable of being removed, the said overseers are directed to cause them forthwith to be removed for further relief and support to the House of Industry.

"*Resolved*, That the overseers of the poor be, and they hereby are directed, as it respects those householders and others, who in their opinion require partial relief, and who may be rendered more comfortable by a small supply at their own houses, than by being wholly supported in a poor house, to grant such partial relief and small supply of necessaries at their own houses.

"*Resolved*, That the overseers of the poor be, and they hereby are directed to see that all poor and indigent persons, having lawful settlement in the city of Boston, and standing in need of relief, other than those belonging to the classes specified in the two preceding resolves, to be suitably relieved, supported and employed in the House of Industry, according to the regulations and under the superintendence of the directors of said house."

INDEX.

66

www.ingramcontent.com/pod-product-compliance
Lightning Source LLC
LaVergne TN
LVHW021104110826
845150LV00001B/165